Robert Desnos, Surrealism, and the Marvelous in Everyday Life

Robert Desnos, Surrealism, and the Marvelous in Everyday Life

Katharine Conley

UNIVERSITY OF NEBRASKA PRESS · LINCOLN & LONDON

Publication of this volume was assisted by The Virginia Faulkner Fund, established in memory of Virginia Faulkner, editor-in-chief of the University of Nebraska Press.

Previously published portions of this book are acknowledged on page xiii, which constitutes an extension of this copyright page.

"Rrose Sélavy," "J'ai tant rêvé de toi," "Infinitif," "Paroles des rochers," "La grande complainte de Fantômas," "Jamais d'autre que toi," "Sirène-anémone," "Je suis passé dans une rue étrange," "La porte du second infini," "Mon tombeau," "Le frère au pétard," "Minute!" "Histoire d'une ourse," "Art poétique," "Vaincre la jour, vaincre la nuit," "Printemps," "Ce coeur qui haïssait la guerre," "Le veilleur du Pont-au-Change," "La voix," "Le paysage," "La cascade," "La plage," "La peste," "Le coteau," "Le réveil," "L'Epitaphe," "Calixto," "La clef des Songes," "Dernier poème," "The Night of Loveless Nights," "Siramour," "Les quatre sans cou," "Aux sans cou," "Cantate pour l'inauguration du Musée de l'Homme" from *Oeuvres* and *Domaine public* by Robert Desnos © Gallimard.

"Le Pélican," "L'Hippocampe," and "La Fourmi," extracts from *Chantefables et Chantefleurs* by Robert Desnos © Éditions Gründ, with kind permission of Éditions Gründ, Paris.

Translations of "Afterword to 'Etat de Veille,'" "Tale of a Bear," "Tomorrow," "Ars Poetica," "This Heart That Hated War," and "Spring" from *The Selected Poems of Robert Desnos* (Ecco, 1991, with William Kulik) © Carolyn Forché and reprinted by permission of William Morris Agency, Inc., on behalf of the author.

"Liberté" from *Oeuvres complètes* by Paul Eluard © Editions de Minuit.

"Front Commun" from *Les Voix intérieurs* by Robert Desnos © Editions du Petit Véhicule.

Library of Congress
Cataloging-in-Publication Data
Conley, Katharine, 1956–
Robert Desnos, surrealism, and the marvelous in everyday life / Katharine Conley.
p. cm.
Includes bibliographical references and index.
ISBN 0-8032-1523-1 (cloth : alk. paper)
1. Desnos, Robert, 1900–1945. 2. Authors, French—20th century—Biography. I. Title.
PQ2607.E75Z65 2003
841'.912—dc21
[B]
2002043038

For Richard

Contents

List of Illustrations ix

Acknowledgments xi

Abbreviations xv

Introduction 1

1. The Automatic Sibyl
   as Rrose Sélavy 15

2. The Sensory In-Between 45

3. Radio and the Mediation
   of the Everyday 87

4. Paris Watchman 121

5. The Marvelous and the Myth 169

Notes 215

Selected Bibliography 241

Index 255

Illustrations

following page 126

1. Desnos in 1908

2. Eugène Atget, *Un Coin des Halles Rue Pierre Lescot,* 1911

3. Eugène Atget, *Rue Saint-Bon,* 1904

4. Man Ray, *Séance de rêve éveillé,* 1924

5. Desnos's automatic drawings

6. Desnos's mermaid

7. Yvonne Georges

8. Youki Desnos

9. Claude Cahun portrait of Desnos, 1930

10. Desnos apartment at number 19, rue Mazarine

11. Bernard Villemot, Trio of Vichy propaganda posters

12. *La Terre ne ment pas*

13. Youki and Desnos on vacation, 1936

14. Desnos and one of his cats, 1943

15. Desnos waking up during the "period of sleeps" by Man Ray, from *Nadja*

16. Desnos in 1943

17. Newly freed prisoners at Terezin

Acknowledgments

Several organizations and many people have been helpful to me in the completion of this book. I wish to thank first of all the Association des Amis de Robert Desnos, Dartmouth College, from which I received a Burke Research Initiation Grant and Junior Faculty Fellowship, the Whiting Travel Foundation for giving me a research grant for this project, the Ramon Guthrie Foundation for helping me with funding for the permissions and the cover art, and the Bibliothèque Littéraire Jacques Doucet, where Desnos's papers are stored. I would also like to thank those generous people whose personal knowledge of Desnos proved to be invaluable in my understanding of his life: first of all, those brave men who suffered with him in deportation, including André Bessière, Pierre Volmer, Henri Margraff, and Clément Degueille; and, second, Babette Godet (Elisabeth Bridault), who worked with Desnos at *Aujourd'hui,* and Dominique Desanti, who met Desnos in the late 1930s and whose own *roman-vrai* about Desnos's life was helpful to me.

I wish to thank Marie-Claire Dumas, whose unfailing support and generosity contributed a lot to my research and who invited me to spend a month in her *chambre d'invités* one summer while I did research at the Doucet Library and allowed me to sleep underneath Desnos's watercolor painting of a mermaid escaping from a bottle on a beach beneath an imposing castle. I also thank Desnos's literary executor Jacques Fraenkel, whose uncle, Théodore, had been Desnos's best friend and whose parents, Dr. Michel and Mme Fraenkel were equally kind and helpful to me. And I thank Fern Malkine for talking to me about her father, Georges Malkine, who was close to Desnos in the 1920s, and for showing me his letters and photographs. I particularly want to thank my copyeditor, Elizabeth Gratch, whose careful work and sympathetic reading made the final stages of revision rewarding and pleasurable.

In France I was encouraged by Pierre Lartigue, who told me the story of his recovery of Desnos's true "last" poem, "Spring," in an interview, by Elisabeth Serment, who generously shared the research she had done for her one-woman show on Desnos's work; by Alain Chevrier, who showed me his manuscript on Desnos's slang poems and allowed me to cite from it; by Olivier Bara and Dominique Carlat, who discussed Desnos's poetry with me; by Linda

Simon at the Maison de la Radio; and by all the members of the Association des Amis de Robert Desnos, particularly the Kopylovs, for producing such lovely editions of Desnos's work with their Editions des Cendres. I also thank the friends who housed me while I pursued my research in Paris, including Jim Rentschler, Marie-Claire and Maurice Dumas, Hélène and Claude Garache, and Jacques Polge.

In the United States I thank William Kulik for generously granting me permission to cite his translations of Desnos. I thank Georgiana Colvile, who introduced me to Desnos in a seminar on avant-garde film in 1987 at the University of Colorado, Boulder, and Warren Motte, who directed my master's thesis on Desnos there, as well as Julia Frey, who inspired me to return to French studies after a long hiatus. I also thank Patsy Carter and Bob Jaccaud, whose help was invaluable at Dartmouth College's Berry/Baker Library, and Deans of the Humanities Barry Scherr and Lenore Grenoble for their help with funding. Over the years I received many helpful suggestions and support from a variety of people, including Jean Alter, Mieke Bal, Tony Campbell, Carolyn Flaherty, Celeste Goodridge, Margaret Darrow, Marian Eide, Lynn Gingrass, Kate Goldsborough, Mary Jean Green, Valerie Hansen, Kathy Hart, Lynn Higgins, Marianne Hirsch, Amy Hollywood, Jim Jordan, Nina Lloyd, Philippe Met, George O'Brien, Melinda O'Neal, Gerald Prince, Maureen Ragan, Marilyn Ranker, John Rassias, Todd Sanders, Amy Smiley, Richard Stamelman, Virginia Swain, Gwendolyn Wells, Kathleen Wine, and Gayle Zachmann, as well as the participants in the Humanities Institute on Cultural Memory, led by Mieke Bal, Jonathan Crewe, and Leo Spitzer, at Dartmouth College in the spring of 1996, who heard early versions of some of the material in this book.

I thank Jacques Fraenkel for his tireless efforts in helping me to obtain the majority of the illustrations for this book. I thank also Jean-Pierre Dauphin at the Editions Gallimard for his help with the photographs and illustrations belonging to the Association des Amis de Robert Desnos. I thank Salomon Grimberg for his help in obtaining permission to use Claude Cahun's portrait of Desnos, owned by the Zabriskie Gallery. I thank Dina Deitsch at the Artists Rights Society. I also thank Jean-Paul Avice at the Bibliothèque Historique de la Ville de Paris for his help in obtaining the Atget photographs, the Association de la Sirène in Blainville-Crevon for sending me photographs of Desnos's mermaid, Renée Devine at the Zabriskie Gallery, and Fabienne Dumont at the Musée d'Histoire Contemporaine.

I thank the Editions Gallimard for granting me permission to quote from Desnos's poetry as well as the poetry of Louis Aragon and Jacques Prévert, the Editions Gründ for granting me permission to quote from Desnos's children's verse currently available under the title *Chantefables et Chantefleurs,* Luc Vidal at the Editions du Petit Véhicule for allowing me to quote from one of Desnos's songs, and the Editions de Minuit for granting me permission to quote from Paul Eluard's "Liberté." I also thank the William Morris Agency for granting me permission to quote from Carolyn Forché's translations of Desnos.

Previous versions of portions of chapters 3, 4, and 5 have appeared elsewhere. "Le Surréalisme médiatisé de Robert Desnos" appeared in the volume *Robert Desnos pour l'an 2000*, coedited by Katharine Conley and Marie-Claire Dumas (Paris: Gallimard, 2000), 13–24. "Against the Grain: Tracing Desnos's *Contrée* in Pétain's France" appeared in the volume *Surrealism in the New Century: Celebrating Robert Desnos*, coedited by Marie-Claire Barnet, Eric Robertson, and Nigel Saint (London: Philomel Productions, 2003). "The Myth of the 'Dernier Poème': Robert Desnos and French Cultural Memory" appeared in the volume *Acts of Memory: Cultural Recall in the Present*, coedited by Mieke Bal, Jonathan Crewe, and Leo Spitzer (Hanover: Dartmouth College–University Press of New England, 1999), 134–47. My thanks to these publishers for granting me permission to reprint this material.

I also wish to thank Kathleen Hart and Paul Fenouillet for housing me during my trips to visit Fern Malkine, Janet and Wingate Lloyd for allowing me to stay in their house on Cape Cod for six weeks, where for days the only sounds I heard were made by boats and wildlife, and Virginia Swain and Harry Beskind for letting me stay in their cottage on the Maine coast, where I was able to finish a draft of the manuscript to the sound of lobster boats and seagulls. I thank my family for their enthusiasm and encouragement as well as all the students who engaged in dialogue with me about "Bobby D," particularly Georgia Reid, who did research for me on this project in its early stages.

Most of all I wish to thank my husband, Richard Stamelman, for his enthusiastic support, his faith in this project, his patience, his countless helpful suggestions, his sense of humor, and his presence in my life.

Abbreviations

CHRD   Centre Historique de la Résistance et de la Déportation, Lyon, France.

D   *Robert Desnos pour l'an 2000.* Ed. Katharine Conley and Marie-Claire Dumas. Paris: Gallimard, 2000.

DSN   Desnos Archive, Jacques Doucet Literary Library

Dumas   Marie-Claire Dumas, *Robert Desnos ou l'exploration des limites.* Paris: Klincksieck, 1980.

Ecrits   Desnos, *Ecrits sur les peintres.* Ed. Marie-Claire Dumas. Paris: Flammarion, 1984.

F   Desnos, *Fortunes.* Paris: Gallimard, 1942.

L'Herne   *Robert Desnos.* Ed. Marie-Claire Dumas. Paris: Editions de L'Herne, 1987.

LL   Desnos, *Liberty or Love!* Trans. Terry Hale. London: Atlas, 1993.

LS   Breton, *The Lost Steps.* Trans. Mark Polizzotti. Lincoln: U of Nebraska P, 1996

M   Breton, *Manifestoes of Surrealism.* Trans. Richard Seaver and Helen R. Lane. Ann Arbor: U of Michigan P, 1972

Mines   Desnos, *Mines de rien.* Ed. Marie-Claire Dumas. Paris: Le Temps qu'il Fait, 1985.

NH   Desnos, *Nouvelles Hébrides.* Ed. Marie-Claire Dumas. Paris: Gallimard, 1978.

O   Desnos, *Oeuvres.* Ed. Marie-Claire Dumas. Paris: Gallimard-Quarto, 1999.

OC   *Oeuvres complètes,* various authors.

S   Desnos, *The Selected Poems of Robert Desnos.* Trans. Carolyn Forché and William Kulik. New York: Ecco P, 1991.

V   Desnos, *The Voice: Selected Poems of Robert Desnos.* Trans. William Kulik with Carole Frankel. New York: Grossman, 1972.

Voix   Desnos, *Les Voix intérieures.* Ed. Lucienne Cantaloube-Ferrieu. Nantes: Editions du Petit Véhicule, 1987.

Robert Desnos, Surrealism, and the Marvelous in Everyday Life

Introduction
Desnosian Surrealism

*1908: In a memorable snapshot eight-year-old Robert Desnos wears
a sailor suit and leans casually against a small table, sizing up the
photographer. He is in short pants, wearing a straw hat and white
gloves, and he holds in his left hand a book with a ribbon around it,
probably a prize won at school. The book anticipates his future life
as a "man of letters." The outfit also anticipates the piratical characters he will invent when he grows older—the intrepid Corsair
Sanglot, for example, who, on the pages of* Liberty *or* Love! *travels,
as the poet himself travels in dreams, to the marvelous land at the
bottom of the sea. (See fig. 1)*[1]

Histories of surrealism always include Robert Desnos as one of the leading
members of the original group. They always acknowledge that Desnos was the
most gifted of all the surrealists at the movement's defining activity of automatism, which involved giving free rein to the unconscious mind. As a result,
it seems logical to think about surrealism through the figure of Desnos, the
most prolific practitioner and star performer of automatism. Before now,
however, no one has made this obvious argument. In all likelihood it is
because Desnos broke with official surrealism in 1930, only six years into the
movement's forty-seven-year history.[2]

Desnos, however, according to his own testimony, never ceased to be a
surrealist. Certainly his work throughout the 1930s and 1940s until his death in
a concentration camp in 1945, a month short of his forty-fifth birthday, bears
witness to his use and practice of surrealist principles—what I call "Desnosian
surrealism." Furthermore, by popularizing surrealism in the media and by
carrying it into Nazi deportation camps, Desnos, a public intellectual by the
time of his arrest in 1944, contributed to the lasting effect surrealism has had
on the twentieth-century imaginary. He also made a significant contribution
to twentieth-century popular culture. In his lifetime and in his "afterlife"
today, Desnos remains exemplary both of surrealism and of his time, as I show
here by resituating Desnos within the history, social history, and culture of the
time in which he lived.

For example, in the opening passage of his antidrug novel *Le Vin est tiré...* (1943), published shortly before his arrest by the Gestapo, Desnos shows the extent to which he maintained his ability and desire to create surrealistic scenes throughout his life. In a prologue that describes a dreamlike event as though it were part of waking reality—the hypnotic encirclement of a North African military encampment by an unidentified white horse—Desnos evokes in sensually heightened prose the other-worldly mood of his Moroccan experience during his military service in the early 1920s:

> The moon glowed. Its light reflected off the deep dark shadows buried between the military huts. The air, the earth, and the night breathed together. Various perfumes wafted up from the tufts of grass and the clumps of dirt. The sentries on guard allowed themselves to be gently rocked by these exhalations and by the languid air of midnight, by the almost imperceptible movement of the planet and by the moonlight which seemed to cause the barbed wires to flower, and to soften the red of their fez hats and belts to an orange color and to give their khaki uniforms the shimmering glow of silk. (*O* 1002)[3]

Within a year of the publication of *Le Vin est tiré . . .* , written after his service in the military during the 1939–40 "phony war" with Germany, Desnos would again see and evoke the equivalent of flowers entwining barbed-wire fences, in his last known poem "Spring," but this time he would see them from inside the walls of the Nazi transit camp of Royallieu at Compiègne.

Desnos in Surrealist Literary History

Studies of surrealism, from Maurice Nadeau's first *History of Surrealism* (1945) to more recent historical works—for example, Jack Spector's *Surrealist Art and Writing, 1919–1939: The Gold of Time* (1997)—have focused on André Breton as the central figure of the movement. Breton coauthored the first automatic text, *The Magnetic Fields*, with Philippe Soupault in 1919; he wrote the first and second *Manifestoes of Surrealism* in 1924 and 1929; and many surrealist gatherings took place either at his apartment or at a café of his choosing. It is no accident that Breton won the nickname the "pope" of surrealism or that Bretonian surrealism and surrealism in general are often understood as synonymous terms.[4] Breton explained surrealism from its start and continued to define its objectives as he published books about it: from *Nadja* (1928) to *Communicating Vessels* (1932) to *Mad Love* (1937) and *Arcanum 17* (1945).

Recently, Georges Bataille's vision of surrealism, as expressed in essays written mostly after World War II and analyzed by such critics as Denis Hollier, Rosalind Krauss, and Michael Richardson, has given rise to a critical and often unsympathetic view of surrealism. Bataillean surrealism could be said to date from the moment in 1929 when Bataille became Breton's rival, rejecting the latter's authority, an act of apostasy to which Breton responded by ridiculing Bataille in the *Second Manifesto of Surrealism* (1929). Bataille got the last word in one of his most vehement rebuttals to Breton, published posthumously in a 1968 issue of *Tel Quel*, two years after the Breton's death.[5] Yet Bataille's view of surrealism, while valuable for the provocative and oppositional insight into Bretonian surrealism that it provides—Bataille accuses Breton of idealism, of favoring what he derisively calls an "Icarian movement" of thought—turns on and is determined by his role as an outsider. Even Bataille himself admits that he was the "enemy within" surrealism and never a full-fledged member of the group.

It is my contention here that Desnos was the person who shaped the very definition of surrealism, who inspired Bretonian surrealism, and through whom, consequently, the movement should be read. He was the laboratory of the surrealist project. His automatic experiences during the so-called period of sleeps—experiments with trancelike, hypnotic states of unconsciousness occurring from September 1922 through February 1923—inspired Breton to declare in the summer of 1924 that "*surrealism* is the order of the day and Desnos is its prophet" (OC 1, 473). A couple of months later Breton stated again, in the first *Manifesto,* that "Robert Desnos *speaks Surrealist* at will" (331; *M* 29). I believe that Breton's definition of *automatism,* which is at the root of his definition of *surrealism* itself, comes from his observation of Desnos's performances while in this semiconscious state, or "second" state as it was called. As psychoanalyst Fabienne Hulak has commented, Desnos's ability to access the truth of his unconscious mind, which through his automatic performances he "offered to the [surrealist] tribe," challenged Breton to define what the group had witnessed, which he proceeded to do in the first *Manifesto* (100). Desnos was better at automatism than Breton. He was better able to disconnect himself readily from rational thought processes and to surrender completely to the random thoughts and marvelous images that flowed from his unconscious mind.

Although Breton wrote automatically—*The Magnetic Fields* is an example—he also wrote analytically. The first *Manifesto of Surrealism* was initially composed as an introduction to, and explanation of, his automatic text *Soluble Fish.* In the first *Manifesto* Breton defined *surrealism* primarily in terms of automatism:

> SURREALISM, *n:* Psychic automatism in its pure state, by which one proposes to express—verbally, by means of the written word,

or in any other manner—the actual functioning of thought. Dictated by thought, in the absence of any control exercised by reason, exempt from any aesthetic or moral concern. (OC 1, 328; M 26)

While Breton was the movement's leader, he was also its rationalist pedagogue. But a pedagogical style, with its need for order, reason, clear presentation, and service to a preconceived idea, is fundamentally antithetical to the practice of surrealism itself and of automatism. Desnos, on the other hand, was naturally and simply surrealist, especially in his resistance to any kind of order, restraint, or preconceived experience, including any kind of hierarchical authority. In terms of his antiauthoritarianism, he resisted the domination of fascism and communism, as much as that of Bretonian surrealism. Desnos was a poet who spoke, drew, and wrote automatically. He did so effortlessly, without having to think about it or plan it. Automatism was part of his everyday experience: he never defined it; he just did it.

Desnos was a pivotal figure between Breton and Bataille as well. His first article in Bataille's journal *Documents* appeared in the autumn of 1929, just as Breton was drafting the *Second Manifesto* for the final issue of his journal, *La Révolution Surréaliste*, which had published Desnos's work throughout the 1920s. Desnos switched his allegiance from one friend to the other at the exact point when the two friends, Breton and Bataille, were turning on each other. Furthermore, it was at this juncture, in the late winter–early spring of 1929–30, that Desnos wrote his own manifesto of surrealism, entitled the "Troisième manifeste du surréalisme." In this text he took for himself the right to open up surrealism to the public and to take exception to Breton's more mandarin conception of the movement. "For surrealists there is only one reality, complete, open to everyone," Desnos wrote (*O* 487). "Surrealism has fallen into the public domain." This was the beginning of his explicit popularization of surrealism: on the radio, in songs, in lyrics for cantatas, in his drawings and paintings, and even as a political prisoner in Nazi concentration camps, where he gave impromptu lectures on surrealism and told surrealist jokes. Desnos anticipated surrealism's ongoing role in popular culture.

Finally, and not at all of the least importance, is Desnos's well-deserved reputation as a love poet. His love poems from 1926, "A la mystérieuse," inspired by the elusive singer Yvonne George, are justly famous as exemplary of the finest surrealist poetry. His most famous of these poems, "J'ai tant rêvé de toi" (I have dreamed so much of you), was so powerfully linked to him in the French cultural imagination that, as I explain in the final chapter of this book, he was thought to have rewritten it at the end of his life, as he lay dying in a newly liberated concentration camp.

Desnosian Surrealism

In asserting his right to present his own popular view of surrealism, Desnos established his "expertise" on his former role as surrealism's star and on his refusal to be co-opted by any authoritarian group, including the one, surrealism, with which he was most identified. With his anti-elitism and his focus on the multiple voices within the self and within surrealism, Desnos resisted Breton's attempt to shape the movement in his own image. At the same time, Desnos was not necessarily trying to create a new surrealism—one that would be substantially different from Breton's initial vision. Desnosian surrealism harks back to the mutually shared tenets that launched surrealism and clarifies its founding ideas. As Marie-Claire Dumas has suggested, the very concept of a movement involves the implicit contribution of several participants (*André Breton* 9). Desnos adhered to the initial ideology of surrealism as a movement fundamentally rooted in collective collaboration and partnership. He lived to the fullest the statement by Isidore Ducasse, so admired by the young surrealists, that "poetry ought to be made by everyone. Not by one person" (244).

Recent studies of surrealism, including those by Jacqueline Chénieux-Gendron, Renée Riese Hubert, Gérard Durozoi, and Martine Antle, have described the movement in terms of a group dynamic.[6] Recent scholarship on the contribution of women to surrealism has also produced multiple readings of the movement, as the plurality of the voices involved has become more apparent. I myself have argued that the evolution of surrealism should be understood in terms of a "conversation," in which ideas, images, and themes circulate and are reconfigured according to the perspective of various members of the group, especially women, who began to manifest themselves in the 1930s.[7] Desnos made a contribution to the surrealist "conversation" as a major player whose inspired performances helped to define the movement. As a consequence, it is fitting to examine the surrealist group dynamic and surrealist principles through the lens of the person of Robert Desnos. He best represents the group because he was unique in persisting in the ideological understanding of surrealism as nonelitist and as a way of life accessible to all. It is his irreverent and continually insurrectionist style that most anticipated the ways in which surrealism became part of our late-twentieth-century aesthetic.

My work would not have been possible without the scholarship of Marie-Claire Dumas. She has done the most significant critical analyses and biographical research on Desnos's work and life to date. She had the chance to interview extensively many of the people who knew him, including Youki Desnos. She organized his papers in the Jacques Doucet Literary Library in Paris, and she has been responsible for the meticulous posthumous editions of his writings, including the recent and indispensable *Oeuvres*. Yet, partly due to fashions in literary criticism, Dumas, like other authors of book-length studies of Desnos, has tended to separate his life from his literary work (although this is less true of her edition of the *Oeuvres*). Also, all previous studies have focused almost exclusively on writings from his explicitly surrealist period, from 1922 to 1930. They include Dumas's *Robert Desnos ou l'exploration des limites* (1980) and *Etude de Corps et biens* (1984), as well as Mary Ann Caws's *Poetry of Dada and Surrealism* (1970) and *The Surrealist Voice of Robert Desnos* (1977), Michel Murat's *Robert Desnos: Les Grands jours du Poète* (1988), and Armelle Chitrit's *Robert Desnos: Le Poème entre temps* (1996).[8]

I believe that the only way to evaluate Desnos's essential contributions to the surrealist movement, to popular culture, and to the arts of the twentieth century is to understand all his work, from the 1910s through the 1940s, in light of his life, which was fully engaged in every aspect of his milieu. This book is the result of my reading of Desnos's life together with all of his works in their biographical, historical, and cultural contexts. Here I reevaluate Desnos's published work alongside his unpublished writings (in different archives), biographical information partly derived from interviews with people who knew Desnos, his historical milieu, and the study of his nonliterary works, including radio productions, songs, screenplays, lyrics for cantatas, children's verse, drawings, and paintings.

For surrealism was more than just a literary or artistic movement. It was a way of life. Surrealism was a way of walking down the streets of Paris and seeing the marvelous in the everyday. My reading of surrealism through the works and the person of Desnos lies at the junction between literature and history. "Change life," Arthur Rimbaud had written. To change life by looking at the world in a new way—with the insight that human beings are dreamers and that what transpires in dreams and in the unconscious plays an integral part in the human experience—was the goal of the surrealist "revolution": hence the attention paid to what might seem like a politically passive activity, namely automatism. In fact, the "transporting" of the senses, which was possible through automatic exploration, was anything but a passive experience.[9] On the contrary, automatic practice made of the surrealist observer an attuned citizen, a phenomenon that was confirmed by the often risky work in the Resistance undertaken by Desnos, Louis Aragon, Paul Eluard, and René Char during the Occupation. This is why Desnosian surrealism must be understood as at once integrally related to Bretonian surrealism and independent of it. For, even though Desnos situated himself in relation to Bretonian surrealism, with his own move into political surrealism during the Occupation of France by the Nazis, he moved the principles of Bretonian surrealism into a more highly engaged domain. A reevaluation of the works and acts of Desnos, surrealism's first "prophet," will enhance our understanding of this formative, interdisciplinary movement as a whole and as it was integrated into the everyday.

The Desnosian Marvelous

Desnos declared in a movie review that the marvelous was "the supreme goal of the human mind" (*Rayons* 67). Breton incorporated the marvelous unequivocally into surrealist aesthetics in the first *Manifesto of Surrealism:* "the marvelous is always beautiful, any marvelous is beautiful, there is no marvelous that is not beautiful" (OC 1, 319; *M* 14). Etymologically, the word *marvelous,* from *mirabilia,* implies first and foremost a sense of surprise or shock. Shock is characteristic of the surrealist image as defined by Breton in the *Manifesto* (a definition borrowed from Pierre Reverdy), which is "*born*" from "*a juxtaposition of two or more distant realities*" 1, 324; *M* 20). The Desnosian marvelous borrows its sense of awe and wonder from the medieval *marvelous,* which, according to Daniel Poirion, bears "the marks of a rupture, of a gap establishing a distance within the represented world" (4). These "ruptures" are sometimes caused by abrupt changes of register in medieval literary texts, by an incursion of what Poirion calls a "popular soul," an *âme populaire.* In his surrealist adventure novel from 1927, *Liberty or Love!* Desnos stages a particularly surrealist textual "gap" between "distant realities" by abruptly juxtaposing the wanderings through Paris of Corsair Sanglot and his lover, Louise Lame, with a lost, white-hatted desert explorer who, upon finding a city in the desert, realizes it is a mirage (*O* 378; *LL* 108). The explorer's uneasiness infuses the Parisian scene with uncanniness. A disquieting sense results from the mixed registers of two different types of narrative, urban romance and exotic adventure.

In her description of the quality of the Desnosian marvelous in his unproduced screenplay, "Minuit à quatorze heures," Dumas argues that the marvelous consists of an integrating force within the present that draws dream realities onto the same plane as ordinary events. Desnos strives "to give more authentic presence to the surreal" ("Scénario" 137). I would go even farther and say that for Desnos the marvelous is part and parcel of everyday life and that everyday life is essentially marvelous, insofar as it is surprising, desirable, and at times tragic and awe inspiring. Desnos finds a strange poetry, for example, in a mountain of vegetables in the predawn light of the Halles market. He defamiliarizes the most ordinary things, showing that what is most ordinary can also be extra-ordinary. Instead of enacting "the power to tear one away from the everyday," as the Bretonian marvelous may be understood, according to his chief editor, Marguerite Bonnet—a transformation of reality that exoticizes the everyday—Desnos enacts a replenishing of the magical within the everyday experience (Bonnet, qtd. in Breton OC 1, 1349 n.5). One must also agree with Dumas about the medieval origins of the Desnosian marvelous, inspired doubtlessly by the poet's childhood spent in the labyrinthine streets of the medieval quarter of the Marais, a part of Paris adjacent to the central market of the Halles, where Desnos's father worked (see fig. 2).

In an article devoted to the fourteenth-century alchemist Nicholas Flamel published in 1929 in Georges Bataille's journal *Documents,* Desnos describes the neighborhood he imagines sharing with Flamel, at a distance of six hundred years, insisting that the smell of sulfur, characteristic of alchemical experiments, still lingers in the Marais air:

> You have to have lived in this neighborhood of Paris in order to recognize the sulfurous odor of magic spells that rises from its streets and its muddy rivulets. For ten years—from early childhood to adolescence—I lived in the house at the corner of the Rue Saint-Martin and the Rue des Lombards. From the upper balcony, every year before Easter, I could see strange men cover over the glassed cupolas of the chapels of the Saint-Merry [*sic*] church with a green fabric which made them look like inflated billiards tables. The multiple odors of the hardware shops on the Rue des Lombards, where racy shadows appear suddenly at night, are still mixed in my memory with the ineffable perfume exhaled by the coffee-grilling shop. I used to play in the square of the St. Jacques Tower, and I've watched three dragons come down from its cornice, as well as Saint Jacques with his smallpox scars. I passed Aubry-le-Boucher Street the very day when Liabeuf was writing his name in red capital letters in the memory of men: in the smoky taverns, dark men still sit elbow to elbow at the white wood tables. When I was learning to read, with *Les Misérables,* it was the neighborhood itself I was learning to spell and I sought traces of the famous riot along the walls of the Rue du Cloître-Saint-Merry and of the Rue des Juges-Consuls. (*O* 456)

Desnos moreover insists that he was visited by medieval ghosts—"Yes, ghosts exist"—before he even came to know their names from studying local history:[10]

> And so it is in this magical landscape towards which we have traveled along the lines of this article, the reader, myself, my fountain pen, and my imagination—one following the other, single file, along this magical landscape of the Square of the Innocents where we arrive towards four o'clock in the morning when the streetlights render even more dazzling the colors of the pyramids of turnips and carrots, where the *white* and the *red* are set against the greenest *green* and against the splendid *black* asphalt.[11] (*O* 457)

The magical, medieval past lives on in Desnos's surrealist present. In this passage Desnos typically equates the line of his writing with a physical space— a twisting path through the Marais's narrow streets, which have retained their medieval contours. This injunction to follow the lines of prose as though they were footpaths compels the reader to accompany the author to a scene haunted by the great fourteenth-century alchemist and to experience the sort of imaginary, alchemical transformation, the Rimbaldian *alchimie du verbe,* sought by the poet. Desnos seeks experiences able to transport him from his familiar urban environment into a suddenly strange and magical place contained within and coextensive with the familiar landscape and thus revealing to the poet and his reader-companion alike the explosion of the marvelous in everyday life.

The landscape in question here—namely, the Square des Innocents, located between the Halles, where Desnos's father worked, and the Marais, where the poet lived until 1926, first on the Rue Saint-Martin and later on the Rue de Rivoli—is, of course, one of the sites in Paris where the very first theatrical performances were enacted, the medieval mystery plays commemorated by Victor Hugo in *Notre-Dame de Paris.* Indeed, such a theatrical thespian heritage, with its make-believe décor and *jeu,* its masquerades and fantasies, so closely linked to the very place where Desnos grew up, may explain the poet's particular gift for masking and disguising himself and may account as well for his close friendship in the 1930s and 1940s with the actors Jean-Louis Barrault and Madeleine Renaud. Is it any wonder that this poet, raised in a quarter of Paris with contrasting faces and voices, where medieval and contemporary worlds collide and past and present voices are continually changing their forms, had a gift for mimicry that verged on ventriloquism (see fig. 3)? According to Henri Jeanson, with whom Desnos would later start a newspaper and write a film scenario in Occupied Paris, Desnos, as a teenager, enacted different personae to the amusement of his friends. His many nicknames included "Robert le Diable, Robert Tête-en-l'Air, Robert Pieds-sur-le-sol, Robert le Fou, Robert de Normandie, Robert-Robert," not to mention Robespierre; these multiple alter egos continued to play a role in his work throughout his life (*O* 32–33).

The different accents or registers of class affiliation that Desnos could capture in his speaking voice were doubled by the different qualities of speech that he was able to project later on the radio. It was as though Desnos, like the Marais, retained an uncanny access to the multiple voices and scenes to which he had been exposed throughout his life and which had been recorded and inscribed for centuries on the façades and in the alleys of his neighborhood. Seizing these traces from his unconscious mind and from the historical unconscious of the cityscape, he used them to surprise and stimulate his listener-readers. This mobility of speech and audition resembles, in a way, the physical experience of walking in the Marais today, where one is suddenly aware of switching from a twentieth- to a fifteenth-century milieu in the time it takes to draw a breath.

Desnosian Surrealism and the Everyday

Desnosian surrealism is embedded in the everyday, in the daily experience of Desnos's life and of French history, particularly Parisian history. What was the "everyday" for Desnos? First, it was the post-Haussmann Paris of the Third Republic. This Paris of Desnos's childhood is well recorded in the photographs of Eugène Atget, whom the poet met as Man Ray's neighbor and about whom he wrote an admiring essay (NH 435–436; see figs. 2 and 3). Second, it was the Paris Métro, opened only two weeks before Desnos's birth on 4 July 1900. This was the everyday of premodern and modern life, the everyday of a nation moving from a rural and agricultural to an urban and industrial society. In the year of Desnos's birth there were still ninety-eight thousand horses in Paris (Marchand 173). With Desnos's generation French was finally becoming the national language of the country and pulling the nation together; the results of the Ferry laws passed in the 1880s were beginning to reverse the tide of illiteracy so commonplace in nineteenth-century France.[12] Compulsory education included an inculcation into a new sense of republican nationalism that did not consistently meet with approval from those who came of age with the disaster of World War I.[13] Changing standards in hygiene led to the taking of more baths and to some brushing of teeth, although running water and electricity were a rarity even in urban dwellings during Desnos's childhood. Electric lamps were more commonly found in theaters, department stores, and government offices than in private homes (Weber, *Fin* 61, 71).

Desnos's interest in the everyday may be found in his use of "low" culture images like the Michelin "Bibendum" man and in his enthusiastic criticism of record albums and films. He admired the popular, larger-than-life characters featured in the movies and comic books, particularly the elegant thieves, Fantômas and Irma Vep (an anagram for the word *vampire*). He wrote in the 1920s that watching films about their exploits was equivalent to dreaming (*O* 411). Furthermore, Desnos's engagement in the everyday may be seen in his job as a journalist, a profession requiring that one work in and with the everyday. Unlike other surrealists, particularly Breton, Desnos was an author of both elite and popular cultural forms. He wrote for the print media in the 1920s and for the radio in the 1930s while forcing himself, especially in the mid-1930s, to compose a poem a day (later collected and published in *Fortunes* and *Etat de veille*). It was his deepest hope that some of these poems would be translated "freely" into songs, which they have been. Desnos also wrote specific lyrics for songs, for cantatas, and even for films. Through the media and through popular performances these works filtered into the everyday consciousness of French culture.

Desnos's involvement with the everyday, therefore, moved in two directions: he culled images from posters visible in the streets of Paris and incorporated them into his writing, and he wrote catchy poem-jingles and songs that flowed back out into the streets of everyday Paris through radio waves. He cultivated the in-between space separating high and low culture: on the one hand, the poetic production appreciated by an elite and, on the other, the popular culture sought after by a segment of the population that may never have read a poem outside of the classroom. Some of his own characters, in particular Louise Lame and Corsair Sanglot from *Liberty or Love!* could have leapt out of the pages of one of the serialized novels or films Desnos loved as an adolescent. The poems he began writing for children in the 1930s, initially for the children of his radio colleague Paul Deharme, reached an even wider and longer-lasting audience. Poems from his 1944 collection, *Trente chantefables pour les enfants sages à chanter sur n'importe quel air,* published after his arrest and deportation, are still memorized by children in nursery schools today.[14] It is rare to meet a French person who cannot recite a line from one of his children's poems and for whom such poems about the ant, the grasshopper, and the giraffe were not an initiation to poetry.[15]

The everyday as a critical category, of course, was not an object of study during Desnos's lifetime, not in the way that it has become since his death. The study of the everyday began with the publication of the first edition in 1946 of Henri Lefebvre's *Critique de la vie quotidienne* and with subsequent works by Maurice Blanchot, Michel de Certeau, Marc Augé, and others. Blanchot focuses on the human and ordinary aspects of the everyday. "The everyday, then, is ourselves, ordinarily," he writes (12). De Certeau studies the everyday in light of the "signifying practices" inherent in the " 'errant' trajectories" of "consumers," which he analyzes in terms of "strategies" and "tactics" (xviii–xix).[16] Augé examines the everyday with regard to models of social relations—of the traveler surrounded by unknown others in such anonymous environments as international airports, superhighways, or supermarkets.[17]

De Certeau, according to Michael Sheringham, owes much to the surrealists, specifically to "ethnographic surrealism" (as James Clifford calls it), in his reading of the "practices" of a city ("Du Surréel" 222). For Sheringham the surrealists enacted "a series of everyday *practices*" ("Du surréel" 223). Such "practices" of everydayness, as in the daily routine of walking one's dog (something Breton, Michel Leiris, and Raymond Queneau loved doing), affected Desnos as well, though he favored and kept cats rather than dogs.

·Desnos's everyday involved the very public work of inventing and actively producing commercial works for the radio and the private work of writing a poem a day. In this daily round of public and private activity, one domain is sometimes recycled into the other: the poetry of a billboard face resurfaces in a published poem, and a commercial jingle is brought to completion through the cadence or alliteration that only poetry can supply.

Of all those who have studied the everyday, Henri Lefebvre was most connected by time and interest to the surrealists. Lefebvre was once a friend of Breton's, whom he cites directly and indirectly in his work. Lefebvre's Marxist orientation gives his everyday a different focus from Desnos's experience because it is concerned more with economic realities than with poetry. Moreover, Desnos, although a leftist, never joined the Communist Party. Where Desnos's and Lefebvre's views may be seen to coincide, however, is precisely in the latter's understanding of everyday life: "We are in it and outside of it. No activity deemed 'elevated' may be reduced to it, but none can be detached from it" (46). Lefebvre later extends his definition: "It is in everyday life and from it that true *creations* are accomplished, those which produce the human and which men produce during their humanization: works" (50). These "works" include both art and acts—both of which demand full cognition in order to be accomplished. For Lefebvre the everyday is poised between "high" and "low," just as it was for Desnos, a poet who never separated himself from his status as journalist, friend, music lover, or antifascist. Desnos's life acts and life works illustrate his view of himself as a creator of both high and low art and of their conjunction and interaction. Perhaps the best example of the blending of the prosaic and the poetic, the popular and the elite, may be found in Desnos's illegal Resistance poems, which incited Parisians to take action against their Nazi occupiers, making his poems instruments for political action with the potential to transform the very condition of everyday life in Paris.

The chapters that follow chart the uniqueness of Desnos's life and work and the unique orientation they give to the trajectory of surrealism in the 1920s, 1930s, and 1940s. As with the introduction, each chapter begins with a vignette from Desnos's life—each one is drawn from known facts, and yet each one, necessarily, constitutes something of a fiction, a projection, as a way of setting the scene as evocatively as possible. The first chapter, "The Automatic Sybil as Rrose Sélavy," examines the origins and beginnings of surrealism and Desnos's role in determining the definition of surrealist activity. It covers Desnos's life and work up to 1926 and focuses on the way in which the experience of automatism takes place according to a temporal understanding of present time that may be seen as fundamentally baroque—as if suspended, as if the moment were endlessly folded within an indefinite present, something that happens in a dream or an automatic experience. While playing with automatism, Desnos also plays at bending gender stereotypes for the purpose of calling into question dominant notions of propriety and the nature of creativity, thus playing into and interpreting cultural anxiety concerning gender roles in France after the Great War.

In chapter 2, "The Sensory In-Between," I concentrate on the period between 1926 and 1931, when Desnos lived in a studio on the Rue Blomet in the fifteenth arrondissement. Desnos was literally "in between" lovers, between the singer Yvonne George, who never returned his love, and Youki, the wife of his painter friend, Tsuguhara Foujita, who did. The chapter examines Desnos's concurrent shift in allegiance from Breton to Bataille and the enhanced sensuality of his poetry.

The third chapter, "Radio and the Mediation of the Everyday," analyzes Desnos's growing role as a public intellectual in France as a result of his increasing visibility in the media. It examines the years from 1931 to 1939, when Desnos and Youki established a household, when his career on the radio took off, and when he began to be more politically active. Desnos's poetry comes to serve a new purpose during this period—a more socially communicative purpose, involving both the advertising of commercial products and the promoting of social causes.

In chapter 4, "Paris Watchman," I focus on the period leading up to Desnos's arrest in February 1944. During this time the poet was mobilized and served throughout the so-called phony war of 1939–1940 between France and Germany that preceded the German Occupation. Desnos also worked for the collaborationist newspaper *Aujourd'hui*, wrote children's verses, and composed both "legal" and "illegal" poetry, that is to say, poetry he was able to publish and poetry for which he could have been arrested. He was active in the Resistance cell "Agir," beginning in 1942, around the time of the first massive roundup of Jews in Paris, which took place in mid-July. Desnos's love poems from this period, dedicated to his endangered country, reveal the way that Desnosian surrealism enters a new phase in which dream and reality merge to create works that articulate a patriotism that defies fascism and strongly upholds democratic ideals.

In the fifth and final chapter, "The Myth and the Marvelous," I investigate the way in which the Desnosian experience of the marvelous infuses his last poems. The chapter treats Desnos's final sixteen months of life, from his arrest in Paris in February 1944 to his death at Terezin, the concentration camp outside of Prague, in June 1945. Both his real and mythical final poems are representative of the Desnosian marvelous: namely, his truly last poem, "Spring," written in the transit camp of Royallieu at Compiègne in April 1944, and his so-called "Dernier poème," which he did not in fact write but which French national memory has preserved as an enduring myth—and as a kind of memory site—with the power to evoke the triumph of the marvelous and of the imagination over the horrors of World War II. Perhaps because of its mythical status, it remains a fitting memorial to him.

Surrealist, poet, journalist, lover, radio personality, and *Résistant*—Desnos embodied what it meant to be young and French in the first half of the twentieth century. His professional and personal trajectory through French history between 1900 and 1945 defines surrealism. His place in the surrealist "conversation" has been modified, retrospectively, by his place in history and by the myth that has enfolded him and unfolded around him. Yet the myth is also a reality. For "Spring" has confirmed Desnos's, and surrealism's, enduring commitment to "change life" in a way that moves from poetry to politics and from love to hope, the hope for the future of humankind.

The Automatic Sibyl
as Rrose Sélavy

1922: Near Place Blanche, in the apartment of André Breton, the lights are out. Only the flashing neon signs from the nightclubs on the Boulevard Clichy eerily illuminate the room. Suddenly the young man, his long hair combed back, slumps in the chair where he has fallen asleep. He electrifies his audience with short aphoristic poems in the style of Marcel Duchamp, whom he has never met. He inspires one participant, Louis Aragon, to describe the assembled group as "surprised utensils" confronted by a poetic voice resonating as profoundly as the voice of the sibyl at Delphi, to which they all feel connected as though by a huge underground sea. (See fig. 15)[1]

Robert Pierre Desnos was born on 4 July 1900 at 6 A.M. His father, Lucien, had moved to Paris from Normandy at sixteen. By age twenty-eight he owned his own poultry and game stand at Les Halles, the huge market in central Paris, and was prosperous enough to propose marriage to Claire Guillais, whom he admired and considered above his station. "Have I perhaps raised my sights too high?" he mused in his letter of proposal. "I was not thinking about the distance that separates us" (DSN 416). She accepted. Their first child was a daughter named Lucienne after her father. The family lived on the Boulevard Richard Lenoir in the eleventh arrondissement until 1902, when they moved to the Rue Saint-Martin in the Marais, at the heart of medieval Paris. The apartment building at number 11, Rue Saint-Martin rises five stories above the ground-floor store—where today books are sold—to end in a roof punctuated with dormer windows. When Desnos was thirteen, the family moved around the corner to the Rue de Rivoli, to a more elegant building reflecting Lucien and Claire Desnos's financial stability and solid middle-class status. The Halles was just a few blocks to the west;[2] to the east the curved streets of the old Jewish quarter wound their way toward the Bastille. As an adult, Desnos wrote about the magical properties of this neighborhood.

Desnos went to neighborhood schools through the age of sixteen and just missed the draft in World War I, unlike his surrealist friends André Breton,

Louis Aragon, and Paul Eluard, who were roughly four years older. He had less formal education than most in his surrealist circle. Although his self-education was extensive, resulting in impressive erudition, Desnos never lost his connection to the working-class milieu in which he grew up.[3] While he may not have seen the war firsthand, he was, however, inevitably marked by the cataclysm that cost the lives of roughly 1.5 million Frenchmen.[4] He was playing Dadaist pranks with friends by the age of eighteen and had already begun to record his dreams and to write poetry. He was a great fan of Victor Hugo, Arthur Rimbaud, and Guillaume Apollinaire, the poet who coined the word *surrealism.*[5]

Desnos began his obligatory military service in the infantry in the Haute-Marne in 1920. Accompanied by Benjamin Péret, whom he already knew, he first met Breton and Aragon while on leave in the spring of 1921. Also present at the bar in the soon-to-be-demolished Passage de l'Opéra, which Aragon later memorialized in *Paris Peasant,* were Tristan Tzara, Georges Ribemont-Dessaignes, Blaise Cendrars, and Raymond Radiguet. To Desnos, as he would recall later, Breton seemed very thin. With his tortoiseshell glasses he looked just like the American comedian Harold Lloyd. Desnos stayed to have dinner with Breton, Tzara, and Péret but was too nervous to say much; he felt foolish: "A disastrous dinner. All I could say was 'of course.' That evening I must have seemed a complete fool" (*O* 39).

Desnos completed his military service in Morocco as a *tirailleur algérien*—the *tirailleurs algériens* were infantry troops located outside of France, made up of local soldiers under the orders of French officers and soldiers. After a brief stay in the infirmary, he befriended the camp doctor and spent the remainder of his military service as the doctor's secretary (Fraenkel 318). In 1922, his military service complete and the awkward dinner all but forgotten, Desnos moved into a maid's room above his parents' apartment at number 9, Rue de Rivoli in the Marais. He easily entered the Dadaist group, thanks in part to his friendship with Breton's friends Péret, Georges Limbour, and Roger Vitrac, and walked straight into a starring role in the incipient surrealist movement.

Surrealist Automatism and the "Hypnotic Sleeps": Desnos as Sybil

Because of the talent he displayed at the poetic and verbal experiments the Parisian Dadaist group began to perform in September 1922, Desnos quickly moved to the center of this band of young men, most of whom would later become surrealists. In his essay "The Mediums Enter" Breton describes how these experiments began with the great poetic potential he and his friends saw in practicing surrealist mediumistic activity in a group—which had nothing to do with communication between the living and the dead, the purpose of most "automatic" activities conducted by mediums—after hearing René Crevel's dramatic depiction of his participation in a séance during his summer vacation (OC 1, 276; LS 92). Breton, along with Crevel, Desnos, Péret, Francis Picabia, Paul Eluard, Max Morise, and Max Ernst, decided to hold séances themselves, primarily in order to explore their own unconscious minds. Among those present on the first night were Simone Breton and Alice Prin, known as Kiki. Eventually others joined them, including more wives and companions: Picabia's companion, Germaine Everling; Péret's friend Renée Gauthier; Vitrac and his friend Suzanne; Gala Eluard, wife of Paul Eluard; Roland Tual, with whom Desnos would later make the movie *Bonsoir Mesdames, Bonsoir Messieurs;* and the Italian painter Giorgio de Chirico. Breton was already calling this activity "surrealism," two years before he wrote the first *Manifesto of Surrealism:* "To a certain degree it is generally known what my friends and I mean by *Surrealism.* We use this word, which we did not coin and which we might easily have left to the most ill-defined critical vocabulary, in a precise sense" (1, 274; LS 90). He and his friends were considerably impressed with Desnos's particular abilities during these experiments. Four years later, writing *Nadja*, he qualified Desnos's utterings at these early séances as possessing "absolutely oracular value" (1, 661; 32).[6]

The first automatist session took place on 25 September 1922. Crevel went into a "hypnotic slumber" and began to speak dramatically, causing Kiki to leave the room in fright. Sounding like a defense lawyer, he told the story of a woman who said she had killed her husband at his own request (Desnos, *O* 129; Breton, OC 1, 276; LS 92–93). Then Desnos's head fell onto his arm. He sighed and, without speaking, began to scratch the table "compulsively" with his fingernails (OC 1, 277; LS 93). When he awoke, he claimed to have no memory of his performance: "I was convinced I had not even moved my hands and that I had been closely watching Morise the entire time" (*O* 129, see fig. 15). Thomas Simonnet accurately points out how all the summaries of the "sleeps" reveal "Desnos's body in action. . . . It communicates and in a tumultuous fashion" (*D* 107–08).

Two days later when they met again, Crevel, having suggested that scratching indicated a desire to write, paper and pencil were placed in front of Desnos. Once again Desnos went into a hypnotic trance, and this time he began to write, dramatically breaking pencils in the process. His first written automatic words were "14 July": the date of the storming of the Bastille. At this point the others began to question him, and he replied. His answer to the first question—"What do you see?"—was "Death," a theme to which he would return regularly.[7] Another such theme was revolution, for Desnos often identified himself in his sleep as Robespierre, one of the main actors in the bloody Terror at the time of the Revolution, whose name sounds like "Robert Pierre."

Within a month, while in a "second" state, he was voicing short, aphoristic poems in the style of Marcel Duchamp's invented alter ego, Rrose Sélavy.

The group continued to meet until mid-October, most often at Breton's apartment at 42, rue Fontaine, in the ninth arrondissement, just off Boulevard Clichy at the base of the Montmartre hills. And they met in November while Breton was out of town in Barcelona, where he gave a talk describing Desnos as the only "man freed from all restraints" (OC 1, 307; LS 125).[8] Based on interviews with the participants, Sarane Alexandrian has explained that Breton would welcome guests with an opened book by a despised author outside his door in lieu of a welcome mat, so that they could wipe their feet on it as they entered (106). A photograph taken by Man Ray in a re-creation of that time for the surrealist journal La Révolution Surréaliste shows Desnos at the focal point (see fig. 4). Crouched down in profile, facing away from the camera, he gesticulates as he speaks. Simone, seated at a typewriter slightly above him and to his right, looks down at him, as do most of the others (Eluard and Chirico look directly at the camera). The group stands in a tight semicircle around Desnos: he is completely engrossed in the automatic experience, while the rest of the participants look on self-consciously.

The accounts given of these sessions of "hypnotic sleeps," as they were called, agree on the disquieting nature of the trances produced. The scene in the Bretons's apartment was "charged with the indefinable presence of paintings, objects, and masks," according to Marguerite Bonnet, who interviewed participants and had access to Simone Breton's letters. The room was uncannily pierced by "the changed voice of the one who spoke while 'asleep,' in particular his exclamations, his cries, his sighs, the very content of his talk: for example the bloody scenes evoked by Crevel, or the constant theme of death brought up by Desnos" (qtd. in Breton OC 1, 1302). Indeed, photographs of the apartment, subsequently confirmed by a private visit, reveal an intimate space jammed with statues, masks, paintings, sculptures, books, and a collection of stones retrieved from riverbeds.[9] There is no doubt that even in the dark an eerie presence must have emanated from the objects surrounding the hypnotized participants. At night the lights from the nightclubs on nearby Boulevard Clichy would have cast spooky shadows on the walls of the darkened room.[10] Furthermore, the testimony of all witnesses and participants points to Desnos as the undisputed master of poetic inspiration and sibylline vocalization.

Characterizing the oral utterances and written texts of these hypnotic slumbers as a kind of "magic dictation" (OC 1, 275; LS 91), Breton used them as the keystone to his definition of surrealism in the 1924 Manifesto: "Psychic automatism in its pure state, by which one proposes to express—verbally, by means of the written word, or in any other manner—the actual functioning of thought" (1, 328; M 26). Indeed, automatism's focus on "pure thought" helped prompt surrealism's autobiographical emphasis: what these poets wrote about was their most intimate selves, about the visions provoked by the inward-directed automatic process. Of all the surrealists Desnos was the one who was best able to speak, write, and draw, at will, the "actual functioning" of his thoughts during this formative automatist period; he was surrealism's purest practitioner. This is why Breton proclaimed in the *Manifesto* that "Robert Desnos *speaks Surrealist* at will" (1, 331; *M* 29).

For Aragon the kind of playful poetic activity so often ascribed to Desnos is an exploration of "words that are mirrors, optical lakes towards which hands stretch out in vain" (*Peasant* 111, 91). Desnos was indeed the master of the "word-mirror," of transformational games played in language and with images, for he could draw as well as write when in a trance. Both media inspired him. Drawings from the 1920s begin as free-form scribbles in pencil over which the blue and black ink outlines of various heads, two "adventurers" in tuxedos, a swan, an "angel," a fish, and a mermaid identified as "Leda" are drawn in a strong hand. Lines of text, lines of images, together produce a map of the creative process: form emerges out of formlessness according to the rules for automatism spelled out in Breton's first *Manifesto*, which calls for opening the mind and allowing unconscious thoughts to flow out onto paper.[11] Other drawings produced by Desnos as a joke prompted Breton to declare in a celebrated footnote to the *Manifesto* that Desnos had proved that automatism could induce visual as well as verbal productions.[12] The drawings were created for "Le Génie sans miroir," an article written as a hoax to mock Weiland Mayr, the conservative managing editor of the journal *Les Feuilles Libres*.

Desnos's wrote "Le Génie sans miroir" and made the accompanying drawings after he failed to provoke Mayr sufficiently by slapping him in public. In the article, published in the January–February 1924 issue of *Les Feuilles Libres* under Eluard's name (in order to disguise Desnos's identity), he purported to reproduce drawings by "madmen" and to do so in a serious "scholarly" study (other contributors to the issue included Tzara, Pablo Picasso, and Pierre Drieu la Rochelle). But the "mad" drawings were automatically produced by Desnos himself. The names of the Polish "madwomen" mentioned in the article, whose poems he supposedly cites, were anagrams of the names of some of Desnos's acquaintances, including Anna de Noaille(s) (Anne Ilda-Salon), Jean Cocteau (Joanna Tucce), and even "Willand" Mayr himself (Maria Delwyn) (*O* 222–29).

In the article he describes the power of madmen to access other worlds through a sense of vision focused on "infinity" and thus anticipates Aragon's conclusion to his version of a surrealist manifesto, *Une Vague de rêves:* "Let infinity in" (L'Herne 84; *Vague* 29). Desnos's drawings demonstrate the same zany humor found in his word poems from the same period. One sketch shows a man's mustache drawn out so far from his face on either side that birds perch on it, while a sun and a moon extend outward from his boots. Another drawing figures a woman (with feet that look suspiciously like drumsticks) doing a handstand. Above her head a bird apparently performs gymnastics, whereas an abstract shape behind her mimes her physical position (see fig. 5).[13]

Just as Desnos's writings and drawings during the early years of surrealism forged the inevitable surrealist link between visual and verbal poetry, conflating plastic and poetic forms into a common aesthetic for the movement, so did Desnos as a person embody an essential duality. He was at once the voice of pure psychic automatism, as his entranced proclamations during the period of hypnotic sleeps attest, and its record, its "book," as Breton notes in the *Manifesto*: "He reads himself like an open book and does nothing to retain the pages, which fly away in the windy wake of his life" (OC 1, 331; M 29). Desnos put his entire self into automatism and into the writing that resulted from it; he joined with it, fusing himself to it. He could "morph" psychically into all the characters he invented and then effortlessly return to his own persona.

In the radio interviews Breton gave in 1952 he described Desnos as unique: "No one else ever rushed so headlong onto every path of the marvelous. . . . Everyone who witnessed Desnos's daily plunges into what was truly the *unknown* was swept up into a kind of giddiness; we all hung on what he might say, what he might feverishly scribble on a scrap of paper" (*Conversations* 67). He was what Breton had been looking for, a spokesman for the collectively creative efforts of surrealism. His ability to lose track of time when he fell into a trance and to become immobilized in a suspended instant reveal how the experience of automatism was lived according to an experience of time that was fundamentally baroque in the sense that sociologist Michel Maffesoli gives it, as a "methodological lever" rather than as a historical time period (154). Gilles Deleuze describes baroque suspension as a fold "that goes towards infinity" (5), an idea upon which Maffesoli elaborates: "Thus, the metaphor of folds, of complication, sends us back to an original ensemble suggested by the baroque: of time immobilized, of time that takes root, of time that folds into itself" (156).

Desnos described this experience of baroque time metaphorically in his 1927 novel, *Liberty or Love!* when the protagonist, Corsair Sanglot, reaches out to his double—his own reflection in the ocean waters—his eyes closed, and gets dragged, unscathed, down to the bottom of the ocean floor, which resembles blotter paper, where he discovers such incredible sights as a mermaid cemetery (O 340–41; LL 60). Corsair's journey, like the experience of automatic trance, evokes a state during which time stands still and marvels hidden deep within the folds of the psyche are revealed. The moment of Corsair's plunge through the surface of his own reflection, eyes wide open, is a moment in baroque time akin to one of Desnos's own descents into alert dream consciousness, eyes wide shut, during the "period of sleeps."

There were those, however, who doubted the authenticity of Desnos's hypnotic performances. In his biography of Breton, Mark Polizzotti describes Desnos's "sleeping fits" as a "psychological narcotic," giving credence to Matthew Josephson's opinion that Desnos was "plainly psychotic" (qtd. in Polizzotti 187). Josephson, an American friend of the surrealists, attended none of the hypnotic sleep sessions, by his own admission, yet in his memoir, *Life among the Surrealists,* he claims that the recitals during those sessions "lacked—shall we say—verisimilitude" (220, 217). Ribemont-Dessaignes and Cendrars, who had been present at Desnos's first meeting with Breton and who admitted to never having attended a session, claimed that Desnos had cheated; even Eluard, in a letter to Breton, makes a dismissive reference to Desnos's being somewhat drunk during one of their sessions (Dumas 47–49).

Nevertheless, everyone who actually saw Desnos in a second state and who attended one of these sessions agrees that his performances were extraordinary. Man Ray insists that Desnos's behavior during the séances "would have been miraculous even if previously prepared and memorized" (223).[14] In 1924 Aragon, addressing the question directly of the authenticity of surrealist mediumistic activity, wondered whether participants like Desnos were really asleep: "Some people ask whether they [the participants] were really sleeping. In their heart of hearts, sceptics want to deny this adventure. The notion of simulation is put on the table. I can't accept it. How can simulating something be different from thinking it. What is thought, is. . . . The shock of such a spectacle necessarily requires wild explanations: the beyond, metempsychosis, the marvelous. The price of such interpretations is, of course, incredulity and mockery" (*Vague* 18–19). Earlier Aragon had stated that "neither laughter nor doubt" could trouble the reality of these experiences. After World War II he told Dominique Desanti, who met Desnos in the 1938, that "'Desnos's ability to work himself up was truly extraordinary. He was often elsewhere'" (interview, 3 Mar. 1999).[15]

Receptivity to hypnosis can require, as Marie-Claire Dumas suggests, some preparatory activity that induces a state wherein simulation and authentic inspiration become confused: "whatever the forms of second states, it is easier to reach them if one wants to do so; and such a desire could not manifest itself better than by means of simulation. . . . [Desnos] certainly took pleasure, on several occasions, in deliberately mystifying his audience; but if he succeeded in simulating so successfully, it probably means that on other occasions he went beyond simulation into a veritable state of auto-hypnosis" (50–51). There is an almost imperceptible frontier, in other words, between simulation and hypnosis (just as later experiments by Breton and Eluard, in *The Immaculate Conception,* would question the fine line dividing sanity from madness), and Desnos, the automatic acrobat, was indeed somewhat responsible for fashioning himself in these sessions. At the same time, those who doubted Desnos's automatist trances were probably expressing an understandable discomfort with automatism itself.

Random thoughts as expressed during the free association typical of automatism can become exaggerated; slips of the tongue, what Sigmund Freud called "parapraxes" in his *Introductory Lectures,* Desnos unconstrainedly, fearlessly, and adventurously let spill out of his unconscious (25). Already in October 1921, during his military service in Morocco, Desnos proclaimed his propensity for automatism—using other words—in a letter to his friend Georges Gautré: "My head is like a piggy-bank in which words, ideas, memories jingle pell-mell. I shake it all up. My mouth releases a coin" (*D* 382).

Performative utterances, according to the linguist François Récanati, often accomplish and bring about, rather than describe, the state of affairs they represent: "What counts, is that the utterance *present itself* as self-verifying, that it *aim* at bringing about the state of affairs it represents" (169–70). When random thoughts are performed with conviction, the form they happen to take acquires gravitas because of the very nature of performativity. If these different kinds of thoughts turn out to be contradictory, which seems inevitable with automatism, then what is revealed is the fact that identity itself, when set free from any restraint, may be called into question. And he performed this automatic activity, with his body and for an audience, leading Dumas to make a most appropriate comparison between Desnos in these sessions and Doctor Charcot's hysterical patient, known as Augustine, who also drew attention to herself with her exaggerated poses (*O* 123).

Desnos bodily acted out through the medium of his person and his own identity, the creative strategy of recycling old materials with a new intent that Elza Adamowicz ascribes to surrealist collage: "the creative transformation of ready-made elements, forging the surreal out of fragments of the real, suggesting the *merveilleux* through the combination of banal and defunct images, clichés and rewritten texts" (17). The elements in Desnos's "collage" of the self were more disturbing to others than Ernst's visual collages at the time, however, because the "ready-made elements" he recycled were the "coins" of the detritus pulled by chance out of his own unconscious, which sometimes involved quoting or imitating the works of others. This recycling aspect of Desnos's automatism was a component in the questioning of Desnos's sincerity in these performances, as Andrew Rothwell pointed out in a recent talk.[16] Furthermore, as media scholar Paddy Scannell argues, sincerity in a performance is inherently paradoxical, because sincerity is more linked to "everyday personal life" than to public life or performance, especially before radio and television—media that privilege sincerity and which tore "down the fence" distinguishing life and art (59–60, 74). Desnos's ability to perform such a private activity as dreaming in front of a group demonstrates how capable he was of occupying the oscillating space in between his private and public selves. It is no wonder he became a masterful radio broadcaster.

By blithely bridging the frontier between consciousness and unconsciousness, Desnos also clearly made others feel uneasy because he revealed the risks of automatism: the danger of appearing foolish as well as the risk of losing one's grip on mental stability or on a coherent sense of identity. Desnos's performances, corporeally embodying his mental journeys, made a mockery of any sort of stable, centered notion of a singular, or "true," self (or even sexual identity, as we will see) that might possibly emerge from psychic experiments. That identity is a slippery, ambiguous phenomenon is most likely the probability that alarmed so many in Desnos's circle and prompted them to question his sincerity. For, in publicly playing with his own identity, Desnos, the automatic sibyl, revealed what others may have feared: namely, that his identity (and, by association, their own) was as various as the voices he playfully or seriously assumed, that it was multifaceted, richer, and therefore threatening in its complexity.

Breton was aware of the more visible dangers incurred by the hypnotic sleeps, which tended to provoke "impulsive activities in certain sleeping subjects that boded the worst." It worried him, for example, when it became increasingly difficult to wake Desnos from his trances (*Conversations* 69–70).[17] His concern was well founded. He brought the period of hypnotic sleeps to a close after Desnos, supposedly while asleep, chased Eluard with a knife around the latter's own house and garden. Another disturbing sign of the danger occurred when Crevel and others tried to hang themselves in the foyer of the house of Madame de la Hire, a friend of Picabia's (70). On 28 February 1923, according to Simone Breton, Desnos, again supposedly asleep, locked everyone into a room and only woke up when Picabia started to take the lock apart from the inside (Bonnet 267). Given the demons that these "sleeps" were releasing and Breton's perception that Desnos wanted to focus all attention on himself, Breton put a halt to these experimental evenings; yet of all the participants it was, Breton admits, Desnos "who indelibly stamped his mark on this form of activity" (*Conversations* 67).

Gender and Identity Anxiety in Interwar France

Nostalgia took on nationalistic dimensions after World War I, as the French romanticized the quality of life they had led before the outbreak of war in 1914. Widespread strikes occurred in 1919 and 1920, and the Left splintered into three parties: the Radicals, the Socialists, and the newly formed Communist Party (1920). The franc was weakened. Prewar life by comparison looked good and was celebrated in popular songs, according to historian Charles Rearick: "In their homes, a large nostalgic public nourished memories by endlessly playing phonograph records of the old songs. People sang along, as they knew the words by heart" (102). The years immediately following the war were indeed difficult, exacerbated by an influx of immigrants from Eastern Europe. One man remembers the end of both 1918 and 1919 as times when "coal was rare, butter impossible to find, it was difficult to get eggs; sugar was an object of great luxury, meat kept getting more expensive and everything cost too much. . . . Disorder reigned everywhere" (qtd. in Becker and Berstein 182). Not before 1919 was an eight-hour workday, six days out of seven, voted into law. Social protections such as social security, health insurance, and pensions were not legislated before 1930.

Raymond Poincaré, president from 1913 to 1920 and head of the government again from 1926 to 1929, coined the phrase *l'union sacrée* in August 1914, the first month of World War I. Poincaré used it as an appeal to the French to present a united front to the enemy: "In this new war, France . . . will be heroically defended by all her sons, who will remain undaunted in the face of the enemy, in their sense of *sacred union*" (qtd. in Becker and Berstein 27). The concept of a "sacred union" was appealing precisely because the country had not been united and needed to be; this struggle for unity would last throughout most of the interwar period.

Succeeding governments between 1920 and 1926 failed to restitute an imperfectly remembered prewar sense of stability, however, including proponents of a governmental policy called the *Bloc national,* in echo of the *union sacrée.* Members of an internally divided Left coalition known as the Cartel des Gauches in turn failed to make the everyday conform to the nostalgic myth of a united France. As a result, Poincaré, still representing France's hope for national consensus, returned to power in July 1926. He succeeded in stabilizing the franc in a movement appropriately known as the *Union nationale.* He incorporated into the new government several leaders from the newly deposed Left coalition, including the socialist Nobel Peace prize laureate Aristide Briand, and thus managed to achieve more of a political consensus than any other government since the end of the war in 1918.

Surrealists responded to the prevailing ambivalent mood with a political act of their own, aimed against those mainstream policies, such as the *sacred union,* intended to shore up patriotic feeling. In October 1924, just as the first *Manifesto* was becoming available in bookstores, Aragon, Breton, Eluard, and Soupault, together with Pierre Drieu la Rochelle and Joseph Delteil, published a scandalous pamphlet attacking the writer Anatole France, revered as the "sustainer of the French language" and widely regarded as a national hero.[18] Publication of the pamphlet, composed of individually written tracts and provocatively entitled *A Corpse,* coincided with the state funeral of France himself, an occasion of national mourning (Nadeau 233–37). France's greatest transgression in the eyes of the surrealists had been his authorship of the kind of traditional "literature" they despised, including his patriotic historical novels. The title of Aragon's contribution to *A Corpse* was the most derisive: "Have You Ever Slapped a Dead Man?" Soupault mocked France for sounding like a "very pedantic schoolmaster." "Your kind, corpse, we don't like," wrote Eluard. Breton accused him of the worst sin of all: namely, the kind of patriotic feeling that had made possible World War I and the loss of so many of his generation.[19]

Three years later, in 1927, Drieu la Rochelle wrote hyperbolically in *La Suite des idées* that Parisian French culture was a "civilization which no longer has . . . sexes" (125). Mary Louise Roberts paraphrases this quotation for the title of her cultural history of interwar France, *Civilization without Sexes.* She argues that, while many men returned from World War I emasculated by the devastating experience of trench warfare, women had become more "masculine" than ever before, at least superficially, by replacing men in the job market, occasionally wearing men's work clothing, and "bobbing" their hair. Yet "masculine" men and "feminine" women continued to be idealized by the government-supported media as the most desirable and patriotic of French citizens.

According to Roberts, the so-called *loi scélérate* of 1920, as a result, tried to force women to return home and to leave the workplace to men, with pronatalist legislation that forbade contraception and any advertising promoting family planning. The primary desired effect of this law was to encourage childbearing because of the drop in the male population in France following the war. In 1911, for example, for every 1,000 men there were 1,035 women; while in 1921 for every 1,000 men between twenty and twenty-four, there were 1,200 women and for every 1,000 men between twenty-five and twenty-nine, there were 1,323 women (Becker and Berstein 156). The restrictive legislation of the 1920 law was further criminalized with a law from 1923, which, according to historian Sian Reynolds, redirected "abortion cases to magistrate's courts instead of to juries, with the aim of obtaining more convictions" (18). Roberts describes the Senate debates over the 1920 *loi scélérate* as "theaters of anxiety," "apocalyptic" in tone because "depopulation as a concept was forced to bear the emotional weight of displaced economic and military anxiety" (110).

Roberts states more globally that "male and female roles were intricately linked in a larger vision of social organization, changes in one profoundly destabilized the other" (33). One reason this "larger vision" of society was linked to gender, of course, was that the nation itself had come to possess a feminine identity, as the art historian Romy Golan explains in *Modernity and Nostalgia:* "The discourse on the reconstituted body of France was a secular and, not surprisingly, overwhelmingly feminized one. Certainly the grammatically female gendering of the name of nations in most Latin languages lay at the root of this practice. But in postwar France, this standard female gendering assumed an almost visceral resonance" (18). Roberts and Reynolds, in the wake of the historians Jean-Jacques Becker and Serge Berstein, describe natalist propaganda sponsored by the government as featuring images that show France as an ailing metaphorical body, most often gendered as female: "By framing the argument in terms of a female social body in mortal need of help, they authorized their right to control the female sexual body" (Roberts 108–09). Female identity in postwar France became "a privileged site for a larger ideological project: how to come to terms with rapid social and cultural change, and how to articulate a new, more appropriate order of social relationships" (5).

In terms of surrealism the generalization could be made that the male surrealist response to the cultural anxiety swirling around gender was to shore up a potentially threatened masculine heterosexuality—and at the same time to refute bourgeois notions of patriotism, which had led to the loss of almost an entire generation of French men—while concurrently examining his own interior sense of femininity, as revealed under the influence of automatism. Heterosexuality was clearly privileged by Breton, even though homosexuals like Crevel were accepted by the group, with a kind of "don't ask, don't tell" policy. Two artists linked to surrealism, Marcel Duchamp and Desnos, chose to dramatize with their own identities the fraught question of gender by creating works of art under the female pseudonym of Rrose Sélavy.

Rrose Sélavy: From Duchamp to Desnos

On 1 October 1922 some word games were published as one-liners in *Littérature,* the antiliterary Dada journal coedited by Breton, Soupault, and Aragon. These word games were attributed to "Rrose Sélavy" but written by Marcel Duchamp. In his biography of Duchamp, Calvin Tomkins explains that "Rose Sélavy sprang full-grown from the mind of Marcel Duchamp during the late summer or early fall of 1920" and quotes from an interview with Duchamp: " 'It was not to change my identity,' he once said, 'but to have two identities.' His first thought had been to choose a Jewish name to offset his Catholic background. 'But then the idea jumped at me, why not a female name? Much better than to change religion would be to change sex . . . Rose was the corniest name for a girl at that time, in French, anyway. And Sélavy was a pun on *c'est la vie.*'" (231). Duchamp's word game poems in *Littérature* play on the nature of homonyms, such as the name Rrose Sélavy, which is a pun for "Eros is life": on the fact that words that sound similar can have radically different meanings. For in automatic poems "a logic of words comes to be, a logic that has nothing to do with normal linguistic communication," as Michael Riffaterre notes (202). The one-line poem "Sa robe est noire dit Sarah Bernhardt" (Her dress is black, says Sarah Bernhardt), for example, only makes "sense" when a listener hears how *sa robe est noire* (her dress is black) sounds like the spoken name Sarah Bernhardt (who may often have worn black because she played male roles) (15). In a later example, "Rrose Sélavy et moi estimons les ecchymoses des Esquimaux aux mots exquis" (Rrose Sélavy and I esteem the bruises of Eskimos who speak exquisitely), the words *estimons, ecchymoses, Esquimaux,* and *mots exquis* all fold over onto one another, seeming to resemble one another, because even with very different meanings these words have similar sounds.[20] Their similarities include spoonerisms, whereby *Esquimaux* is transformed into *mots exquis.* Inside one meaning another meaning or identity is hidden—exquisite words are buried within the Eskimo people; one person or personality is veiled by another, as in the double personae of Duchamp and his cross-dressed alter ego, Rrose Sélavy. With Rrose Sélavy, Duchamp performs what Amelia Jones calls one of his "equivocal sexualizations of the . . . author-function" (33).

Marjorie Garber argues in *Vested Interests* that the cross-dresser enacts a kind of "third sex" and that this concept of the "third" is an important and subversive "mode of articulation, a way of describing a space of possibility. Three puts into question the idea of one: of identity, self-sufficiency, self-knowledge" (11). The concept of the third, neither one or the other, also comes into play in Duchamp's staging of Rrose Sélavy in Man Ray's photographs, specifically in the photograph entitled *Belle Haleine* (Beautiful Breath), that they created together in 1920 for the cover of *New York Dada. Belle Haleine* is a photograph of a bottle recognizable as a flacon of eau de toilette but labeled "eau de voilette" (veil water). The flacon's label also has a picture of Duchamp as Rrose Sélavy and the initials RS artfully drawn with the R in reverse, so that the two letters, the R and the S, look like mirror images of each other.

The title's substitution of something that you put into your mouth to have "beautiful breath" for something you put on your skin in the interest of smelling good creates a visual and verbal joke. Another substitution, the term *eau de voilette* (veil water) for *eau de toilette* (toilet water), also functions as a joke on two levels. On the one hand, *eau de voilette* may be easily misread as *eau de violette,* or "violet water" (by simply reversing two letters), which is in fact a kind of eau de toilette. On the other hand, the smell of an actual eau de toilette can work as a veil over the skin, so the reference is also literal. Similarly, Duchamp's masquerade in the photograph serves as a veil for his everyday, if not necessarily "true," masculine identity. The reversed initials on the label function as a visual metaphor for all the reversals at play in the photograph: from the way, for example, Duchamp "looks" like a woman named Sélavy to the *Belle Haleine* that "sounds" like *belle Hélène,* beautiful Helen of Troy or Pierre de Ronsard's "Belle Hélène" from his well-known sixteenth-century love poems.

It could be argued that, even though it is Duchamp's masculine self that is disguised by this photograph, it is nevertheless that same masculine self that is dominant in the perception of the viewer who reads through the (thinly disguised) "veiled" fiction of Duchamp's outward appearance. According to this reading, it is Rrose Sélavy who is the masked, if powerful, "alter" self. Such an interpretation accords with the understanding of surrealist automatic writing as coming from a part of the psyche that has been traditionally gendered as feminine because it is irrational, non-Cartesian, emotional. In other words, Duchamp's Rrose Sélavy could be seen to act out the inner experience of the predominantly male practitioners of automatism in the early days of surrealism—the experience of "letting go" of their masculine surface identities in the effort to release their creative, feminine sides in automatic writing and drawing of whatever surfaced from their unconscious minds while self-hypnotized or asleep.[21]

The different layers of sexuality in the image of Duchamp as Sélavy remain visible, which enables them to be read together. In "Womanliness as a Masquerade" (1929) Joan Rivière describes a comparable layering of images in the formation of gender identity and as used by women as a strategy of self-protection. Rivière argues that "a particular type of intellectual woman" with aspirations to a position in a masculine world may disguise her "masculinity" by masquerading her own "womanliness": "Womanliness therefore could be assumed and worn as a mask, both to hide the possession of masculinity and to avert the reprisals expected if she was found to possess it" (35, 36). At the core Rivière's "intellectual woman" is a woman who possesses masculinity, putting her in the position of possibly being "seen" as a man because of the masculinity that threatens to veil her innate femininity, and who, consequently, displays her inner womanliness as an outer "masquerade" in order to disguise the masculine aspect overlaying her feminine interior. Duchamp disguised as Rrose Sélavy but still recognizably Duchamp in most of Man Ray's photographs also projects a layered sexual identity that runs from the masculine to the feminine and back to the masculine again.[22] His purpose, however, unlike that of Rivière's masquerading woman, is not to disguise what Rivière calls "the bisexuality inherent in us all" but, rather, to expose it (35). His "playful subversion would not work," as Jennifer Blessing has observed," if we were not in possession of the knowledge that he is a man wearing women's clothes" (23). Duchamp's masquerade of femininity reinforces his masculine identity while nevertheless questioning the relevance of such distinctions within society.

In one of her regular letters to her cousin Denise, Breton's wife, Simone, describes Desnos on 9 October 1922, about a week after Duchamp's short poems appeared in *Littérature,* as possessing certain feminine characteristics as he speaks, writes, draws, and prophesies; he was, Simone writes, "even more impressive [than the Greek sibyls] because he is not a nervous woman, but a poet, impregnated with everything that we love and believe approaches the ultimate word of life" (qtd. in Bonnet 265). This indirect equation of Desnos's performance with that of "a nervous woman" recalls Duchamp's cross-dressed appearance as Rrose Sélavy. For Desnos is "not" a nervous woman just as Duchamp is evidently "not" Rrose Sélavy.[23]

Two months later, in December 1922, Desnos published an eight-page series of short word game poems in the same style and in the same journal but signed with his own name and using Duchamp's pseudonym as the title: "Rrose Sélavy."[24] Beneath the feminine veil of the title, Desnos's masculine identity remains visible through the signature—and authorship—of his own name. Like Duchamp in the Rrose Sélavy photographs (such as *Belle Haleine*), Desnos's appropriation of Duchamp's alter ego is more the case of a man in drag than that of someone intent on truly "passing" as a woman. And this is doubly true for Desnos, since the persona of Rrose was already sexually ambiguous, already double, when he adopted it for himself.

Desnos intends his own identity in the "Rrose Sélavy" poems to be multivalent. Like Duchamp, he holds on to the power of his heterosexuality by textually cross-dressing in an obvious fashion. At the same time, Desnos's Rrose Sélavy retains the subversive power of drag because the female persona he "wears" in his poems—Duchamp's Rrose—was already in drag, already a masculine-feminine hybrid, and not purely feminine. Garber explains that cross-dressing, or transvestism, is a "disruptive element that intervenes [and enacts], not just a category crisis of male and female, but the crisis of category itself" (17). Duchamp's Rrose already occupied the position of Garber's "third sex," which defies all categorization; Desnos's Sélavy doubly and self-consciously occupies that same category-defying position.

Desnos's identity games may be read through Arthur Rimbaud's formula for expressing the self objectively through poetic language—his celebrated declaration that "I is another", *Je EST un autre*—which may be seen as an unconscious animation of what Richard Stamelman calls "a stirring of selves within the self" (Rimbaud 345; Stamelman 20). Desnos's concern in enacting multiple personae and identities, in a staging of selves, has to do, in other words, with the referentiality of language itself.[25]

The wordplay of Desnos's title, "Rrose Sélavy," announces the nature of the text that follows because the name of his title "looks like" something different from what it "sounds like." As in Duchamp's games with the name Rrose Sélavy (he signed plastic works with this pseudonym as well) and in Man Ray's photographs, both verbal and visual elements are at play, although in the Desnos text the accent is more clearly on the verbal. The name looks like a woman's ordinary name: Rose was and is a regular French surname. But the doubling of the letter *r* (which is erratic in Duchamp's writing of the name, particularly when he first started using it), when pronounced aloud, with the *R* of "Rose" doubling itself as it rolls off the glottis at the back of the mouth, yields a phrase with a legible meaning: Eros is life, *éros c'est la vie,* or, more romantically, love is life.

Thus a name (Rrose Sélavy) that has no real "signified" in language, except through the allusion and illusion of a pun, and which therefore circulates opaquely within the economy of communication, finds its opacity partly effaced and becomes something else—a message, a phrase, a meaningful expression. Like an experience of the "double take" when one looks once then twice at something to verify a perception, the experience of seeing Duchamp as Sélavy compels the spectator to take another, second look. Similarly, the double take experience of understanding the punning, masked meaning of the name Rrose Sélavy comes only after hearing the name spoken aloud. Such a conscious process involving repetition linked to gender recalls Judith Butler's formulation of gender as an "act" that is only skin deep: "The parodic repetition of gender exposes as well the illusion of gender identity as an intractable depth and inner substance" (146–47). Duchamp's name and Desnos's title resonate doubly—hence parodically—and serve as reminders of Duchamp's playfulness and Desnos's priorities about love, for example, as the most essential and surrealist pursuit of life.

With this name and this title, Desnos cedes, as a man, the authority of authorship to a sexually ambiguous alter ego in a way that opens the door to legitimizing women's claim to authorial authority. When Breton and Soupault published *The Magnetic Fields* with a double signature, they put the authority of the author and his or her signature into question, thus challenging the reification of established authors in French culture. They theoretically opened up authorial authority to anyone who wished to claim it, including women. With the name Rrose Sélavy, Desnos offered a more explicit invitation to women to step into the authorial position. In a manner that anticipates feminist textual gestures from the late twentieth century, Desnos, through the sexual ambiguity of his title and the invitation to reread his multivalent short poems, clearly celebrates textual (as well as sexual) multiplicity in the poems he composed as Rrose Sélavy. This work resists French culture's attempts to fix identity according to gender in ways parallel to the resistance of Breton, Aragon, Soupault, Eluard, Drieu la Rochelle, and Delteil to the cultural desire to fix the equation of great art with patriotism, through the widespread admiration of Anatole France. Desnos's questioning of gender as a distinct category continued well into the 1920s.[26] Desnos and Duchamp's parodies exposed the fundamental mobility of sexuality in a society eager to reestablish categories after the destabilizing effects of war.

With Rrose Sélavy "Words Are Making Love"

Desnos's "Rrose Sélavy" poems in the December 1922 issue of *Littérature*—published two months after Duchamp's "Rrose Sélavy" aphorisms and three months after the first experiments with hypnotic sleeps—were introduced with an admiring essay by Breton, "Words without Wrinkles," which concluded with a felicitous homage to Desnos's abilities as a wordsmith: Breton implies that in Desnos's hands "words are making love" (OC 1, 286; LS 102). What exactly did Breton mean by "words are making love"? When words meet automatically on the page as a result of that "magic *dictation*" called surrealism, they generate meanings of their own, propelled not by logic but by the unconscious mind and by the collision of words. "In such a game," as Dumas states, "language signifies as phonetic matter, susceptible to various arrangements or constructions" (311). How do the poems work? Let us look at some examples. The first of them was produced by Desnos orally while in a trance in Breton's apartment in response to Picabia's demand that he, Desnos, make a "Rrose Sélavy–type poem": "Dans un temple en stuc de pomme le pasteur distillait le suc des psaumes" (In a temple of apple stucco, the pastor distilled the sap of psalms) (O 502). As is phonetically evident, the complex rearrangement of syllables—*stuc* morphing into *suc, pomme* into *psaumes*, and so on—discloses Desnos's gift for phonetic homony.

Other such one-line automatic poems were produced orally or in writing, like the wonderfully symmetrical "Le Temps est un aigle agile dans un temple" (Time is an agile eagle in a temple) (O 504). This poem demonstrates well Desnos's method of substituting one for the other, at either end of the poetic line, words or syllables that resemble each other, thus creating anagrammatic poems.[27] Here the X shape of the chiasmic structure turns on the assonances of the paired words at the center of the line, *aigle* and *agile*. From these two words, waves of the poem's sounds move outward like ripples from a stone falling into water, thus emphasizing the visually motivated, mirror-effect of the two substantives *temps* and *temple*. The sounds and structure work in tandem to suggest at once the fluidity of time—most certainly an experience of temporality characteristic of the automatic experience—and the primacy in the twentieth century of what is unquestionably a cult of chronological time.

Another possible reading of this short poem focuses on the exchange of the two spatially allied semantic pairings, *eagle time* and *agile temple*, for *eagle temple* and *agile time*. This exchange resists assigning hierarchy to one combination of syllables over another, a resistance further underscored by the ways in which these pairings may be interpreted.[28] For, even though the transposed combinations, *eagle temple* and *agile time*, might seem the more logical of the two pairings because of the nobility of the eagle and the flexible nature of time as experienced in dreams, the strength of this transposed reading is counteracted by the order of the first reading, that is, *eagle time, agile temple*. In a work "under" a woman's name and yet signed or authorized by a man, these competing readings, which stand up to one another and emphatically transgress meaning itself, highlight the way language speaks in a gender-neutral voice.

Five more "Rrose Sélavy" poems reveal moreover how the double take effect so evident when one glances for the first time at Man Ray's photographs of Duchamp as Rrose Sélavy and momentarily doubts what one sees occurs on the very level of a language:

— *O mon crâne étoile de nacre qui s'étiole.*
— *L'acte des sexes est l'axe des sectes.*
— *Si le silence est d'or, Rrose Sélavy abaisse ses cils et s'endort.*
— *Apprenez que la geste célèbre de Rrose Sélavy est inscrite dans l'algèbre céleste.*
— *Le plaisir des morts, c'est de moisir à plat.*

— Oh my mother-of-pearl star-head which withers and becomes dull.
— The sex act is the axis of sects.
— If silence is golden, Rrose Sélavy lowers her lids and sleeps.
— Learn that the famous song-cycle about Rrose Sélavy is inscribed in celestial algebra.
— The pleasure of the dead is to rot lying down. (*O* 502–07)

Then there is the one, a spoonerism of sorts, that acknowledges the true "author" of Rrose Sélavy: "Rrose Sélavy connaît bien le marchand de sel" (Rrose Sélavy knows the merchant of salt well). The *marchand de sel*, when read with the syllables reversed, yields the name Marcel Duchamp (*O* 503).[29] Years later Michel Leiris would comment about his own word game poems, partly inspired by Desnos, that they made the reader "feel the voice in the writing" because of their "sonorous and phonetic basis" (*Langage* 125).[30] Indeed, these poems need to be spoken aloud to be fully understood, yet there remains a significant visual component to the exchange and reversal of syllables and phonemes as well: Desnos insists upon the signifier's autonomy, Marie Paul Berranger comments, "in order to render more visible the physical existence of words" (106). Their repetitions, resembling each other but not completely—the way Duchamp as Sélavy looks almost but not entirely like a woman—stimulate the eye as much as the ear in a game that challenges the reader to untangle a coherent meaning from them.[31]

Desnos's "Rrose Sélavy" poems call out for an interpretive unfolding, as in "O mon crâne étoile de nacre qui s'étiole" (Oh my mother-of-pearl star-head which withers and becomes dull). The final word, *étiole*, draws the reader's eye back to the fourth word, *étoile*, since the reader experiences a momentary doubt about whether *star* (*étoile*), has been repeated or changed—a perfect example of the poetics of the double take (*O* 502). The words must be consistently *reread* to be appreciated: at first glance, for example, the word *sectes* in *l'acte des sexes est l'axe des sects* (the sex act is the axis of sects) seems like a repetition of the word *sexes* (509). A second look, reveals, however, that, on the contrary, *sectes* just looks like and sounds like *sexes*. There is also a third effect, a shock of laughter or recognition, coming from the semantic dimension of the wordplay, as one realizes with a sort of mental double take that most religious sects, in attempting to regulate sex (or *l'acte des sexes*) and to suppress its pleasures, only succeed in the reverse of what they intend: in turning sex from taboo to clandestine transgressive delight. Such a reverse effect, of course, is implicit in the short poem's structure, in which each half of the "equation" is an anagram, a baroque mirror image or double, of the other: *acte-sexes, axe-sectes.*

These short poems exist at the border of intelligibility; they explore and test the limits of that quintessentially surrealist "in-between" state in which meaning and incoherence touch, what Garber calls "the space of possibility," and they make those limits visible. They inhabit and cast light upon the in-between, the space between sense and non-sense. They highlight, as art historian Heinrich Wölfflin observed about the baroque, "the relation of oscillating balance" (130). They play the role of a baroque fulcrum between two meanings, two word identities, in the way that Duchamp, crossed-dressed as Sélavy, is both one and the other, a man and a woman, in a game in which each half of the double ego pokes fun at the other. They resist categorization and mastery.

Like tongue twisters or school-yard jokes, these poems may be decoded according to their verbs and nouns and understood to refer to death, to speed (the automatic process is necessarily tied to rapidity, to the rapid capture of the processes of unconscious thought), to childhood games, to anticlerical feeling, to iconoclasm, to dream, to pure fantasy, to cataclysmic events ("Au fond d'une mine Rrose Sélavy prépare la fin du monde" [At the bottom of a mine Rrose Sélavy prepares the end of the world]), and to the names of specific people.[32] Most of the names refer to Desnos's friends and acquaintances among the proto-surrealist group (for example, *Paul Eluard: Le poète élu des* draps [Paul Eluard: the chosen poet of sheets]; *élu-draps* mixes up the phonetic syllables in the name Eluard and refers to Eluard's reputation as a lover) (*O* 505).

One of these poems was written in English, "From Everest mountain I am falling at your feet for ever, Mrs. Everling," in homage to Picabia's companion, Germaine Everling (*O* 505). Desnos had spent a month in Kent, England, in the summer of 1914, just before the outbreak of World War I. His English had helped him to obtain his first job translating pharmaceutical prospectuses at the Darasse general store in the Marais two years later, when he was sixteen.[33] Duchamp had also used English to make visual jokes, since he was living in New York. His "readymade" *Why Not Sneeze, Rrose Sélavy?*, for example, consists of a birdcage containing "sugar cubes" made of marble, with a thermometer sticking out of it. It turns on the English phrase "to catch a cold." Using a similar technique, Desnos makes an implicit verbal joke that subtends the explicit poetic line. The phrase "head over heels" floats just beneath the surface of his short poem, implying somewhat humorously that not only does he imagine falling chivalrously at the lady's feet but that he has fallen as precipitously in love with her as a fall from the top of Mount Everest might suggest.

Most of these poems reflect the automatic nature of their production. They take place in an immobilized present—in baroque time—as a result of their dependence on the verb *to be*. They function like equations, with the verb occupying the place of the equal sign, and lie suspended between the world of consciousness and the world of "genius" and "madness" evoked by Desnos in his "mad drawings." Dumas explains that Rrose Sélavy "says the same thing twice, and in so doing, causes her discourse to coincide with itself, to fold back on itself, in a process of reiteration. . . . [T]he utterances of 'Rrose Sélavy' put into play an ensemble of elements on equal footing" (310–11). Furthermore, these word games, as Dumas concludes, tend to undermine the stable relations that seem assured between words and their meanings but without destroying language itself. Such a practice shows how "language is capable of transforming its own rules without exploding into incommunicability" (323).

The "Rrose Sélavy" poems map out a particularly Desnosian terrain in which the magical properties of words themselves and of writing as an almost sacred activity remain dominant and will remain so throughout the rest of Desnos's career. Words have a plastic and material aspect for Desnos. Words can make love when they have double meanings. Out of one come two, which together engender a kind of play, of (nonreproductive) lovemaking, which spins out multiple readings (the way procreative lovemaking might spawn new genetic combinations). In the opening to his essay on eroticism, "De l'érotisme," Desnos links love with language in terms that spell out his own experience of written language as an infinitely maneuverable and protean substance:

> Love and poetry have the privilege of being able to name human beings and everything related to them; for anyone who forgoes the triviality of the majority, words are more malleable than wax. Despite their living bony edges and the wounds that may be incurred by clumsy handling of them. There is not a single one that may not be decomposed into the dust of the working gears of a watch, more precise and more fragile than the gears of a chronometer. For those who can master words, the dragons of the secret entryways will be frozen at their lookout posts and the best-armed fortresses will be more welcoming than the wind-mills of commonplaces. (*O* 179)

In this passage words are compared to wax, to tangible matter, which may be shaped by human hands. They have a baroque materiality—in the sense of the baroque pearl at the etymological root of the word *barocco*, which, through its three-dimensionality and corporeal irregularity, emblematizes the mate-rial world.

Words are understood as "spiky," as possessing "edges": they function at frontiers at which two worlds, two faces, meet—sites of the in-between. They may be used as precision instruments, and yet, like the gears of a watch or a chronometer, they are fragile. They may be reduced to dust in all their precise fragility and, consequently, mastered. Once mastered they may be manipu-lated at will—as Desnos proves in his own poetic word games—the way clichés or the commonplaces of everyday life may be used to mean more than one thing at a time. Desnos does this in his early poems from "Prospectus," in which common proverbs or touchstones such as *Liberté, Egalité, Fraternité* signify both the architectural decoration on the façades of French buildings and the more abstract expression of the republican ideals of the Revolution.

For Desnos the process of understanding language in a corporeal sense happens in the mouth, in the air of a breath, of a voice. The "Rrose Sélavy" poems in particular rely on the lips, on respiration, and on timing. In his description of how these poems highlight the human voice, René Plantier observes that they "represent the daily work of the modern poet" (52). Their double meanings are only fully realized when spoken by an animate body. Desnos, in other words, both "embodies" surrealism and creates a "body" of language connected to the body—a *corpus* that is a *corps*—requiring the participatory activity of speaking, laughing, listening. If language is the "agent of transformation" in surrealism, as Mary Ann Caws argues, then Desnos is that agent's representative. In his person he characterizes "the shape-shifting tenets of the baroque" to which Caws refers, and, like surrealist language and art, he presents "an image that *faces both ways,* crossing the boundaries of expectation both public and private" (*Look* 311).

From Rrose Sélavy to the Drama of the Self

Much of Desnos's early poetry, including the "Rrose Sélavy" poems, reflects an obsessive fascination with the poetic effects of baroque time on the self and on the multiple "I" 's that may emerge from the vertiginous sense of suspended time and folded identity. In "Confessions d'un enfant du siècle" (Confessions of a child of this century), published in 1926 in *La Révolution Surréaliste,* Desnos explains: "I have said that I live a double life. Alone on the street or amongst people I constantly imagine unexpected events, desired encounters. . . . I thus pursue, while awake, my nocturnal dream self" (*O* 301). Through hypnotic trances and automatism Desnos explored the multivalent aspects of his own shifting identity in keeping with Freud's understanding that identity is rooted in the unconscious. He represented textually what Suzanne Guerlac has called "the exploded subject of avant-garde art" (46). At the same time, around 1920, Desnos began to sketch the drama of "I" and "you" so characteristic of his poetry from the mid-1920s on. Yet it is only with *Mourning for Mourning,* from 1924, that a textual exploration of a relationship with another person truly anticipates the poet's future work.

Desnos stages his various baroque doubles in writing and does so with particular assiduousness in his early work, "Prospectus" (written in 1919). The title is a reference to Apollinaire's statement in "Zone" from 1913 that prospectuses "sing out loud" as "the poetry of the morning" as well as an inside reference to the prospectuses Desnos worked on translating for his first job.[34] The poems of "Prospectus" are significant because they played a role in Desnos's entry into, and acceptance by, the surrealist group: manuscripts of "Prospectus" may be found among the papers of Breton, Aragon, Eluard, Ernst, Péret, and Morise, indicating that Desnos was interested in his new friends' opinions. They resemble Apollinaire's "poem-conversations" from *Calligrammes,* such as "Monday in Christine Street," in which Apollinaire, incorporating phrases overheard in a café, sought to create a poetic record of everyday life: "Louise forgot her fur piece / Well I don't have a fur piece and I'm not cold" (55).

Desnos, in "Prospectus," incorporates, seemingly at random, phrases that are captured from everyday signs: "NO SPITTING"; "IF YOU WANT CHOCOLATE PUT TWO COINS IN THE MACHINE"; "ENTER WITHOUT KNOCKING"; "DEPOSIT REQUIRED"; "LIBERTY EQUALITY FRATERNITY." Here is an example of a complete poem:

I passed by a strange street
where blond children were pissing on their swaddling clothes

On the door of a restaurant
a sign was posted:

FOOD MAY BE BROUGHT HERE

On the door of a furnished hotel
a sign was posted:

LOVE MAY BE BROUGHT HERE (*O* 20)

His agility with wordplay is evident here especially in the way that *love* substitutes for *food* in the imagined hotel sign, copied from an actual hotel sign. When used with the preposition *de,* the verb *pisser,* of medieval origin, from which the word *compisser* is derived—as in the line "where blond children were pissing on their swaddling clothes" (*où des enfants blonds compissaient leurs langes*)—can mean, figuratively, to speak or to write copiously, as in *pisser de la copie* or *pisser du Plutarque* (*Petit Robert*). Like the blond children "pissing" in the poem, Desnos fools around with the resemblance of the word for swaddling clothes, *langes,* to the word for "tongues," *langues,* in the form of "language." The kids—possibly playing in the earthy language of slang, as their soiled swaddling clothes suggest—are also producing their own private "languages."

Desnos appropriated signs from the walls of shops, restaurants, the Métro, in his neighborhood of the Marais (see fig. 3). His inclusion of these posters and graffiti in poems effects a process of alchemical transformation (in the tradition of Rimbaud's *alchimie du verbe*), whereby the ordinary becomes the extraordinary and the commonplace shines with poetic "gold." Furthermore, a slogan such as "Liberty, Equality, Fraternity" underscores young Desnos's solidarity with the republican, anticonservative, and anti-Catholic views he would espouse for the rest of his life. Unlike Apollinaire's capturing of overheard phrases in "Monday in Christine Street," Desnos's use of signs is visual as well as auditory. Written in all capital letters, they resemble, as much as possible, their originals and stand out in a typographic form different from that of the rest of the poetic text. Consequently, the poems have something of a collage-like quality about them. Fragmentary and spontaneous, they seem already semiautomatic. Words themselves drive these poems, as in the title poem, wherein *potiches* (vases) leads to *postiches* (hairpieces) in a way that anticipates the wordplay of Desnos's "Rrose Sélavy" poems three years later.

The Inkwell Periscope

"Door to the Second Infinity," a poem Desnos wrote in 1923, represents a shift away from word games and at the same time reveals some of the tensions inherent in his practice of automatic writing. Published first in *Littérature* (nos. 11–12), it was later included in *C'est les bottes de 7 lieues cette phrase "Je me vois,"* which was illustrated with etchings by André Masson, and published in 1926, the year Desnos took over Masson's studio in the fifteenth arrondissement.[35] Like the "Rrose Sélavy" poems, however, "Door to the Second Infinity" continues to focus on the poetic process by which identity undergoes alchemical transformation and on the pivotal point found in between states of being. Here is the poem in its entirety:

> The inkwell periscope lies in wait around the bend
> my fountain pen goes back into its shell
> The sheet of paper spreads its huge white wings
> Before long its claws
> will tear out my eyes
> I won't see anything but my late body
> my late body!
> You had the opportunity to view it in full dress
> the day of all ridicule
> The women put their jewels in their mouths
> like Demosthenes
> But I'm the inventor of a telephone
> made of crystal and
> English tobacco
> with a direct line
> to fear!
> (*O* 290; *S* 2, translation modified)

Death and loss of control are highlighted in "Door to the Second Infinity." The inkwell stares the poet down so mercilessly that his (phallic) fountain pen pulls back into its shell. The inkwell doubles as a "periscope," indicating that its "eye" is controlled by an invisible power that is literally under the surface of the ink in the well. The blank page, whose untouched whiteness recalls Stéphane Mallarmé's obsession with the void and absolute potentiality of the empty page, metamorphoses into a predatory bird that rips out the poet's eyes. Putting oneself in a state receptive to those subterranean forces of the psyche that surge out in automatic states is, in other words, a risky business, because such a state attacks a sense of the whole person: the body disappears. And yet here the sublimation of the body into writing is presented in concrete images that have the effect of paradoxically materializing the process of sublimation and consequently of negating it.

Another image of sublimation concretized in a way that turns the sublimating process into a joke is that of "the women" putting their jewels into their mouths "like" Demosthenes. Demosthenes's oratorial "jewels," put on display in his eloquent declamations, are here feminized and interiorized: the art of oratory and poetry and the result of the automatic process of discovery and salvage are manifestly made feminine. The "I" is, subsequently, a subject whose gender identity, having now been called into question, invents a new, unheard-of means of communication. Unlike the periscope and the retracted and useless pen, this new method allows for *les deux yeux* (two eyes)—and, by implication, *les deux je* (two "I" "s)—to "see," or rather to "hear," since it is a telephone the "I" invents. The auditory replaces the writerly; telephone supplants pen.

This means of auditory communication, because it is made of glass, also has visual properties. The telephone is transparent, allowing one to see its inner (or psychic) workings. The automatic literally becomes clear. Hearing and sight join as in the "Rrose Sélavy" poems, which must be both seen and heard in order to be understood. The Bohemian glass telephone does, however, work more like the periscope than it might seem, for instead of connecting the "I" with another person, as a telephone would, it connects it only to "fear." The reader is left with the uneasy feeling that the telephone, like the periscope, is now in communication with another world, that of "the Second Infinity," that of the afterlife, or that of the autonomous and automatist infinite second state that is the unconscious itself. Such a sense, although disquieting, has the curious effect of negating the obvious blindness that the paper bird has engendered in ripping out the poet's eyes. The poet is left, like Tiresias, with a "second" sight based now on hearing and audition—on the auditory imagination—which thus explains the transition from periscope to telephone, from sight to sound, as the figured medium of communication.

The telephone in "Door to the Second Infinity" serves as a metaphor for the surrealist experience of hearing, listening to "the actual functioning of thought" and to disembodied voices coming from the beyond deep within the self. Its presence in the poem anticipates the growing importance of the voice (including the disembodied voice on the radio) in the work of Desnos, a poet who, more than any other surrealist, became closely identified with his voice. The telephone functions as the intermediary or the agent permitting a disembodied voice coming from a distant origin and across space to be heard "live" directly, or "en . . . directe." It relies on the voice as the essential medium between one body and another, between one self and another, and in this way represents a communication that is more immediate than that of sight (as facilitated by a periscope) or that of writing (as produced by a pen). The telephone was a relatively new invention when Desnos wrote this poem. Eugen Weber reports that even ten years later, in the early 1930s, "interurban communication continued [to be] primitive" (*Hollow* 63).[36]

Telephone technology is staged in "Door to the Second Infinity" as the point between one state and another and as the "door" to the "second infinity," that other dimension accessible only through a second state or automatist experience exterior to chronological time. For, if the telephone is in fact connected to this second infinity beyond life, then the afterlife is also actively connected to the everyday world; the lines between both realms are permeable, open. The two worlds coexist just the way the murky bottom and the top surface of the ink in the inkwell are part of the same fluid body. The "I" of consciousness floats and moves between the two spaces as the image on the surface of a milky or wavy mirror sometimes reflects and mirrors a recognizable self and sometimes only disfigures it.

Later, in *Liberty or Love!* in a chapter initially published in the July 1925 issue of *La Révolution Surréaliste,* the inkwell becomes an explicit image for the liquidity of creativity that at times clouds the mind and at other times facilitates it. Identifying himself as Robert Desnos within the text, the poet explains that all of his characters are but "ghosts flying out of the still night of the ink-well" onto the "arid plain of a manuscript" page (*O* 351; *LL* 73). And while that "still night" does "nothing except make stains" on his fingers, "stains appropriate for leaving fingerprints on the painted walls of dreams," nevertheless the process has persisted in leaving him with "the stupid hope of transmuting paper into a mirror by means of magical and effective writing." Only with the alchemical transformation of ink and paper possible through automatism and dream might such a hope become realized.

For Mourning's Sake

In 1924, the year of Breton's first *Manifesto* and Aragon's *Une Vague de rêves,* Desnos published his first long prose piece, *Mourning for Mourning.* It is an example of "psychic automatism in its pure state," Desnos's particular gift, and is structured as a sequence of twenty-four poetic prose episodes, loosely interrelated like a series of dreams occurring over a single night of deep sleep.[37] Animate and inanimate characters are equally humanized in the narrative. There are three recurring characters: a "fair-haired virgin"; her suitor, a "soft blue dolman" (a hussar's jacket); and a poet-narrator, who, as might be expected in an automatically produced fiction, discovers he is, at times, at the mercy of his own creations. Thus the "literariness" of this text, as Riffaterre has observed about Breton's automatic writing, springs from the way in which it mimes unconscious thought processes instead of merely recording them (232).

In *Mourning for Mourning* Desnos celebrates the exhilaration and freedom that can result from automatism. It resonates with a cheerful morbidity, typical of Desnos in the 1920s. Characters die and resurrect. Death is like a dream, an altered state, from which one may awaken and carry on.[38] Desnos dramatizes himself in the character of a poet-narrator, who exclaims midway through the narrative: "The surprising metamorphosis of sleep makes us equal to the gods" (*O* 210, 39). This poet-narrator yields to free association in fantastic detail, even allowing his imagination to run wildly from the most ordinary and trivial of stimuli, like the sound of a dripping faucet. In the thirteenth episode his mind runs backward from drops of water falling into his kitchen sink to the city pipes from which the water comes: "From time to time, a prolonged shiver runs through the water. It is a fair-haired virgin washing herself after love-making. . . . Happy the drops destined for intimacy with her body, but happy also those who feel the rustle of mermaids close to the reefs or the ripping of armour-plated bows through the ocean" (*O* 208, 35–36). Giving free reign to his imagination, Desnos allows the sound of water dropping steadily into the poet-narrator's sink to accelerate until it becomes an absolute flow rushing beyond the city where he lives, all the way to the fantasized bodies of mermaids and battleships in the ocean. Clearly, this image contains a metatextual allusion; Desnos represents the powerful flow of the stream of unconsciousness itself under the liberating effect of automatism.

As in a real dream, however, in *Mourning for Mourning* the poet-narrator does not always maintain complete control over his own dream reality:

> On the table, a glass and a bottle are laid out in memory of a fair-haired virgin who in this room experienced the disturbing menstrual wound for the first time and who, raising her right arm towards the ceiling and pointing her left towards the window, was able to make triangles of moving pigeons flutter in the air to her heart's content. . . . While waiting, the fair-haired virgin dips her blonde tresses in my coffee; it is midday; the statutory litre of wine which has been deposited next to the ribbed glass in front of me turns into a dove. (*O* 201, 24)

The poet has little control over the "fair-haired virgin," even though he has invented her, because she is a character in his automatic dream, to which he himself is completely subject. Like a genie in a bottle, she has psychic powers: in particular, the ability to move objects at will. Desnos shows his readers what he sees, and how he sees, when he falls into a hypnotic trance. As in a dream, everything in this world of automatist reality has an effect on everything else.

The fair-haired virgin and the soft-blue dolman jacket function clearly within what is dream reality. The virgin dons the dolman jacket, travels to the Sahara, and engages in adultery (*O* 203; 27). In the eleventh episode she may have died mysteriously, for she and her lover wander in the sky above their empty tombs (*O* 207; 33). By the following episode, however, they have, characteristically for Desnos, survived shipwreck: "the fair-haired virgin and a pirate in a pale blue dolman lay clasped together on the seaweed on the deserted ocean floor abandoned by the waters at the very moment that The MARVEL, the liner on which they were passengers, was being engulfed" (O 207; 34).[39]

The characters in *Mourning for Mourning* participate in events that control the poet as much, if not more than, he controls them. This is because he is so deeply immersed in, and possessed by, the automatic trance that it is nearly impossible for him to break away from the tyranny of the unconscious and return to everyday reality. In the ninth episode, for example, the poet-narrator sets the action in motion with a kind of St. Elmo's fire ignited by his cigarette, which he throws into the water, yet his characters—an animated pearl and the wreck of the steamship *Marvel,* already at the bottom of the sea—move independently once the story sinks below the sea's surface. The pearl and the shipwreck together progress from the sea floor, dramatizing the idea Desnos expressed elsewhere that "shipwrecks are born from the ocean" the way that poems and dreams may be "born of the night."[40] Pearl and shipwreck emerge above the water's surface, sail up a river and then into a virgin forest, where they will take up residence: "And the pearl, eternally transfixed to the wheel, will be amazed that the boat remains forever immobile under an ocean of fir-trees unaware of the magnificent destiny that was bestowed on her equals in civilised lands, in towns where bar huntsmen have dolmans the colour of the sky" (*O* 204, 29). The "eternally" immobilized ship and the pearl's coexistence with other pearls "in civilised lands" enact a significant aspect of Desnos's own automatic experience. In a hypnotic trance time is suspended and seems to stand still, as occurs in baroque time when all life around the entranced poet remains active, changing, dynamic and mobile within chronological time. Caught in a dream such as this one, the poet may indeed feel "immobilized" for what seems like an "eternity," although in fact the dream itself might last only a few minutes.

Only in the penultimate episode does the "I" relate to a fellow human being. The poet sleeps, while an unnamed beloved woman watches over him: "The woman gets up and sits pensively at the window where our dream follows her," comments the poet-narrator, while sounds interrupt the quiet of the "deserted street" outside (*O* 219, 56). He opens his eyes just long enough to see her at the window and to mistake her for a shooting star. The episode ends with the phrase *it is sleep* repeated three times, which suggests an even deeper level of dreaming buried within this dream narrative. The shared moment between two human beings is fleeting yet remarkable because it only happens this one time in all of *Mourning for Mourning*. And, in fact, the very last episode focuses once again solely on the poet's singular and isolated experience of deep dreaming. There is the suggestion, moreover, in this last episode that the poet-narrator has crossed the limit separating dream from death: the "I" becomes confused with a corpse transmogrified into paper—his *corps* literally transformed into a *corpus*—and held in place by the "paper-weight" of an inscribed granite tombstone that will, by its funerary and epitaphic writing and its link to paper and language, offer up the "mourning" to which the title of *Mourning for Mourning* alludes (*O* 220, 59).

Mourning for Mourning is an example of automatic writing in its most condensed form, mixing romance with fantastic voyage and making the unconscious synonymous with depth and oceanic experience. As a text, it answers Breton's call in the first *Manifesto* for a reaffirmation of the power of the imagination. It also flows directly out of the unconscious, opened up through automatist means, without any kind of pedagogical explanation or philosophical interruption (as one finds more often in Breton and Aragon than in Desnos). It contains its own self-reflexive and self-referential mirroring or *mise-en-abyme:* a poet who is a character in his own right in this dream narrative wakes and dreams and invents other characters who take on a life of their own and who then drag him into their extended dream. In *Mourning for Mourning* Desnos shows that he is adept at living in baroque time, at transforming himself into a "word-mirror" (as Aragon later wrote), by fictionally letting himself be drawn into yielding to the linguistic play that unmoors words from dependence on meaning or sense. By inserting himself so completely into the dream text, Desnos puts himself in the same field as his creations. In terms of his relation to others, to an audience, this text remains an example of a poet at play in the magnetic field of his own unconscious. And yet the phantom love relation intimated briefly here between the "I" and the beloved woman suggests a new desire for communication with another. *Mourning for Mourning* anticipates *Liberty or Love!* and it also anticipates the love poetry to come, for which Desnos will become famous.

The poems Desnos wrote after 1926 reveal a poet less preoccupied with dramatizing his own divided psyche than with moving beyond the inner world of the dreamself and engaging in a communication with others. Language, the experience of a split personality, the questioning of gendered identity, and the challenging of mental, social, and psychological categories—of writing, culture, identity—would remain persistent interests for Desnos's work through-out the 1920s. His linguistic preoccupations would, however, be supplemented by a broader vision in the years to come, a vision extending outside of himself, outside of the confines of the surrealist circle, as Desnos, with greater con-fidence, began to define further his own beliefs and his own view of the world in a wider and more panoptic manner.

The Sensory In-Between

1927: Robert Desnos, thin from lack of money and food, lives in a drafty studio inherited from André Masson, in Montparnasse. His best friend, Georges Malkine, is such a frequent guest from Nice that he is practically a roommate. On the walls hang a couple of works by Francis Picabia and photographs by Man Ray as well as a current watercolor-in-progress by Desnos. A wax mermaid hangs on the wall where Desnos can see her when he awakens. Her realistic head tilts backward, the eyes closed, as if in a swoon, while long hair tumbles over her shoulders and bare breasts; her torso is covered in sequins, while her delicate, curled tail seems to be made of silk (see fig. 6). Jazz plays on the gramophone perched on the huge table among piles of books and objects collected at flea markets: seahorses, a starfish in a jar, a crystal ball. Seated opposite each other, Desnos and Malkine work on a book with an English title: "The Night of Loveless Nights." They were so close at the time, Malkine would observe later, that he could just as well have written the poem and Desnos have drawn the illustrations.[1]

Across Paris from Breton: Life at the Rue Blomet

André Masson explains in a retrospective article on "45, Rue Blomet," that when he occupied the Rue Blomet studio, which Desnos would eventually inhabit in 1926, his door was always unlocked: "One entered this studio as though it were a windmill. There was a door, and there was a lock on the door, but there was no key" (80). Thus, Masson would awaken on several occasions to find friends such as Antonin Artaud or Jacques Doucet seated at the foot of his bed.[2] Michel Leiris, in his own article entitled "45, Rue Blomet," presents the group that met in the studio, which included Georges Bataille and Desnos, as having goals parallel to those of the surrealist group. Also in the group of friends were Roland Tual, who had been present at the sleeps and with whom Desnos would later make a film, and Armand Salacrou, a boyhood friend of Desnos's with whom he would later work for the radio—who lived in the neighborhood and was translating Byron at the time (Miró 101–02). Leiris notes that the Rue Blomet gang around Masson could have become "a new school if our host had had the ambitions of a leader" (*Zébrage* 225). It was, Leiris remembers, an "old, humble building in the XVth whose inner, irregularly paved, courtyard housed two abutting studios." In these two studios—Masson's being more "bohemian" than that of his neighbor Joan Miró—Leiris "saw the borders between art and life disappear, as if I'd been allowed to enter one of Picasso's early paintings, and to break bread with its colorful itinerants, whose poverty took on an enchanted charm" (219–20).

Desnos himself describes the Blomet studio he moved into after Masson as occupying an old farm, where his father remembered buying melons (*Rue de la Gaîté* 20). He evokes the courtyard in an article dedicated to Miró: "A previous tenant had abandoned two marble medallions in the grassy courtyard, supposedly left there by a marble mason from the Montparnasse cemetery, which were slowly sinking into the ground next to a pile of old ironwork, which bled rust onto them. . . . In the summer, birds sang in this patio. In the winter, the snow stayed white longer there than anywhere else in Paris" (*O* 308). The increasingly dilapidated state of the site inspires a philosophical meditation: "Houses die the way men do, and it's only just. To regret a lost house is to aspire, prematurely, to a funereal domicile, to the coffin and the tomb, which are also destined for destruction. And who amongst us is tired of living?"[3]

Desnos and Georges Malkine were, according to Malkine's daughter, "thick as thieves." The poet and the painter were "inseparable" in those years (Waldberg, qtd. in Aragon, *Hommage*); Malkine painted the most memorable portrait of Desnos.[4] Fern Malkine elaborates: "I remember Patrick [Waldberg] telling me about how different my father and Desnos were in this one anecdote. He said they were all sitting at a table reciting poetry. My father said some sort of very somber, short, succinct kind of poem, using only a few words to express a lot. When it was Desnos's turn, he got up and he stood on the table. He was performing his poetry. Everyone was laughing and having a good time, but that's how different they were." Moreover, she remembers the close collaboration of her father and Desnos as they worked on "The Night of Loveless Nights": "In one letter my father wrote: 'we were such close friends at the time, we could practically have done the reverse, he could have done the drawings and I could have done the poetry.' So it was a very important relationship in his life" (interview, 20 Apr. 1996).

Marcel Duhamel, who lived with the group of surrealists installed at the Rue du Château where the "exquisite corpse" game was first invented, also remembers Desnos and Malkine as a pair: they inhabited, he recalls, "a bizarre studio which must have been, originally, a building-site shack. . . . The two of them lived a wakened dream. Of course, surrealism itself bathed in a dream-

ROBERT DESNOS

like atmosphere, but Desnos and Malkine literally transported with them a kind of dream cloud. Desnos's drawings and poems are impregnated with it. As for Malkine, he painted like a seer" (qtd. in Aragon, *Hommage*).[5] As in Masson's time, the studio was never locked.[6]

The studio was curiously furnished, as Youki Foujita Desnos, Desnos's companion from 1931 until his death, writes in her memoirs, *Les Confidances de Youki*. Thrown together were a large stove, a couch, and furniture bought secondhand. It was, she writes, an extremely pleasant place to live, because of the large windows, and a fine place for conversation or listening to records or poems (128–29). By 1928, in addition to his beloved wax mermaid, Desnos had acquired paintings and a drawing by Picabia, a watercolor by Masson, and a painting by Giorgio de Chirico.[7] He also set up canvases there for his own paintings. There is one sizable painting by Desnos that features a disproportionately large sand dune covered with shells and sea rocks, with an ordinary beach ball at its base. Incongruous sticks looking like denuded trees perch on top of the dune, casting long shadows down its side. Behind it stands a dagger, hilt up, with its blade fixed in a planter; small fish, anchors, and multicolored stars swarm around it.[8] His friend Théodore Fraenkel characterized these works as fantastic landscapes where "ships, streets, stars, and monsters" intermingled (319).

In moving across the Seine to the Left Bank, away from Breton's apartment on the Right Bank and away from the Right Bank Marais neighborhood where he had lived most of his life, Desnos came closer to friends who were accustomed to meeting at the Rue Blomet, including Bataille. By 1926, at the time of his move, he had already fallen in love with Yvonne George, whom he had in mind when he wrote the love poems entitled "A la mystérieuse" during that same year. It is likely he met her in 1924, at Chez Fyscher, the fashionable cabaret where Yvonne, a Belgian blonde sensation, had made her début as a singer (see fig. 7). Lucienne Cantaloube-Ferrieu describes the cabaret: "Even if the darkness of the room was not as complete as at the movies, it was nevertheless sufficient to encourage dreamy illusions. . . . In short, the place, the hour—'the triumphant midnight' [Desnos, *Le Soir*]—the lighting helped the sense of confusion between waking and sleeping" (*Textuel* 58).

Everyone who knew Yvonne George remarked on "the paleness of her face, the intensity of her look, the dazzle of her mouth, and the whiteness of her hands." Cantaloube-Ferrieu quotes a contemporary as saying that she gave off an air of "utterly natural femininity" (*fémininité sauvage*) (59). In *Le Vin est tiré . . .* Desnos's description of Barbara, the character modeled on Yvonne, portrays a person from whom the odor of luxury perfumes would emanate, even if she were naked, and who had been dressed by too many elegant dresses for "her body not to take on the lines of the great *couturiers* who had designed her clothes" (*O* 1039). For Desnos she was beautiful, a "modern woman," a "flame," but most of all she had a voice that was evocative of the marvelous and of the ocean: "The voice of a woman . . . and the ocean unfurls on the stage with all its actors, tragedies, and legends" (282). Desnos, the poet renowned for his own voice, wrote that her "sailor songs" performed at the Olympia "could make your heart leap out of your chest" (*Rue de la Gaîté* 19). She was no doubt the model for his music hall *chanteuse* from *Liberty or Love!* the one whose voice could bring "tears to my eyes" (*O* 342; *LL* 61).

In May 1925 Georges Malkine wrote Desnos from Nice: "My dear Robert, I know who Yvonne George is and I see you together *very well*, truly" (collection of Fern Malkine). Youki Desnos explains in her memoirs: "Robert loved her in an almost supra-terrestial manner. For him she wasn't a woman but an immaterial creature, which is why he sublimated her into the Star." Youki describes Yvonne retrospectively as tall and beautiful, with an expressive face and unusual, violet-colored eyes. She explains matter-of-factly that Desnos was not Yvonne's type, physically speaking (131). This is not surprising given that she had a reputation for preferring women to men as sexual partners (Desanti 173–74).[9] In a photograph from the time, Yvonne wears her hair bobbed and slicked back with a single lock falling over her forehead; she has a long nose and circles under eyes that are focused on a distant object, eyes that seem themselves to project distance.[10] She appears inaccessible, even in this image. Indeed, Desnos's love for Yvonne was neither happy nor reciprocated, as Théodore Fraenkel, one of his best friends, reports: "She lived usually in Neuilly in a ground-floor apartment with a garden. The sophisticated décor was faded and dusty. She received public figures there, and writers. Desnos's love for her was extreme, violent, painful, and tirelessly attentive. It was never a shared love. For almost a decade he lived only for her, and did errands for her which were at times dangerous. It was like this until she died in a sanatorium" (*O* 279). The "decade" Fraenkel mentions actually lasted only about five years, since Desnos met Youki Foujita in 1928 and slowly transferred his affection to her. The dangerous errands Desnos carried out for Yvonne included procuring drugs, during the time between 1928 and 1930 when George fought off tuberculosis and was trying to recover from an addiction to morphine and opium (Dumas 570 n.42 n.77).[11] He spoke from experience in an article on heroin, "goddess of dreams and death," published in *Paris-Soir* in 1926: "Heroin, in the name of adventure, is pitiless towards its lovers" (*O* 1153). The day of her cremation, on Saturday, 26 April 1930, Desnos noted simply in his diary: "They burned Yvonne today 4:45 P.M.–6:15 P.M. (DSN 878.108).

Desnos had a series of girlfriends from the 1920s through 1930, including the ill-fated Florence, who died in a car crash and to whom he dedicated a poem in *Corps et biens,* and a South American singer named Bessie (Dumas 81, 90). Yet his poetry attests to the fact that he had only two real loves in his life, Yvonne and Youki. In an undated notebook entry he links both lovers in the expression "the two Y's." This note is accompanied by two drawings. The first is of a heart with an arrow plunged vertically into its dip with the feathered end above it, making two clear Y shapes. The second is of a Y made from the Y-shaped tails of intertwining fishes. At the top of the page are the following lines: "Yvonne gave me a mermaid / I gave one to Youki!!" (DSN 878). (It was Yvonne who gave Desnos the wax mermaid hanging on the wall of his Rue Blomet studio.) Marie-Claire Dumas links these lines to another statement in the same notebook in which Desnos comments that a photograph he had seen of Youki, before he had ever met her, showed her emerging from the water in a bathing suit; and "Youki," Dumas observes, "was thus a marine creature, a 'swimmer,' a 'mermaid,' just as Yvonne George, who sang of the sea and surrounded herself with boats, had become the starfish" (99).

In Desnos's novel *Liberty or Love!* a poet loves unrequitedly a "music-hall *chanteuse,*" Yvonne to be sure. At the conclusion to "The Night-Watch," however, the opening, liminal poem to the same novel, written in alexandrine verses, there is a symbolic figure who prefigures Youki in Desnos's life: in the final line a strong woman swimmer who approaches the shore swimming, "Til love be reconciled with liberty" (*O* 323; *LL* 36).[12] Yvonne becomes a constellation of shooting stars in the love poem from "A la mystérieuse," "If You Only Knew": "Far from me, a shooting star falls into the poet's nightly bottle. He corks it right away and from then on watches the star enclosed in the glass, the constellation born on its walls, far from me you're so far from me" (*O* 541; *S* 17). Youki, on the other hand, the more interactive "swimmer," became identified as a mermaid in Desnos's iconography of love. Only with Youki did this idealized symbol have a human element—the mermaid is half-human—and only with Youki did Desnos himself take on the symbol of the seahorse, a companion to the mermaid. As a result, only with Youki, who reciprocated the poet's love, did Desnos finally find a partner.

Star-Struck, Love-Struck

Desnos's poems from 1926, "A la mystérieuse," were published in June 1926 in *La Révolution Surréaliste.* They include "J'ai tant rêvé de toi" (I Have Dreamed So Much of You), for which he is justly famous as a love poet. In this poem he comes close to his ideal of reciprocal love but not close enough. The voice he adores enchants him in the poem, but he cannot touch its source—the body of the woman he desires. As the poem opens, he is actively dreaming, and he reveals that he has dreamed so much of her that, paradoxically, she is beginning to lose her reality. Here is the poem in its entirety:

I have dreamed so much of you that you are losing your reality.
Is there still time to reach this living body and to kiss on this
      mouth the birth of the voice that is so dear to me?
I have dreamed so much of you that my arms, used to
      embracing your shadow, and finding my own chest,
      would not be able to bend around the contours of your
      body, perhaps.
And that, despite the real appearance of the one who has
      haunted and governed me for days and years, I would no
      doubt become a shadow,
Oh sentimental scales.
I have dreamed so much of you that there is no doubt no time
      left for me to awaken. I sleep standing up, my body
      exposed to all the appearances of life and of love and
      you, the only one who counts for me today, I could less
      touch your forehead and your lips than the first lips and
      the first forehead to present themselves to me.
I have dreamed so much of you, walked so much, talked, slept
      with your phantom, that all that is yet left to me perhaps,
      is to be a phantom among phantoms and a hundred
      times more of a shadow than the shadow that walks and
      will continue to walk gaily on the sundial of your life.
      (O 539)[13]

He fears that by dreaming so intently of the woman he loves he has inadvertently turned her into a mere shadow. Conversely, he wonders whether, having embraced her shadow so often, he might finally succeed in embracing the real woman he loves. Yet other worries assail him. Because of the intensity of yearning and dreaming so much, of physically feeling through his fantasized embraces the presence of the other, he risks losing his own reality and disappearing into a dreamworld. He wonders if he would not himself become a shadow were he to see "the real appearance of the one who has haunted and governed me for days and years." How could he still have any material body if he lives only in dream and only to dream?

At the midpoint of the poem such questions remain unanswered; indeed, the two protagonists are on the verge of becoming shadows. This state of being is implicit in the poet's question, "is there still time to reach this living body?" with its reference to the beloved, and in his fear with regard to himself, that "I would no doubt become a shadow." That hovering moment between shadow and body, dream and reality, is portrayed in the poem as a scale, as "sentimental scales." At the pivotal center of the poem this short line—"Oh sentimental scales"—stands out by its brevity. The other lines seem, literally, to extend and expand from it in both directions. The scale emphasizes the hovering equilibrium of the moment and the precarious space that separates dream and shadow from waking reality. It also immobilizes reality. The addition of the word *sentimental* adds weight to the concrete scale, bolstering it with the intensity of emotion implicit in the *so* of "I have dreamed so much of you." The still moment situated precariously in time and space, which this scale represents and which occurs before the two protagonists can join together, crystallizes the Desnosian view of love. In the immobile balance of the emotion-filled scales, poised in the surrealistic eternal present of an instant's duration, lies the perfect harmony with the beloved that the poet seeks.

The scales represent two realities in emotional balance, captured in a nonchronological baroque time, an oasis of calm. And yet the *Oh* at the beginning of the line already predicts the outcome. The delicate balance is threatened by too much hope, too much desire. The "sentimental scales" are tipped by the moan of the *Oh*. In the very next line, in effect, the conditional supposition, stated in the previous line—"I would no doubt become a shadow"—has come true. The imbalance in their emotions and desires has tipped the scales (and their love) away from each other. The poet can no longer awaken: "I sleep standing up, my body exposed to all the appearances of life and of love." In reality he has become lifeless, no longer able to govern his movements. He can no longer touch the beloved, having himself lost consciousness and become a shadow. His beloved, on the other hand, has, by the poem's last line, emerged from his dream into a conscious reality. She walks in sunny daylight, while he can only follow her as the shadow that he has become, "a phantom among phantoms." He has become much more of a "shadow" than she ever was in his dreams. As her shadow—the shadow on her material, visible "sundial," her reconstituted body—he is now finally united with her. There is even the hint of the fulfillment of a desired possession in the suggestion that she keeps him alive by thinking of him, the same way he thought so intently of her at the poem's beginning.

"I Have Dreamed So Much of You" represents Desnos's closest contact with reciprocal love in the 1920s. There is no doubt that he hopes for a state of exchange with the woman he loves and for a shared experience. The *sentimental scales* make this clear. And yet happy, reciprocal love remains an elusive goal in real life, to be realized only in fantasy. *Liberty or Love!* published a year after "A la mystérieuse," presents love couples as well: Corsair Sanglot and Louise Lame, who are doubled by the autobiographical "I" and the music hall singer he loves. The foursome enacts a scenario similar to that of "A la mystérieuse": Corsair Sanglot and Louise Lame are able to make love with freedom, while the poetic "I" and the chanteuse, remain as separate as the "I" and "you" of the poems dedicated to the *mystérieuse*. Love is strong enough to stop time in *Liberty or Love!* and also powerful enough to transform the writing process into a phenomenon of magic, especially when the authorial "I" participates in the adventures of his alter ego, Corsair Sanglot.[14] Love's power comes from its intractable nature, from its force—at least as powerful as automatism—which is felt experientially through the body and through the imagination's fantasies. For, like automatism, love can inspire visions, dreams, and poetry.

In the Star's Shadows

In December of the same year, when he wrote the first poem of his next collection, "Les Ténèbres" (The Shadows) (1927), Desnos had begun to accept more realistically the hopelessness of his love for Yvonne George. The second poem, "Infinitif" (Infinitive), linguistically links the poet and his beloved: the first letters of each line spell out the name *Yvonne George*, and, as Dumas first discovered, the last letters spell out the name *Robert Desnos* (Dumas 519; *O* 547). "Infinitif" expresses a desire to suspend time with its title, with its use of infinitive verbs, which represent actions and states of being outside of chronological time, and with its theme of love that outlives death—"not to die yet and to see the shadows last / to be born with fire." The body may pass on and pass over the transmitting of "my name to the years," but the poet's ardor is as eternal as it is infinite. This contradiction is played out rhetorically as well as grammatically in the spelling of the lovers' names; while these names coexist in the same poem, they remain at opposite ends of each line, fixed at a distance from one another.

That the "shadows," *les ténèbres*, of the title of this group of twenty-four poems are still linked to the "star" of Yvonne George is confirmed yet again in the twenty-first poem, entitled "Never Anyone but You," in which the poet states, "The further you go the bigger your shadow gets" (*O* 563–64; *S* 44). "Les Ténèbres" includes love poems but also poems focusing on narrative and on sensory experience. The Desnosian sensuality that will become more marked in the works to follow "Les Ténèbres" is evident in a passage from "Never Anyone but You": "It's the Sunday marked by nightingales singing in the tender green woods the boredom of little girls staring at a cage a canary flutters around in while in the empty street the sun slowly moves its thin line along the hot sidewalk" (*O* 564; *S* 44). A mood is conveyed here of concentrated suspension—the boredom of little girls on Sunday afternoons, which can seem endless, and the languor of the slow-moving sun. It is conveyed through the senses—that of sight, as in the vision with the soft green woods; that of hearing, as in the song of the nightingales, rendered more nervous by the agitated canary in the cage; and that of touch, as in the heat of the sun and the hot sidewalk. This image rooted in sensual experience reminds the reader of the extent to which the hallucinatory visions prompted by automatism flit through the body as well as the mind, as though on a screen. Desnos has translated the physicality he had always demonstrated in his trances into his poetic images.

Desnos taps into the sensory power that automatism unleashes in another poem from "Les Ténèbres." In "Words from the Rocks" the "you" is absorbed into an allegorical plural, "heads of hair" (O 562; S 41). A particular temporal moment is again described, "a night of nights," "a night of all seacoasts," which, by its absolute quality, could be any night. Touch and sound are communicated brutally by the empty bottles the poet crushes loudly with his feet: "The empty bottles I smash into tiny dazzling shards." These senses are enhanced by the odor of cork and of nets from the sea: "The smell of cork tossed back by the sea / Nets of fishing boats imagined by little girls." Sight then disappears into infinite space, in a surge of baroque time in which the instant and the eternal remain in suspended animation: "Heads of hair the eternal infinities are shattered!" The dizzying sense of space then spirals back into the material present, metamorphosed into the glass shards the poet can feel underfoot.

Desnos in Everyday Paris, 1926–1929

From 1926 to 1929 Desnos was increasingly connected to the contemporary everyday world of Paris as a journalist and as a critic of art and of film. Work as a journalist clearly suited Desnos, although it caused problems between him and Breton, who felt that journalism was a surrealistically unacceptable profession. Desnos applied for a union card in 1926 and received it in 1927 (Dumas, "Robert Desnos, journaliste" 279 n.6). Already in 1923, Simone Breton reported in a letter to her cousin Denise that Breton had had a "severe" conversation with Aragon and Desnos and that the surrealist group held them responsible for everything printed in their newspapers (Daix 180). Journalism as a profession had probably appealed to Desnos since his childhood because of his admiration for the serial films by Louis Feuillade, *Les Vampires* and *Fantômas*, whose investigator-heroes, Philippe Guérand and Fandor, are journalists. Furthermore, as Christian Delporte explains in a recent book on journalism in France, there was a French myth of the journalist, dating back to the beginning of the Third Republic—the journalist as a "knight of liberty, crusader of truth," who "nourishes himself on the Revolution"—that may have conformed significantly to Desnos's own republican ideals (127).

Paris in the late 1920s regained at last something of the lost prosperity that had predated the war. Raymond Poincaré, the author of the "sacred union" of 1914 and of the "national union" of 1926 and once again head of the French government from 1926 to 1929, succeeded in strengthening the franc. A renewed optimism had settled on the nation, and the 1920s were being called *les années folles*. It was a period of expansion that flourished until the Wall Street crash of 1929 and the subsequent world economic crisis. Poincaré resigned in 1929 for health reasons and was succeeded by the socialist Aristide Briand, whose struggle for peace over the course of his political career had won him the Nobel Peace Prize in 1926. Briand's government in turn fell on 22 October 1929, just days before the Wall Street crash. In December 1929 the decision was taken to fortify France's northeastern border with Germany by constructing what became known as the Maginot line, a concrete wall, five years in the making, which, because it did not extend to the Belgian border, would leave France vulnerable to invasion in 1940.

With the fall of Briand in October 1929, the older group of politicians who had taken turns running France since before World War I ceded their places to a new generation. As the 1920s closed and the 1930s began, two new leaders emerged on the Right, André Tardieu and Pierre Laval. Tardieu was in power essentially from 1929 to 1932 and Laval from 1934 to 1936. Laval would later become one of Marshal Pétain's prime ministers during World War II and an object of ridicule in one of Desnos's illegal poems written in slang under the Vichy regime. France under Tardieu and Laval no longer followed the model of consensus that had been at the root of Poincaré's sacred union (Becker and Berstein 312). The Left, dominated by the Radical Party since 1902, was perceived by some as an outmoded vestige of another century. Those on the Left did not trust Tardieu and Laval. Moreover, disputes between Left and Right became sharper. As the historians Dominique Borne and Henri Dubief note: "The false courtesy which had marked the often high-level debates of the National Block and even of the Left coalition gave way to violent speeches, which, until then, had been limited to the extremes of the Right and the Left" (18).

Tardieu, with the support of the nation's president, Gaston Doumergue, led France through the worst of the Depression. Being opposed to the parliamentary system, he wished to transform the government into a "strong state which would annihilate the parties" (75). The first to suffer from the Depression's unemployment were immigrant workers, and the second were women, whose "natural" place was seen, once again, to be the home. The standard of living for rural workers and members of the lower middle class fell sharply; "The 'time of hatred,'" as Borne and Dubief remark, "had set in" (43). It is against this backdrop of a strong swing to the Right by a younger generation of leaders who believed in authoritarian rule and who gave "violent speeches" that Robert Desnos's and André Breton's friendship dissolved. As in French national politics, in which Left and Right became polarized and disagreements erupted into street violence, the differences that broke out between Desnos and Breton were ideological as well as emotional and personal.

The year of the Wall Street crash brought the first phase of the surrealist movement to an end. Conflicts, which had been developing under the surface, exploded, leading to the expulsion of some of the founding members of the group, including Desnos, and the induction of new individuals, such as Salvador Dalí, Luis Buñuel, René Char, and Alberto Giacometti. There had already been exclusions: in particular, of Artaud, Philippe Soupault, and Roger Vitrac, one of the poets instrumental in introducing Desnos to the surrealists. The marriages of André Breton, with Simone, and Paul Eluard, with Gala, came apart. The group was already divided over the question of whether or not to join the Communist Party. Eight surrealists (Breton, Aragon, Péret, Eluard, Leiris, Duhamel, Jacques Prévert, and a newcomer, nine years younger than Desnos, Pierre Unik) resolved to join the Communist Party on Christmas Eve, 1926. Breton became a party member in January 1927, together with Eluard, Georges Sadoul, and Marcel Noll. Several surrealists who did not share Breton's new allegiance included Desnos, Malkine, and Max Morise, who had been present at the first session of the period of sleeps. Morise also had a long-term affair with Simone in the late 1920s, an affair that coincided with Breton's own troubled affair with Suzanne Muzard, whom he had in mind when he wrote the last section of *Nadja*. This was the historical and surrealist backdrop for the split, which took place between January 1929 and March 1930, between Breton and Desnos.

Moving toward Bataille: February–March 1929

On 12 February 1929 Breton and Aragon sent a circular letter to seventy-three people, including current and former surrealists, Belgian surrealists, and some independents friendly to the surrealists such as the sociologist Henri Lefebvre, author of *Critique de la vie quotidienne*. Desnos's response to this letter would once and for all seal his disaffection with Bretonian surrealism, which he found too authoritarian, and would signal his growing sympathy for the greater realism and materialism of Bataille, an ideological shift that, as we shall see, also manifested itself in his poetry. Recipients of the Breton-Aragon letter included members of the group that had published the left-wing journal *Clarté* and who had collaborated with the surrealists in 1925 in their joint condemnation of the war of the Rif, France's colonial campaign against Moroccan rebels. Desnos was one of several surrealists who wrote for *Clarté*. The list of recipients receiving the Breton-Aragon letter extended to members of the Grand Jeu, a group of former school friends whose focus on dreams made them interesting to Breton but of whose interest in hallucinogenic experiences and in mysticism he was wary.

The letter, requesting that written responses be sent to Raymond Queneau, asked whether collective action—creative, political, or otherwise—was, generally speaking, even possible. Such a question to members of the surrealist group, whose ideology had been founded on collective action, might seem redundant. Yet there were significant differences between these members, as revealed, for example, by their disagreements over the Communist Party. For several years, moreover, the number of issues of the official surrealist journal, *La Révolution Surréaliste,* had been declining: one issue in December 1924; four issues in 1925; three issues in 1926; a double issue in 1927; and one issue in March 1928. This decline was indicative of growing fissures within the group. By their letter Breton and Aragon were, in a sense, seeking to reconfigure the group in a way that would incorporate more explicitly their new political agenda. In precise terms the letter asked whether it might be possible to set aside personal differences in the interest of the collective; it posed the yes-or-no question—"Do you think . . . that your activities can, or cannot, be conducted on an individual level?"—and requested a follow-up: (1) either a justification of a yes answer to the desire to work individually; or (2) the clarification of a no—meaning, in fact, a yes to communal work, with specifics about the kind of "communal activity" that might be "continued or taken up again" and with whom (Breton OC 1, 954).

Of the answers received, four were openly hostile to the idea of communal action (including those from Bataille, Masson, and Leiris). Four were undecided (including answers from Miró and the former Dadaist Georges Ribemont-Dessaignes). Thirty-six were in favor of the idea of communal activity, although expressed with varying degrees of enthusiasm. Malkine gave one of the most positive responses. Few respondents named names in answering the question concerning with whom one might work collaboratively, but one who did, the painter Emile Savitry, specifically mentioned Desnos, together with Aragon, Breton, Malkine, and Man Ray. Desnos's answer could be qualified at best as lukewarm. He did not side with those opposed to communal action: "Most definitely, even in cases which are impossible to determine in advance, I do not refuse to collaborate in communal activity, but I refuse to accept orders and a discipline which is too often arbitrary" (Breton, OC 965). Yet his endorsement of the possibility of communal activity, couched in a negative phrase ("I do not refuse to collaborate in communal activity") was hardly enthusiastic. In his brief letter Desnos also made reference to personal differences with Breton: "I'm not in the mood to overlook [*faire abstraction de*] personal questions."

This personal tension was reflected in the notes and letters from January 1927 through 1928 that Breton sent to Desnos. The correspondence was brief, and there are no extant answers by Desnos. (Whereas Desnos kept Breton's letters, those from Desnos to Breton were in all probability lost during Breton's self-imposed exile in the United States during World War II.) In one letter, from 3 April 1928, not quite a year before the Breton-Aragon question-naire was sent out, Breton protested that Desnos had been saying nasty things about him and Marcel Noll. He told Desnos that he strongly disapproved of the latter's attitude toward work, no doubt a reference to Desnos's new career as a journalist, which made Desnos, in Breton's eyes, the dupe of capitalist newspaper owners. Breton stated, moreover, that he alone, and not Desnos or anyone else, had the right to break all ties between them (Doucet Library).[15]

It seems also that at this time Youki Foujita, who had a completely open relationship with her companion, the Japanese painter Tsuguhara Foujita, had begun an affair with Marcel Noll. At the beginning of April—it must have been the first or second—Youki ran into Desnos, who was dressed in a tuxedo. Even though he knew she was seeing Noll, Desnos flirted with her and tried to charm her with a paper spider he had made, showing her how to make it move. Youki was not impressed. In his biography of Breton, Henri Béhar reports that when Youki recounted this incident to the surrealists assembled in the Radio Café, near Breton's apartment, Breton immediately fired off his letter of 3 April to Desnos (212). In the letter he made it clear that he, as the moral arbiter of surrealism, would not tolerate the kind of behavior between friends that would involve trying to steal another man's girlfriend. In her description of the incident Youki claims that she begged Breton not to send the letter (127). In any case it is obvious that she liked Desnos better the next time she met him.

A letter sent to Desnos just three days later, on 6 April, showed a more con-trite Breton trying to work things out with his friend. He insisted that human relations are important, implying that he was not exclusively preoccupied with ideological questions. He made it clear that he wanted to talk things through with Desnos. Breton's words were written with courtesy and warmth. On one occasion, between the summer of 1927 and the winter of 1928, Breton stated that friendship is more important than anything else. He sent Desnos cheerful telegrams signed by both himself and his lover, Suzanne Muzard.[16] By the following spring, however, Breton's mood may have been increasingly swayed against his old friend.

On 6 March 1929 Breton and Aragon sent out a second letter asking all those who had replied to the first to attend a meeting at the bar on the Rue du Château. This meeting represented a turning point, the event in the aftermath of which official surrealism would change course. Called to address the ques-tion of a communal attitude toward the Russian revolutionary leader Leon Trotsky, the meeting failed to find a way to respond to Trotsky's expulsion from the Soviet Union, which had occurred three months earlier.[17] The eve-ning deteriorated into an exchange of criticism and rejection, as provoked by the Grand Jeu group. Roger Vailland, for example, was singled out and excoriated for having authored a newspaper article that seemed to praise the repressive, right-wing prefect of police, Jean Chiappe, who would play an infamous role in street clashes during the 1930s. Vailland's comrade in the Grand Jeu, Roger Gilbert-Lecomte, seemed to attack him by agreeing with Breton that writing for a newspaper implied complicity with its political policies. Vailland protested that he needed to earn a living—no doubt echoing the tone of conversations often repeated between Breton and Desnos. Aragon, in his response to Gilbert-Lecomte, defended Vailland by defending his surrealist friends who were also journalists, in particular Desnos and Benjamin Péret, claiming specifically that these two "had never published anything for which they need feel embarrassed" (Breton, oc 1, 983). Nevertheless, Vailland's article may have seemed to Breton proof of his point against Desnos: that dependence on an official organ of the bourgeoisie represented a compromise of integrity.

Desnos expressed his feelings about the meeting by not attending it, thus indicating his growing distance from Breton and his increasing rapprochement with the opinions of the Rue Blomet group (namely, Bataille, Masson, and Leiris). Turning away from the pressure Breton and Aragon were exerting on surrealists to join the Communist Party and to participate in prescribed communal action, Desnos chose instead to keep for himself his freedom of choice. Only later, in the 1930s, would he become more politically active, taking a more explicitly antifascist stance. Desnos's absence from the meeting at the bar of the Rue du Château revealed, perhaps more than anything said or written by or about the protagonists in the drama, the loss of the esprit de corps that had defined the surrealist movement in the initial heady days of its birth in the autumn of 1922. At those first group meetings, all eyes had been focused admiringly on Desnos. But his absence at the Rue du Château meeting now surrounded him with negative attention and spoke poignantly of his future separation from the movement. For, while in March 1929 Desnos was still very much a member of the surrealist movement, by December he no longer would be.

Awakening from the Bretonian Dream

Breton and Aragon published the entire proceedings of the 11 March 11 meeting, including the original letter of invitation, the responses, and a summary of the discussion, under the title "A Suivre," in a special issue entitled "Surrealism in 1929" of the journal *Variétés*, published in June 1929. (A fragment of Desnos's long poem "The Night of Loveless Nights" was published in the same issue.) Aside from the mention of Desnos's response to the original letter, the inclusion of his name as a desirable collaborator in Savitry's letter, the reference to his honest work as a journalist by Aragon, and the absence of his name from those present on 11 March, there was no further discussion of Desnos in the text. In June 1929 the first *Manifesto of Surrealism* was reprinted with Breton's old praise of Desnos. There were no indications, no signs at this point, that Desnos might join the list of excluded surrealists. And yet he was, at that time, closer to the outsiders than to the insiders of the group. Continuing to work as a journalist, despite Breton's disapproval, and refusing to join the Communist Party, Desnos had less and less in common with his old friend. Furthermore, one month before the appearance of the special issue of *Variétés* and the reissue of the first *Manifesto*, Desnos's name appeared in the list of collaborators to a new journal, *Documents*.

The appearance of Desnos's name in *Documents*, a journal devoted to material culture and run by Georges Bataille, along with the names of Leiris and Masson, must have struck Breton like a surrealist slap in the face, or an act of war. Bataille, Leiris, and Masson, like Desnos, had been absent from the meeting at the Rue du Château bar. In "A Suivre," prepared for publication before Breton had a chance to assess fully the consequences of a new review like *Documents*, Bataille's original answer to Breton and Aragon's letter-questionnaire was published, and its defiance of Breton was unsubtly expressed in a savage one-liner: "Too many idealist jerks" (*Beaucoup trop d'emmerdeurs idéalistes*). But Bataille was not the only defiant naysayer published in "A Suivre." Leiris compared Breton's call for collective unified action to Poincaré's conservative catchphrase concerning the sacred union, and he did not mince his words: "The politics of the 'sacred union' seem worthless to me" (*OC* 1, 962). Masson's answer was similarly insulting. Bataille represents, as the surrealist José Pierre comments, a kind of "anti-Breton" (Breton, *OC* 1, 1587). To Breton's pure and idealist surrealism, as Denis Hollier observes, Bataille presented a force of opposition that *Documents* and its "aggressively realist" ideology would articulate (*Documents* xxi).

In working side by side with Bataille, Masson, and Leiris, all of whom, unlike him, had categorically refused the idea of communal action with Breton and Aragon, Desnos essentially revised his answer to the Breton-Aragon questionnaire. His choice to publish in *Documents* represented a de facto change in the stance he had expressed in his written response to the questionnaire: he moved by his actions from ambivalence about the possibility of communal activity to a rejection of it, specifically with the circle surrounding Breton. By October, when Desnos's first article in *Documents* appeared, Breton had already started to write the *Second Manifesto*, in which, in a diatribe extending over three long columns of type, he ostracized his old friend from surrealism. The manifesto was published on 15 December 1929, in the twelfth and final issue of *La Révolution Surréaliste*.[18] In the *Second Manifesto* Breton reiterated his exclusion of Artaud and Soupault and confirmed the exclusion of Joseph Delteil, contributor to the 1924 pamphlet *A Corpse,* published to mock Anatole France. Ribemont-Dessaignes, Masson, Georges Limbour, Jacques Baron, and Roger Vitrac, whom Breton called a "a veritable slut of ideas" for his theatrical work with Artaud, with whom Vitrac founded the Théâtre Alfred Jarry in 1926, were also on the list of the marginalized and excluded (oc 1, 789; *M* 134). Limbour, Baron, and Vitrac, in addition to Masson, had all been Rue Blomet regulars. Not surprisingly, another friend from the Rue Blomet was also singled out: Georges Bataille. It is significant, moreover, that Breton devoted particular attention to Desnos in his list of denunciations, according him more space than anyone else.

Claiming to have given Desnos "an incredible amount of time" to recover his critical faculties and find the true surrealist path, Breton commented that he found himself "forced to say to Robert Desnos that, as we no longer expect anything whatsoever from him, we have no choice but to free him from any commitments he may have made in the past with us. I must confess that it saddens me to some degree to do this" (oc 1, 811; *M* 164). Desnos's journalism provoked Breton's ire, for it was "one of the most dangerous activities that exists" and what had "completely consumed" Desnos's poetry (1, 812; *M* 165). Breton mocked Desnos's affection for Victor Hugo and his identification with Robespierre. He singled out "The Night-Watch," Desnos's liminal poem from *Liberty or Love!* admiringly attributed to Rimbaud and written in traditional verse form. He cruelly dismissed it as plainly "bad" (oc 1, 813; *M* 167). "The excessive use of his verbal gift" was, he suggested, what had caused Desnos to burn out (1, 815; *M* 169). In the *Second Manifesto*'s final form, which was published as a book in June 1930, Breton extended his critique of Desnos, drawing attention to his drinking, making him sound like a drunk, and adding the condescending exclamation, "What a pity!" He expressed fury, moreover, that Desnos would have had the gall, as a surrealist who should have revered Isidore Ducasse, the count of Lautréamont, to nickname a shady (and presumably smelly) Montparnasse bar "Maldoror," after Lautréamont's famous antihero (1, 814; *M* 168).[19]

Part of Desnos's genius in the early days of surrealism had been his ability to stay poised at the in-between, liminal frontier between his unconscious and conscious minds: sufficiently able to remain in touch with his unconscious so as to see the marvelous mysteries unfolding there and equally in touch with his conscious mind so as to speak, write, or draw and to translate his visions and sensations into language. Desnos was able to focus his consciousness on that fleeting moment of transition—the in-between—during the process of translation in which one "language," in this case of images, feelings, and impressions, shifts into another, in which one kind of legibility becomes another. For

Desnos, as we have seen in chapter 1, language was a living and malleable presence. Yet language also resisted him, requiring ceaselessly renewed efforts of the imagination, as this letter to Youki from July 1931, two years later, reveals: "I am wary of words. So often they do not resonate properly, or the way they should. They can seem excessive and, as a consequence, mean. They can be insufficient when they should be tender. And I hold you too high in my esteem to be content with a vocabulary that has proven itself and yet which I find unworthy of our feelings for one another. How I would like to invent a special language, clear, precise, absolute, in order to tell you even the smallest things" (L'Herne 289). By 1929 Desnos's sense of language had shifted from an abstract appreciation of its formal possibilities, as evidenced in his "Rrose Sélavy" poems, to a more realist and materialist vision, a vision closer to Bataille than to Breton. By 1929, after six years of working as a journalist, Desnos's relation to language sprang more from a desire to communicate clearly with others than from a wish to see what happens when language is allowed to play freely and with a certain narcissism in the imagination.

The desire for clearer communicativeness was one factor in Desnos's disaffection with Bretonian surrealism. No longer the same person, he hoped to use his gifts in ways that were incompatible with Breton's current interests. Desnos, a poet associated with voice from the start of his career, was finding his own voice as an adult, as he turned twenty-nine in the twenty-ninth year of the century. Dominique Desanti confirms that Desnos felt that "Breton had become despotic and that he had no understanding of people like Soupault and himself, who needed to earn a living" (interview, 3 Mar. 1999). Desnos had liked belonging to the surrealist group, but he also wanted the freedom to express himself with the confidence he had acquired through his own professional and poetical development. Breton, unlike Desnos, was still seeking a metaphysical spiritual reality, a mysterious unknown, what he would call a "a certain point of the mind" (in the Second Manifesto), where "life and death, the real and the imagined, past and future, the communicable and the incommunicable, high and low, cease to be perceived as contradictions" (OC 1, 781; M 123). With this declaration at the beginning of the Second Manifesto, as José Pierre notes, Breton "opens the text with the affirmation of the metaphysical dimension of the surrealist quest" (OC 1, 1587). Even twenty-five years later, as Pierre points out, Breton's abstract idealism was viewed by Bataille as evidence of an excessive attachment to "sovereign truth" (1, 1589). Desnos's orientation, at this time closer to Bataille's than to Breton's, reflected his own movement away from abstractions and toward more concrete modes of poetic and surrealistic communication, in more sensual, material forms.

Desnos made clear his rejection of Breton's abstract idealism by joining forces with Bataille as of the second issue of Documents, which appeared in

May 1929. Subtitled "doctrines, archeology, fine arts, ethnography," *Documents* was an illustrated journal devoted to material culture with articles, at least in the first two issues (Apr. and May 1929), ranging from appreciations of Sumerian statuary, of Gallo-Roman coins, and of recent paintings by Pablo Picasso to an "ethnological study" of the work of Masson. The third issue, published in June 1929, contained articles on "L'Etude des civilisations matérielles: Ethnographie, archéologie, préhistoire" and on etchings and paintings from the eighteenth and nineteenth centuries as well as an article by Bataille entitled "The Language of Flowers." The issue also included for the first time what would become a continuing feature of the journal: a critical dictionary, offering new definitions of words such as *absolute, materialism,* and *metaphor.*

Bataille's concluding sentence to his definition of the word *materialism* shows how distant his perspective was from Breton's: "When the word *materialism* is used, it is time to designate the direct interpretation, *excluding all idealism,* of raw phenomena, and not a system founded on the fragmentary elements of an ideological analysis, elaborated under the sign of religious relations" (16). This focus on the material over the ideal is well illustrated in his essay "The Language of Flowers" (10–14). While acknowledging that the "language" of flowers is often linked to the language of love, Bataille does not accept, however, the coincidence of beauty in a flower and a pretty girl, to whom the flower may be offered in love. He refers instead to the way love is already part of the flower's natural symbolism: "love can be posited from the outset as the natural function of the flower" (11). For Bataille this "natural function" draws attention to the way flowers grow, propagate, and then, decomposing, become hideous and pathetic before they die; they incarnate "this death-drama, endlessly played out between earth and sky" (12).

The language of flowers, like the language of love, has a materialist and realist subtext: "*love smells like death.*" Flowers are symbols, not so much of love but of the episodic power of erotic seduction and mortality, inextricably linked to the duality of base and sublime that flowers reveal. The "nobly elevated" sun-touched bloom visible above the ground depends upon, and is connected to, the "ignoble and sticky roots" that "wallow in the ground, loving rottenness just as leaves love light" (13). In his philosophical analysis of baseness and formlessness, *l'informe,* Bataille examined the hierarchy between high and low in all natural forms, including the human body, in which pride of place is given to the head over the feet.

It is impossible, states Bataille, to eliminate this opposition between the bloom and the root of a flower. When we speak of flowers as though they were all "cut"—severed from their roots—we are using abstractions to hide and avert our glance from their underlying, base "natural forms." Bataille's fascination with the natural, founded in eroticism, is diametrically opposed to

Breton's idealistic and spiritually pure notion of "elective love." Bataille's essay was published just months after Breton's *Nadja*, in which the latter idealizes his new love, Suzanne Muzard, identified only as "X." For example, in a veritable litany of praise for X's qualities, Breton exclaims: "You who know of evil only by hearsay. You, indeed, ideally beautiful" (oc 1, 751, 157). In Bataille's view such idealism is wrongly placed. For every long-stemmed rose there are grappling roots to which dirt and decomposing matter cling. Bataille seeks to understand the "real presence" of the flower, whether that of the floral or that of the feminine world, as determined by the dialectics of high and low.

Everything that is considered "noble, sacred" in our culture is also mistakenly seen as solely and purely "elevated," in Bataille's view. For whatever is elevated is always in opposition to *bassesse,* the impure, like the flower whose blossom may epitomize perfection in form but whose roots function as an example of the *informe,* formlessness. Bataille elaborated these oppositions throughout the 1930s as part of the ideological foundation of the College of Sociology, which he created together with Leiris and Roger Caillois. The transgressive power, if not "nobility," inherent to the impure exists in inverse proportion to the symbolic power of the pure, as Rosalind Krauss explains: "This notion of *informe* does not propose a higher, more transcendent meaning through a dialectical movement of thought. The boundaries of terms are not imagined by Bataille as transcended, but merely transgressed or broken" ("Corpus" 65). In his article on "The Big Toe," published in November 1929 and accompanied by enlarged photographs of big toes, Bataille praises this lowly part of the human anatomy as "the most *human* part of the human body" (20–23). Because the toes are far from the head, the traditional seat of intelligence and a privileged symbol of humanity, especially within French Cartesian thought, they are closely linked to the earth and to dirt—to human mortality. And it is precisely our mortality, Bataille argues, that makes us human.

Breton might believe that what lies buried beneath consciousness holds secrets pertinent to understanding humanity. He might scorn Enlightenment thinking for having overlooked the irrational powers of dreams and the discoveries of the unconscious mind. But, as stated in the *Second Manifesto,* he had no tolerance for Bataille's materialization of these oppositions, which for Breton were almost exclusively connected to the mind. It is not difficult to imagine how angry he must have felt with Desnos when he saw his old friend's name in Bataille's journal. It raises the question as to which of the two, Breton or Desnos, took the first step in breaking off the friendship. Seeing Desnos's name on the masthead of Bataille's journal must have looked to Breton like proof that Desnos had given up on the life of the mind, on the interior life lived on a higher, oneiric, and unconscious plane.

Desnos was, in fact, devoting himself increasingly to questions of the everyday, not only in his journalism but also in *Documents*. His first article, as mentioned in the introduction, was devoted to the alchemist Nicolas Flamel and to his own childhood neighborhoods of the Halles and the Marais. While extremely poetic, the article has a historical and autobiographical focus. There is no sign of automatic virtuosity here. Instead, a distinctive voice noticeably takes pleasure in expressing clearly, for a wider audience, its enthusiasm for the chosen topic at hand. Desnos's second article, "Imagerie moderne," in the December 1929 issue of *Documents*, addresses a higher, more spiritual reality but in jest only. The article praises the comic book heroes from his youth, especially that masked and caped man, Fantômas, whom Desnos sees as an influence "on the morality of our era" because his "apparition in the oneiric-erotic universe of children," and his own childhood, have had an effect on "feminine sensuality in 1929," namely that of predisposing women of Desnos's generation to an attraction to dangerous men. He credits the *Fantômas* series for being a great monument of "spontaneous poetry" as well as an accurate record of aspects of everyday life before World War I in Paris, "the life of the little people." Most important, he discerns in this popular detective series, in which the criminal is the hero, "the first presence of a marvelous particular to the twentieth century" (*O* 460).

Desnos seems to substitute his childhood memories of popular culture heroes for the moral seriousness of Breton's interests. He has returned to the effervescent humor that characterized the productions of the young surrealists when they were still Dadaists. He places irreverent names and heroes in his pantheon of "divinities" in a gesture that opposes his Fantômas or the advertising poster baby Bébé Cadum to Breton's poetic heroes, such as Lautréamont and Maldoror. In "Pygmalion et le sphinx," an article from *Documents* from early 1930, Desnos imagines the marble statue of Bébé Cadum at the center of a city and wonders whether "these contemporary fetishes [have not] earned their day in the sun, at least as much as this poet, that general, or the other scientist?" He also pokes fun at those, like Breton, who take their heroes too seriously: "I also regret that there have never been statues raised to ordinary everyday objects like the cooking pan, the bottle, the wheel, the wheelbarrow, etc." (*O* 465).

In December 1929, presumably right after the *Second Manifesto* was published in *La Révolution Surréaliste*, Bataille described Breton in a letter that was not published at the time as "that old surrealist priest" and "exactly the type of the great religious hypocrites" (*oc* 2, 51). Both Bataille and Desnos perceived Breton's behavior and attitudes as restrictive and authoritarian. Desnos's light-hearted contributions to *Documents* in 1929 and 1930 echo Max Morise's response to Breton and Aragon's circular letter: "I deplore the profound extent to which humor seems to have been forgotten" (Breton *oc* 1, 966).

Bataille's anger with Breton still resonated thirty-nine years later, when his scathing essay "The 'Old Mole' and the Prefix *Sur* in the Words *Surhomme* [Superman] and *Surrealist*" was published posthumously in an issue of *Tel Quel* from 1968 (32–44).[20] Given the lasting influence of the journal and its role in the importance of critical theory in French Studies in the United States over the past thirty years, it is perhaps not surprising that Bataille has often been more highly respected than Breton in American university circles. In "The 'Old Mole' and the Prefix *Sur*" Bataille condemns surrealism as pretentious and idealist; he accuses Breton of abusing "his mob like a priest" (107, 42). He mocks the surrealists in general and Breton in particular for having "scurrilously disguised" "claims from below" (such as the unconscious or sexuality) as "claims from above" and thus of misunderstanding and misrepresenting their own spiritual and elevated project, which Bataille describes as having a "magnificent Icarian pose"—an Icarian solipsism characteristic of the surrealists that Bataille explains as follows: "the Icarian movement consists precisely of acting and even thinking as if they had attained without laughter the violent spiritual elevation that is only the empty rumbling of their words" (39–40).[21]

Bataille's angry language may seem extreme, except if one considers that this piece was written in response to an equally scathing condemnation by Breton. In the *Second Manifesto* Breton accuses Bataille of being "vague" in defining *materialism*. He adds insult to injury by suggesting that Bataille has only "a small number of specific ideas" (OC 1, 825; M 183). Bataille, Breton claims, has a "fly on his nose," a criticism that implies that Bataille's interest in the phenomenon of attraction and repulsion as inspired by excrement is in fact merely an interest in excrement itself. Breton's condescending language indicates his surprise that Bataille can reason at all, given his fascination with the lowliness that *bassesse* represents: "M. Bataille's misfortune is to reason: admittedly, he reasons like someone who has 'a fly on his nose,' which allies him more closely with the dead that with the living, but *he does reason*. He is trying, with the help of the tiny mechanism in him which is not completely out of order, to share his obsessions" (OC 1, 826; M 184). Bataille, according to Breton, has a "phobia" about " 'the idea' as soon as he attempts to communicate it." Breton's attitude is personal and mean-spirited, especially as regards Bataille's professional activities: "He who, for hours on end during the day, lets his librarian fingers wander over old and sometimes charming manuscripts (it is common knowledge that he exercises this profession at the Bibliothèque Nationale), at night wallows in impurities" (OC 1, 826; M 185).

Aside from the absurdity of Bataille's writings there is the problem, Breton says, of his having composed them when he must have been "simply very tired." The final critical coup de grâce comes when Breton accuses Bataille of having no understanding whatsoever of one of Breton's heroes, the Marquis de Sade. Responding to the gloriously provocative image from the final line of "The Language of Flowers"—which evokes the Marquis de Sade, "locked up with madmen, who," Bataille writes, "had the most beautiful roses brought to him only to pluck off their petals and toss them into a ditch filled with liquid manure"—Breton retorts somewhat haughtily that "the rose, stripped of its petals, remains *the rose* and moreover . . . the dancing girl goes on dancing" (14; Breton OC 1, 827; M 186).

1930: A Second *Corpse*

Desnos and Bataille may have provoked Breton, but they were both furious with his response in the *Second Manifesto. Documents* paid for a rebuttal pamphlet entitled *A Corpse,* an intentional echo of the pamphlet published by Breton with Eluard, Soupault, Aragon, Drieu la Rochelle, and Delteil in 1924 in scorn of the recently deceased Anatole France. This second *Corpse* also made clear that, as far as the authors were concerned, André Breton was "dead" as well, partly because he was beginning to sound more and more as if he took himself to be a national institution, like France.

A *Corpse* was published in the first three weeks of January 1930. Jacques-André Boiffard, who was responsible for many of the photographs in Breton's *Nadja,* made the photomontage on the first page; it showed Breton looking like a corpse with his eyes closed, wearing a sacrilegious crown of thorns. The pamphlet's contributors included Bataille, Desnos, Ribemont-Dessaignes, Leiris, Baron, Limbour, Vitrac, and Alejo Carpentier. Morise, Queneau, and Prévert apparently joined in out of loyalty to Simone, who had just divorced Breton. There were, Gérard Durozoi points out, some contributors whose absence from *A Corpse* was noticeable: namely, Masson, Artaud, Soupault, and Pierre Naville (192).

In turn, Breton once again responded, in February 1930, by publishing a tract entitled "Before, After" in which he quoted contradictory statements that Desnos, Ribemont-Dessaignes, Limbour, Baron, and Vitrac had written about him. Read alone, it makes the authors of *A Corpse* sound like hypocrites. Breton's pamphlet is signed by the surrealists of the time, including new members René Char, Salvador Dalí, Francis Ponge, and Tristan Tzara, a founder of Dada who had come back into the surrealist fold. Not to be outdone, Desnos answered Breton with a "Troisième manifeste du surréalisme," published in *Le Courrier Littéraire* on 1 March 1930. In this document Desnos sounds wounded and upset. He speaks of betrayal. He compares Breton to the right-wing politicians of the day, Poincaré and Tardieu. His fury is sarcastic and bitter: "I think I loved a pig," he writes (O 486). With this statement he is also perhaps ironically citing a footnote from Breton's "Surrealism and Painting" essay from 1928, in which Breton wrote, "God, whom one does not describe, is a swine" (*S&P* 10). Desnos is perhaps implicitly accusing Breton of putting himself in a godlike position. Explicitly, like Bataille, Desnos accuses Breton of priestlike behavior: "Breton . . . is no different from the Pope." "I do not share the ideas of Breton, this priest who does not laugh, who has no idea what it means to laugh, he is so devoured by envy," Desnos continues (309). He declares himself an "atheist" in the Bretonian "religion" (*O* 487).

Desnos's most telling and significant statement comes at the end of the "third" manifesto, in which he proclaims that "surrealism has fallen into the public domain": "I, who have some right to speak of surrealism, I declare it here, the surreal exists only for non-surrealists. For the surrealists there is only one reality, complete, open to everyone" (*O* 487). With this statement Desnos categorically rejects Bretonian surrealism, finding it too centered, elitist, and autocratic. He institutes his own form of surrealism, a more populist surrealism open to a much wider public than ever before. The last word in this pamphlet war, however, went to Breton, who added a brief announcement to the book-length version of the *Second Manifesto*, published in June 1930. Here in this *prière d'insérer* he gave the names of fifteen surrealists who had remained loyal to him. One of the names was that of Desnos's former best friend, Georges Malkine.[22]

Betwixt and Between

By choosing Bataille over Breton in 1929, Desnos chose material reality over the surrealist dream. He broke away from a friendship that had propelled him to the center of the most influential avant-garde group of the twentieth century. How did this come about? Desnos remained both poet and journalist during these years. In 1929, between April and June, he published at least eighteen articles in a newspaper run by his patron, Eugène Merle. Desnos's articles for *Le Merle* included pieces on film (*Les Mystères de New York*, *Le Cabinet du Docteur Caligari*, *Nosferatu le Vampire*, *Un Chien andalou*, Man Ray, and the film star Harry Langdon), photography ("Adget" [*sic*]), jazz ("Le Chanteur de jazz"), and his friend "Kiki," performer and singer. He had a knack for picking classics. (The *Merle* was replaced by *Le Courrier Littéraire* in December 1929, the newspaper in which Desnos would publish his "third" manifesto of surrealism.) Attempting to maintain friendships with both Breton's cronies and the group around Masson and Bataille, Desnos found himself caught between conflicting occupations and circles of friends, trying to participate in several domains and torn by difficult choices.

Breton's condemnation of Desnos must have seemed particularly cruel since Breton seemed in part to be condemning him for exactly the same qualities—his "verbal gift"—for which he had praised him in 1924. Had not

Desnos's verbal facility been one of the primary motors of surrealism in its early days? Yet in 1929 Breton accused Desnos of using this gift to "veil a serious lack of thought" (oc 1, 815; *M* 169). Automatism, according to Breton, had to be used partly for philosophical and political ends. Aesthetic production for its own sake, like a poem in traditional alexandrine verse (specifically Desnos's " Night-Watch," for example) was for Breton a hollow, meaningless creation. But, in Desnos's eyes, his experimentation with twelve-syllable alexandrine lines was an innovative, even revolutionary act, filling a classical poetic form with subversive surrealist content and thus similar to the formal experiments of the "Rrose Sélavy" poems, for which Breton had lauded him. How unfair Breton's apparent change of heart must have seemed.

Desnos's tone of hurt in his 1930 responses to Breton echoes the emotions often associated with romantic breakups. Indeed, it is safe to say that Breton had been Desnos's best and closest friend after they first met. From February 1927 through February 1928 the wealthy couturier Jacques Doucet commissioned Desnos to write a personal history of Dada and surrealism, published posthumously in *Nouvelles Hébrides*. Not much more than a year before the fateful meeting at the bar of the Rue du Château, Desnos describes Breton for Doucet as a man lit by an inner flame. He concludes with this evaluation of his friend: "Whatever happens, Breton will pursue, with a pure soul, an exemplary life which will always remain attached to poetry, revolution, and love" (*NH* 299). Desanti confirms that, when she talked to Desnos in the 1940s, he told her that, despite the angry exchanges of 1929–30, "Marcel Duchamp was the man he admired the most, after André Breton" (interview, 3 Mar. 1999). In the end Breton still came first in Desnos's estimation.

In his biography of Breton, Mark Polizzotti suggests that Breton had called the meeting at the bar of the Rue du Château partly in response to the breakup of his marriage and the difficulties he was experiencing in his relationship with Suzanne Muzard: "In 1929, as Suzanne became more elusive and the divorce from Simone entered an especially bitter phase, Breton's attempts at maintaining control would turn increasingly strident. . . . Overwhelmed at home, Breton responded by further tightening his hold over his own protectorate" (311).[23] Love problems were affecting Desnos as well; sadly, he had to acknowledge his failure to win the love of Yvonne George. Both Breton and Desnos were in a similar position of insecurity with regard to the women they loved, but they responded in very different ways: Breton by surrounding himself with friends; Desnos by seeking a more independent life.

Breton is asked, in the radio interviews he gave in 1952, if there was not a contradiction in his effort to enact both an aesthetic revitalization and a political reorientation for surrealism. Breton answers no, but the question remains as to whether his ambitions for surrealism at the time were even possible, whether the reconciliation of art and politics within a tightly knit group of people who had as many differences as they had points in common could ever come to pass. Was Breton trying to console himself for personal failures with ever more grandiose and idealistic goals in his intellectual life? Was he being unrealistic at a time when Desnos was trying to become more grounded in material and everyday reality? In the same interviews Breton points out that in the 1946 edition of the *Second Manifesto* he had added a prefatory statement concerning Desnos that revised the harshness of his earlier judgment. In this 1946 text he states that in light of the "recent events" of the war he hopes that the negative opinions he had once expressed concerning his old friends, Desnos and Artaud in particular, will be discounted (OC 1, 836). With characteristic honesty and a willingness to revise once fiercely held views, he acknowledges that his past judgments had at times been somewhat "hasty." The 1929 *Manifesto* carries, he admits, "distressing traces of nervousness" (1, 835).

In this 1946 preface Breton also makes specific reference to tumultuous times, to the unavoidable return, around 1930, of "the worldwide catastrophe" that the rise of fascism had initiated. Certainly, the "nervousness" to which he refers came from his own mood at the time. But 1929 was also the year of the Wall Street crash. The era of the stable franc under Poincaré had been short-lived. Throughout the 1930s politicians of the Right and the Left would try unsuccessfully to regain that elusive sense of stability. The extreme reactions of Breton and Desnos to their differences seems eerily in tune with the more "violent speeches" taking place in political debates at the time. The anxiety working through the public domain seems incontrovertibly to have slipped into the exchanges between these friends.

As far as Desnos's ongoing relationship with Georges Bataille is concerned, it seems to have flourished during the 1930s, at least according to the account of Georges-Henri Rivière, director of the Musée de l'Homme in the 1940s. In an interview with Juliette Darle, Rivière remembers sharing a memorable friendship with Desnos, Bataille, and Leiris:

> "That Desnos! I loved the guy," he said, almost to himself. "He was a man from the Parisian working class, a man full of popular sap running underneath extraordinary refinement. We shared a frank camaraderie. He was incredibly kind and always discovering things. It was marvelous to see him, full of whimsy, with Leiris and Georges Bataille. There was between us a fountain of communication that was permanent and direct. With them I was less in my role as a curator than in my role as a musician—I was choirmaster at Saint-Louis-en-l'Ile.

Desnos amazed me with the richness of his vocabulary, the
niceness of his character, and his whimsy, which always en-
livened our work." (Qtd. in Darle 47)

Yet Desnos remained closer to Leiris than to Bataille. Bataille's name does not
figure in Desnos's personal date books and agendas from the war years. Moreover, Bataille's intellectual interests as expressed in the books he was working
on in the 1940s—*L'Expérience intérieure* and *Le Coupable*—became increasingly esoteric, in contrast to Desnos's growing concern with and engagement
in the everyday.

As for Bataille and Breton, they reconciled briefly in 1935, within the
context of Contre-Attaque, an anticapitalist "union of revolutionary intellectuals" that included both Marxists and non-Marxists. This short-lived cooper-
ation points to the fact that, despite all their differences, they had a lot in
common—they would have invested less in their rivalry had it mattered less to
them. Bataille had initially been drawn into the surrealist circle, after all,
because of shared interests, among them an early appreciation for the "dream
paintings" created by Miró in his Rue Blomet studio in the 1920s. In one of the
most beautiful among them, *The Birth of the World* (1925), Bataille saw an
example of formless marks, *taches informes,* as Briony Fer observes, whereas
Breton saw the work of an artist who was "perhaps the most surrealist of us
all" (qtd. in Fer 245). Even when they agreed, they saw the same work from
differing perspectives. Desnos's place in their relationship had been to ally
himself first with one view and then with the other, to see and to create
according to aspects of them both.

The Mermaid Swims Ashore

If Robert Desnos was in between friends in 1929, he was most certainly in
between lovers. The "in-between" as both the point of friction, the sparking
short circuit, typical of the shock of the surrealist image, and the point of
union, the elimination of all contradictions, was enacted in Desnos's personal
life through his conflict with Breton, on the one hand, and his contact with
Youki Foujita, on the other. Desnos met Youki in April 1928. Unlike the distant
Yvonne, poetically symbolized by a star during Desnos's Bretonian years,
Youki, the mermaid, became Desnos's lover and companion (see fig. 8). As
Desnos moved in friendship from Breton to Bataille, he concurrently left the
astral domain and came down to earth in his love relationships, pursuing a
love that existed in Bataillean material reality, in a shift from the spiritual to
the material that his long poems of the time clearly reveal.

Born Lucie Badoud in Paris in 1903, Youki, like Yvonne, grew up in Belgium. Upon returning to the "City of Lights" in 1921 at the age of eighteen, she

quickly attracted the eye of Foujita, a successful Japanese painter living in Montparnasse. In her memoirs she explains how they both fell in love at first sight the minute Foujita saw her at La Rotonde, a café at the Vavin crossroads, diagonally across the Boulevard Montparnasse from La Coupole, where she would meet Desnos seven years later. With his thick bangs and tortoiseshell glasses, Foujita swept Lucie off her feet; he left his wife for her. He renamed her Youki, which she claims means "pink snow" in Japanese, and made her famous in a large nude shown in Paris in 1924 and entitled *Youki, déesse de la neige* (48). She never went by the name Lucie again. When Picasso met her at the Salon d'Automne, he said, according to Youki, that she was even more beautiful in person. A photograph from 1930 shows her with a heart-shaped face, dramatic eyes, and a sensuous mouth. Her hair looks dark and short, although she describes herself as a blonde with very long hair.[24]

At first Desnos clearly delighted in Youki's friendship as part of the couple she and Foujita made. The Foujitas lived extravagantly in a house next to the Parc Montsouris, so close in fact, Youki writes, that they had the feeling that the park belonged to them (143). When they moved into this house they had a "Calder soirée" in honor of the sculptor, whom they had just met at the Dôme and who had recently completed his famous work, *The Circus*. Youki had her own chauffeur to drive her around Paris in their Delage convertible. She probably accepted Desnos's admiration as she had accepted the admiration of others, by sleeping with him from time to time but not exclusively.

In 1928 Desnos wrote an unproduced play, *La Place de Petoile*, in which the protagonist gazes at a starfish in a jar while longing for reciprocated love. In March, he went on a press junket to Cuba, where he was introduced to Cuban music, politics, rum, and his lifelong friend Alejo Carpentier. When he left Paris, his friend Man Ray was in the process of making a short film inspired by a poetic scenario by Desnos, entitled *L'Etoile de mer* and starring Kiki. Desnos himself has a walk-on role—filmed before his departure—in the surprising position of the guy who gets the girl away from the film's protagonist, played by André de la Rivière. The entire film takes place as if in a bottle—the opening and closing shots are of a porthole opening and closing in such a way that it resembles the top of a bottle, while the content of the dreamlike images are frequently shot through a lens coated with Vaseline (to protect it from censorship), which draws attention to its glasslike property. The woman is compared to shooting stars and starfish, the symbols linked to Yvonne George. Yet the ending suggests that already Desnos hoped that his luck was changing and that for once he might win the woman he loved.

Polizzotti reports that in the summer of 1928 Youki favored Desnos with enough attention that a jealous Marcel Noll tried unsuccessfully to "win Youki back from Desnos," by stealing money from the Surrealist Gallery and then trying to drown himself in the Seine (305–06). Desnos himself, in a November 1928 article in *Le Soir* in honor of the phonograph, evokes a time when he and both Foujitas listened to records until dawn (*Voix* 159). Kiki also remembers parties at the Foujitas's house, "where Robert Desnos played old records for us which he had bought with Youki at the Flea Market" (Prin 190).

In 1929 Foujita made tattoos for Youki's and Desnos's bodies: on her thigh, a mermaid in honor of the fact that already in 1929 Desnos referred to her as his *sirène,* or mermaid, and, on his arm, a bear and a band of stars, an allusion to the constellation Ursa Major, so important to Desnos's subsequent poems "Tale of a Bear" from 1936 and "Calixto" of 1943 (*Confidences* 169). (Youki used her tattoo as a model for personalized bookplates [interview with Dumas, 3 Mar. 1999].) Three years later Desnos published an article on tattooing in which he claimed that tattoos bring good fortune (*O* 732). Youki and Desnos also began a joint dream diary in 1929. Most of the dreams are hers, but there are poems written in his handwriting, including one entitled "My Mermaid," later published in *Destinée arbitraire* (Ms. 6670; DSN 899; *O* 677; *S* 62–63). At the same time, however, Youki was still happy with Foujita, and they celebrated their union by getting married in January 1929.[25]

But in August 1929 Youki's life with Foujita changed dramatically. As a foreign national, he had never paid taxes to the French government, even though he had become very successful as a painter in France. When problems over taxes surfaced, Foujita and Youki went on an extended trip to the United States and Japan. Desnos wrote them letters into which he incorporated decals as part of his messages. One decal shows a series of waiters serving a feast, with the word *gala* on top of it. Adding words and letters to the decal, Desnos produced the following message: "During your *galas,* do not lose your memories of home" (DSN.C.450). He also makes a reference in the same letter to his and Youki's tattoos—next to his signature at the end he wrote: "There are no mermaid decals but my big bear continues to be well, Robert Desnos."

In February 1930, when Youki and Foujita returned to Paris, Desnos's first articles in *Documents* had been published as well as Breton's *Second Manifesto* and Bataille's *Corpse.* Desnos's third manifesto would be published within weeks. That August, to celebrate the publication of his first book-length collection of poems, *Corps et biens,* Desnos persuaded the Foujitas to accompany him on a walking vacation in Burgundy—a trip that included as much eating and wine drinking as it did exercise (snapshots from the trip show them enjoying both activities [*O* 600]). By then Desnos's official connection to Bretonian surrealism had been severed. Yet his life as a surrealist, according to his own statements, continued but in a more materialized form, as his title *Corps et biens* indicates. A transformation of the stock expression *corps et âmes,* "body and soul," into *corps et biens,* "body and goods" (which also refers to losses in a shipwreck), materializes the soul, embodies it, and suggests the sensual awakening of the title's creator from the ephemeral nature of his previous surrealist activities.

When the Foujitas went to the Côte d'Azur in September, Desnos wrote individual letters to Youki that show that his feelings toward her were deepening and that he found their separation intolerable. He begins his 3 September letter with "Ma chérie" and continues: "I received your letter and your card with so much joy that I understood just how much your absence weighs on me. I would like it if you could tell me that my absence bothers you a little" (DSN.C.452). But he remained loyal to Foujita, too, and, when the painter went to New York during September and October to raise money, Desnos wrote asking him to return to Youki, who needed him (Dumas 92).

In 1931 Desnos was so poor that he and his friend Carpentier shared a pair of shoes, since they wore the same size ("L'Homme" 490). In need of money, he turned to a new profession and took a job as a real estate agent for Leon Schwob. His primary responsibility was to mediate arguments and transactions between tenants and landlords. In his new capacity Desnos rented an apartment for the Foujita couple on the Rue Lacretelle in the fifteenth arrondissement.[26] That summer, when Youki left alone on vacation, Desnos wrote to reassure her that Foujita would soon follow: "Foufou will leave as soon as he can. You can count on me to see to it." And he also wrote to tell her how much he missed her: "I'm bored far away from you and I'm always afraid that you'll forget me. You are so extraordinary, too, like a summer sky where a storm, the sun, and rain all follow one another in unpredictable ways" (DSN.C.467). While Youki was away, however, Foujita met Mady Dormans.

Youki returned to Paris from her vacation in early September 1931; by late October Foujita had left the country with Mady, without even saying goodbye. Fraenkel explains how one day Foujita just disappeared: "Foujita went out to buy cigarettes and he left for Japan, from which he returned for a brief visit only several years later" (320). Foujita left farewell notes for Desnos and Youki, giving them his blessing to live together. "You now have your faithful friend Robert," Foujita wrote his wife, "he is nice and he has so much admiration for you! He never leaves your side, he has taken my place, deep down you live with him, and for him you are the dearest person in the world." To Desnos he wrote: "To Robert, Thank you for everything you did for me, and to Youki you will continue to give your loyal friendship. Thank you, thank you, I don't need to stay here any longer; you have the destiny of taking care of Youki. Thank you. Foujita." On 31 October Foujita mailed Youki a final short letter from Marseille: "Youki, adieu, I'm leaving. Be well, let me go and don't come after me, have pity on me. I'm leaving for good. I kiss you one last time and be happy" (qtd. in Dumas 97–98). Soon afterward Desnos gave up his studio in the Rue Blomet and moved in with Youki in the Rue Lacretelle. In 1932, in celebration of their love, he took a Japanese blank book with a silk cover and folding pages, calligraphed and painted it, and gave it the title "Le Livre secret de Youki." Inside, in painting and in verse, he represented Youki as a mermaid and himself as a seahorse, finally joined together.

From Double to Couple

Three long poems characterize this amorous period in Desnos's life. In them multiple characters seek true love: "The Night of Loveless Nights," with its English title, was started in 1927, when Desnos was still in love with Yvonne George, and finished in 1928–29, after he had met Youki; "Sirène-Anémone," from 1929, was written toward the beginning of his love affair with Youki; "Siramour," from 1931, coincides with Desnos's finally moving in with Youki.[27] Each of the three poems experiments with form but in ways that differ from the "Rrose Sélavy" poems of the early 1920s. Desnos again uses the traditional alexandrine verse line, as he had in "The Night-Watch." Such traditional, classical versification was anathema to the surrealists; a poem in regular verse was clearly the opposite of a poem produced by automatic writing. Yet in Desnos's hands the alexandrine gained a double power: at once canonical and free, especially considering the liberties he took with this classical and rational form of French verse. Any poetic constraint, for Desnos, represented a form to be bent to his will, to be transformed, so that, in his hands, fixed form could metamorphose into free verse and then back again into formal verse.

The *prière d'insérer* for *Corps et biens* (1930), a volume including all of Desnos's official surrealist poems and "Sirène-Anémone," anticipates and responds to any criticism that might come from surrealist quarters. It praises Desnos's poetry for being a reflection of everyday life: "Freed from all rules, all constraints, the poetry of Robert Desnos is written in the image of life, insofar as life and poetry can be free" (*O* 589). Responding to Breton's 1929 accusation in the *Second Manifesto* that Desnos's alexandrine verses were "bad (false, padded, and *empty*)," the *prière d'insérer* declares that Desnos's understanding of his own *art poétique* could be summarized in just two words: "Every liberty" (*Toutes licences*) (Breton *oc* 1, 813; *M* 267; *O* 589).[28] Finally, it situates Desnos's poetry within the experience of the quotidian, claiming that his poems constitute a veritable "journal written in the margins of his life, a singularly sincere diary, exact and adapted to the least shift (*revolution*) of his sensibility."

Desnos was absolutely correct in attempting to preempt the criticism of the Bretonian surrealists. Aragon wrote a scathing review of *Corps et biens* in the first issue of the new surrealist journal, *Le Surréalisme au service de la révolution*, launched right after the publication of the *Second Manifesto*. He claims that Desnos mistakes the "vulgar" for the "popular," unless Desnos, he dismissively implies, has confused *popular* with little imitative folkloric songs (13). Aragon also accuses Desnos of shameless imitation, unconscious pastiche, and sentimentality. He takes umbrage that Desnos would include his "Rrose Sélavy" poems, which were no more than "clinical documents" and never true poetic texts. He denigrates Desnos for his lack of formal education and intellect: "it would be difficult to imagine a man with so little ideology who is nevertheless so satisfied with himself in his ignorance" (15). The ideology Aragon finds lacking in Desnos in 1930 was, of course, communism, as reflected in the new journal's title.

Desnos's style had changed in the final poems of *Corps et biens*. Regular rhyme schemes, fixed rhythms, and regular quatrains do not appear in the earlier poems composing "A la mystérieuse" and "Les Ténèbres." Yet, as the even earlier "Rrose Sélavy" poems demonstrate, Desnos had always been interested in experimental as well as traditional verse forms. Two of his earliest poems from 1919, "Le Fard des Argonauts" and "Ode à Coco," were written in rhymed quatrains of alexandrine lines. This interest in fixed forms and in all possible ways to transgress them persisted from the beginning to the end of his career. (By the war years Aragon would change his mind about fixed-form verse, just as he would change his mind about his old friend Desnos.)

In "The Night of Loveless Nights," "Sirène-Anémone," and "Siramour" Desnos experiments with voices and symbolic masks that he assigns to himself and the women he loves. Not until the last of these poems, "Siramour," does the poetic "I" finally find its mate. In the first poem, "The Night of Loveless Nights," however, the poet is alone as the allusion to lovelessness in the title indicates. The first line of "Night of Loveless Nights" sets the scene: "Putrid, glacial, horrible night" (*O* 904). It is written partially in regular verse form—rhymed, alexandrine quatrains—which in no way belies their automatic inspiration, for Desnos could "speak in alexandrines" for hours, according to Malkine (Ottavi 75–76). While the style of individual lines and quatrains in "The Night of Loveless Nights" might suggest a return to conventional forms, the overall architecture of the poem is far from standard or traditional. Long sections of rhymed quatrains are broken up either by sections resembling prose poems or by passages in italics with irregular quatrains.[29] It ends with a detached final line that exclaims: "Oh Revolt!" (*O* 923).

The poem is a veritable drama, an agon, with multiple and competing voices and dialogues in which the principal poetic voice speaks sometimes to others, sometimes to himself. Its theatrical setting is enhanced by explicit references to mythical personae often connected to the theater. Don Juan (who is also *not* Don Juan) and Bacchus appear (see fig. 9).[30] In the character of Don Juan a human meets his fate and goes to hell. In the mythic form of Bacchus-Dionysus, in whose name dramatic festivals were held in antiquity and who "represented the force of life in all growing things," a deity continues to renew himself (Stapleton 69). With Don Juan a mortal, chronological timeframe is announced. With Bacchus-Dionysus an eternal, baroque sense of time reigns, in keeping with the dream setting of the poem.[31]

The speaker addresses a ghost, a "fantôme," whom the "I" discovers in his mirror. This baroque double lives in a dimension that is doubly different—a phantom on the other side of the mirror and on the opposite side of life, since he is a suicide. Incarnating the speaker's self in a more advanced state of dreaming, the phantom points to the night as the space of dreams and to this poem as a record of the various depths and stages of sleep. Like the speaker, this ghostly dream double yearns after seductive, punishing women, "the severe ones." He will (in the future tense) pursue, and be tortured by, these women. The ghost's torment illustrates the fact that death is not final but, rather, a new existence in a different dimension.

This drama of servitude to indifferent women is played out under the governance of a character referred to as *l'unique* who controls love, like Cupid from Renaissance poetry or Don Juan, the mythic seducer and master of disguise who, in Molière's play, descends directly into the netherworld, thus both emblematizing and escaping mortality. He is a character whose "story" ends with his departure from mortal life but who inhabits the same world as the *fantôme* from the opening quatrains. Yet "this is not the Don Juan" of Molière's play, claims the poem's speaker: "It is Bacchus," reborn. Love is as natural as the regenerative life cycle in nature and just as inescapable; it permeates our unconscious in a manner that resembles automatism or intoxication, with whom Bacchus, god of the vine, and his Roman counterpart, Dionysus, are connected.[32] It is appropriate that Desnos, the surrealist most responsive to the "surrealist voice" during the period of sleeps, should invoke Bacchus-Dionysus in later poems, since Bacchus, unlike Apollo, god of poetry and images, was the god of rhapsodic song and unbridled dance.[33] In effect, the "I" in "The Night of Loveless Nights" is caught in an extended present moment, in "*this always nocturnal ravine*" in which he hears the sounds of hunters, evocative of the "hunt" often depicted in Renaissance sonnets of love (908–09).

Once the speaker's identity has been established through the double personae of his doubles—a dead man and another spectral character, a condemned prisoner—the "I" disappears and sinks into the impersonal infinitive, a universalist verb form, at once infinite and eternal, which may be used by any speaker. The infinitive is neither subjectified nor personalized, remaining free of any given moment, tense, user, or pronoun.

Expressed in the infinitive, a new section of unrhymed italicized quatrains (inserted after much of the poem had already been composed) invokes a deep desire:

> *To sleep with her*
> *For the sake of sleeping side by side*
> *For the sake of parallel dreams*
> *For the sake of a double respiration*
> *To sleep with her*
> *For the singular and surprising shadow*
> *For the same warmth*
> *For the same solitude*
>
> *To sleep with her*
> *For the shared dawn*
> *For the identical midnight*
> *For the same ghosts*
>
> *To sleep, to sleep with her*
> *For absolute love*
> *For vice, for vice*
> *For every possible kind of kiss. (O 912)*

In this, the poem's central part, which includes some of the most lyrical love verses ever penned by Desnos, the poet reveals that he desires to "commingle" with the beloved, who also exists "in the heart of the lover." The italicization gives the impression of a whisper, as though the words were barely emerging fully formed from the page. As in Breton's lapidary phrase, "words are making love," language here speaks the lover's emotions, thus unconsciously allowing his deepest desires to surge out of a welter of feelings, thoughts, and associations and to define themselves the way a coherent image can slowly appear from the confused lines of an absent-minded, automatic doodle on the page.

After this central, hypnotic section, the speaker finally initiates a dialogue with his beloved: "For so many long months, my dear, I have loved you" (*O* 915). He pleads for her attention and rails against the hopelessness of his fate:

> I am tired of struggling against a fate that keeps escaping me
> Tired of attempting to lose myself in forgetting, tired of
>   remembering
> The least perfume emanating from your dress
> Tired of hating you and tired of blessing you. (916)

Finally, near dawn, the poem metamorphoses into an incantation to "night," which echoes the earlier section built on a litany of repeated negative *ni, ni* expressions. For this is a night of the negation of love, a "night of loveless nights," resolving itself at dawn into a final dialogue that the speaker conducts with himself:

> Be quiet, put down your pen and close your ears
> To the slow, heavy footsteps coming up the stairs.
> The night is already fading but this dawn is similar to
> Dead butterflies at the base of candles. (921)

Exhorting himself in the final quatrain to "call the mermaid and the star with loud cries/If you cannot sleep with your mouth shut and your hands clasped," the speaker presents Desnos's amorous *états d'âme* of the time, by calling attention to siren and star. Desnos probably wrote the conclusion to "The Night of Loveless Nights" in 1928–29 after he had met and begun a love affair with Youki.[34] He anticipates Youki's rivalry here in his pantheon of love with the "star," with Yvonne, who, like the cold "adorable phantom" of the poem, refused to return his love. This was not the first time, either, as we have seen, that a siren approached the poet. Desnos had already evoked a human female creature swimming toward shore in "The Night-Watch." Yet the speaker in "The Night of Loveless Nights" is predominantly alone. The poet's interlocutors—the phantom, the condemned prisoner—have no substance; they do not answer him. Ultimately, surrounded by doubles of himself, he is a captive to his own dreams, making it difficult to return to reality. But, as Desnos begins to disengage himself from his solitary obsessive passion for the elusive Yvonne George, so too do his poems reflect a greater possibility for connection with another.

The second in Desnos's 1927–31 sequence of long love poems, "Sirène-Anémone," was written in 1929—the year that Youki had herself tattooed with the mermaid symbol ascribed to her by Desnos—and published in *Corps et biens* in 1930. The suggested interaction between the speaker and double objects of affection, the mermaid and the star, from the conclusion to "The Night of Loveless Nights," is taken up again in this poem. Such a repetition is clear from the title. "Sirène-anémone" identifies the exotic female, the double creature to whom the poem is dedicated, as a mermaid-anemone. The mermaid and the flower—already inherently double, since *anemone* designates both floral and aquatic blossoms—represent double beloveds, in contrast to the speaker, who remains singular here. Moreover, the flower absorbs into herself the star from previous poems. From the poem's start the anemone is at once floral, mineral, and celestial: the "anemone of the skies" as well as the "anemone of the nights/Who plunges her roots/Into the shallow water of the wells/Into the shadows of mines" (*O* 567). The drama has thus changed from one man (in "The Night of Loveless Nights") split into multiple doubles of himself because of his unhappiness in love to that of one man (in "Sirène-Anémone") seeing "double" as he contemplates the multiple aspects of the woman he loves.

The connection to the beloved is much more intimate in "Sirène-Anémone" than it had been in "The Night of Loveless Nights." The poet now speaks through the female character's multiple selves, as the first quatrains show:

> So who could see me
> I who am the strange flame
> The anemone of the evening
> Flowering underneath my ferns. (*O* 567)

This anemone is mineral, floral, human, like the starfish in Man Ray's *L'Etoile de mer,* who is beautiful like a woman and also like a "glass flower," a "flesh flower," and a "fire flower" (Hedges 216–17). Her charms are not fully sublimated, but they are not quite yet as poisoned with mortality as in Bataille's vision of love and nature. She is a double and a hybrid, an in-between, insofar as she is the semihuman, semianimal mermaid. She is also observed by a fellow earthbound creature: an aging horse who, like her, has human characteristics. She is as carnally realized as he is. Mermaid and horse breathe and live on the earth.

Like "The Night of Loveless Nights," "Sirène-Anémone" is composed of a series of sections written in divergent styles. Midway through the poem the "I" turns out to be a "sleeper" in love with a "lover" whose hair sweeps across his forehead and who kisses his closed mouth and eyes. These sensations send the dreaming "I" into another world, into the eye of a storm, the "night of shipwreck" (*O* 570). The dream drags the dreamer close to death yet is merely the result of "a night of fresh ink." It leads to the mundane desire for a pillow "for my tired forehead," "for kisses" and "caresses," "To console a heart that has worked too hard" (573).[35]

The speaker wonders whether the lover here might not finally be the one:

> Who will forgive my past my heart my scars
> For having explored alone moving countrysides
> For having been tempted by tentative voices
> For not having met her sooner
>
> Will she be able to forget my former dreams
> The lost fortunes and the tears shed
> The merciless star shining in the dark woods
> And the bruised desires and the senseless nights. (*O* 573)

He sounds as if he were asking his new love to forgive him for having loved another—a heartless "star," for whose love he has lost many nights of sleep, "nights of loveless nights." He has finally matured and has grown to expect love and forgiveness.

As the poem continues, a Desnosian sensuality emerges linked to smell in the form of "flowers which dropped their petals onto the fruits of autumn" and linked to touch through the brand marks left on the flank of another Desnosian double, the wild horse (*O* 573):

> I am marked for life by my loves
> Like a wild horse escaped from the Gauchos
> Who, finding freedom on the prairie,
> Shows the mares his flank burnt by the branding iron
>
> While far away with grand virile gestures
> The mermaid, singing to a carbonated sky
> In the middle of barrel-ripping reefs,
> In the heart of the swirling waters, brings forth an anemone.
>   (574)

In light of Desnos's emotional life in 1929, these verses, which evoke the wild horse "finding freedom" and sufficiently inured to his love scars to show them off to the sympathetic mares on the prairie, illustrate how Desnos closed the book on his unhappy love affair with Yvonne. These lines also reflect Youki's physical distance in 1929, for she had just married Foujita and left with him on a long trip away from France. She was indeed "far away" from Desnos when he realized that he loved her, across "swirling waters," in the United States and Japan. Yet her willing acceptance of Desnos's admiration for her—as witnessed by her mermaid tattoo and by Noll's jealous escapade of the previous summer, pointing to a full-blown love affair between her and Desnos—made of her a responsive lover, unlike Yvonne.

Desnos's love for Youki rescues him from being a lover only in his dreams and holds forth the hope of the birth of a new anemone, a new flowering love. Like the flower in this poem, his new love affair, even though in 1929 it still had an uncertain future, was firmly rooted in a sensuality redolent of the odors of fruits, autumn petals, sea salt, and sea breezes. Desnos's change of heart in his love affairs, as reflected in this poem, harmonized with his concurrently shifting political agendas as well—from Bretonian to Bataillean and eventually to Desnosian surrealism, which effectively combined the idealism of the first with the materialism of the second.

The final poem in this series, "Siramour," signals with its title a shift in attitude. A neologism that combines the words for "mermaid" and "love"—

sirène and *amour*—the word *Siramour* joins them solidly; there is no doubling. These two words, feminine (*sirène*) and masculine (*amour*), are sol-
dered together in the title.[36] Dating from 1931, the year that Foujita finally
abandoned Youki and in which she and Desnos decided to live together, the
poem firmly asserts a union in the personal pronoun *we,* which shouts out at
the beginning of the third complete sentence: "We will go to Lisbon, with a
heavy soul and a light heart" (*F* 11).[37] And yet the "we" in the poem—the "I"
and the "ideal, living mermaid," who is "a flesh and blood figure"—are not
fully united until the poem's final lines. The "I" takes time out from describing
his love for the mermaid to address a "you" (in the long central section), who
is clearly not the mermaid but, rather, the recently dead star from his poetic
cosmos: namely, Yvonne George.

The six-syllable quatrains that follow the opening free-verse section resonate in tone with the memory of Yvonne George because they have the sonorous semblance of popular songs of the day—in particular the kinds of
songs Yvonne liked to sing. Cantaloube-Ferrieu argues that many of Desnos's
poems from the 1920s resemble, in the way they use lyric apostrophe, unfinished sentences, and anaphora, a form "fundamental to the genre of song."
In these songlike forms, Cantaloube-Ferrieu hears "an echo between poem
and song" according to which Desnos created "a duo between the *chanteuse*
and the poet," which was the only way he was able to unite "his voice to that of
the beloved" (66). This duo effect may certainly be read as intentional in
"Siramour," in which Desnos speaks to the recently dead Yvonne, explaining
that, while he still loves her, he now also loves another "her."

The mermaid, whom the poet credits with inspiring Don Juan in his
ambitions as a lover, is also the heroine of a fairy tale, told in italics within the
poem and unfolding over the course of several episodes. The scene, which
Desnos also painted in watercolor, opens on a beach, at the foot of a castle,
where the mermaid is held captive in an abandoned bottle.[38] A female mythic
figure, she is known in dreams as *la Fantômas.* By her name she incarnates a
female version of the elegant and wily masked thief who consistently eludes
the journalist Fandor and the Paris police in the Feuillade films Desnos so
loved and about which he wrote in *Documents.*

In the section after the first episode of the fairy tale, the mermaid's mate
appears: the seahorse. He is the aquatic double of the horse branded by love in
"Sirène-Anémone." He is also the double of the poetic "I" identified here as
"the drinker, drunk with song" who hears the mermaid singing from inside
the bottle: he "drinks" the song and "liberates the mermaid," thus fusing
himself with the object of his love: "That nothing in this circle which isolates
them/May separate the mermaid from the seahorse" (*F* 16). Mermaid and
horse could not live on the same terrain, even if their moods might have
coincided. But the mermaid and the seahorse can possibly share a future.

In the second episode of the fairy tale of the mermaid, the "I" returns and declares his loyalty to her: "*Oh mermaid! I will follow you everywhere*" (*F* 19). Suddenly, however, she rises into the sky and becomes a flame, a star. The symbol for Youki metamorphoses into her predecessor, Yvonne. Here the "I" addresses a familiar "you" through a personal letter written in verse, in which the "I" remembers a night when "she put her hands around my neck and, looking me in the eyes with that look which my own eyes absorb, she said: 'You are the one I should have loved.'" At the same time, he grants her the right to reject him: "I kiss your hands; you have the right not to love me" (20). This calm reaction to Yvonne is then explained in terms of the wax mermaid that had once hung in Desnos's Rue Blomet studio:

> And you,
> Do you remember that wax mermaid that you gave me?
> Already you saw yourself in her and in the one who resembles
>   you.
> You do not die as a result of the transfiguration of my love, but
>   you live
> on in it, she perpetuates you.
> For love is stronger even than you, even than her.
> And you will only truly be dead
> The day when I will have forgotten that I loved.
> That mermaid that you gave me, it is she. (21)

In "Siramour" the poet informs his dead beloved that his new lover, like her, appreciates "the little bistros, the zinc bars at dawn in the working class neighbors, the joy of workers when they're happy." The resemblance is so strong that it becomes unclear whether the "you" in the poem is still the star, who is gone, or the mermaid, who is alive. The poet specifies that these two female figures represent "the two faces of my love, of my unique love" (*F* 22).

In truth, "she," Youki, does perpetuate "you," Yvonne. Soon, the metamorphic transition is finally completed; the "I" indeed addresses his new love in an extended apostrophe:

> You will say goodbye for me to the little girl on the bridge
>   to the little girl who sings such pretty songs
>   to my old friend whom I've neglected
>   to my first mistress
>   to those who knew the women you know about
>   to my true friends, whom you will readily recognize
>   to my glass sword
>   to my wax mermaid
>   to my monsters to my bed

Whereas to you, whom I love more than anything in the world
I will not say goodbye yet
I will see you again
But I am afraid of not being able to see you for very much
      longer. (*F* 26)

The "I" expresses hope for reciprocated love, one tinged nevertheless by the unfounded fear of "not being able to see" the beloved for much longer. The poet soon makes light of his own fears, however, identifying his poem as "a song" written "to amuse the one I love." Having first conflated the two women he loves, he then separates the one he loves in the present from the one he loved in the past. This rhetorical gesture is confirmed in the last episode of the fairy tale; the mermaid now shines in the heavens as a star and then, in one single leap, leaves the celestial world behind her: "*the mermaid dives into the sea in the midst of a cresting wave so bright that the Milky Way pales beside it*" (28). She swims toward shore like the "swimmer" from "The Night-Watch." The "I" fears losing sight of her as she heads toward the bottle left on the beach, but then the poet's double, the seahorse, takes his place beside her in the final strophe. The "I" may hesitate in real life to confirm his position in the life of the mermaid he loves, but in the poem, at least, Desnos manages to imagine in the end a happy couple. The two aquatic creatures can live together in the same watery element, in the same alternate world of dreams and the unconscious.

With "Siramour" Desnos finally projects a love scenario with two compatible protagonists who finish the story together, as the poem's final strophe announces: "Oh nothing can separate the mermaid from the seahorse!" (*F* 30). The seahorse gets his mermaid, just as Desnos, in real life, finally gets the "girl" he will love until he dies. Using the metered constraints of traditional verse forms to mimic the constraints he feels as a "prisoner of love," eager to break out of his bonds, Desnos experiments with breaking the rules and standards of French versification. In reverting to the classical verse forms with which he had experimented as a youth, was Desnos knowingly sealing his break with Breton and the official surrealist movement? Michel Murat points out that Breton, Eluard, and Aragon, in their respective surrealist collections, *Clair de terre*, *Capitale de la douleur*, and *Le Mouvement perpétuel*, had also used alexandrine lines ("Desnos" 48). For them to say that Desnos was no longer surrealist because he wrote in fixed verse forms can be interpreted as the height of hypocrisy. Murat suggests that Desnos was out of sync with Breton, Eluard, and Aragon, because he was already experimenting with poetry in new ways, as they had proposed that the group should do (51). To explain why his work from this period drew so much criticism, one need only look to his unwillingness to be forced to march in step with the group. And that problem—the conflict between the individual and the collective—was, in fact, the true cause all along of Desnos's troubles.

In conclusion, it was not Desnos's poetry from this time that separated him from the rest of the surrealists. It was his growing desire for intimacy as well as a developing sense of confidence in the strength of his own voice as a poet, as a journalist, and as a player in the intellectual and cultural dramas of Paris at the end of the *années folles*. During the years Desnos lived in the Rue Blomet studio, from 1926 to 1931, he was between roles as a public surrealist and as a public intellectual. He explored the in-between materially in the heightened sensuality of his poetry, which concretized the spatial and temporal experience of baroque time. He also lived an in-between dilemma on several practical fronts: in his friendships, in his love affairs, and in the tension between his desire for privacy and for increased visibility. Once he emerged from this transitional state, he sought greater contact with the larger social and cultural world around him—both in his personal life with Youki, which became increasingly social, and in his new, more public life on the radio and in politics.

Can it be said that by 1931 Robert Desnos was no longer "surrealist"? Perhaps not in name, but it was surrealist of him to experiment with poetic form. It was surrealist to write about dream experiences, captured retrospectively in the manner of paintings by René Magritte, Max Ernst, and Salvador Dalí. It was surrealist to recognize an unconscious life in which the singular identity evident during waking life is multiplied and complicated by the plural identities generated by conflicting desires, fears, and hopes as unleashed by dreams. It was surrealist to take a strong stance against group pressure—of the increasingly doctrinaire surrealist group itself. It was surrealist, in other words, to maintain a firmly revolutionary stance, even, if need be, against surrealism.

To use Friedrich Nietzsche's distinction between Dionysian and Apollonian principles, surrealist automatism has its source, it could be said, in nonimagistic intoxicating Dionysian experience, which is then translated into intellectual images. In *The Birth of Tragedy* Nietzsche describes Dionysian ecstasy as nonimagistic and as linked to music. In fact, his description of the Dionysian state strongly resembles that of the communal automatic state, which Desnos had perfected during the period of hypnotic sleeps:

> In song and in dance man expresses himself as a member of a higher community; he has forgotten how to walk and speak and is on the way toward flying into the air, dancing. His very gestures express enchantment. Just as the animals now talk, and the earth yields milk and honey, supernatural sounds emanate from

him, too: he feels himself a god, he himself now walks about enchanted, in ecstasy, like the gods he saw walking in his dreams. He is no longer an artist, he has become a work of art: in these paroxysms of intoxication the artistic power of all nature reveals itself to the high gratification of the primordial clay. (37)

Robert Desnos, as exemplified in the poems written between 1927 and 1931, was of all the surrealists the one who most identified with the sensual and ecstatic experience of Bacchus, and he had always been the one who best heard the murmur of the surrealist voice. It was in response to that inner voice that he willingly left the movement in 1930, striking out on his own to follow its sounds and attuning his own speech to it over the course of the next decade.

Radio and the
Mediation of the Everyday

1936: On a Saturday night in a large nineteenth-century apartment just blocks from the Seine, Robert Desnos, a glass of red wine in his hand, holds court at his weekly open house. He is surrounded at different times by friends and acquaintances from across Paris and beyond France's national borders, including the actor couple Jean-Louis Barrault and Madeleine Renaud, the Cuban writer and composer Alejo Carpentier, the Doctors Théodore and Michel Fraenkel, Ernest Hemingway, whom Desnos had met through their shared sympathy for the Republicans in the Spanish Civil War, and the singer Damia. Quick to anger, though just as quick to reconcile, this Desnos, together with his beloved Youki, alternates rumbas, jazz, and tango records as guests come and go. He listens closely to songs that he will play on his radio show the following week or inspire the poems he hopes musicians will feel free to set to their own music.[1]

Changes in Private and Public Life

The personal everyday experience of Desnos in the 1930s was focused on his intimate relationship with Youki, who was, along with Kiki, one of the "queens of Montparnasse." Desnos cut a handsome figure in these days. With eyes the color of "spoiled oysters" behind thick glasses with heavy frames and short hair, he blended a facility with the accents and slang of his childhood working-class neighborhood of the Marais with an elegant style of dress.[2] Youki, for her part, loved to dress in the latest fashions. By 1934, when Robert and Youki moved into a large sunny apartment at number 19, Rue Mazarine, in the Saint-Germain-des-Prés section of the sixth arrondissement, Desnos had begun to allow his private life to become increasingly public.

The Saturday night open house parties at the Desnos residence were legendary. Dr. Michel Fraenkel, Théodore's younger brother, described them in an interview: when Desnos had the means, red wine and food were abundant; when he had less money, there was less on the table, but the door was always open (interview, 23 July 1993). Théodore Fraenkel described the Mazarine apartment as being filled with books and a magnificent collection of records, due in large part to the music and recording reviews Desnos wrote (see fig. 10). Of the Saturday gatherings Fraenkel wrote:

> In the big black-and-white-tiled dining room, a long table is covered with a black waxed cloth, and crowned with liters of red wine. At dinner there are rarely fewer than eight or ten places set, sometimes as many as twenty. The food, usually prepared by Youki, at times with Robert's help, especially for the lobster *à l'américaine*, arrives in earthenware plates, which are sometimes positively huge. The biggest parties are on Saturdays; after dinner more friends arrive. They are all received with warm cordiality and kissed by Youki; some of the guests don't even know their hosts by sight! (321)

The novelist Alejo Carpentier, Desnos's regular collaborator on the radio, offered his own description: "Every Saturday there was a traditional party where the guests had the absolute right to do anything they fancied: to play music on the phonograph, to examine the collections of rare objects, to climb up onto the library ladders, to cook, drink, perform acrobatics, flirt with one of the women guests—as long as they weren't interfering with someone else's interests" (qtd. in L'Herne 333). Alain Brieux, who hid in the apartment during the Occupation, remembers that the walls of this room were decorated with paintings by Miró, Klee, Duhamel, and Malkine (26).

In March 1928, having gone to Cuba as a reporter on a press junket arranged through his contacts with South and Latin American painters and writers living in Montparnasse, Desnos had met the dissident composer and author Carpentier, whom he helped to escape Cuba by hiding him as a stowaway on the return trip to France (*O* 433; *Confidences* 156). Once back in Paris, Desnos published a series of articles on Cuba and Mexico in *Le Soir;* he also brought back records of Cuban music and a fondness for rum. Carpentier claims to have met at Desnos's Saturday parties such disparate figures as Langston Hughes, John Dos Passos, "the Lecuona Cuban Boys, who improvised concerts with drums and maracas in the library," and Georges-Henri Rivière, a contributor to Georges Bataille's journal, *Documents,* and, in the 1940s, the director of the Musée de l'Homme (L'Herne 333).[3] Michel Leiris met Carpentier at the Desnos's along with the Guatamalan author Miguel Angel Asturias and Léon-Gontran Damas, who was one of the originators of the negritude movement and whose work Desnos appreciated (368).[4]

Kiki would sometimes continue her popular nightclub act at these parties; she loved the bohemian atmosphere and the mystery created by the piles of dusty objects: the glass canes, postcards, unframed paintings, and old shoe-boxes filled to the brim with papers, notes, and manuscripts (Mollgaard 266). The dancer Julia Tardy Marcus was a regular (Ferdière 141). Georges Hugnet and André Verdet told Dominique Desanti that on those Saturdays "everybody brought what they could, including rabbits to cook and wine to drink" (interview, 3 Mar. 1999). Psychiatrist Gaston Ferdière, who later counted Antonin Artaud, Hans Bellmer, and Unica Zürn among his patients, would come for dinner and spend the night (Ferdière 108). By the 1940s, judging from Desnos's diaries, the names of Paul and Nusch Eluard; Pablo Picasso; Jean Galtier-Boissière and his wife, Charlotte; Simone de Beauvoir, and Jean-Paul Sartre were added to the guest lists, as were those of Robert Antelme and Marguerite Duras (DSN 878.188). Throughout this period Desnos also remained loyal to his family. Carpentier asserts that Desnos "adored" his father and never missed family Sunday dinners in the old neighborhood of the Marais (L'Herne 364).

Just as Desnos's private apartment became a public meeting place, so too did his work become increasingly public. With a half-hour talk entitled "Initiation au surréalisme," Desnos began his radio career (at the invitation of the radio pioneer Paul Deharme) at 7 P.M. on 14 June 1930, just two and half months after the publication of his "third" manifesto of surrealism had sealed his break with Breton and Bretonian surrealism. By 15 November 1932 he had begun working full-time for Deharme's *Information et publicité* radio service. "It took me thirty years to find a job that I love and I even get paid for it!" he was later to write in a letter (qtd. in Dumas 198). To Desanti he said: "I owe to Paul Deharme the recovery of myself, after the shipwreck of my friendships within the Bretonian group" (272).

In shifting "the transmitter from the psychotechnical device of his own body to the crowd," as Douglas Kahn describes the poet's move from private and poetic to public and radio automatism, Desnos changed the emphasis he gave to his surrealistic voice (26). And yet, even though radio does indeed reach "the crowd," it does so more often than not on an individual level, as former surrealist Philippe Soupault, who also worked on the radio in the 1930s, remarks: "Radio addresses men in isolation, men who are neither influenced nor encouraged nor limited by the reactions of the crowd or of their neighbors" (173). With his radio work Desnos sought to reach both the crowd and the individual. By 1938 he developed a dream interpretation program called "La Clef des songes," an interactive show that responded on the air to dream narratives sent in by individual listeners. At the same time, in *Radio Magazine* he expressed the desire to use the show as a way of accessing the collective unconscious, or, as he puts it, "a veritable collective dream" (qtd. in Alexandrian 279).

Broadcasting was indeed the ideal profession for Desnos, since, as Paddy Scannell points out, it is "part of the orderly, unremarkable ordinariness of everyday life," and yet nonetheless, in the early days especially, radio injected magic into everyday lives, as a British listener in the 1920s attested to in *Radio Times:* "It's a real magic carpet" (95, 90). This is because, Scannell argues, radio creates "new possibilities of being: of being in two places at once, or two times at once. This magic *shows* most clearly for us when we experience mediated occasions in the fullness of what they presence for us" (91). Radio allowed Desnos to work daily and literally at the marvelous in everyday life, in which he had always believed, with his voice, his body, as a medium with which to reach a mass audience. Before addressing the nature of Desnos's increasingly public everyday life in the 1930s, I would like to turn to the phenomenon of the auditory imagination, so poetically developed in Desnos, and the power of this imagination to affect others through the radio.

The Auditory Imagination, Part I: The Affective Power of the Voice

Automatic experience, particularly when practiced in a group environment, takes place simultaneously on a self-involved, narcissistic level and on an "other"-oriented, collective level. Psychic energy, released by the group, is funneled by each participant into his or her interiorized "listening" to the "voices" awakened by the self-induced trance within the unconscious. Desnos—the most gifted of all the surrealists in putting himself into a trance and then, while unconscious or semiconscious, communicating to those around him the words and images he "heard" from deep within himself—was indisputably the most in touch with what might be called the auditory imagination. Like the visual imagination, the auditory imagination generates fantasies, but, unlike its visual counterpart, it is stimulated by sound and expressed by voice.

In some ways the auditory imagination is more sensual and more corporeal than the visual imagination, more linked to the physicality of the body, to a corporeality that finds expression in the voice. For voice—which literally moves out of the body, propelled by breath coming from the lungs and formed by sounds as air passes up through the throat, over the tongue, and out into the world—carries an articulation of "body-ness." Sound technician Daniel Deshays insists that "sound remodels the body, it 'gets' us in the gut. To work with sound is to work with bodies. The body of sound as well as the body of the auditor. . . . It is in this space [of the body] that games with sound are inscribed" (222–23). This is what Roland Barthes calls "the *grain* of the voice," an "erotic mixture of timbre and language" in which the fleshiness and sensuality of the body are articulated: "its aim is not the clarity of messages, the theater of emotions; what it searches for (in a perspective of bliss) are the pulsional incidents, the language lined with flesh, a text where we can hear the

ROBERT DESNOS

grain of the throat, the patina of consonants, the voluptuousness of vowels, a whole carnal stereophony: the articulation of the body, of the tongue, not that of meaning, of language" (*Pleasure* 66–67). And this erotic carnality carried by the voice defeats the "tyranny of meaning" and logical clarity (*Responsibility* 273). The graininess of the voice substitutes pleasure for signification. In the materialist sounds of speech that come to him via the voice, Barthes hears "the breath, the gutturals, the fleshiness of the lips, a whole presence of the human muzzle," which project "the anonymous body of the actor [and the speaker] into my ear: it granulates, it crackles, it caresses, it grates, it cuts, it comes: that is bliss" (*Pleasure* 67).

Just as Desnos used his body as the primary medium with which to contact the voices within him, he used his speaking voice to project to others a vivid sense of his own presence. The voice is the strongest marker of a person's identity and, as such, is capable of tremendous affective power. After a time lapse of many years, one might be less likely to recognize an old friend face to face than to recognize his or her voice on the telephone—to hear the once familiar voice in isolation from the face as changed by time. Barthes's description of an individual's response to the voice focuses on its subjective affective power: "there is no human voice in the world that is not an object of desire— or of repulsion: there is no neutral voice. . . . Every relation to a voice is necessarily erotic [*amoureux*]" (*Responsibility* 280). Barthes identifies the voice, which is a sonorous incarnation of the body, as fundamentally erotic; listening inspires eros: "I am determined to listen to my relation to the body of someone who is singing or playing [and speaking] and . . . that relation is an erotic one" (276).

When Desnos went to work on the radio, he used his familiarity with his own "interior theater," to use Deharme's expression, to awaken the auditory imagination of others. This radio work was, in some ways, his most surrealistic work, and he was as fearless faced with the microphone as he had been confronting, and transmitting, his dreams under automatist conditions. For fearlessness was required in the days when all radio was live, as Soupault observes: "We are in the presence of an instrument that one cannot fool. It is faithful and that faithfulness is frightening. It attacks directly, without any intermediary, and it permits neither correction nor regret" (173). By voicing directly, "live" and every day, the emotions, colors, and moods of his own inner experience and by doing so through words, nuanced intonation, pauses, nonverbal exclamations, and sound effects, Desnos was recalling for his listeners the primal cries and sighs of their own remembered inner dramas. His voice doubled that inner voice, familiar to listeners from their own dreams and reveries and even from their experiences of reading in which the voice mutely "speaks" a text as the eyes follow the lines. Such auditory stimulation, when transmitted by a disembodied voice over the airwaves and heard by an audience of thousands but also by individuals (sitting each before his or her own radio), can succeed in arousing shared auditory hallucinations—"is it not the truth of the voice to be hallucinated?" Barthes asks (*Responsibility* 272)— such as those experienced by the small surrealist group sitting in Breton's apartment and taking its lead and inspiration from Desnos, during the period of hypnotic sleeps.

The full presence of the person speaking may be sensed, literally, by just hearing the specific timbre of his or her voice. Into that singular sensual experience of listening to a voice in isolation, other senses rush in to develop and embody what is initially being aurally expressed and evoked. Although one is only listening, one can also see, taste, smell, and certainly feel any number of sensations and emotions, set in motion and provoked by the auditory imagination. One sense, namely audition, in isolation from the others has the curious effect of enhancing sensual perception. The isolated sense is heightened by its primacy in the given moment, while the other senses are channeled into that heightened and expanded consciousness, producing a kind of magnification similar to a hallucination that gives the illusion of a totalizing experience. Vivid and emotional memories "of lost time" flooded Proust's mind in *A la recherche du temps perdu* (*Remembrance of Things Past*), when later in life he tasted the madeleine crumbled into linden tea that he had drunk as a child. Marcel, his autobiographical hero, closes his eyes and evokes in great detail his early years at Combray. Similarly, many years (and volumes) later, his tripping over an uneven paving stone in St. Mark's Church in Venice brings back more insights and remembrances, powerfully triggered by a memory stored in his body and resuscitated by an accidental movement of that body and its enhanced sense of touch. For the body contains memories that can be most effectively awakened without visual stimuli. A sound, a taste, a smell, a touch, can set off a chain of free associations leading back into the past, in an act of sensual recovery that, temporarily, gives one the illusion of reliving that past in the present.

The way that one sense experienced in isolation prompts a compensatory enhancement of the other senses has been described by film theorist Michel Chion as a hallucination of wholeness: "So in explicitly depriving us of one element, both radio and silent cinema cause us to dream of the harmony of the whole" (125). That "dream of the harmony of the whole" is conjured particularly well by the sense of hearing because it is the first sense to be fully developed in infancy. Indeed, insofar as it determines the formation of identity, listening even takes primacy over seeing, because it begins before birth with the fetus listening to the mother's voice inside the womb. A psychobiological study done in 1995 confirms that newborns respond most to their mother's voice, because they respond best "to the language that they heard in utero."[5] And Barthes associates voice with mother speech, with maternity, as well; it is "the materiality of the body speaking its mother tongue" (*Responsibility* 270).

Unconsciously, the act of listening is bound to the memory of the mother's voice through an act of remembering and a hallucination of recovery that constitute a primary and primal memory of sensual pleasure, what Barthes calls bliss, *jouissance,* and the "space of pleasure, of thrill" ("Grain" 183, 187).[6] For the maternal voice, according to psychoanalyst Guy Rosolato, is "the first model for auditory" pleasure (81). Reversing Rosolato's idea, one could claim that all subsequent auditory pleasure is an echo, in some fashion, of the "primordial listening" every human being experiences with his or her mother and in response to which identity is initially formed. Barthes would seem to concur: "The human voice is, as a matter of fact, the privileged, (eidetic) locus of difference" (*Responsibility* 279). Therefore, it supplies the vocal distinctiveness that identifies a person's individual, unique subjectivity as it stands out necessarily from that of all others. Structurally, the pleasure of listening in the present is always linked to a memory of the past, whether that memory is actual or lost, real or fantasized.[7]

In *The Acoustic Mirror* Kaja Silverman argues that fantasies associated with the voice may be linked to that first voice ever heard: the maternal voice.[8] In her analysis of "the maternal voice as a blanket of sound" in the cinema, Silverman shows that the voice, as Rosolato and Mary Ann Doane have discovered, "is a 'sonorous envelope' which 'surrounds, sustains, and cherishes the child' " (72). She makes a compelling argument for the maternal voice as "the original prototype for the disembodied voice-over in cinema." Accordingly, a case may be made for the maternal voice as the original prototype for the radio voice, which is even more powerful than the "disembodied voice-over in the cinema," since it works in isolation and is definitely not accompanied by an image. As Amy Smiley has argued with regard to Soupault's radio work, "the voice, which the radio disincarnates, could be considered as an incarnation" (107).

As an "incarnation," the radio voice projects its power. As the recalling of a preverbal state of subject formation, it is nearly primal, as Silverman observes: "Psychoanalysis tells us that the mother's voice is usually the first to be isolated by the infant from other noises, and that it is by imitating the sounds she makes that it produces its own initial articulations. Hers is the voice (at least within a traditional family scheme) that first charts space, delimits objects, explains and defines the external world. . . . Because her voice is identified by the child long before her body is, it remains unlocalized during a number of the most formative moments of subjectivity" (76). Silverman posits the notion that some of "the most formative moments of subjectivity" for each individual are linked to a powerful disembodied voice. This emphasis shifts the focus, which Jacques Lacan had given to the sense of sight in identity formation in "Le Stade du miroir" ("The Mirror Stage"), and recognizes the significance of the sense of hearing in the formation of subjectivity. Moreover, the research of Didier Anzieu has shown that the optically or visually determined theories of subjectivity proposed by Lacan's and D. W. Winnicott's work are incomplete because they fail to consider "the even more precocious existence of a sonorous mirror," which, as research indicates, shows that "the baby is linked to his/her parents by a truly audio-phonic system of communication" (162, 167). Silverman reiterates the point even more clearly: "Since the child's economy is organized around incorporation, and since what is incorporated is the auditory field articulated by the maternal voice, the child could be said to hear itself initially through that voice—to first 'recognize' itself in the vocal 'mirror' supplied by the mother" (80).

What the listener does when hearing a radio voice is to experience, subliminally, the hallucination of recovery of something precious and pleasurable that has been lost and that comes from a deep psychic past. A process is triggered by the senses that directs a listener's consciousness inward onto the interior stage of the imagination. This trajectory mimics the automatic practice by which one travels into the self in order to "recover" traces from the past, secrets from the present, and even anticipatory flashes of the future, which lie buried in the unconscious mind. Who better than Desnos would know the inner workings of such a surrealistic activity? And who better than Desnos could communicate through his own affectively powerful voice such a surrealistic process to a larger collective community, which, in the 1930s, extended to all radio listeners of France?

The Auditory Imagination, Part 2:
From Mental Telepathy to Wireless Telegraphy

Desnos was literally the most vocal surrealist, the one most identified with his voice, beginning with the period of hypnotic sleeps in the 1920s. Louis Aragon described the power of Desnos's voice during these early years of surrealism as so hypnotic it drowned out all other ambient sounds: "In a crowded, well-lit café, amid the noise of voices, Robert Desnos has only to close his eyes and he speaks; amidst the beer bottles, the saucers, the entire Ocean surges in, with its prophetic roar and its steamships decorated with long banners" (O 140).

When Desnos first recited his aphoristic "Rrose Sélavy" poems in the style of Marcel Duchamp, he claimed that Duchamp's voice spoke to him telepathically from the other side of the Atlantic, thus miming the technology of the radio, which, in 1922, was only just barely beginning in Paris (although it was more advanced in New York, where Duchamp was living). Desnos supposedly "heard" Duchamp's disembodied voice, according to Breton, only "if Duchamp is wide awake" (Breton, *oc* 1, 286; *ls* 102). He thus made of his own body a medium—a kind a microphone over which could be heard his own voice and that of Duchamp.[9]

Radio developed relatively slowly in France, compared with the United States. In 1922, when French stations first began broadcasting, there were already two hundred stations and over fifty thousand radios in the United States (Jeanneney 148). The first Paris radio broadcast in November 1921 was of Yvonne Brothier singing the "Marseillaise" (Sebbagh 30). Radio Tour Eiffel was one of the first stations to broadcast on a regular basis (Jeanneney 152–53). Owned initially by the army, its programs were limited to the weather, stock reports, and some "radio concerts." The government-run Radio PTT and the private station Radiola, which soon became Radio-Paris, also started in 1922. Radiola, where Desnos would work in the 1930s after it became Radio-Paris, went on the air for the first time at 8 P.M. on 6 November 1922 with the following statement: "*Bonsoir mesdames, bonsoir messieurs,* your Radiola speaker has the honor of announcing that you are about to hear the first Radiola concert" (Sebbagh 31). Desnos used this emblematic opening for the title of his film in 1943. Within five years Radiola/Radio-Paris had added sports reporting, and French radio listeners were able to follow the Tour de France, stage by stage and day by day (39).

Legislation passed in November 1923 encouraged the growth of more private stations, and thus Poste Parisien was created in 1924. By 1928 there were thirteen private and fourteen public stations, a situation that Jean-Noël Jeanneney in *Une Histoire des médias* calls "anarchic" because of numerous conflicts and a competitive struggle over acquiring radio frequencies. By the 1930s, when Radio-Paris was bought by the state, the distinction between private and public stations became clearer. Advertisements were transmitted only on the private stations, according to the principle, "private funds for private stations; public funds for public stations" (Jeanneney 154).[10] State-run radio, under Georges Mandel, the minister of the Postes, Télégraphes, Téléphones (PTT), underwent a process of systematic modernization and restructuring so that, by the year prior to the outbreak of war in 1939, Radio-Paris was the most powerful radio station in Europe (Eck, *Guerre* 17).

The ubiquity of news coverage, to which we are accustomed on the radio today, was completely foreign to France in the 1920s because of government censorship. Radiola, which had just been transformed into Radio-Paris, proposed a "Journal sans fil" on 26 October 1923, but it was censored at the last minute by Pierre Robert, the undersecretary of state at the PTT. Robert, Jeanneney explains, was "mistrustful faced with a novelty he was unsure of being able to master: it was better not to allow anything to be said!" (156). Maurice Privat of Radio Tour Eiffel got around such censorship in 1924 by delivering news without calling it "news," just as he surreptitiously disguised publicity as editorial material (Jeanneney 166). Even if, as Christian Brochand explains, "the creation of the spoken news was not yet a fact," Privat nevertheless introduced into his programs "news of the day which developed slowly" (26). Yet radio news in the 1920s was read by "speakers," not journalists; thus, even when news was eventually included in broadcasting, it had "the fixed format of official communiqués, of lectures, and only gave an attenuated echo of what was happening in the world" (Sebbagh 40).

Poetry and Politics in 1930s Paris: Desnos's Totem Bear

Starting in the 1930s, during the time when his radio career was in its early phases, Desnos connected his more personal intimate self with the outside world through various kinds of voicing. He attuned his ear, for example, to the rhythms of popular songs, which he wrote for the voices of such singers as Fréhel, Mireille, and Marianne Oswald. He also collaborated with singer-songwriters such as Charles Trenet. Like Trenet, who would later compose songs for François Truffaut's movies, Desnos wrote lyrics for soundtracks, including eight songs, set to music by Cliquet-Pleyel, for the film *Panurge* (1933), starring Danielle Darrieux, and a song for *Les Mutinés de l'Elseneur* (1935), set to music by Arthur Honegger. He thus satisfied his love of music by mediating it through the performances of others. For, even though he had "a very fine musical ear" and loved to sing, he could not sing on key (as he was well aware) (Carpentier, "La Havane" 44). In the afterword to *Etat de veille* from 1943, Desnos stated that he hoped that his poems would be set to music and played as popular songs, which they eventually were: by Juliette Greco and Yves Montand in the postwar period and in the 1980s and 1990s by such musicians and actors as Michel Arbatz, Francis Dudziak, Chantal Galiana, and Elisabeth Serman.

Desnos also gave voice to his political allegiances through songs. As a passionate antifascist, he joined the Common Front against Fascism, the group started in 1934 by Gaston Bergery, and wrote a rallying song called "Front Commun":

> To fight with our brothers,
> Today! Not tomorrow!
> Today!
> Against the exploiter, Common Front! (*Voix* 111)

Desnos's fervor against Francisco Franco's troops in the Spanish Civil War may be heard in this verse from "No Pasaran," set to music by Paul Arma:

Who drags chains?
Who sows hatred?
Fascism and all its bankers
They have gold, they have cannons
But we fight for the entire world
We will crush them
No! No pasaran! (*O* 825)

France had looked as if it were on the brink of civil war in 1934. Political groups on the Left and Right claimed different Parisian spaces: whereas the Right colonized the Rue de Rivoli, with its statue of Joan of Arc, the Left occupied the Place de la République, along with the Faubourg Saint-Antoine, from Nation to the Bastille (Borne and Dubief 125). Desnos's song reflects the rebellious sentiment felt by many strikers in the mid-1930s toward their bosses, who had come into a position of power during the Depression. Desnos's militant words against the "gold and steel barons" and his call for them to "bend" to the workers' needs reflect what the historians Dominique Borne and Henri Dubief call the sudden birth of a spirit of "trade-unionism on a massive scale" (150–54).

Desnos's allegiance switched in 1936 from the Common Front to the more powerful Popular Front.[11] He signed various documents protesting France's policy of "nonintervention" in the Civil War in Spain. He had been friends with Federico García Lorca and participated, together with Pablo Neruda, in an homage to Lorca after the Spanish poet's death (Dumas 249–50).[12] For the struggle of the Republicans in the Civil War Desnos wrote "Sangre y sombra" in addition to "No Pasaran" (*O* 825–26). By 1936 he had become an intellectual of the Left who, along with Aragon—the two former friends had worked out a rapprochement—believed that a pacifist stance could not prevail against the threat of fascism (Desanti 288). He kept a tract about the problem posed by Adolf Hitler in his papers, from June 1935, produced by the Vigilance Committee of Antifascist Intellectuals (DSN 887).

At this time Desnos became the literary director of the Foniric radio studios on the Rue Bayard, where Carpentier, called "Carp," was the artistic director (L'Herne 24; *O* 767). Like his apartment on Saturday nights, Desnos's office became a kind of crossroads. It was, as Théodore Fraenkel remembers, practically buzzing with activity, with secretaries all around and Desnos trying to answer at once the two telephones on his desk: "you could hear his resonant voice, nothing was ever done fast enough for him" (321). Desnos's approach to radio work was "hands on," to say the least. Samy Simon, with whom he worked closely, remembers seeing Desnos "emerge victorious from one of those fascinating struggles during which the poet in him was at war with a reputedly insoluble technical 'problem'" (O 788). And Guy Brun recalls that in the studio "no technical difficulty could stump him" (2). But Desnos invariably found time to have a drink with a friend and, late each night, to write a poem. Beginning in 1936, as he explains in the afterword to *Etat de veille*, "I forced myself to write a poem each evening, before falling asleep. With or without a subject, tired or not, I faithfully observed this discipline" (O 998; S 133). One of these poems, "Tale of a Bear," reveals much about Desnos's state of mind and his understanding of his own work during this time (O 984–85).

In his public life Desnos had transformed himself into a mediator—between friends, between acquaintances, in print journalism, on the radio. Underneath his public persona, however, Desnos still exhibited the same passionate romanticism that had inspired his love poems from the 1920s. These public and private selves are emblematized in "Tale of a Bear," in the form of the myth of the Great Bear, yet another mobile, changeable female figure, like Rrose Sélavy, and one that Desnos wore tattooed on his body. "Tale of a Bear" is the tale of a bear's walk through a Paris beset by massive street demonstrations. The story is inspired by the myth of the beautiful nymph Callisto, who attracted the attention of Zeus and bore him a son. Furious that Callisto had broken her vow of chastity, the goddess Artemis turned her into a bear. But when Callisto's grown son, Arcas, mistakenly hunts a bear, unaware that she is his mother, Zeus protects them both by transforming them into mother and son constellations: the Great Bear and Arcturus, the Guardian of the Bear (Stapleton 50). In Desnos's poem the private body of the nymph-Bear becomes universalized, available for everyone to see, the way Desnos's own private voice, as expressed during automatic experiments, became audible to everyone who owned a radio.

Callisto as the Great Bear has multiple identities; she is a vulnerable woman and a lover first hidden under the outer body of a bear and then transformed again into a celestial constellation. In Desnos's poem the story of the bear's walk through the busy city and her subsequent "aspiration" into the starry sky is linked by audition to the political aspirations of the crowds marching through Paris in response to the victory of the Popular Front during the spring of 1936.[13] Historically, the year 1936 was eventful. In January ministers of the Radical Socialist Party all resigned, forcing the head of government, Pierre Laval, out of office and into retirement, from which he would not emerge before France lost the "phony war" to Germany in the summer of 1940. In March Hitler's troops reentered the Rhineland in clear violation of the Versailles Treaty and the Locarno Pact of 1925. Although concerned, France did not react.[14] New elections brought the Popular Front into power, with Léon Blum at its head, in May. Blum revolutionized everyday life for workers in France with his new policies, including a forty-hour workweek, the right to belong to a union, and a fifteen-day paid vacation (Borne and Dubief 155–56).

The streets of Paris, which had been the setting for over one thousand parades and demonstrations since February 1934 and the political and financial scandal of the Stavisky affair, now in 1936 belonged to the Popular Front.[15] Actor Jean-Louis Barrault, with whom Desnos improvised poems to accompany Barrault's mimes in the streets, describes that spring as intoxicating: "We went to read poems in the factories" (79, 90). A new culture, as Borne and Dubief explain, was created in the street: "Photos of the period do justice to an atmosphere in which gestures from the past—from carnival or traditional charivari events where social roles are inverted—fuse with more modern gestures such as raised fists . . . which a new mass culture had invented" (153).

At the beginning of "Tale of a Bear" the bear moves invisibly within the crowd:

> A bear made her way into the city.
> She walked heavily
> And waterdrops shone in her fur
> Like diamonds
>
> She walked unrecognized
> Through the streets
> In her furry coat.
>
> The crowd went by.
> No one watched her
> She was even jostled. (*O* 984; *S* 136)

Once she leaves the streets and reappears in the sky bedecked with stars, as a ghost raised to a higher power and plane named "Great Bear," she sails through the universe, passing over meadows, forests, and cities, glimpsed only by a few astronomers and by prisoners through barred windows. She metamorphoses into a moving reference for navigators and fortune-tellers. In an echo of the swimmer from *Liberty or Love!*, she shifts into a hopeful symbol for a day in the imminent future when liberty and love will be reconciled: "But when day comes / Freedom and love will be born" (*la liberté et l'amour*).

The poem enacts the private and public aspects of Desnos's own poetic self in the 1930s. Like the bear, he felt at once "unrecognized" and anonymous among the street demonstrators, and, like the bear again, in her radiance as a constellation, he saw himself as the voice emitted along not waves of light but, rather, frequencies of radio. In his private life he sometimes felt anonymous as well, since he had to struggle with Youki's insistence on her right to free love— to take and discard other lovers as she pleased. (Desnos wrote her in 1933: "I would be so happy to have a Youki who felt free enough not to fear losing her freedom every time I kissed her" [DSN.C.477].) Nevertheless, in his public life his visibility and auditory fame were increasing.

Announced in the poem by the movement from visual to aural evocation and with the declaration that the Bear now has even more sparkle than the sound of a hammer hitting an anvil, the popular uprisings of the spring of 1936 echo throughout the conclusion to "Tale of a Bear":

> I hear heavy steps in the night
> I hear songs, I hear cries
> The shouts and songs of my friends.

Like remembered steps in a dream or the filtering into dream consciousness of voices in an outer room, these footsteps and euphoric cries and songs slip into the poem. They grow louder and louder, causing the poet to exclaim: "Throughout the world I sense the rising/Of the great invasion, the great tide." The Great Bear is glimpsed one last time in a visual and auditory crescendo joining the Bear to the uplifted voices in the final stanza:

> Great Bear you're shining
> In the night sky as I listen for
> The cries, for songs of my friends. (O 985; S 137)

Desnos may literally have gone out onto his balcony and admired the Great Bear in the sky while simultaneously hearing the sound of men and women marching through the streets of Paris. In "Tale of a Bear" the extraordinary is naturalized, and the connecting link between totemic legend and everyday crowds is forged with sounds. The Great Bear's footsteps, transformed into the crowd's steps, represent the hope for a dawn that will reconcile *la liberté et l'amour* and echo the beat of past revolutionary marches. These footsteps promise an even broader distribution of rights and freedoms to the people of France than those that had been gained by previous uprisings. The poem's emphasis on shouts, cries, and yells, its insistence on audible and vociferous insurrection, its blend of starlight and street sound, of the visual and the vocal, point to the growing importance of voice and of sound in Desnos's consciousness. Paradoxically, it was published only in April 1943, semiclandestinely, in *Etat de veille,* at a time when the popular uprisings of the mid-1930s had become memories emblematic of a freedom of expression no longer tolerated by the French state and in the same year that he completed his next poem about the Great Bear, "Calixto" (O 980).

Surrealist Voice and Technology

In "Mon tombeau," an early poem from "Prospectus," Desnos had already emphasized the experiential importance of listening. He anticipated the way that Breton would describe the automatic experience as an act of listening in

"The Mediums Enter": an act that allows the ear to be penetrated by the "murmur" of "our own unconscious" (*oc* 1, 275; *ls* 91). Listening—especially to the surrealist "voice" (Breton, *oc* 1, 329; *M* 27)—is generative of surrealist experience. "The words, the images are only so many springboards for the mind of the listener," Breton wrote (*oc* 1, 336; *M* 35).[16] Such listening is meant to be fundamentally receptive, for "we, who . . . in our works have made ourselves into simple receptacles of so many echoes, modest *recording instruments*" (*oc* 1, 330; *M* 2–28).[17]

The voice in "Mon tombeau," whether disembodied or from beyond the grave, issues strangely from a phonograph:

> My grave, my pretty grave,
> will be painted with enamels
> with boating tackle
> and a sailor's tattoos.
>
> On my grave a phonograph
> will sing night and day
> the sad song of the Kaffir warrior
> distressed by a licentious wink.
>
> On my grave a record-player
> will recite this epitaph
>
> LIBERTY EQUALITY FRATERNITY (*O* 20)

Desnos's love of music is evident. The "singing" phonograph—an anthropomorphic machine—"sings" a song belonging not to him but to an exotic stranger. It embodies the rhetorical principle of prosopopoeia in two ways—as the personification of an inanimate thing and also as a figure of speech in which an imaginary, absent, or deceased person is represented as speaking. For substituted for his own voice is the mediated voice of the Kaffir, a warrior from what is now northern Afghanistan, who represents Desnos's life-long fascination with adventurers, like Fantômas, and who may have been inspired by a comic book adventure story from Desnos's adolescence. Since the Kaffir's song is followed by France's revolutionary slogan *Liberté, Egalité, Fraternité*, presented as a vocalized epitaph, the warrior is a stand-in for the Revolutionary-era French citizens who longed for social change. The phonograph, which, on top of the poet's grave, sings a song belonging to someone else, emblematizes a double act of ventriloquism on the part of the poet. His own disembodied voice is mediated twice, once by the phonograph and once by the Kaffir warrior's song—and perhaps even a third time, insofar as the "song" is not necessarily original to the warrior but acts as a screen or an appropriated vehicle or mode of transmission for the warrior's distress. From beyond the grave, in other words, the poet hopes to be heard, thanks to technology (the phonograph) and also through the voices of others, no matter how distant and foreign they may be.

The interposition of a relatively new technological innovation—the phonograph—between the poet and his listener-reader and the emphasis on technologically mediated poetic language anticipate Breton's image of the "modest *recording instruments.*"[18] Desnos's phonograph, like Breton's *recording instruments,* speaks not only for him but also to him, in a voice from his unconscious auditory imagination that is utterly familiar and yet strange enough to "sound like" that of a shy foreign warrior. Again like Breton's instrument, Desnos's phonograph requires interpretation in a manner similar to that of the words and images springing unbidden from the surrealist's mind during the automatic process.

Desnos's image of the phonograph incorporates the surrealist preoccupation with machine aesthetics carried over from Dada. It represents a system of communication that functions in a way that symbolizes how automatic surrealist telepathy moves the desires of the buried self (in other words, the unconscious) through the barrier of the earth (the body) and into the visible, colorful grave (the poet's *tombeau*—referring to his physical grave and to the traditional form of posthumous poetic homage called *tombeaux,* for which Stéphane Mallarmé was well known) in order to find expression through the phonograph (the voice).

Like a radio voice, the voice in this poem is disembodied. Deharme explicitly describes the radio "speaker" as someone who must become "a sort of phonograph" (417). Moreover, the radio voice resembles Breton's idea of the surrealist voice, which emerges similarly from the unconscious without any connection to an exterior, visible body and haunts the listener, insofar as it calls to mind something or someone else. In "Mon tombeau" the voice is an enactment of fantasy, a mise-en-scène of roles by which the poet can play at being an exotic foreign sea adventurer in the form of a Kaffir warrior or a long-dead French republican citizen, evoked by the capitalized revolutionary slogan, which, because of its insistent, bold typography, suggests loudness. The poem implies that the poet's desire to slip into a series of disguises is powerful enough to extend beyond chronological time and even mortality, to articulate a spiritual and psychic enigma. Because the voice emanating from "*my* grave" seems to be the poet's own, despite the death to which the grave itself attests, the reader is left with the poet's fantasy that deep-seated (and disembodied) longings, desires, and wishes are immortal and will continue to haunt the earth, even after his mortal body has been put into its grave. A disembodied voice, like the disincarnated radio voice, writes Allen Weiss in

Phantasmic Radio, is evocative of "ubiquity, panopticism, omniscience," and causes "the radio work to return as hallucination and phantasm; it is thus not unusual to find the radio fantasized as receiving messages from the beyond. . . . [W]ith no visible body emitting the sound, and with no image whatsoever to anchor the sound, the radiophonic work leaves a sufficient space for fantasizing" (32).

The Interior Theater of the Mind

Desnos's radio career took off in November 1933, when he created a publicity campaign on Radio-Paris for a revival of the legendary pre–World War I superhero-thief Fantômas.[19] Desnos's poem "La Grande complainte de Fantômas" was the centerpiece of an important radio show—with original music by Kurt Weill, dramatic direction by Antonin Artaud, and music by Carpentier—produced at the Foniric Studios (*O* 739–57). Youki explains how Desnos mobilized such friends as Georges Gautré and Lise Deharme to help with the production by singing songs in the background in addition to "a real street singer" and "a baritone from the Opera" (241). Artaud himself read the role of Fantômas and was, as many testified, unforgettable. The poem was interspersed with dramatic sketches.[20] The show opened with an invitation to remember the year 1913–14 then moved into the clamor of voices in a busy bar, where the customers' orders were interrupted by the cries of newspaper boys calling out the headlines, including the repeated name of the notorious criminal, "FANTÔMAS." Desnos's poetic text then began by exhorting the listener to pay attention: "Listen. . . . Be quiet" (*Ecoutez . . . Faites silence*) (*O* 739–41). Playing on the emotions, it aimed to thrill its listeners with fear experienced as pleasure, since the show was scheduled for the peak time of 8:15 P.M., an hour when it would be heard by most auditors in the controlled and safe environment of a household.

In brief, the "Complainte" told the hair-raising story of a murderous master of disguise, whose ruses even tricked death. Arrested for murdering over one hundred people, Fantômas escaped the guillotine by sending another in his place. Arrested again for daring to attack the queen of Holland, "he nevertheless escaped / a just punishment." Arrested a third time by the English police, he escaped yet again. Fantômas impersonated the czar of Russia, hid a treasure in the entrails of a murdered Englishman, robbed a bank—"Do you remember that? . . . / He master-minded it"—and sank an ocean liner: "Who did that? Fantômas." Fantômas killed his mistress's husband and the mother of Fandor, his police-reporter pursuer: "he didn't have a heart / That vile evildoer." Finally, the steamship onto which the reporter Fandor and the Paris policeman Juve had followed Fantômas sank, but no one knew for certain if all three had died in the wreck—"No one found their bodies." Desnos's final lines were intended to send a shiver down the spines of his listeners (via Artaud's dramatic voice). With a reference to shadows lengthening over the world and over Paris, he concluded with this spooky question: "Fantômas, could it be you/Rising over the rooftops?"

On the day the "Complainte" was broadcast, the program's raison d'être was supported theoretically by Deharme in an article that emphasized the auditory power of radio drama: "In truth, it's less a question of compensating for the absence of sight and more a question of using that absence; the music and certain motifs nourish the imagination, and work even more effectively because we hear them with our eyes closed, so to speak" (qtd. in Dumas 201). Desnos had met Deharme through the latter's wife, Lise, with whom Breton had been very much in love before her marriage. Desnos describes him as a tall, handsome man with a clear gaze, "at once confidant and daring."[21] Desanti remembers that Desnos told her that he had met Lise when he and Breton were still friends because "Breton's friends would pay court to her, so as to please him" (interview, 3 Mar. 1999). Long after Breton had given up his pursuit of Lise, Desnos became friends with Deharme, and they remained close until the radio pioneer's premature death in 1934; Desnos even wrote some of his first children's verses for the Deharme children.[22]

Deharme believed that radio voices had the power to touch and spark the auditory imagination of listeners. "Words," he wrote, "are at the same time sonorous facts and symbols, therefore they are producers of images and of simultaneous sensations" (qtd. in Lescure 1703). Words that are heard are evocative in similar ways to words that are read, but, because of their voicing on the radio, they transmit other "sensations," such as the awareness of a breathing body whose mood may be palpably intuited from what Barthes would call the "graininess" of the voice. Voiced words become part of a broader vocabulary projected into the imagination of listeners and including such nonverbal "sonorous facts" as sighs, gasps, laughs, coughs, and silences. This sensual, nonvisual, fleshly "language," as we have seen, can create the illusion of recovering something that has been lost (most notably the "sonorous envelope" of the mother's voice heard by every infant in the womb) and can therefore rekindle a primal, deep-seated pleasure linked to identity formation. Deharme's goal in his radio theory and in his effort to harness Desnos's surrealist energy was to increase the auditory pleasure of listeners and to maximize the powerful effect of the new medium of the radio.

Desnos showed his creative mastery of radio's nonverbal language in a short presentation called "Essai d'anesthésie," created for his 1938–39 show "La Clef des songes" (The Key of Dreams).[23] These few minutes of Desnos's recorded voice (now in the archives of the Maison de la Radio) evoke an anesthetized state. He creates the effect of a ghostly echo chamber with his voice, his timing, and sound effects. There is one sentence—"You will not suffer," *Tu ne souffriras pas*—that is repeated four times, followed by the intermingled sounds of tolling bells and crickets. The first time, the sentence is so indistinct that it cannot be understood and sounds more like a nonverbal cry than like language. By the fourth time the sentence finally becomes clear, but the listener is left unsure, at the first hearing, whether this greater comprehensibility springs from greater clarity in the recording or from the stirring within the self of a more finely attuned aural acuity. The impact on the listener is eerie, like hearing a voice from another dimension, a voice "from the depths of a dream," as his friend Samy Simon notes.[24] Weiss comments that "there exists a point, unlocalizable and mysterious, where listener and radio are indistinguishable," which is exactly what Desnos accomplishes here (7). The echo chamber effect, combining Desnos's voice with silences, tolling bells, and crickets, causes one to doubt one's own hearing and prompts a straining to hear more, to compensate, with other imagined, remembered, or hallucinated senses. In an article written in defense of the artistic and technological creativity evident in radio publicity, Desnos himself described the echo chamber as "capable of giving to a phrase the amplitude of a call in a cathedral or a shout on a hike up in the mountains" (*O* 791).

Deharme's sympathies for surrealist goals were clear. In his 1928 article "Proposition d'un art radiophonique" he even sounds like a surrealist theorist. Listeners to the radio, he states, need to pay attention to their own individual *théâtre intérieur,* and his desire was to encourage this process (Deharme 414). He goes so far as to link his ideas explicitly to surrealism: "In effect, surrealism draws its source and life from the subconscious (as it is called today). And it is indeed in the subconscious that we hope, with radio, to arouse feelings, directly, without awakening the interference of consciousness" (415–16).

On a practical level Desnos worked with this idea of the interior theater in his plans for broadcasts. In notes made for a radio spot advertising Saint-Michel cigarettes, for example, Desnos proposed to recreate the noises and the atmosphere of a cabaret (where people, of course, smoke), and to include "cabaret" performances of "first-class stars" (he mentioned by name Marie Dubas, Damia, Mistinguett, Fernandel, Tino Rossi, and Maurice Chevalier), which would permit the "advertisement" to function as a kind of mini-concert. The scene was to be suggested by "the habitual sounds of a *cabaret*" in order to "create an atmosphere, an ambiance," so that listeners could close their eyes and pretend they were present, listening to "the most important part of the show . . . constituted by the singer and the songs he or she might sing" (DSN 415). He consciously set out to evoke the aural effect of "being in two places at once" for his listeners, of what Scannell considers the *magic* of radio (91).

"La Grande Complainte de Fantômas," mixing poetry and commerce, was a major success, ensuring Desnos's future on the radio. By 1934 he was working full-time for Deharme at Radio Paris. Together with Carpentier and Paul Clérouc, he had a regular show called "La Demi-Heure de la vie pratique," which was broadcast during the popular 7:30 to 8 P.M. time slot. Desnos contributed a section of the broadcast entitled "Ephémérides radiophoniques," which were short sketches based on the date. For example, for 2 January 1935 he invented a sketch situated on le Pont-des-Arts, the pedestrian bridge across the Seine not far from his apartment. It featured the embodied ghost of the Académie Française (a building not far from the Left Bank end of the bridge), who comically defended himself (itself) from the listeners' disbelief by exposing the academy's patriarchal prejudices: "If you do not wish to admit that I am the ghost of an institution, you might admit that I am the ghost of several women of great talent who could not join the Academy because of their sex. . . . Madame de Staël, George Sand, Marceline Desbordes-Valmore, la Comtesse de Noailles" (DSN 459).

For 25 August 1935 Desnos celebrated historic inventions that had had an influence on Parisian everyday life. On that day in 1837, for example, the railroad linking downtown Paris to the outlying town of St. Germain had been inaugurated. "Horses were indignant, furious, humiliated," commented Desnos. "Apparently they revolted against this new invention." After the railroad, what most "enchanted" Parisians on 25 August, according to Desnos, were the newly lit boulevards: "From the Church of the Madeleine to the Rue Montmartre, the two alleyways of candelabra from which pure white light flashed created a marvelous effect" (DSN 456). With this last bit of historical Parisian ephemera, Desnos was presenting to the interior theater of his listeners a vision that was positively surrealist. For a public grown accustomed to electric lights, the image of a grand path through Paris lit with flashing candelabra was, indeed, "marvelous" insofar as it introduced into the present a scene from the outmoded past, thus momentarily rendering the familiar strange.

By 1934 Desnos was selling publicity on a regular basis as well on the private radio station Poste Parisien, thanks to the help of an old friend, turned businessman, Armand Salacrou. As teenagers, Desnos and Salacrou had liked to play Dadaist pranks. At the end of the war, in late 1918, they would ring doorbells randomly in the Latin Quarter (safely across the Seine from where Desnos lived with his parents) and shout "DADA" (Salacrou 39). By the 1930s Salacrou had become a successful capitalist and gave Desnos full responsibility for advertising all of his pharmaceutical products. In addition, Desnos was able to persuade Salacrou to allow his brands of fortifying drinks (such as "Vin de Frileuse" and "Thé des Familles") to sponsor "concerts," featuring popular

French singers such as Damia, Tino Rossi, and Maurice Chevalier as well as American singers, jazz composers, and musicians such as Bessie Smith, Duke Ellington, Louis Armstrong, Sidney Bechet, and Benny Goodman.[25] Already his style of programming included the listeners, since in the shows he honored their musical requests and dramatized the letters and stories they sent in (Dumas, "Avant Propos" 9).

Desnos's love of jazz is particularly easy to understand, since it is a musical form that involves a kind of improvisational talent similar to his own gift for automatism. In jazz themes are transposed in ways that sound like, but are not, exact repetitions: such play with notes resembles the kinds of play with words at which Desnos excelled both in his early word game poems and in his 1930s advertising slogans. Just as jazz riffs involve key changes, Desnos was adept at changing registers with his voice and his facility with slang and different accents. With Carpentier again, Desnos produced several concerts organized around a theme. "Chansons de l'Empire française" was one; another was "Persil—Trois siècles de chansons" during which Desnos presented local songs from different towns and provinces in France. Another concert, "La Rue de Paris," was devoted to the popular songs of Parisian streets (Dumas 210–11).

In addition to his work writing advertising copy and organizing radio concerts, Desnos was responsible for two memorable nonmusical radio productions: the first reflected his politics, the second his popularization of surrealism. Symbolically, on 4 July 1936, his birthday, Desnos staged a radiophonic enactment of the American poet Walt Whitman's "Salut au monde." Carpentier hailed this memorable production as a "film without images" (L'Herne 333). Germaine Blondin gave it a rave review in Radio-Magazine, calling it "an admirable sonorous fresco" and crediting Desnos with a mastery of "radio art." With "professional intelligence" blended with poetic gifts, she wrote, "Robert Desnos has found sounds, songs, and music that appear to have sprouted from the same place in his brain as his verse" (qtd. in Dumas 215). For the success of this production Desnos was rewarded with a regular weekly show. Also entitled "Salut au monde" and broadcast from May through August 1937, this program was devoted to presenting the customs and habits of different cultures and countries.[26]

Six months after "Salut au monde" went off the air in August 1937, Desnos inaugurated what was his second and most memorable (and surrealist) radio program: "La Clef des songes." It ran from February 1938 through June 1939 and was devoted to the surrealistic activity of interpreting listeners' dreams. It was Desnos's most successful experiment with interactive radio, a notion to which he was completely committed.[27] Echoing Deharme's philosophy of radio production, Desnos claimed in a magazine article written to promote the show and to invite listeners to submit their dreams for dramatization and interpretation that he and his collaborators, Jérôme Arnaud and Colette Paule, wanted to create "a poetic drama in order to restore to the radio a domain [namely poetry] which fundamentally belongs to it" (*O* 846). In the interactive play of interpretations and reader's responses, Desnos encouraged the poetic possibilities arising from such verbal exchange. Desnos's article concludes with a teasing incitement to readers and listeners to respond to the show by giving free rein to their own auditory imaginations. For "an invented dream," he writes, "delivers the same secrets, carries the same portents, as an authentic one. Dream on then, Dear Readers" (848).[28]

Desnos wrote a song for the show, "La Clef des songes," which opens with an explicit invitation to Parisians from all walks of life to pay close attention to their dreams. The first verse, while summarizing his hope that his radio show will reach a broad enough audience to include cooks, businessmen, poets, and carpenters, also reveals how close Desnos had remained to his earliest surrealist belief that dreams are essential to life:

> Cook or poet
> Businessman or carpenter
> Everyone loves laziness
> Leisure, sleep, and dreams
> For dreams are spectacles
> A dream is a lucky ticket
> That the night gives as a gift to the dreamer
> Luck that is our due
> It's an everyday miracle
> A night without dreams
> > Without love
> > Is lost. (*O* 849)

Desnos may have broken with Breton, but clearly he never broke with the surrealist philosophy that dreams constitute a vital element in the existence of human consciousness. Furthermore, as surviving scripts for the show reveal, Desnos and his collaborators believed that, just as listeners' dreams could support the show, the radio, in turn, could generate their dreams.[29] An exchange between Paule and Arnaud clarifies the functioning of this interrelationship:

> C.P.—Well, in the mail we received this week, there were many
> dreams inspired by songs heard on the radio.
> J.P.—It's not surprising! It's completely natural that the radio,
> that voice which extends everywhere, would have an
> influence on dreams, since, in short, the radio *is* the home
> delivery of dreams. (DSN 448)

Each show began with the dramatization of a dream; the only extant recording lasts for about ten minutes.[30] This particular dream dramatization demonstrates how the disembodiment furnished by the radio offered Desnos a satisfying outlet for his fascination with disguises, allowing him, through the use of different voices, to don multiple aural "masks." Without the distraction of the face (even a masked face), the listener (as opposed to the spectator) must focus on a different kind of theatricality, one that is necessarily privileged by the medium of the radio, as Deharme claimed with his idea of the *théâtre intérieur*. Desnos, who from childhood had loved to assume different identities and who continued to explore multiple identities in his surrealist dramatizations of the self, was well prepared for the radio's theater of the imagination and for mediating his understanding of it to others.

This remaining recording begins with the sound of wind blowing. Then Desnos's lively and cheerful voice commences a narration in the first person and in the present tense: "I find myself suddenly in a strange country where the wind is blowing strongly." The sound of an approaching marching band with one man's voice singing in the lead is heard. Desnos continues: "We were in a group [*nous étions toute une bande*], walking along and singing." At this point the man from the marching band sings a refrain. He is joined by a crowd of people. Desnos goes on: "The others were walking very fast but I couldn't seem to keep up, despite all my efforts." Then a faint voice is heard in the background crying plaintively: "Wait! Wait for me" [*Attendez-moi, attendez-moi*].

The band plays on, and then Desnos's voice exclaims, "Suddenly . . . ," and a strange roar is heard in the background. It sounds like a noise made by a large animal, possibly an elephant. Then, just as suddenly, music from a jazz song overrides the animal's roar, followed again by Desnos's voice saying, "In front of us. . . ." But he is interrupted by the impatient voices of two men muttering to one another: "But what *is* this!" "It's a hippopotamus. They're all fat hippopotamuses." Then Desnos explains: "And they all began to run away." Desnos's voice continues: "But I could not move my legs. . . ." Then another strange cry erupts, a human cry of agony, which Desnos clarifies: "I was in the process of stepping on Max Rénier, who was lying on the ground! He was thirty meters long and covered with spots like a giraffe." Interrupted yet again, this time by cries that are not human, Desnos resumes the narrative: "The two hippopotamuses were headed straight for us and, at the very instant they were going to flatten us . . . ." More cries are heard, followed by Desnos's voice, apparently speaking from a place of safety: "I saw from behind a tree a surprising parade. All the wild animals in the world were in it, a real menagerie. At that moment a storm blew up. The wind, the rain, the storm, made the wild animals run away." Storm sounds take over, carried along by what seems to be a full orchestra musically imitating a storm. Desnos then elucidates the situation: "The storm had become a storm of music and the forest had been transformed into a bathroom. There was clapping and yet there was no one there." Orchestral music continues in the background, together with the sound of clapping. The clapping then morphs into gunshots, and other sound effects give the impression of a war.

"The clapping became deafening," Desnos continues. "It sounds like shooting." And, in fact, shooting is heard, over which, eventually, a woman is heard crying out, "Help! Help!" Faintly, behind her, a man's voice echoes hers. Then another woman's voice exclaims authoritatively: "Enter here, you'll be safe" [vous êtes à l'abri]. "Enter here. But why don't you come in?" "It was the female usher at the concert hall," explains Desnos, "who was pushing us into a padded room. The room was, in fact, a bomb shelter into which all the surprised spectators were tightly crowded [tassés comme des sardines]. Above our heads, the concert hall was collapsing, the shooting continued." Here the sound of a worried crowd and the report of shots anxiously underscore Desnos's voice. "In the shelter, everyone was complaining that they were going to suffocate." Two voices interrupt: a woman cries "Help!" and a man calls for "Air, air!" Bombs or explosions go off in the background. Continuing the narrative, Desnos concludes: "I myself was about to be smothered when I woke up breathless, my pillow over my head."

This dream narrative is fascinating for several reasons. First, Desnos's voice is remarkably vibrant; if he could have sung on key, he would have had a resonant singing voice. Second, the theatrical realization of the dream has the vocal pace and auditory excitement one might expect from a man whose great hope for the liberation of the unconscious lay in the power of the radio. It is remarkable how, with minimal sound effects and few extra actors, one narrative voice could create such a full, almost symphonic sound. In fact, it is the listener's mind that, through the auditory imagination, at once hallucinates and completes the scenario suggested by the sounds. Desnos gives the impression of a three-dimensional theater by contrasting voices and sounds in the foreground and background and with the addition of short asides by actors in secondary roles and sound effects evoking wind, marching, a band, an orchestra, crowds of people, and gunshots. He interrupts his own narrative in a realistic way, as though the action were happening simultaneously with the narration. He manipulates effectively that nonverbal sensual language suggested by Deharme with his use of pauses, breathlessness suggesting panic, and noises—from the animal roar in the beginning to the multiple voices of the frightened people crowded into the bomb shelter at the end. Finally, the dream shows the extent to which the political demonstrations of the 1930s had marked Parisians. As in "Tale of a Bear," the everyday sounds of marching feet seem to have pervasively infiltrated the collective unconscious of the city of Paris. These demonstrators certainly commanded Desnos's attention during these years, as his selection of the dream for dramatization indicates.

The few remaining scripts for the remainder of "La Clef des songes" shows suggest that Desnos's interpretations of dreams, "according to the Key of Dreams from Antiquity" (based on the work of Artimedorus of Ephesus), were almost uniformly upbeat. For example, a Mademoiselle Jeannette from Gap dreamed of a stream full of blood and of a young man who had committed suicide. Desnos cheerfully advises her that she "will see her secret desires come true, and furthermore she will learn of the marriage of a friend, but she must watch out for colds and the flu." A Madame A.B. from Marseille dreamed that she saw a chick come out of an egg and then a great quantity of little chicks walking calmly down the middle of a busy street. Desnos reassures her that it was an "excellent dream: a sign of birth, a sign of happiness, a sign of peace" (DSN 448.3). With a young woman who dreams she escapes the guillotine by entering a convent, however, Desnos is more cautious: "Mademoiselle G.D. must be depressed just now and seems to need more exercise in order to recover her sense of mental and physical equilibrium." Desnos also offered more general dream interpretations. For example, one week Colette Paule explained that some listeners had experienced "maritime dreams," concerning ocean liners, naval combat, shipwrecks, and so on. Desnos suggests an all-purpose interpretation: "In general, the sea signifies the wife or else people who, by their power and authority, have an influence over our destiny. Usually for a young man, a sea voyage dream is a sign of marriage. For a young woman, such a dream is a warning to beware of coquettish behavior" (448.9).

Desnos's exploitation of the "theater of the mind" in "La Clef des songes" constituted his most surrealist work in the 1930s because, on a mass level, he was able to ignite the senses and illuminate the inner landscape of millions of his listeners by guiding them to focus on their own capacity for dreaming. With his cheerful interpretation of his listeners' dreams he was able to encourage them to pursue their "dreams," that is to say their hopes. By emphasizing the creative potential of images produced by dreams, he encouraged listeners to understand the fundamental surrealist idea that human beings are dreamers as much as they are rational thinkers. With his radio show Desnos asked listeners to recast Descartes's classical explanation for man's humanism ("I think therefore I am"), which was founded on the primacy of thought, as "I dream, therefore I am," based on the primacy of dream, and to apply this surrealist formulation to their own everyday lives. This was his way of popularizing surrealism, once and for all. For who better than Desnos knew how vivid the inner theater could be? How strangely appropriate, then, that his attempts to compel listeners to focus on the theater of the mind should be lost to posterity, for, in those early days of radio, programs were mostly un-recorded, and scenarios, frequently improvised on the spot, as Simon and Jacques Prévert attest, turned out to be as fleeting as the visions Desnos himself had regularly witnessed within his own automatist inner theater.

Echoes of Rrose

Desnos's radio advertisements closely resemble his automatically inspired po-etic word games. Simon confirms that it was perhaps "with the advertising slogan that he best exercised his virtuosity as a word acrobat: his prodigious, scientific mastery of compression, of the well-placed word, allied to a true sense of popular poetry for which he was never at a loss." The voice of Rrose Sélavy, the poetic cross-dresser who, while in a hypnotic trance, invented such one-line poems as *Les Lois de nos désirs sont des dés sans loisir* (The laws of our desires are restless dice), was heard over ten years later in Desnos's advertising slogans. His old friend Salacrou described Desnos's slogans for his phar-maceutical company as "radiophonic poems" (*O* 788–89).

In a list of "signs of good fortune," for example, assembled by Desnos as part of an advertising campaign for the National Lottery, the poet suggests: "If your cat starts to purr for no reason, pet him. . . . It's a sign of good luck," *Si votre chat se met à ronronner sans raison, caressez-le. . . . C'est signe de chance* (DSN 383). Poetic assonances may be heard in the guttural r's repeated in *ronronner* and *raison* and in the soft *sh* sound of the purring *chat* who brings *chance* to its owner. The rhythmic similarity of the phrases *sans raison* and *signe de chance*, the repeated *s* sounds in *sans* and *signe*, the chiasmic structure of the word *sans* in relation to the voiced ending of the word *chance* (in which the nasal and the sibylline sounds are reversed), highlight how *chance* works without *reason*, just as the surrealists had always believed it did. In his poetic word games Desnos created poetry automatically. In his advertisements he was doing the same thing, except that he was explicitly marketing a product.

With the radio Desnos's voice-motivated virtuosity found its medium. He gave full rein to his playfulness, proposing, for example, in advertising copy for André Brun furs that to hang from the "shoulders of elegant women" was the "destiny of splendid foxes" (DSN 331). For Marie Rose flea powder he proposed for fleas "a perfumed death" (*la mort parfumée des poux*). He trans-formed stock sayings such as "tell me what you eat, and I'll tell you who you are" or "tell me whom you frequent, and I'll tell you who you are" into "tell me what brand of shoes you wear, and I'll tell you who you are" (347). Thus, listeners could hear in the advertisement an echo of the more familiar cli-ché phrase (and, as a result, remember the product).[31] For proverbs and set phrases "liberate language from the obligation of referencing, or, rather, liber-ate desire within language," Marie-Paule Berranger observes (105). Desnos's strategy of inventing phrases with double meanings goes back to Rrose Sélavy, whose name means "Eros is life," to Desnos's play on Marcel Duchamp's name, the *marchand de sel* (*Rrose Sélavy connaît bien le marchand de sel*), and even to Desnos's totem bear with her multiple identities, one hidden inside the other.

His subtle understanding of, and his facility in using, the musicality of language enabled Desnos to write slogans that could be sung, including this ad for the painkiller Finidol:

> Pains fly away
> when one takes Finidol
> pains are silly
> when one takes Finidol
> Finidol, monopoly of anti-pain.

> Les douleurs ça s'envole
> quand on prend Finidol
> les douleurs sont des folles
> quand on prend Finidol
> Finidol, monopole de l'anti-douleur.

In an article from 1939 Desnos credits Deharme with the idea of putting radio publicity slogans to music (*O* 790). Desnos's mastery of his own mellifluous voice may be heard again in the assonance of one of his commercial slogans for Parfum Sauzé: "Sauzé perfume/makes elegance easy," *un parfum Sauzé/ rend l'élégance aisée* (DSN 418). He uses rhyme and rhythm, moreover, in an advertisement for Lu brand "petit beurre" cookies in which he links freshness with good flavor:

> made with fresh butter
> with fresh milk
> Lu *petits beurres* are perfect.

> au beurre frais
> au lait frais
> les p'tits beurres Lu sont parfaits.

In still another example, the jingle for Pupier Chocolat, Desnos creates rhymes out of words with similar sounds:

> For children, it is without equal
> A true treat
> Pupier Chocolate . . . is available to everyone.

Pour les enfants, il est sans égal
Un vrai régal
Le Chocolat Pupier . . . à la portée de tous. (354)

What Desnos claims for Pupier Chocolate—namely, that it is "available to everyone"—expresses precisely what he is trying to do through his voice: to make poetry accessible to all owners of radios in France, who, by 1935, numbered almost two million and close to four million by 1937 (Jeanneney 155).

On the radio Desnos was finally fulfilling his dream of becoming a truly popular poet. He passionately wanted to create, as Youki explains in "Desnos, poète populaire," "songs that could be heard on the streets, sung by delivery boys, for example, or murmured by lovers into each other's ears" (*O* 792). In effect, his jingles were set to popular and familiar songs such as "Auprès de ma blonde," Charles Trenet's "Les Oiseaux de Paris," and the children's song "Cadet Roussel." In testimony to his being what he called "the most listened-to poet in Europe," he himself would offer the slogan he wrote for Salacrou's fortifying drink, Vin de Frileuse, which, played to the tune of "La Cucaracha," had the most air time of any of his advertisements (Desauti interview, 3 Mar. 1999):

To feel well
Drink *vin de Frileuse*
To feel well
It's the strongest fortifier.

Pour être bien portant
Buvez du vin de Frileuse
Pour être bien portant
C'est l'plus fort des fortifiants. (52)[32]

He believed that musical radio advertisements were inspired by popular culture but that they also contributed to it. He thought that these jingles helped bring French folklore, in the form of proverbs, songs, and music, back into circulation: "Radio advertisements will deserve a nod when the renaissance of French folklore is analyzed" (*O* 790).

Desnos's mobilization in the 1939 war against Germany brought his work on the radio to an end. When he returned to Paris in the late summer of 1940, after the phony war's armistice, the radio had become an organ of the Vichy state, and working in the service of state propaganda constituted too great a compromise for him. Radio-Paris became an essentially "German" medium after the June 1940 defeat (Eck, *Guerre* 13). Desnos did, however, continue to work on "La Clef des songes," but in print, in the women's magazine *Pour Elle*—under the comical pseudonym Hormidas Beloeil (DSN 449).

From Disembodiment to Headlessness: Celebrating Liberty

The only new volume of poetry Desnos published in the 1930s, *Les Sans cou* (The Neckless Ones), with illustrations by André Masson, reflected his fascination with the disembodied voice and with the phenomenon of disembodiment in general.[33] The title of this collection, *Les Sans cou*, referring both to those French citizens guillotined for their political beliefs during the Terror and, as a homonym, to the expression *les cent coups*—which can mean frantic behavior or even the sowing of wild oats—also describes headlessness. The impression given in these poems by Desnos's mythical headless men, who, like walking hallucinations of the "harmony of the whole," wander the streets and "haunt" Parisian bars, is of humankind rooted more in the body than in the mind.[34] When these headless men speak, their voices are disembodied, not unlike radio voices. Poetically, these poems confirm Desnos's mediumistic focus on the senses and anticipate his more political poetry of the Occupation.

Les Sans cou (later published in *Fortunes* in 1942) includes two poems with titles linked specifically to the title of the collection: "Les Quatre sans cou" (The Four Neckless Men) and "To the Headless." Ideologically, both these poems refer to the revolutionary periods of the eighteenth and nineteenth centuries, to past times that resonated with the upheavals taking place in France during the 1930s. They reflect the hope that the republican ideals of the past still haunt French citizens enough to result in a more egalitarian society.[35] Both poems feature headless protagonists.

The headless heroes in "Les Quatre sans cou" have names comically reminiscent of swashbucklers from nineteenth-century historical novels: "Anatole," "Croquignole," "Barbemolle," and "encore Anatole." "Les Quatre sans cou," in particular, uses repetition and anaphora to create a chantlike rhythm (*O* 923–25). Such a poem, describing the adventures of the four dashing headless men, could easily have been spoken by Desnos while marching the streets of Paris in the multiple street demonstrations occurring during these years:

> When they ran, it was like wind
> When they cried, it was alive
> When they slept, it was without regret. (924)

These characters, like legendary daredevils from the past, embody, first, the freedom to break social rules, as recalled by the pun of the title—*quatre cent coups* (four hundred blows) refers to getting into trouble, to wild, unruly behavior—and, second, the sensual intensity of an existence lived uniquely through a body separated from its head and therefore from reason.

The poem begins with an evocation of the revolutionary past:

> There were four of them who had no heads
> Four whose necks had been cut
> They were called the four headless men. (*O* 923)

These four men are heroes from the republican past who loved love ("But when they spoke, it was about love") and whom Desnos resurrects during the current struggle to establish democratic freedoms: "The four headless men are still alive, that's for sure" (924). Through them he creates a new myth, as Marie-Claire Dumas suggests, that of the proto-surrealist revolutionary "who denies hierarchy and authority in the name of a community founded on different ideals" ("Guillotine" 75).

In the second poem, "To the Headless," the headless men from the past live on in an imaginary bistro Aux sans Cou—enacting a play on the two uses of *aux* as "to" as in a tribute and as "at" as in the name of a restaurant or store (*O* 938–39; *S* 107–08). Using the first-person, Desnos personally salutes one of the bar's headless patrons, who is not a revolutionary hero but an ordinary outlaw, a common criminal, *de droit commun*: "You have the best wishes of Robert Desnos, Robert le Diable, Robert Macaire, Robert Houdini, Robert Robert and my uncle Robert" (*O* 939; *S* 108).[36] He identifies himself through the multiple disguises and names he had used to mask himself during his adolescence. And he does so here, in this poem, through voice: the salutation is in quotation marks, indicating that he is speaking to this man, who, when he replies, does so in a headless and thus disembodied fashion.

Through the medium of the *sans cou* from the past, ordinary men buried in "a common grave" who congregate in his imaginary neighborhood bar, the poet gives voice to the aspirations of the anonymous Parisians of the 1930s whose bodies thronged the streets. The poem implicitly expresses the hope that these lost men will live on "in tomorrow's revolutions," that the current street "revolutions" will live up to the legacy of bravery inherited from these men of the past, and that the poet's lament that these earlier heroes were "born too soon, forever too soon" will be belied because it will turn out that they have now been reborn in the idealists of Desnos's own generation, true successors to their republican forebears.

A further example of Desnos's commitment to human liberty and dignity may be found in the lyrics he wrote for the cantata composed by Darius Milhaud for the opening, on 11 October 1937, of the Musée de l'Homme, the new ethnographic museum where Desnos's friends Leiris and Rivière were working. In 1937 Leiris was busy developing, with Bataille and Roger Caillois, the Collège de Sociologie, a group that would dedicate itself to studying and applying to contemporary prewar France the lessons learned from sociological and ethnographic studies of so-called primitive societies by such venerable French scholars as Emile Durkheim and Marcel Mauss. According to Georges-Henri Rivière, Desnos was himself involved in the work of the museum:

> It was Professor Paul Rivet who had founded the Museum, by combining the Chair of Anthropology from the Natural History Museum and the Trocadero Ethnographic Museum, in 1928. It was at that time that he asked me to work with him. The Museum was to be inaugurated in 1937, in the euphoric time of the Popular Front, of which Paul Rivet was also a founder.
>
> I was friends with Darius Milhaud, Michel Leiris, Robert Desnos. I had hired Desnos at the Musée de l'Homme, where he worked on scientific research files and helped with our move. I remember he was there the day when, together with Leiris, we broke a host of horrible mannequins. (Qtd. in Darle 46)

The "Cantate pour l'inauguration du Musée de l'Homme" expresses some of Desnos's most heartfelt sentiments about humanity. Against a small chorus of four voices and six instruments (including a saxophone), a speaking voice narrates the poem, which traces the development of mankind from disparate, mute, isolated, and inarticulate beings to creative, productive members of a social entity. The first performance was played by the Radio-Lille Orchestra, and the speaker was Madeleine Milhaud, wife of the composer (Darle 45). Against a historical moment of upheaval Desnos invokes a hopeful future:

> In the morning light
> At the source of life
> Where destiny quenches its thirst
> Old horses from the prairies,
> We will run to the edges of the rivers
> To wash away our nightmares
> Here is the new day
> And its treasures of chance.

The cantata closes with a call to others:

> Come quickly comrades
> Life is no longer uncertain
> Let us all sing, comrades!
> Come to the great harvests
> The earth finally submits
> The seasons to our comrades. (O 808)

The old love-scarred horse from "Sirène-Anémone" reappears here, the "wild horse escaped from the Gauchos" who showed the mares on the prairie "his flank burnt by the branding iron" and the stigmata of former loves (574). The horse is reconfigured in this poem both poetically (in the plural), as "old horses from the prairies," and politically, as a hopeful emblem for a renewed society. Desnos, the morose poet from the 1920s who flirted with death now turns toward life, even in the face of fascism's real danger, and does so with greater optimism than ever before. In a flyer for the play *Numance de Cervantès,* which his friend Barrault directed, partly in response to the Spanish Civil War, which Desnos helped to finance with an advance on his own salary and which was produced in the spring of 1937 with scenery and costumes by Masson—he again voices this life-affirming optimism: "I believe in the persistence of the spirit, of liberty as a given" (Barrault 95; *O* 844).

The Act of Remembering a Lost Voice

Of Desnos's voice only about twenty minutes remain, because radio broadcasts were not routinely recorded until after World War II. Those minutes have a haunting sound, emanating from the voice—the disembodied presence—of someone who died tragically over fifty years ago. When the newspaper *L'Etoile* announced a radio prize in Desnos's honor in November 1945, only months after his death at the Terezin concentration camp in Czechoslovakia, Guy Brun, who had worked with him *devant le micro,* "in front of the microphone," wrote that "radio leaves no trace. Once finished, the show vanishes, pushed into oblivion by the following show. The prize founded by *L'Etoile* will be the last homage rendered to Robert Desnos, to him whose radio work is gone forever, and who was able to write between the spaces of words as lightly as a fragile bird" (2). What does it mean, then, to think about Desnos's past voice in the present, especially for us today who did not know him? Such retrospective imagining constitutes an act of memory for which radio may serve as a metaphor. For, no matter how vivid an actual memory may be, it is necessarily already in the past.[37] To remember a voice on the radio is to remember a sound, which is the transmission of a momentary human presence—a bodily pleasure—by means of the movement of breath and sound lasting but an instant, in a present quickly lost and therefore irrecoverable.

To remember the quality of Desnos's voice, even for those who have never actually heard it, accords well with the very nature of surrealist perception. Like a dream in which time escapes its chronological boundaries, a speaking voice, with all its nuances and pauses, is as volatile and as free-form as an automatic poem, particularly a spoken automatic poem. The radio, as Jean Lescure wrote in the 1950s, offers no chance of a second reading: "It has to marry movement with emotion. In this sense, it is, in effect, a spectacle" (1703).

In a memorial article on Desnos in *Les Lettres Françaises*, Eluard writes that "of all the poets I have known . . . Desnos was the most spontaneous, the most free, always inspired, and capable of speaking the way few poets know how to write. He was the most generous of men."[38] Prévert, with whom Desnos worked on a radio drama, "Histoire de baleines" (Story of the Whales), confirms the power of Desnos's improvisational talents in a poem dedicated to him twenty years after his death, a poem written specifically for radio broadcast:

> And I'm talking to you as I did years ago
> on the Rue Saint-Merri, at the bar of a bistro
> or at the terrace of Cyrano
> a Cyrano of Montparnasse and not by Edmond Rostand
> just the way we did on the radio for Deharme
> when we experimented with improvised advertisements
> every week, two idiots talking about whales.
> Was it a project for a soap brand,
> an umbrella or a corset?
> Do I know?
> We created instantaneous foolishness
> the absurd wasn't even in style yet
> it hadn't been cataloged,
> we laughed, we laughed
> and now you are dead. (466–67)

The memory of Desnos's voice is evocative precisely because of the corporeal trace it leaves behind; it reminds the listener of the body attached to it. There is no language without body, argues Barthes (*Grain* 5). And Desnos, the surrealist poet most identified with voice, is suitably remembered for the uniqueness of his voice. Remembering him on the radio is to remember him at his most surrealist, since it is to remember him according to his own principles, those that define Desnosian surrealism, whose fundamental tenet was that surrealism is a reality that has become part of the "public domain," as stated in his "third" manifesto and echoed in his jingle for Pupier Chocolate: "one reality, complete, open" and "available to everyone," like the voice itself (*O* 487; DSN 354).

4

Paris Watchman

1943: A man, looking perpetually tired, with a short brush haircut, horn-rimmed glasses, and a herringbone tweed overcoat, shoulders his way to the back of a crowded café, where he manages to find two seats before going to the counter to order drinks for himself and his companion. Waiting in the back of the café, which he has not entered in some time, absorbing the familiar smells and sounds, sits Dr. Michel Fraenkel, the younger brother of Desnos's friend Théodore. He hopes that his yellow star fails to draw attention to the fact that, according to the laws of Vichy France, he has trespassed into a space forbidden to Jews. He wonders as well if anyone knows that the man ordering their drinks is at once Robert Desnos, "Pierre Andier," and "Lucien Gallois," pseudonyms for the author of militant, provocative, and clandestine poems, published at considerable risk.

"It is not poetry that has to be free, it is the poet"

On 10 May 1940 Hitler's army invaded Holland and Belgium, crossing the natural northern borders of the Somme River and, eventually, the Ardennes Forest into France, in what became known as the "lightning war" (*la guerre éclair*) or the blitzkrieg. Within a month the French army, together with the British and Belgian forces, were backed against the English Channel at Dunkirk and forced to surrender. The French capitulated, and by 14 June the German army was in Paris. For the French army, led by the victorious military heroes of World War I, was well prepared to refight the war of 1914–18 but unprepared for battle with Hitler's well-equipped troops, tanks, and bombers.[1] More significant than France's equipment, which was adequate, according to Henry Rousso in *Les Années noires*, was its lack of mental preparation: France refused to play the role of aggressor (26). Within a month ninety-two thousand French soldiers were dead (21). Between 15 May and 20 June six million French fled their homes and took to the roads with as many of their belongings as they could carry. "To some extent, the exodus stemmed from deep ancestral terrors," remarks historian Jean-Pierre Azéma (38–39). Children were put on trains headed toward the south; some took months to find their families.

On 16 May Paul Reynaud, the head of state, recalled the eighty-four-year-old World War I war hero Philippe Pétain from his post as French ambassador to Spain and asked for his help. The government left Paris for Bordeaux on 10 June. Reynaud stepped down on 17 June and was replaced by Pétain, who, the same day, called for a cease-fire. Pétain established his cabinet and immediately requested from Germany the necessary conditions for an armistice. The next day, 18 June, Charles de Gaulle broadcast a "Call for Resistance" from London, a now-famous radio transmission that was heard by few at the time. Pétain signed the armistice with Germany on 22 June and wrote that, in his view, it was "the necessary condition of the perpetuity of Eternal France" (qtd. in Peschanski, *Vichy* 19). One of the stipulations of the armistice was the division of the country into Occupied and non-Occupied zones. Paris, although no longer the center of government, was nonetheless at the heart of Occupied France.

Public opinion began to turn against the Vichy régime as early as 1941, yet Pétain himself remained admired and incontestably in power until the end of the war in May 1945, as the arrest of Desnos for Resistance work in February 1944 attests.[2] A note in the diary of Desnos's friend Jean Galtier-Boissière describes the chilling circumstances of everyday life in Paris in early 1944: "Roundups in the big cafés and at the entrance to cinemas. Immediate deportation" (172). The French responded the most strongly to the extensive roundups of Jews in the summer of 1942, according to Pierre Laborie, for in their wake came the organization of "chains of silent solidarity and complicity in a profoundly shaken population" (238).

Before his arrest by the Gestapo on 22 February 1944, Desnos completed for publication a series of twenty-five classically inspired poems under the title *Contrée*.[3] He was already writing these poems in 1942, at a time when he was increasingly interested in another language of fixed forms, the language of mathematics, as he explained in his "Author's Note" to *Fortunes:* "I would like to take up again the study of mathematics and physics" (he did take private math lessons in the 1940s) (*O* 976). From the liberty and constraint practiced by Desnos in his "Rrose Sélavy" poems to the opposition between liberty or constraint evoked by Desnos in *Liberty or Love!* Desnos in the 1940s moved more fully toward a reconciliation of the two, to poetic liberty within constraint, to freedom in formality.

Desnos wrote a letter to Paul Eluard in October 1942 about his attraction to the precision of the sonnet form, using a mathematical image: "I dream of poems that could be no other than what they are. Which no one could imagine following a different course. With a force as implacable as the resolution of an equation" (*O* 1156). He was talking about poems that were like his "Rrose Sélavy" equation poems from 1923 in the sense that they were poems in which two readings, two meanings, could be neatly folded into one multivalent structure. In the afterword to *Etat de veille*, published semilegally in 1943 and including everyday poems from 1936 to 1942—written on a daily basis with a "quasi mathematical" discipline—Desnos declared: "it is not poetry that has to be free, it is the poet" (*O* 998; *S* 134).[4] His final poem from this collection, "Tomorrow," is a fixed-form poem from 1942 that insists optimistically on maintaining a persistent "hope" in a dawning "tomorrow" that "will prove that at last we are living in the present" (*O* 996; *S* 144).

For Desnos, within an inevitable, destined format, within the discipline of a fixed-form poem, every liberty of the imagination was possible. One form could yield a variety of interpretations—literal, fanciful, aural, visual, legally sanctioned, and clandestine. He had not come that far from the declaration of the *prière d'insérer* for *Corps et biens*, which had also included fixed-form verses: "Every liberty!" (*Toutes licences!*). The poetic liberties taken by a poet whose own liberty was compromised equal the most moving verses written by the younger poet in complete freedom, during the Paris jazz age of the 1920s.

Against the Grain of Pétain's France

Given the circumstances under which the poems of *Contrée* were written, their every aspect may be considered in a symbolic light. A close reading of *Contrée* reveals the voice of the Resistant poet thinly veiled beneath rhetoric that resembles, but not quite, the polemical imagery of Marshal Philippe Pétain's Vichy state. Even the title may be read as an adjectival variation on the past participle of the verb *contrer*, "to situate oneself against," as Marie-Claire Dumas has remarked (*O* 1156). In effect, Desnos's *contrée* was very much against the grain of the patriotic homeland envisioned by Pétain.

Contrée was published "semilegally" three months after Desnos's arrest by a man only in his twenties, Robert J. Godet. Godet's books were "legal" in the sense that they were sold in bookstores. On the other hand, the print runs were small enough, roughly two hundred copies, and the imprint, "For My Friends," *Pour mes amis*, intimate enough, for the books to escape the notice of the censors who monitored the lists known as the "listes Otto" (after Otto Abetz, the former German ambassador to Paris), which inventoried any books expressing anti-German sentiments.[5] It was Godet's second book of Desnos poems. In April 1943 he had already published *Etat de veille*, which included "Tale of a Bear."

As of 1 July 1940, only a week after the armistice of the *drôle de guerre*, the "phony war," between France and Germany, a rule was established stipulating that all publishers had to submit copies of every book to be published to the Press Office of the German Military Authorities and receive authorization (Loiseaux 71). Any book expressing anti-German sentiment was outlawed and its author in danger of arrest. The Nazi Propaganda-Stafel censored books in France through the control of paper as well. From 1941 to 1944 publishers were allowed 28,000 tons of paper for 112 million volumes, as against 152 million volumes published in France in 1938 alone (Peschanski, "Politique," 69). Godet used the widespread paper shortages to his advantage, printing just enough copies to drop off at those bookstores in Paris willing to risk selling books of questionable content but not enough to attract too much attention. His wife, Babette, also knew Desnos because of her job as a typist at *Aujourd'hui*. In an interview with me, she explained how Godet published five books under the imprint *Pour mes amis* (which made the books seem "private"), "without authorization, with paper unearthed heaven knows where, and printed by printers who took serious risks" (interview, 17 Nov. 1999).[6]

In *Contrée*, published with an etching by Picasso, there is one poem for every hour of the day, in addition to a final poem entitled "Epitaph." In a more symbolic fashion than his daily "everyday" poems from the 1930s, with poems referring to moments of the day such as "Le Réveil" and "La Sieste"—waking and siesta—these twenty-four poems express the everyday experience of the French during the Occupation in often necessarily oblique terms.[7] One of them, "The Voice," evokes a national voice that seems to address most specifically the "shaken" population to which Laborie refers in his evaluation of the shift in public opinion that took place in the summer of 1942—a population in need of reassurance of the existence of a shared "solidarity and complicity" (238). Desnos's "voice" here comes from the past and resonates through the sequential seasons of the *contrée* into the present, with a message of hope and faith in an imminent liberation:

> A voice, a voice from so far away
> It no longer makes the ears tingle.
> A voice like a muffled drum
> Still reaches us clearly.
>
> Though it seems to come from the grave
> It speaks only of summer and spring.
> It floods the body with joy.
> It lights the lips with a smile.

I listen. It is simply a human voice
Which passes over the noise of life and its battles
The crash of thunder and the murmur of gossip.

And you? Don't you hear it?
It says "the pain will soon be over"
It says "The happy season is near."

Don't you hear it? (*O* 1171; *V* 80)

The voice here is not the voice of the poet known for his voice in person and on the radio but that of France itself. The distance traveled by the voice is one of time transmuted into space. France is humanized by the fact that her voice beats, the way a heart does, like a "muffled" drum. The rhythm must be muffled because, within the perspective of the poem, France is alive only clandestinely. The "clear" sound of the voice and of its heartbeat rhythm, which, like a drumbeat, is capable of stirring the hearts of those willing to tune into its message, is available only to those who choose to listen. A choice must be made to hear a drumbeat different from the one that predominated in France at the time: the sound of Pétain's National Revolution and of his voice on the radio, which preached a future in which France would be subsumed into the "new order" of a greater Europe controlled by Adolf Hitler's Germany.

Doubling this mythological voice, of course, were other, human radio voices coming from England, calling to the French to resist Pétain's policy of collaboration with the Nazi régime, beginning with Charles de Gaulle's call for resistance on 18 June 1940, four days after the entry of the victorious German army into Paris and the day after Pétain formed his cabinet and requested an armistice from Hitler.[8] These real voices of resistance were at war with grandfatherly Pétain's voice on the radio throughout the Occupation enjoining the French to "remain confident in Eternal France."[9] The voice of France in Desnos's poem is similarly eternal but with a chronological memory of the times it has moved through in order to reach the ears of those discouraged citizens under the Vichy régime in the present: across "the noise of life and its battles / The crash of thunder and the murmur of gossip." This Desnosian voice of France takes into account the natural landscape as well as the dramatic and ordinary quotidian experiences of the French people.

Finally, with its active act of questioning a plural *vous,* twice—"And you, don't you hear it? . . . Don't you hear it?"—the poem encourages the sense that there are people waiting and listening for the voice. It suggests to the individual reader that he or she is not alone in reading this poem. By hinting that those who long for change are numerous, the poem functions as a call to arms and may be understood to be asking the reader to listen even more attentively, to be prepared to take an active part in bringing "the pain" to an end and hastening the approach of the "happy season."

As part of his effort to displace Paris as the locus of power and culture not only toward the spa town of Vichy, where the wartime government presided, but in a general move toward decentralization, Marshal Pétain encouraged a "return to the land" policy, calculated in part on the assumption that agricultural workers, unlike the urban working class, were inherently more conservative and easier to manipulate (Loiseaux 358). Urban society was understood to favor "individualism, disorder, licence of all kinds, divorce, and social contestation" (Faure 120). It was the Parisian working class, after all, that had supported the Popular Front, a disruptive régime in the eyes of those on the Right of the political spectrum. Pétain was supported by a class of people who were nostalgic for rural France and for local ecclesiastical power (Sapiro 83). The land, for the Vichy régime, "was also the earth of the homeland, of a hurt and defeated country in need of refreshing itself in its past" (Gervereau 121). This was the sense of the last part of the Pétain's Vichy slogan: "Work, Family, Homeland" (*Travail, Famille, Patrie*), which replaced the Republican slogan of the Third Republic, "Liberty, Equality, Fraternity" (see fig. 11).

Under Pétain liberty, equality, and fraternity became outmoded concepts replaced with the moralizing, hierarchical values of work, family, and the notion of a mythical homeland led by the patriarchal Marshal. For, even if the government became increasingly unpopular between 1940 and 1945, Pétain managed to retain an aura of authority that commanded loyalty. Jean-Marie Flonneau affirms that "a fundamental, heart-felt loyalty to the Marshal [*un maréchalisme de base et de sentiment*] persisted up until the very end" (520). The farmer and the artisan became the idealized archetypes of the "new society" envisioned by Pétain with his national revolution, an ideological move that, according to Christian Faure, found favor with French farmers who were resistant to an increasingly mechanized and industrialized society: "Mythical symbol of a 'natural' order of men, the land [under the Vichy régime] came to represent a world closed to difference of any kind. The idea of rooting oneself in the land, in a particular region, or in the nation was associated with the exaltation of the concept of a [French] 'race of farmers' whose virtues were inherited from the past" (118).

Desnos would have seen this nostalgic evocation of France as an idealized, conservative "homeland" all around him in Paris in the 1940s. He would have had another perspective on it as well, through his friendship with Georges-Henri Rivière, who, because he was second in command at the National Museum of Popular Arts and Traditions, kept his job. Paul Rivet, under whom

Fig. 1. Robert Desnos in 1908. (Courtesy of the
Association les Amis de Robert Desnos)

Fig. 2. Eugène Atget, *Un Coin des Halles Rue Pierre Lescot,* 1911. (BHVP/Leyris.)

Fig. 3. Eugène Atget, *Rue Saint-Bon*, 1904. (BHVP/Leyris.)

Fig. 4. Man Ray. *Séance de rêve éveillé* (1924). "Waking Dream." *Seated:* Simone Breton. *Around her, from left to right:* Max Morise, Roger Vitrac, Jacques-André Boiffard, André Breton, Paul Eluard, Pierre Naville, Giorgio de Chirico, Philippe Soupault, Jacques Baron, and Robert Desnos. © Man Ray Trust / Artists Rights Society (ARS), New York / ADAGP, Paris / Telimage, 2002.

Fig. 5. Robert Desnos's automatic drawings for "Le Génie sans miroir."
(Courtesy of the Association les Amis de Robert Desnos.)

Fig. 6. Desnos's mermaid, from the former collection of Anatole Jakovsky.
(Courtesy of the Collection of the Association
La Sirène–76116 Blainville-Crevon, France.)

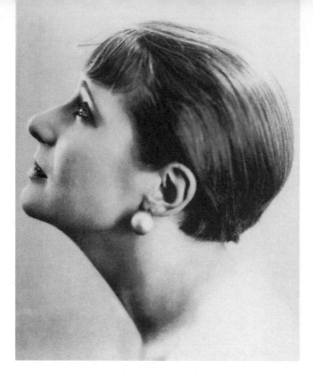

Fig. 7. Yvonne Georges. (Courtesy of the Association les Amis de Robert Desnos.)

Fig. 8. Youki Desnos.
(Courtesy of the Association les Amis de Robert Desnos.)

Fig. 9. Claude Cahun. *Portrait of Robert Desnos*, 1930. (Courtesy of the Collection of Zabriskie Gallery.)

Fig. 10. Desnos apartment at number 19, Rue Mazarine. (Photo Alain Brieux.)

Fig. 11. Trio of Vichy propaganda posters by Bernard Villemot (1941) used in 1943 for a "train of propaganda." © 2002 Artists Rights Society (ARS), New York/ADAGP, Paris. (Courtesy of the Collection of the Musée d'Histoire Contemporaine-BDIC/Archipel.)

"LA TERRE, ELLE, NE MENT PAS"

Je hais les mensonges qui vous ont fait tant de mal. La Terre, elle, ne ment pas. Elle demeure votre recours... Aux heures les plus sombres, c'est le regard possible et décidé du PAYSAN FRANÇAIS qui a soutenu ma confiance... La TERRE DE FRANCE n'est pas moins riche de promesses que de gloire. Il arrive qu'un paysan de chez nous voit aux champs dévasté par la grêle. Il ne désespère pas de la moisson prochaine. Il avance avec le même foi le même sillon pour le grain futur. Croirait-on que les Français refusent à la France l'amour et la foi qu'ils accordent à la plus petite parcelle de leur champ ? UNE FRANCE NOUVELLE JE VOUS LE JURE, NAITRA DE VOTRE FERVEUR ! (Paroles du Maréchal - 1940)

IMAGERIE DU MARÉCHAL - Imprint : LIMOGES 1941

Fig. 12. *La Terre ne ment pas* (The Earth Does Not Lie). Anonymous. From *Imageries du maréchal*, Limoges, 1941. (Rights reserved; collection of the Musée d'Histoire Contemporaine–BDIC/Archipel.)

Fig. 13. Youki and Desnos on vacation in 1936.
(Courtesy of the Association les Amis de Robert Desnos.)

Fig. 14. Desnos and one of his cats in Paris in 1943.
(Courtesy of the Association les Amis de Robert Desnos.)

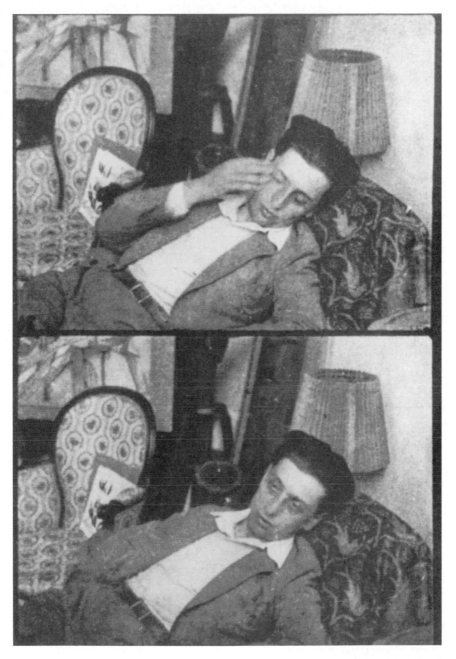

Fig. 15. Man Ray. Photographs of Desnos waking up during the "period of sleeps," published in *Nadja*, by André Breton (1928). © 2002 Man Ray Trust/Artists Rights Society (ARS), New York/ADAGP, Paris. (Courtesy of Mark Austin-Washburn.)

Fig. 16. Desnos in 1943 in Paris.
(Courtesy of the Association les Amis de Robert Desnos.)

Fig. 17. Photograph of newly freed prisoners at Terezin in May 1945. Desnos
is thought to be in the *center*, leaning on the shoulder of the man in the black
coat. (Courtesy of the Association les Amis de Robert Desnos.)

Rivière had worked at the Musée de l'Homme in the 1930s, was, with other museum heads in 1940, forced to resign (Ory in Rioux 232). Ethnography in the form of the study of popular culture in all forms had been on the cultural agenda of Blum's Popular Front, and, because of Pétain's focus on the French "homeland," it continued to flourish under Vichy. Pierre Pucheu, at the Ministry of the Interior, together with Jérôme Carcopino, archaeologist and director of the Ecole de Rome, sent out a circular in April 1942 to regional prefects stipulating that the "intellectual élite of our cities . . . must know better the life of the French provinces" (Dumoulin 246–47). Thus, ethnographic research continued without interruption from the 1930s to the 1940s, only with the purpose of mythifying rural France for political purposes rather than simply to study it.

The land evoked by Desnos in *Contrée,* like the publication of the book itself, lies symbolically in the middle ground between the French agricultural landscape so prized by Pétain and a different France, one valued by the French for its heritage of egalitarianism and independence. This latter view of France is well represented by the conclusion to one of historian Marc Bloch's Resistance essays, "Pourquoi je suis républicain," from 1943: "There is no liberty of the people without sovereignty of the people, that is to say, without a Republic" (220).[10] This Republican landscape is not fertilized by the healthy cows or tilled by the contented farmers from Vichy propaganda posters (see fig. 12). It is an agrarian landscape that, while also beautiful and productive, has been ravaged and silenced by war. "La Vendange," a sonnet, elegiacally evokes a land that is absolutely quiet because the wind, bells, cicadas, and thunder have been silenced (*O* 1171). It is "drunk with blood" and fertilized by the rotting corpses of soldiers. Yet this land is nevertheless bountiful in its wine production, that intoxicating fruit of the "grape harvest." The poem reads as an apostrophe to "Oh Wine in your barrels," which will "dye our mouths" "according to your magical colors" before the inevitable passage into a pre-Christian underworld.

The Greek god of wine, Bacchus, makes a specific appearance in another poem, "La Plage," which describes a scene on a beach where two men meet to exchange a one-word message: "Corinth"(*O* 1172). One of them leaves under the cedar trees at the hour when "Bacchus prepares his conquest." Yet Bacchus in the poem, like France, fails to conquer and becomes overwhelmed and penetrated by space: "Space passes through him." Meanwhile, on the beach the messenger lies dead with a knife in his back. His message continues to resonate, however, and, in response, "the earth moans with languor and fear." Here a landscape linked to Bacchus is anthropomorphized as afraid. For the name Corinth refers to a once rich and powerful Greek trading port that then, like France, lost its influence to neighboring invading powers. In Desnos's *contrée* the message of "Corinth" still provokes fear because it portends enhanced vulnerability, as the melancholy land itself senses.

Another anonymous person passes by the narrator's house in the sonnet "La Peste," which compares fascism to the Plague (*O* 1169–70). During a night lit only by shining constellations, the unnamed poet asks:

> Where is he going, the walker who comes close
> slowly and stops for an instant? Here he is in front
> of the house. I hear his breath behind the door.

The walker has left a black and yellow poster glued to the speaker's door with one word on it: *Plague,* for the "I" inside the house has been singled out, soundlessly accused of breaking the understood rules of national collaboration. Danger, fear, anticipation, resignation, are emotions in which the poems of *Contrée* are steeped. In another part of the overall geography of *Contrée,* in "Le Coteau," a child is killed while his dog barks in vain:

> This place is fated.
> Nothing is real here except this smell of a forge
> Which rocks us, makes us drunk, and reddens our eyes. (1160)

The poem expresses the same fear of being branded and hunted down evident in "La Peste," a fear legitimately shared by many. Even the noun chosen for the title, *coteau,* rather than the more benign term for "hillside," *colline,* presages violence because of its resemblance to *couteau,* the word for "knife." It is "in vain," once again, that

> the barking and the child's cries will pierce
> The thickness of the night, the thickness of the ashes
> Which fill our hearts, which burn our foreheads.

The poet reveals his own personal frustrations in *Contrée* as well. In "Le Réveil" a sense of foreboding is evoked by the repeated phrase "It's late" (*O* 1174). Seeming to address another with the injunction, "Get up," the poem is addressed to the poet himself, who needs to bathe after rubbing "hands stained by ink" and after brushing teeth that have had to hold in until they rot: "So many words held back like ships at anchor,/So many songs, truths and secrets." It is late in the poem for the poet, and yet his anxiety cannot be compared to those for whom it is irrevocably "too late," for whom there will be no more "awakening": "those who are dumb and deaf/For they are dead, assassinated, at dawn."

The landscapes in these poems link France to its Greco/Gallo-Roman heritage. They are wealthy in crops and natural beauty, as is France in Vichy propaganda. Yet they are not visibly inhabited by Demeter, the Greek goddess of the harvest, who was reactualized by Vichy as a demure and stoic symbol for France, a feminine counterpart to the warrior myths of the Germans (Faure 273; Muel-Dreyfus 30–31). Nor do the men who traverse these landscapes accord with the passive agrarian population nostalgically idealized by the Vichy régime. These anonymous men respond not to the ideal of rational manhood encouraged by either Vichy or the Third Reich but to the god of life and wine, Bacchus-Dionysus, who represents and encourages ecstasy, sexual promiscuity, and mystical delirium. There is no hierarchy between them; Pétain's "natural order" is nowhere visible. These men live in a landscape marked by centuries of wine cultivation, by the creation of lyric poetry, by the ancient Greco-Roman tradition of democracy, and by the traditions of three French Republics since the 1789 revolution. Their anonymity in fact belonged to the everyday culture in which Desnos lived when he wrote these poems—it was dangerous for any Resistant to know what his or her companions were doing. Thus, Babette Godet explains that she knew little of her husband's meetings with Desnos, because it would have been dangerous for her to know: "I know nothing. I am kept in the dark, on purpose. It was an indispensable protection. If not, a single tug on a single thread and the entire network would unravel" (interview, 17 Nov. 1999).

Accordingly, an unknown person passes through a safe house in "La Maison," in which an "I" listens without seeing and merely imagines what the stranger looks like:

> He comes down the staircase, he's already in the foyer.
>
> The porch opens onto the crater of the nights.
> I listen and imagine him. He walks, he goes out, he escapes,
> He flies into a sky pierced with peninsulas. (O 1168)

Once again the landscape itself intimately reflects a mental cartography of anxiety experienced by those secret sharers who struggled against Nazism. The night is a multitude of dangerous "craters" for the person who works in the Resistance, whereas the only "peninsulas" of solid ground apparent to the wary eye are those that, like mirages, "pierce" otherwise volatile skies.

Within the landscape of Desnos's *contrée* the poet also speaks of love, as in much fixed-form sixteenth-century French Renaissance poetry. In "The Landscape," a sonnet in alexandrine verses with a traditional rhyme scheme, the land is explicitly linked to the theme of love:[11]

I had dreamed of loving. I still love but love
Is no longer that bouquet of lilacs and roses
Filling the woods with their fragrance
Where a flame lies at the end of paths which do not bend.

I had dreamed of loving. I still love but love
Is no longer that storm where the lightning superimposes
Its pyres on castles, routs, convulses, illuminates,
While fleeing the parting of the ways.

It is the spark of flint under my footsteps at night.
The word no dictionary in the world has translated
The foam on the sea, that cloud in the sky.

With age all becomes rigid and clear,
Streets without names, ropes without knots.
I feel myself harden with the landscape. (*O* 1168–69; *V* 65)

"The Landscape" describes an emotional landscape in more sensual terms than in Desnos's earliest love poems. The speaker in the poem admits that he used to dream and that he dreams no longer, not because those dreams no longer charm him—clearly, they are still redolent of beauty and life in its full cycle, from the fresh smell of lilacs to the ephemeral odor of decomposing leaves in a storm—but because dreaming, like loving, has become dangerous. For the illuminating flame of an *amour fou* could overwhelm the spark under-foot in the night of Occupied France, where the darkness and secrecy of the "streets without names" had to be kept at all cost when faced with the danger of the hangman's "ropes without knots." One slip, and everything, everyone, could be lost.

The poet and the world he inhabits are threatened with rigor mortis, an imminent danger that sharpens the mind like the sparks from the underfoot "flint"—that illuminates the beauty of what has past, both the natural beauty of the spring landscape and the dreams of love past and lost. In the present moment is a walk in the dark in which each step on flint kindles sparks that cannot be translated into words but which serve as silent reminders of human-kind's Promethean ingenuity in defiance of fate. The fate in question here is linked to political danger born of a political passion. Even the natural images linked to youthful passions—"a flame [that] lies at the end of paths which do not bend" and the "lightning" that ignites and demolishes—function like alarms in the reader's mind. This political love represents the binding tie among those who alone recognize the passwords exchanged between Re-sistance fighters living under siege, "the word that no dictionary in the world has translated."

The "Landscape" here is the landscape of the *maquis,* where the armed resistance fighters struggled to free France. With the memory of lilacs and roses giving off their heady perfume, this landscape is filled with nostalgia for a view forbidden to a Parisian, whose freedom of movement was severely restricted. Furthermore, this reference in 1944 to these specific flowers must be read as an intertextual reference to Desnos's friend Aragon's well-known poem from 1940, "Les Lilas et les roses." Another fixed-form poem, "Les Lilas et les roses," as Max Adereth explains, "owes it title to the two flowers which symbolise the two stages of the May–June 1940 war, the lilacs greeted the French troops in Belgium as the people 'smothered' them with flowers because they expected instant Allied victory, and the roses which retreating French soldiers and civilians found everywhere they went as they fled towards the south of France" (15–16). In Desnos's rural *paysage* the bountiful vegetation so scarce in Paris may still be found and prized, especially by a poet who loved to collect mushrooms, to cook, and to eat well.[12]

The fixed-form poems of Renaissance Pléiade poets also echo throughout the opening sonnet from *Contrée,* "Cascade." Like Joachim Du Bellay and Pierre de Ronsard, Desnos uses poetry in French to defend the nobility of France through the beauty of its poetic tradition. But, whereas the Pléiade poets were defending French against Latin, the poets of the Resistance were, of course, defending French literature against the ascendancy of German culture. "Cascade," like "La Plage," is located on a coast: a natural frontier that highlights the perimeters of the contested *contrée* in question and the dangerous activities situated along its borders. Like many sixteenth-century poems, this fixed-form poem showcases a hunt as a central metaphor. But, whereas French Renaissance poems commonly deploy the hunt as a metaphor for the pursuit of the beloved, the hunt in "Cascade" relies on the reader's expectation that the apparatus of the hunt—the arrows, the wound, the hunter—will refer to love in order to veil the fact that the hunt in question represents the political pursuit of armed Resistance fighters hidden in the landscape of France, to whom the poem is addressed:

> What sort of arrow split the sky and this rock?
> It quivers, spreading like a peacock's fan
> Like the mist around the shaft and knotless feathers
> Of a comet come to nest at midnight.
>
> How blood surges from the gaping wound,
> Lips already silencing the murmur and the cry,
> One solemn finger holds back time, confusing
> The witness of the eyes where the deed is written.

Silence? We still know the passwords.
Lost sentinels far from the watch fires
We smell the odor of honeysuckle and surf
Rising in the dark shadows.

Distance, let dawn leap the void at last,
And a single beam of light make a rainbow on the water
Its quiver full of reeds,
Sign of the return of archers and patriotic songs. (*O* 1159; *S* 170)

Although not a member of the French armed Resistance, Desnos, once again, clearly writes this poem in solidarity with those individuals who risked their lives in the *maquis* of the French *contrée,* who were *contre* the men running France. Against a backdrop of fog and night sky one person is wounded, while that person's companion watches in stunned silence. The shock of the arrow, like a comet or a cascade, combines swiftness with natural beauty and with violence. The two anonymous individuals are alone and vulnerable because they are away from their camp, and yet they are supported by the knowledge that they belong, as did Desnos, to a fraternity united in opposition and danger, which shared passwords. But what exceeds the danger and the impact of the flesh wound—the cometlike shock of the arrow—is the sensual beauty of the landscape itself.

Verbs in the poem such as *quivers, spreading* (or *fans*), *surges, rising,* and *leap,* all refer to renewal, to a new "renaissance." Such a reference, in a French fixed-form poem, must also refer to the beauty and nobility of the French poetic language itself, in a reference to Du Bellay's 1549 treatise "in defense" of the French language. And, in effect, the substantives referring to the arrow— *arrow, feathers,* (quiver of) *reeds*—wind up linking the powerful wounding weapon to the potential power of the writer's pen. This interpretation of the pen as a weapon is confirmed by Picasso's etching. Dumas cites Youki Desnos as describing the etching as "a seated knight, leaning on books— doubtless a symbol for a struggle in which both books and weapons were viable" (*O* 1159). For a Resistance poet's pen could function as a weapon in the propaganda wars, and such a poet could be arrested for the words penned by his quill.

A corporeal wound may have been incurred in order to protect the landscape from any invader or occupier, but the smells of that landscape, its light at dawn, and the hopeful omen of the rainbow upon its vast and silent distances inspire the poet to address it intimately, in the original French. Here is my own more literal translation of the final stanza:

When finally dawn springs up through your chasms,
Distance, and when a ray is drawn on the waters,
It is an omen of the return of the archer and of hymns,
A rainbow and its quiver of reeds.

With the second-person singular possessive adjective *your,* in "*your* chasms,
Distance" (my emph.), the landscape's "distance" is transformed into an intimate space. Within this newly intimate distance is concentrated the entire
physical landscape evoked, which is also a poetic geography.[13] For it is only in
the final quatrain that there is a "false" rhyme—between *abîmes* and *hymnes*
(chasms and hymns)—establishing a distance between the two substantives
linked by the rhyme. In effect, threatening "chasms" will have to be negotiated
before fresh poetic "hymns" will be possible in the lovely yet dangerous countryside emblematized by the *cascade* of the title. Yet the mood is ultimately
hopeful. The "cascade," which is also a rocky, wet rendezvous in the predawn
landscape, has turned out to be a meeting site that the "we" succeed in leaving
alive. The emotion that radiates from the final six lines, from "we smell"
(meaning also "we will feel"), is one of pleasure and hope akin to love, which
suggests that in fact "the archer" from the penultimate line is not the enemy
who has inflicted the wound in the second quatrain but that other, older,
mythological, archer "Love" in the form of Cupid from sixteenth-century
verse, who will return to the landscape and once again reinject fixed-form
poems on the theme of the hunt with human and sensual love.

For a substitution occurs in the poem between passionate love for a woman
and a similarly passionate love for a landscape. This substitution operates
logically with the situation of "Cascade" on the first page after the dedication
of the collection, "To Youki." For the interlocutor "Youki," the poet's human
beloved, is substituted the interlocutor "you," which refers in the poem to the
land the two individuals are seeking to protect. Desnos is still writing poems of
love, but this time his love extends beyond the person of the woman he loved
the most to include the nation for which he lost his life.

Desnos's Everyday "Phony" War

At the outset Desnos's experience of the war with Germany was as traumatic
and as banal as that of most of his friends. He and Youki were vacationing in
Brittany, on the island of Belle-Ile, with their friends Gaston and Simone
Ferdière, when they heard the news of the outbreak of war (Ferdière 141; Youki
Desnos 280; see fig. 13). Ferdière was the psychiatrist who treated their mutual
friend Antonin Artaud during the war at his clinic in Rodez (where he also hid
members of the Resistance passing between the Occupied and non-Occupied
zones). Although just past his thirty-ninth birthday, in September 1939, Des-

nos, together with his friends Fraenkel, Eluard, Trenet, Barrault, and others, were mobilized. He was obliged to leave Paris on 6 September for Brittany as a sergeant, in the first company of the 436th Regiment of Pioneers. From 1 September 1939 until his return to Paris on 20 August 1940 Desnos wrote to Youki almost daily (frequently signing his letters "kisses, kisses, kisses"), describing his experiences in the army as best he could, despite censorship, throughout the entirety of France's peculiar "phony war," or *drôle de guerre,* with Germany.

Even though France had signed the Munich Accord of nonaggression with England and Germany in October 1938, under Edouard Daladier, France followed England in declaring war on Germany on 3 September 1939, two days after Germany invaded Poland. The major preparation for such a war by the French had consisted in the construction of a protective wall along France's eastern border, known as the Maginot line. It did not extend to the north as far as Belgium, however, since the dense Ardennes Forest was supposed to provide a sufficient natural barrier against attack. Desnos spent much of his time in the army at the northeastern edge of the Maginot line, in Lorraine.

On 1 September Desnos wrote to Youki, who was away in a hotel in Corrèze. He begged her to be careful with money and not to drink too much yet reassured her that he was taking care of everything and that they would see each other again shortly.[14] The next day he wrote to her from the Deux Magots café, opposite the Church of Saint-German-des-Prés in the heart of their neighborhood, about his plans to send on her jewels, furs, and the cats and whom to contact if she needed cash; he told her that Théodore Fraenkel, who had also been drafted, had already left town (*D* 388–90; see fig. 14). He found the wait for his departure for Nantes annoying because of Paris's odd emptiness: "The house is empty, the streets are empty, the time is empty" (390). From Nantes, back in Brittany, he informed her that he would not be sent to dangerous places and that he would mostly be responsible for "accounting work." He told her that the whole experience seemed unreal: "we are all living as though in a dream" (393–94). As he traveled northeastward, he sent her short postcards to reassure her and finally, on 20 September , another letter in which he insisted that, despite the fact that he could not tell her where he was "or the letter would not reach you and would be stopped by the censors," she should not worry: "First of all, my regiment is not an attack regiment but a regiment of workers, mostly made up of farmers from Brittany and the Vendée with a few Parisian officers. I'm an Accounting Sergeant of the First Company, which has certain advantages." Returning to the strangeness of the experience, he noted: "I'm participating in a war without having any notion whatsoever of its reality. I find it bizarre, disturbing. It's a bit like a dream" (398).

In his letters Desnos worried about household details such as coal for heat and whether Youki was spending money too quickly. Occasionally, he wrote on postcards preprinted with the following message: "This card may not contain: any indication of location; any explanation of military events; any names of leaders." He sent her some Alsatian wheat, perhaps as a hint regarding his location, and asked for her to send him wool sweaters and a warm sleeping bag. He meditated on how to earn money when he got out of the army and suggested to Youki that he could always write fairy tales and songs, already choosing pseudonyms for himself. He mentioned a plan to write a book for the *Nouvelle Revue Française:* "I will not be, we will not be, in any way, the victims of this story" (*D* 413). In a later letter he wrote about his plan to write for American magazines, with the help of his friends John Dos Passos, Ernest Hemingway, and Evan Shipman—a plan that was not realized (432–33). But his letters were censored, and this frustrated him. When a song he sent to the singer Mireille was censored and returned to him, he forwarded the letter and envelope to Youki, with the following diatribe: "I must have hit a hairsplitter. If he dissects all the letters like that, it's not surprising that the mail is late." He imagined the boring job the censor must have held in peacetime and then satirized the censorship process, crossing out his own words: "I've reached Z, in the region of X, state of H, and I'm planning to leave for A, and to pass by C" (416–17). He managed to meet Jean-Louis Barrault in a field between their two encampments, after hoping for such a meeting for a long time in his letters to Youki. Then in January 1940, after a lot of paperwork, he was able to go home to Paris on leave.

In effect, for the first eight months of France's war with Germany nothing much happened, hence the adjective *phony* attributed to it by the journalist Roland Dorgelès, reporting for the weekly *Gringoire* (Sapiro 345). Desnos's letters reflect the boredom and frustration of this peculiar phony war: "Calm, nothing new" (7 Oct. 1939; *D* 406); "Our cannons shoot a lot. Last night, [they did so] without stopping. No response from the German side" (18 Oct. 1939; *D* 414); "Nothing, Nothing, Nothing is happening. I won at bridge yesterday. I'm bored but my health is good" (16 Feb. 1940; *D* 458). Two more cards from late February repeat: "still nothing happening (a familiar tune)" and "Still nothing happening!" (*D* 463).

Then, in mid-May, conditions changed radically. Desnos wrote to Youki that he had heard the news of the blitzkrieg battles in Belgium, Holland, and Luxembourg and also of bombings in Paris, Lyon, Pontoise, Nancy, and Colmar, "which leave us breathless" (*D* 486). Four days later he advised her to leave Paris for the country. At the end of May he counseled her to sell certain objects like his gold watch and their silver vases "intelligently," in order to raise scarce cash (504–05). By 26 June Desnos wrote that he had left Alsace for Normandy: "and we arrived in time for the rout." He reassured Youki that he was in good health, waiting to be demobilized, and concerned not for himself but for her well-being in Paris (510–11). He wrote a description, published only after his death, of the walk through Normandy after the defeat as a hallucinatory experience, the men exhausted from days of exertion with little sleep:

> At a stopping point, near a farm, a white cat jumped out of a window and seemed to dissolve into the multiple odors of earth and air. From then on, from milestone to milestone, white cats jumped in and out of the steps of the battalion of men. They seemed to be born and to disappear, to multiply, to replace one another. . . . These cats had emerged from eight hundred brains walking through the countryside with tired bodies.
>
> Perfumes multiplied. Some of the soldiers recognized them as we passed by and used them as names for imaginary paths and châteaux: honeysuckle path, sweet pea château, rose path, thyme path, tarragon path, spicy mint path. Fields, thickets, and forests arranged themselves throughout the dark night, to the sound of feet dragging on pebbles, to the shock of a rifle butt against an empty bin. And the human voice, when a cry was heard, seemed unreal, as if invented by the far-away echoes. (O 862)

As Desnos reached Normandy, Pétain's government moved to Vichy. Within a week, on 3 July, the day before Desnos's fortieth birthday, he wrote that his regiment had allowed itself "foolishly to be taken prisoner, almost on orders" (D 512–13). On 10 July the National Assembly voted to give Marshal Pétain the mandate (les pleins pouvoirs) to establish "a new constitution of the French State" (Rousso 31). Two weeks after that, Desnos wrote from the Dordogne that all he needed was the necessary paperwork to return home (D 515–16). He was lucky, at least at the time, because many troops taken prisoner that summer were transferred to German camps as prisoners of war and not released until 1945 (Rousso 21).

By August Hitler had annexed Alsace and Lorraine, reclaiming land lost to France after World War I. The French beret and the French language were immediately outlawed (Azéma 107). This contested territory had previously been won by Germany during the Franco-Prussian War, which had brought about the downfall of the French Second Empire and led to the establishment of the Third Republic in the 1870s. The ascension to power of Marshal Pétain effectively dissolved the Third Republic of France. Pétain, in the view of Azéma, sought literally to wipe out France's republican spirit, its "destructive individualism" founded on over sixty years of democratic rule and centered in

Paris, in order to replace it with a new focus on rural and "natural hierarchies" (51). Rousso goes even further and states that Pétain's régime sought to create a worldview "in which individuals were no longer free and equal in the eyes of the law, no longer sovereign, but subordinated, hierarchically, to 'natural bodies' underneath the authority of a supreme leader" (37).

Pétain did not waste any time establishing the repressive parameters of his new authoritarian National Revolution: in August all "secret societies," including Freemasonry, were outlawed; in September anticommunist measures were made explicit; in October all French Jews were distinguished from the rest of the population by a particular status, and all foreign Jews were subject to detention in French internment camps; in November unions were disbanded (Azéma 58–61). Other changes included the closing of the elite universities for teachers, the *écoles normales* (a gesture protested by Desnos in *Aujourd'hui*); the censorship of the media, which included the complete shutdown of several publications; food rationing; and the guillotining of abortionists. In December a law establishing a "Peasant Corporation" was declared with the stated goal "to promote and manage the common interests of peasant families in the moral, social and economic domains" (qtd. in Azéma 61).

In October 1940 Pétain's minister, Pierre Laval, and then Pétain himself met with Hitler. Shortly after his own meeting with the German führer, Pétain spoke on the French radio and explained his views to the French people: "It is with honor and in order to maintain French unity—a unity that has lasted ten centuries—and in the framework of an activity that will contribute to the new European order that today I enter into the path of collaboration" (qtd. in Gervereau and Peschanski 190). Pétain closed his speech with the following injunction: "I have used with you, until now, the language of a father. Today I use with you the language of the leader. Follow me. Keep your confidence in Eternal France." Not all the French were dismayed by Pétain's speech. One journalist who would play a role in Desnos's fate, Alain Laubreaux, became famous for having declared, back in September 1939: "I can wish only one thing for France: a short and disastrous war" (qtd. in Ory, *France* 54). By October Desnos was back in Paris with Youki, faced with the necessity of earning a living any way that he could.

Nursery Rhymes and National Spirit

While in hiding from the Germans in an attic in the Dordogne, Gilbert Lamireau, a friend of Desnos's, remembers hearing children playing outside and reciting from Desnos's newly published book of nursery rhymes, *Trente chantefables pour enfants sages à chanter sur n'importe quel air:* "Hop, hop, grasshopper (*Saute, saute, sauterelle . . .*) (41).[15] Unbeknownst to him, Desnos had already been arrested and deported—Desnos's poems for children appeared in print the month that marked his stay at Auschwitz-Birkenau and his passage through Buchenwald on the way to the work kommando at Flöha near the German-Czech border. As already noted, Desnos had envisioned writing fairy tales as early as 1939, while waiting through the long months of the phony war. This project was a natural outgrowth of children's verse he had written and illustrated in the 1930s for the children of his friends Lise and Paul Deharme and Darius and Madeleine Milhaud—who had mailed him a hand-knit scarf while he was in the army.

These Mother Goose–style rhymes exhibit Desnos's typically fanciful sense of humor. Inevitably, they are in fixed forms: the rhyming stanzas made up of regular octosyllabic lines are easy to remember and to set to music (as they have been by multiple composers, including, notably, Jean Weiner). One of the most memorable ones, "Le Pélican," displays well Desnos's humor:

> Captain Jonathan
> Who was eighteen years old
> Captured, one day, a pelican
> On an island in the Far East.
>
> Jonathan's pelican,
> In the morning, laid a white egg
> And out of it came a pelican
> Who resembled him amazingly.
>
> And this second pelican
> Lay, in turn, a white egg
> From which, inevitably,
> Came out another one, who did the same.
>
> This can go on and on for quite some time
> If we don't make an omelet first. (O 1338)[16]

The short poem at once suggests the dreamlike delirium of the endlessly reflected images of pelican eggs and the deliciously irreverent suggestion that this dizzying continuum of reproduction could be stopped quite simply by cooking up the eggs in an omelet. Just such a bloodthirsty touch is typical of seventeenth- and eighteenth-century fairy tales, which generally delight as much as frighten young children. What could be more delightful than a Far Eastern baby pelican? What more tasty and familiar than a fresh omelet?

It is no coincidence that Desnos wrote verses that hark back to Charles Perrault fairy tales and Mother Goose folk rhymes. Those older poems and stories were similarly written in coded language, as a method of conveying morals, jokes, and frightening truths through suggestion and indirection, a method that Desnos would practice with fluency in several forms through the Occupation years. Little Red Riding Hood, for example, suggests that unaccompanied young women risk being snapped up, if not literally eaten, by wolflike courtly seducers, a moral that any worldly seventeenth-century reader would have recognized without further explanation. Desnos's short poems, directed toward children, quickly became standbys of the popular culture of his own time. A recent essay in praise of Desnos begins with the author's admission that, for him, one of these *chantefables* had been "the first poem" (Adelen 138). These poems also contain occasional hints of Desnos's overall mind-set at the time of the Occupation.

One such poem, "L'Hippocampe," dedicated to a seahorse, the aquatic animal with which he strongly identified in his poetic portrayals of himself with Youki, his seductive mermaid, may be read as an indication of Desnos's own frame of mind:

> Hip Hip Hooray for the handsome seahorse,
> Marine horse, horse of damp temper,
> Which no jockey has ever ridden,
> Which no coachman has ever harnessed.
>
> Hip! Hip! Hip! for the seahorse.
>
> Hip Hip Hooray for the handsome seahorse,
> In a pocket, on his belly,
> He carries and cocoons his eggs.
> There, his young are comfortably at home.
>
> Hip! Hip! Hip! for the seahorse. (*O* 1331)

Here it is as though Desnos were insistently claiming freedom from any kind of subjugation. Certainly, the freedoms he permits himself in these short rhyming verses constitute a poetic parallel to his living conditions in Paris: for while his life was outwardly constrained, like the constraints of rhyme and rhythm in these poems, his imagination remained resolutely free.

Within the confines of regular meter and facile rhymes, a vivid imagination sings forth, revealing that, far from imprisoning the poet, these historical, regularized poetic forms liberate him in spirit to reach his most playful heights. For, in effect, through these regular verses he proselytizes the pleasures inherent in maintaining a lively imagination. It is not surprising that during this same period, in January 1944, he wrote: "beyond automatism there is the intentional, that beyond poetry there is the poem, that beyond poetry received there is poetry imposed, that beyond free poetry there is the free poet" (*O* 1204; *S* 178). The delightful short poem dedicated to a ridiculously large and well-educated ant, "La Fourmi," carries within it implicitly the injunction to ignore reason and imagine things:

> An eighteen-meter-long ant
> With a hat on its head
> Doesn't exist, doesn't exist.
> An ant dragging a cart
> Full of penguins and ducks
> Doesn't exist, doesn't exist.
> An ant speaking French
> Speaking Latin and Javanese
> Doesn't exist, doesn't exist.
> And so? Why not! (*O* 1330)

In fact, within a month of his return to Paris in the summer of 1940 Desnos began to imagine unimaginable things such as, for instance, a future after fascism, which must, at times have seemed almost impossible in Occupied Paris. At the daily newspaper *Aujourd'hui* he used book and record reviews and columns as a stage for his perpetually free and distinct voice, despite censorship and the evident dangers of free speech. He also used them to send messages to enemies and friends alike, including, among the latter, Louis Aragon, who had once reviled Desnos for writing alexandrine verses, when *Corps et biens* was first published in 1930. By 1940, however, Aragon had changed his mind radically and had himself come to embrace historical French verse forms, for many of the same reasons as Desnos.

The Politics of Fixed Forms

Aragon turned back to fixed-form poetry as a soldier in 1940, ten years after Desnos, as revealed by "Les Lilas et les roses." This poem, composed of rhymed stanzas in alexandrine verses, was written to commemorate the traumatic loss suffered by the French to the Germans in Belgium, from May to June 1940. First published in *Le Figaro* in September 1940, the second stanza describes the illusions of victory that ill prepared the troops for the shock of defeat:

> I will never forget the tragic illusion
> The procession, the cries of the crowd the sun
> The tanks charged with love and the gifts of Belgium
> The air atremble and the road set to the buzzing of bees.
> (*Crève-coeur* 45)

Even more significant than the elegiac tone of the poem, however, is its archaic form, which Aragon defends explicitly in "La Rime en 1940," first published in

April 1940, while Aragon was still in uniform. In this essay Aragon defends regular rhyme against free verse such as the type of poetry practiced by the surrealists. He rejects surrealist poetry yet makes an exception for Desnos's "Rrose Sélavy" poems, which Aragon dubs "possibly the masterpiece of explicitly surrealist poetry" because they succeeded in combining freedom and constraint (72). Aragon writes: "Freedom, whose name was usurped by free verse, takes back its rights, not in the sense of letting go, but in the sense of the work of invention" (76). Aragon himself, after Guillaume Apollinaire, adopts the fixed forms he had once criticized and, like his old friend Desnos, proceeds to take his own "liberties" with the long-held rules, thus adapting those forms for himself.[17]

Max Adereth's explanation for Aragon's political purpose in returning to fixed forms illuminates an agenda doubtless shared at the time by Desnos. With reference to the twelve-syllable alexandrine, the octosyllabic, and decasyllabic lines Adereth writes: "these forms belong to an ancient French tradition and so are best suited to the 'French' poems Aragon wants to write in his German-occupied country. Moreover as they are familiar to most French people, they can help readers to memorise the poems without having to keep them, a quality not to be despised when Resistance poetry became illegal and one could be arrested for having 'subversive' literature in one's possession" (55). In effect, these forms practiced by both Desnos and Aragon provided a rhythmic link to France's great literary past. Aragon presented this argument in "Du sonnet" from 1954—that traditional French fixed forms arose out of a desire to elevate the national language, beginning with the first sonnets written by the sixteenth-century poets of the Pléiade and culminating in his own poetry and that of his friends during the Occupation (1, 5). For any French poet writing in fixed forms meant writing in a form that was particularly French. It represented a kind of nationalism in the face of the "new European order" represented by the Occupation. Thus, it was not surprising that Aragon's poems and his treatise on rhyme met with furious controversy, which pointedly contextualizes Desnos's own fixed-form poetry from the 1940s.

Aragon's old friend Pierre Drieu la Rochelle, who had contributed to the issue of *Feuilles Libres* in which Desnos presented his hoax drawings and writings of madmen in January 1924 and who had also contributed to the October 1924 *Corpse*, gave Aragon unhoped-for publicity in the controversy over his new poetry. Drieu published a damning and revealing review in *La Nouvelle Revue Française* when Aragon's poems came out in book form as *Le Crève-coeur* in October 1941. With the patronage of his friend Otto Abetz, Drieu had taken over the NRF from Jean Paulhan in late 1940. Paulhan had tried to persuade Gaston Gallimard to allow the review to be published in the non-Occupied zone, but Gallimard had been told by Dr. Kaiser at the

Propaganda-Staffel in November 1940 that the Gallimard publishing house would be closed down unless he agreed to allow the NRF to continue publication under Drieu's leadership. Those who contributed to the journal in the war years tended to invoke, as their excuse, either "the cause of art" or the maintenance of *l'esprit français,* the French mind/spirit (Sapiro 60).

Drieu's review "marks the passage from a counter-attack to a denunciation," argues Gisèle Sapiro in *La Guerre des écrivains,* because of the way he reveals his own collaborationist politics in his concurrent defense of his own literary journal and attack on Aragon's tribute to medieval poetry (441). Sapiro quotes Aragon's friend and biographer Pierre Daix as saying that in the literary circles in Paris, this denunciation " 'contributed, in fact, to the revelation of Aragon's true position' " (Sapiro 443). For far from being himself a collaborator, as rumor had had it at the time, Aragon was, on the contrary, calling for "a new French dawn" that would result in the defeat of Germany. Sapiro concludes her narration of this literary battle between two former friends with the fact of Drieu's suicide after the Liberation in 1945, which she presents as "the dénouement, if not the consequence," of their fight; once fascism had lost the day, Drieu succumbed to despair.[18] It was in this climate that Desnos himself continued to work in fixed forms. At the same time, Desnos scoffed at the notion that the poetry he was writing during the Occupation was somehow more valid than what he had written previously: "Poetry reborn! At its age! Those who are saying that poetry is undergoing a renaissance are the same ones who said it was dead several years ago" (*O* 1205). The only book of poetry he published in the 1940s with Gallimard, with whom he had published *Corps et biens,* was *Fortunes,* a compilation of the poems he had written mostly in the 1930s.

The Everyday in Occupied Paris

Having no desire to work for the propagandist radio upon his demobilization, Desnos joined up with his old friend Henri Jeanson in an effort to create a newspaper that could keep its integrity despite the political landscape. Jeanson reminisced in a June 1965 radio show produced by Samy Simon in honor of the twentieth anniversary of Desnos's death that the two had shared a code, dating back to 1918 when they first met, which they would repeat to each other throughout their friendship and which symbolized their shared love of peace. It was the first line of the very first poem ever written by Desnos, "Aquarelle" (Watercolor), from 1915 and published in February 1918. Jeanson misremembers the line on the radio as "They destroyed the farm and burned the chateau" (it was literally "The soldiers burned the farm and the chateau" [*O* 15]), in reference to the destruction of the French countryside by German soldiers during World War I. Again in 1940 they were hoping for peace following another French victory over Germany and the avoidance of further harm done to the French landscape. The *Aujourd'hui* of Jeanson would be short-lived, however, as Jeanson himself was arrested in November 1940. Desnos's ongoing contributions to *Aujourd'hui* show a veiled but undaunted continuation of the spirit in which the newspaper had been founded.

Life in Paris during the Occupation was characterized by a radical shift from prewar time. To begin with, the hour literally changed: Paris clocks were set on German time. Swastikas decorated the Tuileries and Luxembourg Gardens (Azéma 93). Furthermore, in his effort to appease the Third Reich so as to be seen as a full-fledged negotiating partner (rather than as the leader of a defeated country), Pétain made a policy of actively collaborating with Germany both politically and economically, a policy strongly supported by Pierre Laval, in an effort to save face and guarantee that "France would only be administered by the French" (69, 48). Pétain and Laval were convinced that the only "peace" possible was a German peace, a belief that Pétain maintained despite Laval's fall from grace between December 1940 and April 1942. Once he came back to power in 1942, Laval conceded French workers for the German war effort and the first choice of French agricultural and industrial products as well (121, 129). These policies sprang from a combination of fierce anticommunism, anti-Semitism, and strong anglophobia. By December 1942 Laval stated unequivocally: "Victory for Germany will save our civilisation from sinking into communism. Victory for the Americans would be a triumph for Jewry and communism . . . I, for my part, have made my choice" (qtd. in Azéma 121).

As an economic consequence of Pétain's policies, there were shortages of everything imaginable throughout the Occupation. Being cold; poorly fed, clothed, and shod; short of soap, glass, and coffee, became facts of everyday life in Paris. Beginning in September 1940, bread, noodles, and sugar were rationed.[19] A year later clothing, shoes, and tobacco were added to the list. Yet many got rich, and impoverished France, by selling goods on the black market (Azéma 99, 98). Others, mostly farmers, only got fatter because, as one man put it: " 'We used to try to let the Germans have as little as possible' " (qtd. in Azéma 100, 101). Money had to be found where it could be, especially by someone like Desnos, whose companion had extravagant tastes.

There seems to be no doubt that Youki's fickle nature, which both delighted and terrorized Desnos, persisted throughout these years. She hated not to wear the latest fashions, for example, or to be deprived of wine. Her friend Julia Tardy Marcus, who spent months at a time living in the Desnos apartment during the phony war and the Occupation, comments: "In order to have a litre of red wine she was capable of a lot, of too much perhaps . . . so she had friends and connections all over the place" (9). One way in which she managed to make do while Desnos was away during the 1939–40 war was to take at least one lover. Later, after he had returned, she may have continued to take as lovers men who could provide her with the luxuries she craved, including stockings and shoes with leather soles, when these commodities were scarce (interview with Dominique Desanti, 3 Mar. 1999).

Marcus insists that, despite her perennial unfaithfulness and despite some tempestuous scenes between the two of them, Youki loved Desnos and that he accepted her as she was (8). Mouloudji, who later became a well-known singer, was taken in by Youki and Desnos as a child and lived for a while at their Rue Mazarine apartment. He performed the child's voice in some of Desnos's radio commercials. He also remembers witnessing their lover's quarrels, in which they were well matched (94).

Youki's unpredictability meant, however, that Desnos was constantly trying to provide adequately for her, for both sentimental and political reasons. Her "luminous" frivolity could be a boon in a dark time, but it could also be dangerous. Marcus adds: "I don't think that Youki knew that Robert was in the Resistance (before his arrest), he must not have told her in order not to worry her but also so that she couldn't do anything foolish . . ." (9). In other words, Desnos would have felt that he had no choice but to stay in Paris during this time (unlike Breton and others, who wisely fled to the United States), because it was inconceivable that Youki could live elsewhere for long, and he did not wish to be separated from her. Thus, he had no choice but to become implicated in the Occupation economy, since there was no other way for the two of them to survive.

Making do was necessary. This did not mean that life came to a complete standstill. Georges Hugnet remembers celebrating the entry of the Soviet Union into the war against Hitler in June 1941 with a party at the Desnos apartment together with Paul and Nusch Eluard and Sonia Mossé; once the curfew was past, they were invited to stay the night ("the hospitality of Youki and Robert being limitless"), and, with blankets covering the windows, they drank and talked late into the night (349; Gateau 271). Galtier-Boissière, who worked with Desnos at *Aujourd'hui,* also describes lively dinners with Desnos and Youki throughout the Occupation (52, 74, 91, 120). In his diary he recounts anecdotes, with typical humor, that illustrate the small acts of defiance that kept many Parisians motivated. For example, there is the story of a newspaper seller who sells a *Fritz,* his daily paper, with a kindly smile and the words: "Here it is, *grand con!*" (big idiot). After inquiring as to the meaning of his morning greeting and being told that it was a diminutive of the expression *grand conquérant,* "great conquerer," the German soldier saluted the newspaper seller the next day with a ready reply. His arm raised he insisted: "I'm not a *grand con,* I'm just a *petit con; Hitler* is the big *con!*" (45).

Collaboration?

The newspaper launched by Jeanson sought to maintain a particularly Parisian sense of humor, an *esprit parisien*, despite the reality of the Occupation. The inaugural issue—a thin, four-page tabloid—introduced the staff to the readers as "French, like you. The collaborators to *Aujourd'hui* belong to your generation. They have had a childhood that resembles your own, like a sister." Babette Godet, who worked at *Aujourd'hui*, says that Jeanson and Desnos "organized the survival of freedom of thought" with their concept for the paper (interview, 17 Nov. 1999). Pascal Ory explains in *Les Collaborateurs* that the spirit of the daily newspaper optimistically seemed to confirm the hope that "France had not been vanquished and that its military conqueror was capable of standing back and smiling magnanimously" (71). Yet Jeanson's ironic, often sarcastic tone, not to mention Desnos's short-lived column entitled "La Revanche des médiocres" (Revenge of the Mediocre People), were not appreciated magnanimously by the military conquerors after all. Jeanson's vision for *Aujourd'hui*, with Desnos as news editor, lasted barely two months—from 10 September 1940 to 22 November, the day Jeanson was arrested for refusing to publish articles in favor of the new Vichy laws concerning Jews (Youki 293; Dumas and Simonnet 8).

After Jeanson's removal from the paper, the editorship was taken over by Georges Suarez, whom Galtier-Boissière characterized as nothing more than a "shoe-shine specialist" (20).[20] Galtier-Boissière and Desnos took smaller jobs; Desnos remained employed at *Aujourd'hui*, writing increasingly shorter pieces, until his arrest in February 1944. Originally, the newspaper was set up on the Rue Réaumur, in the office space of a former newspaper, *L'Intransigeant*, which had ceased publication during the Occupation. Later, after Jeanson was dismissed, the offices were moved to a site directly across the street from the German Kommandantur, at the head of the Avenue de l'Opéra (Godet, interview, 17 Nov. 1999).

Which groups were most receptive to active collaboration?:[21] the far Right, including right-wing Catholics, anticommunists, even authors of traditional fiction—in other words the same sorts of people routinely criticized by the young surrealists twenty years earlier for having supported the patriotic view of France, which resulted in the massacre of World War I (the people most offended by Breton and Aragon's *Corpse* in 1924).[22] But, whereas the generation to which the surrealists belonged was antiwar during the war of 1914–18, most of the former and current surrealists, including Desnos, Aragon, and René Char, in the 1940s believed that war, or at least resistance, had become a necessary choice in the face of Hitler's fascistic regime. These former surrealists, then, positioned themselves distinctly against all those who tolerated or willingly accepted collaboration. These included long-term enemies, such as the journalist Alain Laubreaux, and former friends, such as Pierre Drieu la Rochelle and even the publisher Jean Luchaire, whom Desnos knew personally as the brother-in-law of Théodore Fraenkel.

What did it mean, then, to "collaborate" on a newspaper that was run by a Laval loyalist handpicked by the Nazi Propaganda Office? Did this act, an economic necessity for Desnos, make of him a collaborator in the sense that Pétain meant in his radio speech from October 1940? Certain purists believed that exile or silence, absolute "refusal," were the only honorable options for a writer during the Occupation. But, if exile seemed unthinkable to someone like Desnos and silence or "refusal" impossible for someone who earned his keep by writing, then what options were there? Any stake at all in the economy of the Occupation represented a compromise with the Nazi regime. Once such a compromise was accepted, what choices then existed? Sapiro explains the various positions very clearly:

> In fact, those writers who abstained from any legal publication whatsoever were rare. . . . For many of the writers of "refusal," the trick was to struggle for the maintenance of *l'esprit français*, but honorably, which meant without compromise . . . : rather than publish nothing, to maintain a presence—first legal, then clandestine—which better illuminates the withdrawal of such writers from certain venues such as *La* NRF as well as their refusal to sign their names in the collaborationist press. . . . [F]or many involved in clandestine publication, total silence [*la non-publication légale*] was not an option. (61, 64)

The option adopted by Desnos was to write in a "coded language" of double entendres, a practice that became more and more common starting in 1941. Great efforts were made to get around censorship; it became a kind of game that created yet a new complicity between writer and reader (Sapiro 63). Furthermore, by 1943 Desnos had ceased signing his pieces in *Aujourd'hui*. Nevertheless, he wrote "legally" for the paper until his arrest, even formulating the desire to publish a selection of his *Aujourd'hui* articles under the title *Mines de rien*, according to Raymond Queneau, who worked as an editor at Gallimard. (Dumas published a selection of his articles under that title in 1985.) To that end he kept a large, red, hardbound notebook (in the back of which are mathematical notations), into which he himself pasted many of his *Aujourd'hui* pieces (DSN 903). Beginning in 1943, he also began to write and publish clandestinely poems for which, had his apartment been searched, he could have been arrested.

Desnos at *Aujourd'hui:* How to Read a Newspaper

While Desnos was at *Aujourd'hui* he wrote book reviews in which he alternately strove to reassure and provoke his readers, albeit in oblique terms. On his third day on the job, 13 September 1940, he suggested to his readers, in a review of Alain-Fournier's *Le Grand Meaulnes,* first published in 1913, that "to provoke the spring is to take on a comforting struggle, which can generate joy" (*O* 866). There can be little doubt, given Desnos's attitude and what Charles Nunley calls his "invitation to read allegorically" in his *Aujourd'hui* book reviews, that "spring" may be read as the hope for a forthcoming shift from Occupation to Liberation and that the "comforting struggle" leading to "joy" may be understood as the hope that the work of the Resistance would lead to an Allied victory (*D* 279). Desnos's friend Pierre Berger testifies that in 1941 Desnos "yelled at people who had lost hope in Victory" because he believed in it so strongly ("Mon Copain" 35).

About three weeks later, on Saturday, 5 October, Desnos published a "how-to" piece in his book review column that put his readers on alert: "Do you know how to read a newspaper? Yes? Are you sure?" He is emphatic about the readers' responsibility today (*aujourd'hui*) and every day during the Occupation: "Reading a newspaper means not only learning what is happening, it means learning how to interpret events, to interpret them for oneself" (*O* 865). Always read between the lines, exhorts Desnos in the short review's subtext, because those of us responsible for bringing you the news cannot tell you the whole story. It was no coincidence that on the page facing Desnos's "book review" was a detailed official explanation of French law concerning Jewish identity, with a diagram showing how to determine Jewish origin. The previous Wednesday *Aujourd'hui* had published German rules against Jews, signed into law in France on that day by an officer representing the "Chief of the Army, the Chief of Military Administration in France." The law stipulated that, as of 2 October 1940, all Jews had to register in their neighborhoods and "Jewish businesses" had to display signs in their stores to identify themselves, and violation of the law would result in imprisonment. Desnos had always hated prejudice. Marcel Duhamel tells the story of the night in 1926 or 1927 when they went to hear jazz together with Frisco, a well-known black tap dancer. They were given a table in the back, and, when Frisco tried to join the other dancers on the floor, he was asked to return to their table, upon which Desnos yanked the tablecloth off, breaking all the plates and glassware. He then proceeded to climb onto the neighboring tables and to smash everything in sight, inspiring his tablemates to do likewise (244–45).

Most memorable from Desnos's years at *Aujourd'hui* were his overtly political columns from late 1940, published under the provocative title "La Revanche des médiocres."[23] In case there was any doubt about whom he meant by the "médiocres," he dispelled it with his book review of Aragon's *Paris Peasant* in October 1940, within a month of the appearance of Aragon's "Les Lilas et les roses" in *Le Figaro*. Clearly, by "médiocres" Desnos meant all those unimaginative, reactionary minds who had been criticized by the young surrealists in the 1920s and who, empowered by the collaborationist policies of Marshal Pétain, were in a position to take their "revenge" in the 1940s. In the review Desnos allies himself with Aragon as a former surrealist. Identifying Aragon's book from 1926 as the surrealist classic that it is, Desnos declares: "Surrealism was, among many things, a revolt against mediocrity. And mediocre people are not disposed to forget it and they remain ever ready to take revenge for the well-earned blows they received at the hands of the surrealists." He thus stresses that he and Aragon shared a desire to revolt in the 1920s, strongly suggesting that they persist in this desire in the 1940s, as antifascists opposed to collaboration with the Nazi Occupiers. He concludes in an unequivocal tone that ostensibly concerns Aragon's work from the 1920s yet obliquely validates Aragon's political stance in 1940: "Read it. You will see on which side lie talent, honest thought, and French genius" (*O* 868). Readers who had taken to heart Desnos's injunction "to interpret" for themselves would have understood which "side" Desnos was on, that in the literary world there were in fact two sides, and finally that Desnos, like Aragon, disparaged everyone on the "other" side—that of collaboration.[24]

Desnos's first "Revanche des médiocres" column directly and openly attacked the practice of denunciation with a model fable against all those petty mediocre people who, long dissatisfied with troublesome neighbors and acquaintances, rushed to avenge themselves by denouncing them to the Nazi Kommandantur in Paris. Entitled "J'irai le dire à la Kommandantur" (I'll Go Tell It to the Kommandantur) and published on 14 September 1940, this article uses humor to mock all those eager to embrace collaboration as a way settling old scores (*O* 866–68). In his first example Desnos describes a man who told his neighbor he was going to denounce her because she allowed her dog to urinate on the second-floor landing of their apartment building. The second example was of a woman who discovered that she had arrived too late at her grocer's to obtain any coffee. She responded: "What? Just an hour ago you sold some to my concierge. OK. I'll go tell it to the Kommandantur." As Desnos puts it: "There exists in Paris a group of pathetic people determined to bother their neighbors." He calls this behavior the "foolishness of human meanness" and ends with a call for dignity. Ian Ousby explains the effect of Desnos's article: "The word the French use for denunciation or laying information with the authorities is *délation*. During the Occupation they also had a phrase, '*j'irai le dire à la Kommandantur*': 'I'll go tell the Germans about it.' It came from the title of an article by the poet Robert Desnos published in *Aujourd'hui* in September 1940, when Henri Jeanson's editorship seemed to guarantee it some freedom of opinion. It bravely appealed to people's 'sense of dignity' to stop them denouncing one another. The appeal failed but the phrase stuck" (146).

Roughly two weeks later, on 26 September, Desnos wrote another fable about the dangers of overeager denunciation entitled "Du temps où l'Abbé Bethléem lacérait les affiches" (From the Days when the Abbot Bethléem Tore Down Posters). He told the story of a cleric who was arrested around 1920 for tearing down music hall posters he considered indecent. Paradoxically, this cleric, Abbot Bethléem, came to trial together with young Desnos and Jeanson, both as fervently atheistic as the abbot was theistic, who had themselves been arrested for a similar crime but with an opposite intent—that of tearing up religious tracts in a bookstore situated inside Saint-Sulpice Church. The confused authorities "condemned, with commendable impartiality, the Abbot Bethléem together with his accomplices (sic), Henri Jeanson and myself, to an eleven-franc penalty apiece" (*Mines* 88). With this moral tale Desnos used himself, Jeanson, and the abbot as examples of how the denunciator could turn out to share the same fate as those he wished to denounce. Denunciation is not only a nasty (even though possibly comical) business; it can be dangerous as well.[25]

Desnos sided with Aragon again in June 1941, with his review of Aragon's *Le Crève-coeur,* the volume of poetry that included "Les Lilas et les roses": "Aragon is one of the most intelligent men of our time and one of those who has the most talent" (*Mines* 125). A couple of weeks later, in his 28 June 1941 "Au Crayon" (Sketches) column, he once again implicitly concurs with Aragon's praise of fixed-form poetry as typical of a particularly French literary tradition: "And then, all the same, is not the history of French literature the history of a unity held together by language? Precious unity, indispensable unity, but a unity never completely realized and always in danger. This is something that, doubtless, we must reflect upon" (138). The "we" of the final sentence draws the reader into the "unity" of all those who share the particularity of the French language—in other words, all those who are not the Occupiers or their sympathizers.

On 3 December 1940, the day that Suarez took over the direction of *Aujourd'hui* from Jeanson, the day that the newspaper became tightly controlled by the Nazi régime, Desnos reviewed the *Essays* of Montaigne. He began with his own attitude: "Not anyone can doubt. And to doubt is an art. To doubt is not an act of mistrust" (*Mines* 55). Reading between the lines, and against the negatives, the reader may surmise that only those who are principled in matters of trust are capable of doubt in the face of a leader of state who tries to persuade his people that the conditions of Occupied France are acceptable. To doubt is to maintain the "trust" of a France nourished since the Revolution on the principle of "Liberty, Equality, and Fraternity." Not to doubt, by implication, is thus to remain intellectually mediocre.

Other features signed by Desnos were published in the columns "Au Crayon" and "Chroniques des temps présents" (Current Chronicles). Two pieces on the nature of time and memory in these columns reveal a more mature and reflective Desnos. In an "Au Crayon" column from June 1941 he points out the foolishness of asking the time. The piece begins with the question, "What time is it from now on [*désormais*]?" An old idiomatic expression, this question delights Desnos because of its regionalism particular to Paris and also because of the way in which it sheds light upon an imponderable of human nature: the question "illustrates well the general tendency to consider as definitive that which is only transient and fugitive." For Desnos the question refers less to the disconcerting sense of time connected to living on German time—a fact of life for roughly twelve months already when this "sketch" was written—than to the wish that it could be possible to live more fully in the present moment, in a new version of baroque time, perhaps: "If, from now on, nothing was understood to last forever? If we accepted to judge, not according to rules and habits, but according to a permanent and pressing necessity? If only we wanted to understand that the hour is dead already, at the instant we read it on the dial?" (*O* 874). In a different voice Desnos shows himself to be preoccupied with the same question here that fascinated him as a younger man experimenting with automatism: how to live most fully and consciously in the present moment. No longer trying to stop time in the same ways, this older Desnos still hopes to savor every moment with his senses, his mind, and his mindfulness of others. Did he not write in another "Au Crayon" column one month later: "And the imagination, wise and mad, tonic and depressing, opens up its cargo of dreams and symbols. In an instant, while fully awake, a man may penetrate the fertile regions of mindful dreaming" (15 July 1941).

A sense of time passing too quickly from the perspective of a man already taking a retrospective view of his life, although only forty-one years old, is reflected again in the "Chroniques des temps présents," from 19 March 1942, with the title "Sous le pied d'un cheval . . ." (Under the Foot of a Horse . . .) (*O* 875–76). In this piece he remembers his childhood neighborhood of the Marais with great tenderness and nostalgia: "I find within the heart of the shadows of 1942 the perfume and echo of nights from long ago." He evokes the apartment in the Rue Saint-Martin where he lived between the ages of two and thirteen: "From my bed, I could see the reflection of a streetlight in the recess which precedes the Rue Saint-Bon as well as its steps where the sounds of insurrections have melted into the past" (see fig. 3). He remembers being lulled to sleep by the sound of hooves pulling horse-drawn carriages through the streets, a sound rediscovered in the nights of 1942 in his apartment on the Rue Mazarine, across the Seine from his old neighborhood. The remembered sound causes him to dream about his childhood and his school, forever marked for him by "the odor of washed and polished wood, the flavor of penny fountain pens, chewed and transformed into paint brushes, the green of the chestnut trees after Easter vacation." (Chestnut trees still line the street outside the Lycée Turgot.) "Let us put our memories under our pillows and not abuse them," he advises. "We must keep them for our dreams. . . ." Later Desnos's "Chroniques" were written simply under the pseudonymous heading "L'Homme de jour" (Man of the Day). As Dumas points out in her introduction to Mines de rien, this last rubric, "L'Homme de jour," was shared by several journalists at Aujourd'hui, thus ensuring the anonymity (and a limited protection) of each individual author (9–10).

Desnos also wrote music reviews for Aujourd'hui, never disguising his love of jazz, a style of music considered "degenerate" by the Nazi régime and Vichy.[26] On 23 December 1940, for instance, he wrote positive reviews of records by Artie Shaw and Benny Goodman (of whose Jewish origins Desnos was doubtless aware); a month later he favorably reviewed records by Louis Armstrong and Count Basie, which he himself pasted into his Aujourd'hui scrapbook. In July 1941 he was more daring, although in an veiled manner: he suggested that young people in the "youth camps" that had sprung up in the 1930s and had become very popular during the Vichy régime be allowed to listen to swing records, in addition to the more patriotic "Maréchal nous voilà" (Marshal, Here We Are). Rousso describes these camps, which every young man of twenty living in the non-Occupied zone was obliged to attend for eight months, as a place where they were made "to celebrate the joys of nature and the catechism of the Redeeming Marshal" (42). Disingenuously "supposing" that "the organizers of these camps where young people sing have thought about the marvelous training offered by the phonograph," Desnos subversively suggests that French youth listen to music considered degenerate by the very marshal in whose honor the camps were created ("Chroniques" 76).

Undaunted by the danger linked to professing a love of jazz, Desnos persisted in his favorable reviews of his preferred musicians, reviewing in December 1941 an "anthology" of the Hot Club of France, including Louis Armstrong, Bill Coleman, Duke Ellington, Coleman Hawkins, and Fats Waller ("Chroniques" 76). In July 1942 he reviewed a particular favorite from his radio days, Django Reinhardt. For jazz fans, sometimes known as zazous, were vulnerable to arrest and deportation. As Yannick Séité stipulates: "In Vichy France, the zazou is the enemy. We know how, in Germany, certain jazz fans paid for their love of jazz with their lives" (66). By January 1943 it was indeed distinctly dangerous to be a jazz fan in France as well. An unsigned front-page article in *Aujourd'hui* from that month disdainfully mocks the *zazous*—"the fruit of seventh-five years of Jewish democracy"—and suggests that they should be put to work repairing roads in the east, a thinly veiled reference to labor in the concentration camps situated to the east of France's borders.

Desnos, who had pleaded with the public to resist the temptations of denunciation, found himself denounced in print, as early as March 1941. Louis-Ferdinand Céline wrote an indignant letter to the editor in response to an unfavorable review Desnos had given his new work, *Les Beaux draps*. In his book review column, newly and significantly retitled "Interlignes" (Between the Lines), in a reference to his 5 October 1940 book review essay on how to read a newspaper, Desnos had deeply insulted Céline by judging his work boring: "Boredom, total boredom forces me to fall asleep from the first pages" (*O* 871). Irate, Céline accused Desnos of "leaving his ritual deposit of filth on the 'clean sheets' of his *Beaux Draps*."[27] Supposedly "reading between the lines" himself, Céline then wondered why Desnos should bother writing reviews at all since what he really wished to say was simply: " 'Death to Céline and long live the Jews!' "(872). He claimed that the name *Desnos* was empty of meaning, accused Desnos of being a *philoyoutre* (a Jew lover), and challenged the editor to publish a photograph of Desnos in profile so that the readers could see his nose (presumably as a giveaway to Desnos's supposedly Jewish origins).

Had Desnos had Jewish origins, he would not have been allowed to hold down his job at *Aujourd'hui*. But Céline was absolutely correct in accusing Desnos of being pro-Jewish and fervently against anti-Semitism. In his response Desnos focused on the fact that L.-F. Céline was only a pseudonym for Louis Destouches, thus accentuating Céline's secretive impulse to hide his own "true" identity. He then ridiculed the criticism that his only critical alternatives were to declare either "Death to Céline" or "Death to the Jews," calling such a choice an "eccentric theory" of criticism (*O* 873). He signed his rebuttal: "Robert Desnos aka 'Robert Desnos.' " This last gesture underscored the fact that he, unlike Destouches-Céline, felt no need to disguise his identity.

In September 1942 Desnos was denounced for the second time, by the collaborationist author Pierre Pascal, for an impudent review of Pascal's translation of Poe's poem "The Raven": "M. Pierre Pascal manipulates French verse with a rare lack of skill and has no feeling for poetry itself. This book, at the paper manufacturer's, will rejoin a certain number of other works without interest which, once recycled, will perhaps allow for the publication of readable works" (*O* 877). This time Desnos received a supportive letter from Jean

Paulhan, written on stationery from the NRF, despite the fact that Drieu la Rochelle was directing the journal at the time (883).

Such public criticism of political foes by Desnos ended with his review of Pascal's translation. From then on he was restricted to writing record reviews and a few anonymous contributions. Desnos collaborated once again with Jeanson, however, three years after Jeanson's ouster from Aujourd'hui. They cowrote the screenplay for a successful film about life at a radio station, Bonsoir Mesdames, Bonsoir Messieurs. It was released on 15 February 1944, one week before Desnos's arrest.

Walking the Tightrope of Legality: Clandestine Writings

Starting in the spring and summer of 1942, around the time he joined the Resistance cell Agir, Desnos began to write clandestine poetry as an outlet for the opinions it became more and more risky to express in public. Resorting increasingly to anonymity at Aujourd'hui, he began to feel a growing need to act side by side with those whose beliefs he shared. While he published the poems he had written in the 1930s legally in Fortunes with Gallimard, semi-legally he was preparing Etat de veille and Contrée for publication with Godet. At the same time, he began to write poetry more overtly "under the coat" of legality.

Laval returned to power in 1942. He was nonetheless widely unpopular at the time, partly because of the policy of collaboration with which he was identified (Laborie 237). As early as November 1940, when he had been in power the first time and within a month of the publication of the photograph showing Pétain and Hitler shaking hands, Laval had encouraged the public to accept the policy of collaboration. He declared in a banner headline in Aujourd'hui: "We have committed ourselves in the interest of France so that harmony might reign in Europe according to a policy which will allow us to improve the country" (1 Nov. 1940). The non-Occupied zone disappeared, and the entire country became occupied by German troops in 1942. Starting in the spring, it was also the year that systematic arrests and deportations on exclusively racial grounds began to occur, culminating in the massive roundup of Parisian Jews on 16 and 17 July and their temporary incarceration at the Velodrome d'Hiver sports arena in subhuman conditions. Known as "Operation Spring Wind," the "roundups of the Vel d'Hiv" resulted in the arrest and deportation of almost thirteen thousand people, including four thousand children (Azéma 112; Rousso, Années 92–93). Laborie insists that there was "a widespread indignation" in response to the arrests and deportations of Jews (238). Flonneau agrees that by the summer of 1942 "Gaullisme was on the way to acquiring the sympathy of the great majority of the French people. . . . [B]y the spring of 1943 there was less of a turning point whereby the population became hostile to Vichy so much as there was the exteriorization and open expression of a hostility that had begun, interiorized, as early as 1942" (509).

In the month that Laval came back into power, April 1942, Desnos publicly slapped Alain Laubreaux, the anti-Semitic journalist for *Je Suis Partout* who had voiced hope for a Nazi victory over Europe, in a surrealist act of bravado for which he would pay dearly later on. That summer Desnos first became active in the Resistance cell Agir.[28] At a theatrical evening on 24 July 1942, although he was among friends, Desnos appeared "moody, stressed," recalls Alain Brieux, the son of Youki's seamstress, Mme Lefèvre. "He must have just heard about the 'roundups of the Vel d'Hiv' which had taken place a few days earlier" (29). He joined Agir the next day.

Desnos took an avuncular interest in Brieux, who became a permanent resident of 19, rue Mazarine, in 1943, because Desnos and Youki were willing to hide him there to escape the Service du Travail Obligatoire, known as the STO. Laval's widely unpopular STO policy, whereby young French men were obliged to sign up to work in Germany, was instituted in 1943. The STO had the unintentional effect of bolstering the ranks of the Resistance with the many young men whose refusal to work in Germany left them no alternative but to become outlaws. While he was living in Desnos's living room, Brieux helped him by photographing documents at night in secret. Brieux had to promise to keep this activity from Youki. Desnos also warned him of its dangers: " 'You must do this without reading any of the documents I give you; turn them upside down when you shoot them so that you can't read them. This means that if you're caught and tortured [*supplicié*] you can't talk.' " Brieux surmises that "Robert must have 'borrowed' pieces from the newspaper and returned them the next day, while transmitting the 'photocopies' to his network" (30–31).[29] By January 1944 Desnos clearly felt himself to be in danger because he asked Brieux to get rid of compromising materials in the Mazarine apartment, including books by the newly created underground press, the Editions de Minuit (L'Herne 29).

For the Agir network, commanded by Michel Hollard, Desnos provided information, garnered in part from his job at *Aujourd'hui* and his access to official press conferences, and he made false identity papers "to help members of the Resistance network and Jews" (*O* 1368). One friend remembers how Desnos, who was able to circulate at night past the curfew thanks to his press pass, would bring him news—the entry of the United States into the war, for example—which they would then seek to confirm by short-wave radio. Even within such a friendship, however, Desnos kept secret his true clandestine activities, as this same friend learned when he unexpectedly discovered Desnos, with whom he had just chatted on the street, at a Resistance meeting

(Jeander 33, 35).[30] Desnos made false papers, including a convincing false identification card for his friend Dr. Michel Fraenkel. Desnos's sense of humor is evident on the card because he gives Fraenkel the name Renaud and changes his place of birth from Paris to Bouzy La Forêt. Renaud, in the verb form *renauder*, means "to protest" and is derived from the sound of the cry of a fox, a *renard*, who, of course, comes from "the forest," as in Bouzy La Forêt. (Bouzy also sounds related to *bousillage*, which has the noun *sabotage* as a synonym.) Fraenkel's photo is a front-facing head shot, instead of the potentially more equivocal profile shot on his original identity papers.[31] Fraenkel had to wear a yellow star starting in 1942, according to a law that infuriated Desnos. Fraenkel remembered, in an interview, that Desnos would illegally sneak him into crowded cafés and order for the two of them (interview, 23 July 1993).

Desnos further walked the tightrope between legality and illegality in 1943. He continued to publish legally: his polemical novel against drugs entitled *Le Vin est tiré . . .* , featuring characters inspired by Yvonne George and himself, came out from Gallimard. As a belated response to the loss of a woman he had loved to drug addiction, the novel may also be read as the work of a man whose career as a journalist resulted in insightful social observation. In the preface he predicted that, "within twenty years, drugs will be found everywhere, perhaps even in the countryside, and it will be too late to control their use" (*O* 1001). He concludes his preface with eerie prescience: "If this vice menaces France as much as any other nation, France is not the nation that is most endangered by this problem." At the same time, the novel may be read as yet another cry for resistance to social oppression: "As long as the social order continues to restrict the free development of the individual, men and women will seek illusory compensations in opium and heroin, the key to a slow suicide." Dumas surmises that this novel summarizes a fundamental notion for Desnos: "it is necessary to know how to resist anything that oppresses the individual, whether it be drugs or the nazi plague" (981).

Desnos also published the semilegal *Etat de veille* in 1943 and completed four other works for semilegal and legal publication, all of which were published after his arrest: *Contrée*, published by Godet in May 1944; *Trente chantefables pour les enfants sages à chanter sur n'importe quel air*, published by Michel Gründ, also in May 1944; *Le Bain avec Andromède*, nine interconnected fixed-form poems on the theme of the myth of Andromeda, illustrated by Desnos's friend and neighbor Félix Labisse and in which Carmen Vasquez sees the "figure of the Occupier" in the myth's monster, published by the Editions de Flore in November 1944 (*O* 1157); and a revised version of his play from 1928, *La Place de l'étoile*, published as an "anti-poem" by his friend the psychiatrist Ferdière in 1945. He also wrote the long poem "Calixto," composed partly in slang and fragments of which would be published the following year.

Desnos went completely undercover in 1943 as well with his first wholly clandestine publications. The struggle to remain afloat mentally had become a struggle to hold onto the bodies and souls, the *corps et âmes*,[32] of French national dignity in the face of the Nazi propaganda machine. Resistance pamphlets urged the French to remember "THESE PEOPLE ARE NOT TOURISTS" and that their own "hearts and minds" were at stake (CHRD). Shortly before Bastille Day 1943, a flyer put out by the Mouvements Unis de la Résistance, the Worker's Movement, and the Communist and Socialist Parties called upon everyone sympathetic to liberty to go into the streets on 14 July and sing the national anthem in unison at 7:30 P.M. in front of the nearest neighborhood mayoral office. It states: "July 14th, 1943 will be the last July 14th of slavery! It must be the pinnacle of the Resistance, the announcer of the liberation." It announces subversively and with pride: "your army, your navy, your air force are fighting for you; you now have a government in Algiers; France has re-discovered her honor; she will re-conquer her liberty."[33]

That same day, 14 July 1943, the newly formed Editions de Minuit clandestinely published an anthology of poems under the title *L'Honneur des poètes,* composed of openly resistant poems written by well-known poets using pseudonyms. Desnos had two poems in the book, "The Legacy," under a version of the names of both his parents, Lucien (his father's name) Gallois (a version of Guillais, his mother's maiden name), and "This Heart which hated war," signed Pierre Andier.[34] Unlike the poems of *Contrée*, these two poems are direct and brash, with what Vasquez has called "an unequivocal meaning" (175). The first of these addresses Desnos's boyhood literary hero, Victor Hugo, and imagines him turning over in his grave at the betrayals of Laval, Pétain, Abel Bonnard, the newly named minister of education (in what Sapiro calls "a victory of anti-intellectualism"), and Fernand de Brinon, the French government delegate to the Occupation authorities. Not only did these collaborators betray republican France by dissolving the Third Republic and allying themselves with Hitler; they also colluded in appropriating phrases by Hugo to support their view of a Nazi "new order." "The Legacy" ends with Desnos's proclamation of Hugo's true "legacy": "Freedom" (*Liberté*) (*O* 1245; *S* 161).

In "This Heart that Hated War" the emphasis is on a heart that beats to remain alive more than to yearn for love. The first two lines feature a singular heart beating for war and the seasons: "This heart that hated war is now beating for the struggle. / This heart that once beat only to the rhythm of the tides, the seasons, and the hours of day and night" (*O* 1246; *S* 160). In the final line this individual heart is joined by others in the service of liberty: "Because these hearts that once hated war beat *for liberty* to the rhythm of the seasons and the tides, of day and night" (my emph.). The equivocal syntax in line 2 ("which *only* beats to the rhythm of the tides") is reversed in the affirmative of the final line, "because these hearts that once hated war beat for liberty," in which the hating heart refocuses its energy into the love of liberty. The crucial question here no longer concerns the surrealistically sanctioned notion of *l'amour fou* but a passionate love of the free.

The evocation of the heart's rhythm in sympathy with that of other hearts serves to remind the listener of the vitality of those who actively resisted collaboration. In addition, the poem's structure, which lends itself to recitation due to its pacing and repetitions, had a practical function—since these poems were easy to remember. It sounds like a song or a chant. Michel Murat appropriately associates these underground Resistance poems with Desnos's voice: "And it is with the force of simple language that he evokes—he who was one of the inventors of radio communication—the voice on the airwaves" (*Robert Desnos* 183). Not only does "This Heart That Hated War" lend itself to the spoken voice, in a marching body, but it focuses on the sound of the collective heartbeat: "it's the sound of other hearts, of millions of other hearts beating like mine across France." This sound is a "noise" akin to a drumbeat that is like "a bell tolling for a riot and fight," and also the sound of "the sea attacking cliffs." It beats as urgently as the tides in its call on "the old angers" needed to galvanize the French people: "And millions of Frenchmen are preparing in the dark for the work the coming dawn will impose on them." The reference to dawn underscores the poet's hope for a new beginning in freedom, yet it also presages an awareness of death, since it is traditionally at dawn that executions take place.

Certainly, the menace of death is present in the poem, since the sound provoked by the beating hearts is a call of revolt: "Rise up against Hitler and death to his partisans!" This view of death presents a striking contrast to the omnipresence of death in Desnos's early work, as in the conclusion to *Mourning for Mourning*, in which Desnos's flirts with death as a metaphor for alternate states of mind in a systematic attempt to free himself from what he sees as the restrictions of daily life (Sheringham, *Moi* 71). Life itself represents a constraint in *Mourning for Mourning*, in other words, and metaphorical sleep or death, a kind of psychic freedom. By the 1940s Desnos's view of life and death has changed, and it is life, emblematized by the anticipated dawn in "This Heart," which confers the freedom to feel deeply. Clearly, death is the price to pay for political principles. He has in a sense reverted to the revolutionary slogan "Liberty or Death!" from which he derived the title *Liberty or Love!* but in the 1940s death was no longer a metaphor for Desnos: it had become a real and a high price to pay. Already in a July 1941 "Au Crayon" column he had written: "For, like you, readers, I do not wish to believe in death, I cannot believe in death" (15 July 1941). His imaginative reality no longer stands in opposition to daily lived reality but enhances it, particularly in the poems published under his own name.

The clandestine poem for which Desnos became most famous among his contemporaries was "The Watchman of the Pont-au-Change" (*O* 1253–56; *S* 166-69). In his deportation memoir Jean Baumel remembers feeling that he was meeting the "Watchman" himself when he met Desnos at the detention camp at Compiègne (130). Louis Parrot, editor of the clandestine journal *L'Eternelle Revue*, tells the stirring story of this poem being read aloud for de Gaulle at the Liberation: "A few days after the deliverance of Paris, in the presence of General de Gaulle, a gala was given at the Comédie Française during which 'The Watchman of the Pont-au-Change' was read by several voices" (88).[35] The first-person poem in the voice of the watchman of Paris was published after Desnos's arrest, in May 1944, in the second volume of *L'Honneur des poètes,* and signed with another variation of his mother's maiden name, Valentin Guillois.

In effect, the poem is a valentine to the poet's endangered city, in the voice of her vigilant watcher, as she awaits her Prince Charming in the form of the long awaited Allied Troops. The poem is addressed to all those who love freedom and directly calls to those who wait in London, "on the banks of the Thames," to the "comrades from all nations," who will be present at the rendezvous of Liberation. Again, freedom is linked to the dawn, to the moment when it will be possible to say *bonjour* to those whom the Watchman calls to the meeting at the Pont-au-Change in central Paris: "Americans of all races and flags," friends from Algiers, Honolulu, Tchoung-King, Fez, Dakar, and Ajaccio, "Norwegians, Danes, Hollanders, Belgians, Czechs, Poles, Greeks, Luxemburgers,/Albanians and Yugoslavs." He calls to them,

> in a language known to all
> A language that has only one word:
> Freedom! [*Liberté!*]

The poem is Desnos's most openly militant and mostly openly evocative of the war. It begins with the identification of the poem's speaker: "I am the watchman of the rue de Flandre/I watch while Paris sleeps." Flanders, of course, is a site where many Frenchmen lost their lives in battles to the Germans in both world wars and most particularly the location where the so-called phony war came to its disastrous end. The poem describes the sound of airplanes over the city, the cries emanating from trains rolling toward the east, the red color of fires burning outside the city, the acrid smell of smoke. It expresses the hope that the liberation of Paris is imminent. In effect, Henri Margraff, who was deported with Desnos and who had worked in the Resis-

tance as a student at Clermont-Ferrand, claims that D-Day had been anticipated already for a long time by 1944: "Because it had been promised, promised for sure for 1943" (interview, 7 June 1996). Called upon to "kill an enemy"
by Resistance pamphlets (*A chacun son Boche*), the poet claims: "I have
slaughtered one of Hitler's men / He is dead in the empty street."[36]

Again relying on sound as a unifying connector between formerly free,
republican France and French people and those Parisians of the present day,
"you who sleep / After your dangerous secret work," the poet links himself to
all fellow travelers with his voice:

> Let my voice come to you
> Warm, joyful, and determined,
> Without fear and without remorse,
> Let my voice come to you with that of my comrades,
> The voice of ambush and the French vanguard. (*O* 1256; *S* 169)

Through the voice of the watchman in the poem Desnos calls out *bonjour* to
all those who will arrive in the new dawn to a free Paris. The poem evokes the
physical pleasures of speaking, as René Plantier has suggested; it constitutes "a
constant appeal to the pleasure of speaking, to the pleasure of recognizing
words and savoring them: science of the mouth, science of the ear, science of
communication, of the physical awakening of song" (73). The literary van-
guard has been replaced with the military avant-garde of Resistance fighters.
This voice insists: "We speak to you not of our suffering but of our hope, / On
the threshold of the new day we wish you good morning." The poem ends in
joyous anticipation:

> Good morning just the same and good morning for tomorrow!
> Good morning with full heart and with all our being!
> Good morning, good morning, the sun is going to rise over
>   Paris,
> Even if the clouds hide it it will be there,
> Good morning, good morning, with all my heart good
>   morning! (*O* 1256; *S* 169)

The closing calls resound with an echo of airwaves, indeed—especially when
"good morning," *bonjour,* is understood simply as "hello"—but this time with
the undercurrent of a two-wave radio used by soldiers making contact in
battle, repeating the address "hello" in an effort to make sure that contact has
been made and the important message relayed. The audience here has moved
from the popular to the strategic and is imbued with the heroism of fighters
willing to sacrifice everything for freedom.

It is in these pseudonymous poems, illegal in their content, clandestine in their form of publication, that Desnos uses his most direct poetic language. Leaving nothing to the imagination, he professes his passionate love for his country, his city. In an echo of the love poems addressed first to Yvonne in the 1920s and then thereafter to Youki, the tone of these poems shifts into the political realm. The emotions expressed and the reactions the poems intend to arouse spring from a similar well of intimate intensity, except that the public addressed is plural and collective. No longer an individual woman, the audience of these poems extends to include all the people of France and all those, friends of France, prepared to fight for its freedom and long-term survival as a republic.

In some respects the "The Watchman of the Pont-au-Change" may represent Desnos's most quintessential political self, to which his popular poetic talents are harnessed. And yet such a direct form, linked as it is to the songs and advertising slogans that Desnos had earned his living writing, necessarily leaves out another aspect of Desnos's poetical identity—the desire to play with language. For the fixed-form poems of the 1940s, despite their loveliness, are still games or puzzles set by Desnos for his readers. Desnos's best readers, like his lover, Youki, a consummate charmer and storyteller herself, were those who could consistently read "between the lines." For them Desnos concocted another category of clandestine poem: the fixed-form poem in slang.

Beauty "under the Cloak" of the Beast

Of the nine Occupation poems written in slang, six and a fragment of a seventh were published in 1944. Six slang sonnets signed "Cancale" were published under the title "A la Caille" (In Anger) in Jean Lescure's semilegal journal *Messages,* in April 1945 (the publication date was November 1944);[37] two more were only published in 1975 in *Destinée arbitraire* (edited by Dumas). Desnos's growing admiration for slang was connected both to his belief that the "theory of double meanings (immediate and secondary)" was "indispensable to poetry" and to his desire to make the spoken word live within written verse; for Desnos slang was "spoken poetry" (*O* 1230). In the notes he typed as he was working on the long poem "Calixto" posthumously called "Notes Calixto," he defines slang as equivalent to poetry: "Slang: the art of inventing new words or of giving new meaning to old words in such a way that whoever speaks slang understands right away. Slang and its meanings, uncertain, vibrant, oscillating. Poetic language" (1229). What better way to speak to a non-German public in France in the 1940s than with what Dumas has called a "secret language requiring an initiation, which plays the role of a signal and at the same time excludes all undesirable readers"? (280).

Desnos was predisposed to slang, having grown up in the working-class environment of the Halles market, where his father owned a poultry concession and the back streets of the medieval neighborhood of the Marais. He never lost his ability to converse in the colloquial French of the streets he had learned as a child, what Alejo Carpentier called his "parler populaire, faubourien" (L'Herne 364), an ability that must have been reinforced by his twelve months spent alongside working-class soldiers during the *drôle de guerre*, "farmers from Brittany and the Vendée" (*D* 398). He mentions slang, "the most common" language, again in his "Reflections on Poetry," written in the month before his arrest: "To wed common language, the most common language, to an indescribable atmosphere, to sharp imagery; to annex domains which, even in our day, seem incompatible with that fiendish 'noble language' which is endlessly reborn in languages ripped away from the mangy Cerberus which guards the entrance to the poetic domain, is what seems to me the work worth doing" (*O* 1203–04; *S* 177).

The six slang sonnets written "in anger" and published in *Messages* were delivered by Desnos to Jean Lescure just days before his arrest in February 1944 (Gaucheron 118). *Messages* was one of a group of journals, including *Poésie, Fontaine, Confluences,* and *Les Cahiers du Rhône,* that played a subversive role during the Occupation by pseudonymously publishing work by authors who "refused" to collaborate (Sapiro 67). Desnos's old friends Michel Leiris and Raymond Queneau were on the editorial board, together with René Char, another poet linked to surrealism who was also a member of the armed Resistance. Desnos's pseudonym, "Cancale," was the name of a coastal village in Brittany, not too far from Belle-Ile, where Desnos had been vacationing when he first learned about the outbreak of war and where he had joked about becoming mayor of the town of Palais (Youki 278). Brittany, a region that retained its original language and culture, had traditionally resisted assimilation into mainstream French culture, just as Parisians like Desnos in the 1940s resisted assimilation into the new mainstream of Pétain's Vichy. By 1944 Desnos's most recent trip to Brittany would have been to Nantes, in uniform, alongside Breton soldiers. In part these poems must have been written for them, in a popular language that was, as Jacques Gaucheron insists in *La Poésie, la résistance,* "readily memorizable" (118).

Three of the sonnets take on the three men most responsible for Vichy's policies: Pétain, Laval, and Hitler. "Maréchal Ducono" (something like "Idiot Marshal") describes Pétain as sleeping poorly because "he already senses that he is hateful and will be caught red-handed / For having swindled the people of France" (*O* 1233).[38] Pierre Laval is identified as "Pétrus d'Aubervilliers," for the town of which he had been mayor since 1923. Hitler is mockingly referred to as "le grand sorcier," "the great witch/warlock" in "Le Bon bouillon" (A Bad Business) (1234–35).

The "Frères mirotons," a frank denunciation of collaborators as willing sexual partners to the uniformed Nazi Occupiers, refers ostensibly to those members of the Parisian gay community who were "very visibly in the collaborationist literary milieu of the time, beginning with the minister of education, Abel Bonnard, who was nicknamed the 'gestapette,' " as Alain Chevrier explains in his unpublished study of Desnos's slang works. Chevrier specifies that a *frère miroton*, could be understood more generally as "human being" or "individual." It is in this sense, I believe, that Desnos's contempt for these willingly submissive sexualized individuals should be read—as anyone who accepted the conditions of the Occupation willingly and was thus "possessed," as in a sex act, acquiescent to the legitimacy of the foreign lover's "dominance."[39]

The last two sonnets, "Le Frère au pétard" and "Minute!" openly and obscenely insult German soldiers as "a group of imbeciles stuffed with stupid lies"; "they think they're chiefs but they're imbeciles"; "they haven't had our whores, they haven't had our wives,/It is not their kisses that wears them out/It is having to repeat to themselves, 'We are the real idiots' [*Nous sommes les vrais cons*)]" (Chevrier, qtd. in *O* 1236–37). Desnos uses slang here to express pure contempt, without the pleasure of sharing a secret language with compatriots that will distinguish "Calixto"; as Anna Jeronimidis points out, therein lies their "true obscenity" (190). Desnos had intended to write twenty-four slang sonnets all together and to include them in a manuscript of poems he was working on at the time of his arrest, which had the title *Sens. Sens*, translatable as "meaning(s)," "senses," or "orientation," may be seen as an appropriate title for a man preoccupied with the multiple meanings possible within the language of slang.

Two fragments of the long poem devoted to Desnos's totem Great Bear, "Calixto" also appeared in 1944 (although the complete poem was not published before 1962). The poem centers on Callisto, the nymph transformed first into a bear by Artemis and then into a constellation by Zeus already celebrated by Desnos in 1936 in "Tale of a Bear" (published only in 1942), as discussed in chapter 3. "Calixto" formally represents the varied nature of Calixto as nymph, bear, and constellation with its construction as a long work incorporating extended sections in slang together with sonnets and other classically inspired poetic forms. Slang also erupts into, and interrupts, some of the more classical portions of the poem in rhymed lines that scan according to a regular rhythm. The key to reading "Calixto" lies in the seventh and eighth stanzas of the opening section:

For a long time you have been acting the Beast
But Beauty is under the coat,
Like the fishbone in the fish
Like the skeleton under the skin
On which the knife blade breaks,
Like the thought in your head,
The light, needed to see.

And the same is true for language
Under which many secrets lie hidden.
Beauty and her luggage
Hide the star of good fortune
And the watchful prisoner,
Dreams of Beauty and of travel
As in the days of the ship Argo
Whose sailors spoke in slang. (O 1217)

As these stanzas show, the clandestine purpose of the poem and the slang in "Calixto" are explicitly announced and explained. The very subject of the poem is clandestinity. It encourages and directs the reader to seek to uncover the various treasures hidden *sous le manteau, sous le langage* (under the coat, buried in the language) and in "the luggage" of Calixto. Furthermore, the embedding of slang in a fixed-form poem with a mythological theme formally emblematizes the simpler strategy deployed in the sonnets published in *Messages:* "under the cloak" of coded words, readable only by the initiated, and further protected by the layer of vulgarity associated with much of the vocabulary, a legible poetic line sings forth expressions of anger at oppression and of appreciation for the heroic beauty of those strong enough to resist it.

Here the nymph's beauty is equated with the "light" of thought within a human head. This hidden light of thought refers, of course, to the conditions of everyday life in Paris in 1943: men and women had to hide their subversive thoughts, especially thoughts that were potentially sharp like a fish's spine. Such thoughts could also be "hard" enough to break the "knife" of an enemy's weapon—such as interrogation or even torture—in the sense that they could be resolute, tempered by political idealism. In this vision of the inner-outer Calixto her final form as a constellation is suggested only by the aura of light emanating from under her coat—from her beautiful, interior nymph-self. This Enlightenment-connected creature masks herself with her fur "cloak," with the "luggage" of the coded language of slang, which functions like a password shield, and yet her brilliance breaks through the barriers imposed by necessary clandestinity. Anyone who catches a glimpse, or hears an echo, of the message of hope flashed from her light-filled person will be able to continue to dream, even if he or she has been reduced to the state of a "watch-ful" prisoner. Such a person will then be like a sailor on the mythological ship the *Argo*—a ship about which Desnos wrote one of his first poems, in 1919, "Le Fard des Argonauts"—a speaker of slang and a practical idealist in search of the Golden Fleece of a once-again free France.[40] For anyone who understands "Calixto," the emblem or the poem, already knows how to read between the lines.

The "Calixto" to whom the poem is addressed in an apostrophe represents neither Desnos himself nor Youki, the flesh-and-blood woman he loved, nor even France (as in *Contrée*). This mythological figure, at once human woman, animal, and luminous constellation, is semidivine and yet retains enough mortality to remain in contact with earthly beings and emotions. This hu-manized Calixto is a watchful mythological guardian who suffers along with France; she embodies the idealism of republican France and of those who believe in liberty. She is upset—her eyes have circles under them and are in tears (*O* 1222). She has become invisible, but her roar may be heard in the desert; waiting for the dawn, in the next section, she cries in fury (1223–24). She is an in-between creature who can only be apprehended and observed in a "light," wakeful sleep. Calixto is the repository for an emblematic state of mind—changeable, humanly fraught with emotions and memories, and yet, like a deity, able to transform herself into a beacon for others. As a beacon, she represents the hope that transformations in both those who watch her and in their environment may be possible.

In addition to the link of slang, "Calixto" is connected to Desnos's slang sonnets by the matter of slang itself. From the earthiness of his word choices in the "A la Caille" sonnets Desnos turns to the earth itself in this poem devoted to a nymph twice transformed, once into an earthly beast and then into a celestial constellation. The opening stanzas, which read as an epigraph be-cause of their situation at the beginning of the poem and because of their typography in small capital letters, reveal Desnos as the mature political sur-realist he had become by 1943. As in a typical baroque poem the four elements are reviewed—earth, wind, water, and fire in the form of light (Chevrier):

> TO FALL ASLEEP LIGHTLY
>
> TO THE SOUND OF THE SPRING, UNDER THE SKY,
>
> DREAMING ACCORDING TO THE PLANETARY RHYTHM,
>
> WE PLUNGE, TOMBSTONE STATUES, INTO THE EARTH
>
> AND IF EVER DREAM TO REALITY
>
> REVEALED SECRETS OR MYSTERIES
>
> IT IS IN SLEEPING TO THE SOUND OF WATERS
>
> AND OF THE WIND CLOSING ITS SCISSORS.

TO FALL ASLEEP LIGHTLY

ON THE EARTH, INTO WHICH MUDDLE,

EARTHLINGS, ARE YOU STUMBLING? FERNS

ARE FALLING INTO LINEN BASKETS

IN A THICKET'S ARMOIRE

EMBROIDERED WITH SILK AND WHERE IS EXAGGERATED

THE LIGHT, OUTSIDE OF THE COAT

OF YOUR FLESH, NYMPH CALIXTO. (*O* 1215)

Desnos reveals himself as a political surrealist here, with his emphasis on "light" sleeping and the suggestion that to sleep deeply would transform the poet into a *gisant,* literally a recumbent "tombstone statue," a figure retaining a human shape but in whom mortal life is absent. To sleep too deeply, in other words, would mean to leave behind everyday French life in the manner of those poets who "refused" all contact with Occupied France either through a "dead" silence or through exile. Sleeping lightly, by a stream on the earth, in a natural world connected to mortality, means, rather, sleeping watchfully, like a military sentinel. The light sleeper rests in between wakefulness and dreams. The light sleeper, like the surrealist in an automatic trance, can bear witness to what transpires in both the worlds of waking and dreaming. Concretized in the universalist infinitive of the verb in the first line of both stanzas, this ubiquitous light sleeper witnesses on behalf of France the struggle to remain alive in deadening circumstances.

In the following long section, the one published independently in *Cahier du Sud,* Calixto is again a humanized deity, passionately nostalgic for her simpler, human past. She is angry for having been banished into the sky and regrets the days when she made love on earth. Through this mythological figure Desnos develops his own elegiac expression of love for France, his regret for her pain, his intense desire to experience the natural bounty of France not in the future or in an afterlife but in the present moment, today. In this section he evokes the arrow from Renaissance poetry, "antiquity's arrow," which symbolized the act of falling in love as fated by mythological destiny, manipulated by the gods: ("For you had some love affairs on earth when you were young/ Before feeling within your flesh, not flesh, but antiquity's arrow"). He evokes the life on earth that she misses, the sexual loves she enjoyed before Zeus seduced her and changed her fate, the life in the French countryside that is celebrated in the poems of *Contrée:* "Oh, may destiny preserve us always from unleavened bread,/From nights without dreams, skies without stars and cellars without wine" (*O* 1223). The only possible life is in the here and now. When the poem's speaker himself dies, as is suggested further in another section, there will be no more consciousness.

Calixto's regret for the simple pleasures of country life arises from her position, caught between earth and sky, just as the poet himself is caught between two worlds, two identities: a legally sanctioned identity as a journalist for a collaborationist paper and an illegal identity as a Resistance worker and writer. This in-between state is emphasized by Desnos in a sonnet section of the poem in which he describes her just as her constellation moves across the sky to vanish with the dawn, and he calls on her to linger there, on the threshold between her constellated self and her former human self:

> On the edge of the abyss where you will disappear
> Contemplate once more the rose, listen to the song
> That you used to sing at the threshold to your house
> Live again an instant in agreement with your own being.
> (O 1225)

The implication here is that by becoming a constellation, a beacon, Calixto has lost an essential part of herself and that that most essential part of herself was connected to what occurred *during* her mortal life, in its most everyday moments, within the being of the human, mortal body. This identification of Calixto, the constellation, with the earth is repeated again later on, when the poet calls her "star of the earth," barely visible in the light, in a section in which he celebrates the lovemaking of "the perfect couple." Yet, although only dimly visible, once dawn has come, for the poet she continues "to serve as a reference on our path towards a faraway goal" (O 1227).

The poem's concluding section, written partly in slang, puts the emphasis on Calixto's mortality. Even though she may be eternally celestial, she is not constantly visible. The poet cannot always see her—when he is fully awake, for example—as he notes in slang: "But you run away, you escape." In the first stanza of this final section he senses that his own departure is near:

> it is time to put everything straight again
> Yes, ok, but at the last train station
> the train will wait for me:
> signed "Canrobert" or "I'm coming." (O 1228)

This train with Desnos's name on it, "Can-robert" (and not "Can-cale," the name with which he signed the sonnets of "A la Caille"), the one that carried him to Auschwitz-Birkenau then Buchenwald, Flossenbürg, and Flöha, was only seven months in the future when he finished "Calixto." The poem and its nymph emblem represent Desnos's idealism tempered by a strong sense of his own mortality, his imminent arrest, and the fragility of an entire country's hopes and dreams.

In the very last stanza and final couplet two possible and opposing outcomes are postulated as the consequence of falling "asleep lightly" from the epigraphic stanzas of the poem's opening: either a liberating awakening or a fateful falling into weightiness, into the deeper sleep of the *gisant*, which can only result in death: "In rediscovering weight / He found his creator." And that "creator" turns out to be, in the final line, not a deity at all but simply "earth and, only the earth . . . ," the only creator suitable to Desnos. His "god" is revealed in this poem to be not the semidivine nymph Calixto or even the Christian Neoplatonic god Amour from Renaissance poetry but, rather, mortality itself, meaning life itself as symbolized by earth, which, in this poem, is the soil of France.

During the Occupation, while Desnos expressed his political views and his political loves most freely in those poems in which his identity was disguised by pseudonyms, his greater flights of imagination and poetic achievement were released by the formality of the neoclassical stanzas from *Contrée* and "Calixto." These late poems are allegorical in the manner that they evoke the familiar images of Vichy propaganda to celebrate France. Yet at the same time they are radically subversive in the ways that their content contradicts the ideology of Pétain's régime. With these poems Desnos walked the tightrope of Vichy censorship: it was conceivable that their pastoral images could have been missed by overworked censors and just as conceivable that their subversive nature would have been detected and condemned.

The poems of *Contrée* represent perhaps Desnos's greatest poetic achievement and fulfill the promise of the alexandrine refrain from the powerful free-verse poem "Ars Poetica" that opens "Sens," the collection of poems left on his desk the day he was arrested: "I am the verse witness of my master's breath" (*O* 1241; *S* 146). As we read the sonnets from *Contrée* and "Calixto," we may see that these formal poems bear witness to the greatness that Desnos achieved at the moment in his life when he, as well as his verses, were most constrained.

The Marvelous and the Myth

1945: One month short of his forty-fifth birthday, an emaciated man with huge dark eyes, wearing a tattoo from Auschwitz-Birkenau and a worn striped uniform, sits in the chaotic former concentration camp of Terezin, outside Prague. Two medical students, Josef Stuna and Alena Tesarova, look over the list of former prisoners, now patients, awaiting transport home. Stuna sees a name he recognizes and looks up at the man, who is weak from dysentery and exhaustion. He approaches him and asks, in French, "Do you know the poet Robert Desnos?" "I am Robert Desnos, the French poet," answers the man at the same time that the Czech student recognizes him from a Man Ray photograph, taken twenty years earlier (see fig. 15).

Ars Poetica

When Desnos was arrested on 22 February 1944, he left a dossier of poems on his desk with the title "Sens." "Sens" opens with "Ars Poetica," his most passionate poem about poetry (*O* 1241–43, *S* 146–48). Anchored with an alexandrine line—"I am the verse witness of my master's breath" (*Je suis le vers témoin du souffle de mon maître*)—the poem reads as a life-affirming cry. It proclaims an intense awareness of the body, intermingling slang and formal language in an ardent oral rhythm. The beat of the lines resonates like the heartbeat of the "I" in the poem, who is not the poet himself but the poetic verse that speaks through him. This premise harks back to the earliest definitions of automatism from the first *Manifesto*, wherein André Breton stipulates that the true surrealist listens to the murmur of his inner voices and is himself merely a "modest recording instrument" of them. Desnos asserts once more in this late poem that, while he may be the "master" who speaks the verse, he is a master whose being is governed by the poetry for which his breath is the medium. With this assertion he maintains the link between breath, passion, and expression articulated in July 1925, in his first of "Three Books of Prophecies" (only published in 1985):

prophet by my passions.
Passions of the heart
Passions of the dream
and by the Breath. (*O* 263)

Poetry, in the classically metered alexandrine refrain, is specifically linked to breath and also vividly associated with earth in the first lines—with mud, spit, vomit, and excrement. The earthy slang shocks, partly because it directly follows the title, which refers back to the classical tradition, dating to Horace, of the poet who transmits his most significant lessons concerning his craft in an *ars poetica*. Boileau's version from the seventeenth century went farther in linking the tradition of poetry with virtue and classical beauty. Desnos's turn at this tradition surprises because its inherently elevated form seems to run counter to the willful irreverence of his word choices, beginning with the opening lines:

Across the snout
Picked up in the mud and slime
Spit out, vomited, rejected—
I am the verse witness of my master's breath—
Left over, cast off, garbage
Like the diamond, the flame, and the blue of sky
Not pure, not virgin
But fucked to the core. (*O* 1241; *S* 146)

In addition to a play on form with its mixture of free verse and fixed-form lines and its high and low language, "Ars Poetica" circles back to Desnos's earliest surrealist writings in another way as well: it also enacts a play on gender. The verse line, the *vers,* which is masculine, is also feminine in the form of *la poésie* at the poem's beginning:

I am the verse witness of my master's breath
Fucker and violator
Not a maiden
There's nothing dirtier than virginity
Ouf! Here today gone tomorrow.

Even though the verse, *le vers,* is masculine, the "fucker and violator" in these lines is in the feminine: *Baiseuse et violatrice.* Masculine and feminine are interchangeable, in a poetic replay of Desnos's Rrose Sélavy double persona from 1923 and in his ongoing rejection of categorization. The voice's sexual ambiguity is interconnected with blatant sexuality and with the lowbrow language of slang often linked to talk about sex. For the language in this poem comes directly from everyday spoken conversation. Poetry is fertilized by popular language and made alive. Once again, as he did with the form and content of his "Rrose Sélavy" poems, Desnos rejects all hierarchies: masculine, feminine, high, and low culture.

Imminent crisis coupled with heartbreaking nostalgia threads through the poem:

> I am the verse witness of my master's breath
> That cracks farts sings snores
> Great storm wind heart of the world
> There is no longer a foul weather
> I love all the weathers I love the time
> I love the high wind
> The great wind the rain the screams the snow the sun the fire
>   and all that is earth muddy and dry
> And let it collapse!
> And let it rot! (*O* 1241; *S* 146)

The collapse of the world runs in tandem with the poet's great love of the world. His love spreads from the world's volcanic center to all those creatures who have ever emerged from its shell. It is steadfast and fearless, in keeping with a statement he made about Paul Eluard's poetry in 1940, in *Aujourd'hui:* "For my part, I prefer the poem to be fearless when faced with bad weather or mud" (*Mines* 43). His passionate Bataillean equation of humanity with mud is a continuation of his identification with the earth, which was manifestly apparent in "Calixto." It was Georges Bataille who wrote that the "Big Toe" is "the most human part of the human body" because it stands in the dirt (297). Desnos proposes his own version of Bataille's idea in this poem:

> A moon from long ago
> Is reflected in this rot
> Smell of death smell of life of embrace.

Sexual love, death and life are linked to the land.

The land creates a home for the poet that reflects a city dweller's appreciation of nature's riches: leaves look like toilet paper (*papier à chiottes*). This land is represented by the four elements: earth, air (breath and also the "great wind"), fire (in the flame linked to the diamond and the blue sky of the beginning), and water—the "I" promises to ride to the sea, where "I will come into your waves/After the worn-out river." These four elements evoke an entire world linked to poetry, as David Fontaine explains in his excellent article on "Ars Poetica":

Genesis of the world, genesis of the poem as well, according to the romantic equivalence between the making of the world and the *poïein* of the work: the language of the street . . . will be "picked up in mud" by the poet who, thanks to his divine breath, will give it the conscious and finished form of poetic verse—"like the diamond, the flame, and the blue of sky" (which is another alexandrine line). More precisely, in the midst of the poem-world, the poet creates the verse in his own image as a being who can witness and testify to it. From then on, the famous alexandrine line "I am the verse . . ." appears as the cogito of the verse. (110)

The urgency of the poet's need to leave behind a testimonial to his poetic being is reflected in the appearance of Orpheus three-quarters of the way through the poem. This Orpheus (a lover, a *baiseur* just as the poetic verse itself was a female *baiseuse* at the poem's beginning) is a broken man, "the skinned-alive one," who, defeated in his attempt to bring back his wife from the dead, is headed for his own violent death. The poet, too, seems destined for an imminent death. But in the interim the "I" maintains a stubborn optimism about walking with another "hand" in his own and seeking *la joie de vivre* with "men worthy of this name" as he emerges from walls guarded with passwords. The presence of passwords at the poem's close reinforces the use of slang, since both form languages that bind men with shared experiences and distinguish insiders from outsiders, strangers from Occupiers. With his mastery of these secret languages, Desnos tries to cross yet another divide, transforming speakers of slang into readers of poetry by infusing "verse" with the "breath" of the human voices from the overlapping communities in which he lived over the course of his life—from the workers at the Halles market in the Marais to the participants in the Dada and surrealist movements in Montparnasse to the working-class soldiers with whom he shared the boredom of the phony war to the anonymous men with whom he traded secrets in the Paris Resistance from his house in Saint-German-des-Prés.

Another of Desnos's last poems, "Vaincre le jour, vaincre la nuit" (not included in "Sens"), most clearly reveals the extent to which he felt himself to be condemned.[1] Its reference to the "I" as a hanged man in the last of the four quatrains evokes François Villon's "Epitaphe," known as the "Ballade des pendus" ("Ballad of the Hanged Men") and suggests that Desnos, like Villon when he wrote his "Ballade," felt that he was under a death sentence. Its rhythm also echoes a melancholic poem by another quintessentially Parisian poet who influenced Desnos: Guillaume Apollinaire's "Pont Mirabeau."

Desnos's poem resembles Villon's fifteenth-century "Ballade" in its tone of entreaty and despair. Villon wrote his poem in a prison cell, not knowing his sentence would be commuted the following day, after which he was exiled from Paris and disappeared. Like Desnos, Villon was of humble origin, proud of his populist heritage, and sometimes wrote in slang. Villon wrote about Paris—about the medieval neighborhood where Desnos grew up—and his voice literally resounds in his poetry, because of the traces of his Parisian accent in the formation of the rhyme schemes.[2] When reflecting on his own slang poetry in his "Notes Calixto," Desnos wrote: "a slang poem always sounds like Villon" (O 1229). Like Villon, Desnos was a scholar-poet-outlaw in the eyes of the French government of his time. He felt he too was fated to be arrested, exiled from Paris, and condemned "to disappear" in the euphemistic sense of the French term, which serves as a synonym for "to die."

The nature of the entreaty in Desnos's "Vaincre le jour, vaincre la nuit," however, differs from the entreaty in Villon's "Ballade." Whereas Villon's poem begs those "human brothers" who will come after him to have pity on him and those due to hang with him the following day—"Brother humans who live on after us/Don't let your hearts harden against us"—Desnos's poem is addressed to the city of Paris itself (Villon 209). The final quatrain cries out to Paris in despair:

> But my time, is it not wasted?
> You have taken all my blood, Paris
> At your neck I am this hanged man,
> This libertarian who laughs and cries. (O 1257)

In Desnos's poem Paris is a woman, a mother. The despair the autobiographical "I" expresses springs from the lonely and exhausting isolation of Resistance work, which he could not share with anyone, most of all his beloved Youki. The poet is despondent at the thought of disappointing Paris, the parent on whose neck he hangs. His sense of desolation is made more acute because, if he fails in his daily struggle for self-mastery, she will be the one he risks betraying. Written in a moment of supreme discouragement, he suggests that all his efforts will merely "plunge" him into the "unknown/Into numbness, into the impenetrable" because his ambitions are so hopeless: "To convert hate into hope/Into saints, evil words." For the despair provoked by the apparent impossibility of reprieve and redemption in Villon's poem, Desnos has substituted the hopelessness of achieving his own impossibly high goal of saving his beloved city of Paris from the moral depravity of collaboration.

The human grief of the speaker in the poem is communicated by its songlike rhythm, evident from the first quatrain:

Vanquish the day, vanquish the night
Vanquish time, which clings to me
All this silence, all this noise
My hunger, my destiny, my horrible chill. (*O* 1257)

This rhythm evokes the melodic refrain of Apollinaire's famous "Pont Mira-beau": "May the night come and the hours ring/The days go by and I remain" (*Vienne la nuit, sonne l'heure/Les jours s'en vont, je demeure*) (*Selected* 65). Apollinaire's poem bemoans the fact that love, once it is gone together with the pain it has induced, leaves no trace. The continuation of everyday life, conveyed by the repetition of the refrain, is seen as the dreaded antithesis to passionate love because it belies the intense illusion loves creates, which causes the lover to believe he will die without it. This sense of the continuation of everyday life is similarly conveyed in Desnos's poem—by the repetition of the words *vaincre, tout,* and *mon* (vanquish, all, my) in a melodic rhythm. The repetitions in Desnos's poem, however, project an opposite message from Apollinaire's: that everyday life could sustain the poet rather than emblema-tize the death of his fading passion. The banality of the everyday is exactly what the poet most desires, because the enduring love is not for a faithless human lover but for an endangered city.

The speaker in Desnos's poem fears that he cannot repress his own pas-sions sufficiently. He can neither strip down his human heart nor squash his active body "full of fables." The repeated words in the first quatrain, *vaincre, tout,* and *mon,* reveal not only everyday life but also the speaker's struggle within it: to control himself, above all. He seeks to master himself so that he might complete his mission: to prevail and not to die a "hanged man." The pure fighter, the poem implies, can persevere only with his heart, body, and mind stripped bare. But this takes "all the blood" out of this particular speaker, who is fundamentally an anarchist in every way, a "libertarian" whose nature resists all attempts to restrain himself, even if it is for a cause, a city, he loves deeply. He cannot make himself invulnerable but continues to laugh and cry. The poem's anguish comes from the poet's self-knowledge: his human vulnerability will most likely be his downfall, forcing him to give his life for "Paris" and for everything his hometown symbolizes.

"May Every Day Bring Joy"

Youki tells the story of Desnos's arrest in her memoir. Shortly after 9 A.M. on the morning of 22 February 1944, Mme Grumier from *Aujourd'hui* called to warn him that the Gestapo was looking for him. Instead of hiding himself, Desnos helped Alain Brieux to escape. Brieux, who had already been living in the Desnos apartment for about eight months at that point in avoidance of the

STO, recalls that Desnos quickly gave him a small packet and told him to throw it into the nearest sewer.[3] As he left the apartment, he "passed the men from the Gestapo on the stairs" (29–31). Desnos had time to escape, writes Youki, but he stayed in order to protect her (295).

Three plainclothed Gestapo policemen arrived at the door asking for Desnos. The officer in charge seemed chagrined to learn that he was at home and explained to Youki, apologetically: "They have forced me to do this police-work, but I am an officer."[4] At 9:25 a.m. the telephone rang. It was Jean Galtier-Boissière, to whom Youki whispered urgently: " 'Call me back in fifteen minutes, will you?' " (Galtier-Boissière 173). The other two agents discovered a handwritten list hidden in the back of a book binding, which included the names, nicknames, and addresses of Desnos's friends in the Resistance. The German officer began to read the list aloud: "Aragon—such and such an address, in Lyon," not understanding the significance of what he had in his hands. Youki claims he interrupted his recital in response to a look from her, thus preventing the other Gestapo "policemen" from hearing it. Asked about the list, Desnos replied: " 'I am not only a journalist; I am a writer and that is the list of art critics who can discuss my work.' " According to Youki, the officer quietly put the list into his pocket while advising Desnos to leave behind his gold watch, chain, and checkbook and to take some toiletries. Nothing seems to have come of this appropriation of Desnos's list; Aragon, for one, was not arrested as a result.

The officer would not tell her where he was taking Desnos but said gently that she should go to the Rue des Saussaies to find out. Youki was horrified to hear the address, since it was there that friends of theirs had been brutally interrogated in bathtubs filled with ice water. Desnos tried to comfort her as he handed her his favorite Parker fountain pen, given to him by Cuban friends in 1928. She collapsed in tears as he descended the stairs, while Mme Lefèvre had the presence of mind to drop onto his shoulders a wool cape that belonged to Brieux, her son. " 'That cape saved my life,' " Desnos later wrote Youki.

On the ninth of that month, barely a fortnight earlier, Desnos had begun a journal in which he seemed to be preparing himself for the inevitability of his arrest. In the ten diary entries Desnos records stirring memories from his early childhood and reflects on his legacy (O 1261–69). In this first entry, on 3 February, he evaluates Jean Giraudoux's legacy after returning from his funeral and indirectly compares it to his own. Of Giraudoux he writes: "The work of Giraudoux is of fugitive quality." His evaluation of his own work is similar:

> What I write here or elsewhere will, in the future, doubtless interest only some curiosity seekers now and then, spaced out over the years. Every 25 or 30 years my name will be exhumed in

certain private publications and some selections cited, always the same ones. The poems I have written for children will have a longer life than the rest. I will belong to the chapter of limited curiosities. But all of it will last longer than a lot of what has been written during my time. (1265)

Work that is "fugitive," however, or what might be called "everyday" writing, has few negative qualities for Desnos. "Why should the fact of being fugitive diminish the value of something?" he asks. He lists the cherished yet "absurd details which nourish memory and which die irremediably," such as the "ammonite I lost in the stables. The doves that nested in the shed. The bouquets of lily-of-the-valley, hyacinths, and also wild garlic!" He values ephemera for the way it focuses the body on the present moment.

At the time, he was preoccupied with a preface he was writing for a book of six Picasso reproductions. His preface, "Les Sources de la création: Le Buffet du Catalan," meditates on a buffet painted twice by Picasso in the restaurant where they used to meet together with Georges Hugnet (O 1177–81). Hugnet remembers that they saw Desnos there almost every night, either to share a meal or to pick up kitchen scraps for his cats (354). Picasso's painting of this piece of furniture invites the viewer to see with his own eyes, to see from "the place of the painter." For Desnos, Picasso's work conveys "veracity, possession, recreation, liberty, sensuality, exaltation," which, comments Desnos, add up to "very abstract contents for a buffet in a restaurant." Yet, in Picasso's abstract invitation to imagine what the buffet contains, there is the authorization to see it as a cornucopia overflowing with material goods, with "all the fruits of the earth and of life."

Picasso's genius, for Desnos, was to paint the potential pleasures of the present moment of looking and freely imagining and thus "to teach us that life does not measure its intensity merely according to the distance which separates birth from death nor upon fragile hypotheses as to life's cause or its end." As he stated in another essay from 1944, this one written in the transit camp of Compiègne after his arrest, "Quand le peintre ouvre l'oeil": "How to translate, with brush and color, the joy of seeing. For it is indeed the exaltation of the sense of sight that is in question and, through that exaltation, the provocation of ceaselessly accelerating pleasures, ever more exquisite and new" (Ecrits 184–85). This last question, of the pure joy of seeing a painting, Desnos posed in a short piece on Jean Py Eirisch, with whom he was by then imprisoned at Royallieu.

Joy and pleasure in the here and now were linked to a preoccupation with mortality. Three days before his arrest Desnos noted the following wish: "May every day bring joy," with the addendum: "If necessary provoke it, premeditate it." Life must be lived fully in the present because life on earth is all there is; we are most human in our mortality. In terms that recall the thinking of his old friend Bataille he wrote: "Man is only man from his birth to his death. Before as afterwards, he is only matter, even if his destiny as a man is determined by this matter" (O 1267).

In these few pages Desnos also recorded moments that had served to establish his own particular perspective in life. His very first memory opens the journal entry of 13 February. He explains that it dates from 1902, when he was only two years old and the family was still living on the Boulevard Richard Lenoir. He wonders if he made it up, from "some stories told in my presence by my parents, when I was five or six." He was being walked on the boulevard in a stroller and can remember that the stroller had a little protective awning over it, which shed a "soft shadow" over his head. Beyond this gentle shadow the sun was blinding, and he recalls seeing "soldiers in red trousers." He follows this early memory directly with another one from the same year, from the day when the family moved from the Boulevard Richard Lenoir to the Rue Saint-Martin. An employee of his father's had accidentally broken a coatrack in the move, and Desnos remembers being held in his cousin's arms and getting a laugh for repeating, in a child's broken French, "Raoul broke it!" (*C'est Raroul qui l'a caqué!*) (O 1267).

The final entry, written the day before his arrest, has the most striking memory, from the years when he was living with his family in the Rue Saint-Martin. He and his mother were returning from their shopping in the Rue de Rivoli when his mother suddenly squeezed his hand. He remembers asking her why. She seemed to come out of a trance, looked at him, and replied: "I thought they had changed you." It was as if she had felt the presence of a stranger in the body of her son. This disconcerting memory, where his own identity was put into question, seems appropriate to the musings of a man who feared his imminent arrest. Had he become someone other than his mother anticipated he would be, than he himself expected to become? In his forty-four years had he been consistent?[5] The remainder of this entry from 21 February 1944 lovingly recreates details remembered from his beloved Marais neighborhood, ending with an eerie memory that, in retrospect, seems to reveal that Desnos knew his world was about to change dramatically, and for the worse.

He remembers looking out at the rooftop of the medieval Saint-Merri Church, which stood catty-corner to his apartment building at number 11, Rue Saint-Martin, and watching men unfurl green shades over the church's glass cupola. It took him years to associate the ritual with the gloom in the church itself on Holy Friday.[6] He remembers the merchants on the Rue de la Verrerie behind the church, the significance of the sign over the candy shop for his child self, the women who plucked the stems off cherries, and the odor of the orange trees. He remembers the construction of the huge Bazar de l'Hôtel de Ville department store, which still stands close by, the beggar who occupied the corner of the Rue Saint-Bon (see fig. 3), the little girl from the Rue des Juges-Consuls, the fire at the local telephone exchange. The last sentence tells of a memory that puts everything that came before into a new context: "One summer Sunday afternoon, the cyclist and his wife (who was seated in a small wicker trailer) were knocked down by the La Villette-Saint-Sulpice omnibus." This is the final sentence in Desnos's diary—the description of two people in a picturesque neighborhood on a sunny summer day, almost literally run over by a bus. What story could better convey metaphorically the abrupt ending to his own happy idyll with Youki in the Paris he loved?

These memories conjure a man at a turning point, poised at an in-between moment in his life. The following morning his anxious wait would come to an end with the arrival of the Gestapo at his door. He was taken first to Fresnes prison, where he was kept for about a month and interrogated twice, and later sent to the transit camp of Royallieu in Compiègne, which André Bessière has called "the antechamber of deportation" (interview, 12 July 1999). At Royallieu, where he stayed a little over a month, Desnos wrote his last poem before being deported to Auschwitz-Birkenau. Ironically, in Desnos's final journal entries Compiègne is evoked as one of his favorite vacation spots. Desnos was intrigued by the many anecdotes linked to the forest in Compiègne. He posed a question about those anecdotes that in retrospect seems to refer to his own life: "How many years will it take before the memory of these human lives will be buried for ever?" (*O* 1265).

Acts of Resistance

Was Desnos betrayed? He was arrested less than four months before D-Day, an event that was widely anticipated (and expected in the Pas-de-Calais region), leading to preventive arrests of people with the reputation of being hostile to the Occupation (Azéma 179). Vichy, transformed into a police state by January 1944, created martial courts with the mandate to judge "terrorists," meaning anyone who was against the government (181). Robert O. Paxton notes that even after D-Day "some 80,000 Frenchmen were deported by the German police in the summer of 1944" (298). There were enough reasons to be suspicious of Desnos for the Occupiers to have arrested him at any point after the summer of 1942, but there is no evidence that he was betrayed. What may have attracted attention to him was his difficulty in silencing himself, as the anguish in "Vaincre le jour, vaincre la nuit" expresses. For, despite his need to keep quiet about his underground activities and his strongly held opinions, he was naturally a man "full of fables," who laughed and cried readily. Dominique

Desanti claims that he referred openly to Marshal Philippe Pétain as the "Maréchal Ducono" (as in his slang sonnet from "A la Caille") on the terraces of cafés; she was worried that he would get himself arrested for nothing (interview, 3 Mar. 1999). Indeed, to Josef Stuna, the Czech medical student who cared for him in his final days at Terezin, Desnos said that he was not arrested for his true Resistance work, his "principal crime"—the information he got through his position at *Aujourd'hui*—but for a "triviality" (DSN 986). Perhaps it was something as minor as his daily greeting at his local café ("This time they're done for"). Had it not, however, been for Alain Laubreaux, according to the accounts of Youki and Gerhard Heller, he might nevertheless have been released and survived the war.

Generally speaking, Desnos was arrested for "acts of resistance."[7] What did it mean to be a member of the Resistance? The first national "act" of resistance occurred very early, on 19 June 1940, the day after Charles de Gaulle's "call for resistance" on the radio from London, when Etienne Avachanne, an "agricultural worker," cut the telephone lines in an airfield occupied by the Wehrmact. He was arrested and shot (Azéma 75). Only in 1941 did Resistance networks and movements truly begin to develop. The major distinction among the groups was between the "exterior" Resistance organized in London by de Gaulle as La France Libre, Free France, and the "interior" Resistance, which was initially subdivided into multiple groups. The two types were not coordinated before 1943, when different groups began to merge and work together.

Jean-Pierre Azéma explains in *From Munich to the Liberation* that between 1942 and 1943 " 'fighting France' was at last emerging from the shadows: the internal Resistance and Free France were converging and their union prompted the various resistance movements to coordinate their action" (158–59). These movements included the Mouvements Unis de la Résistance (MUR), a movement that combined Combat, Libération, Franc-Tireur, and others, created in January 1943; the Conseil National de la Resistance (CNR), de Gaulle's group, created in May 1943 and presided over in France by Jean Moulin; and the Mouvement de Libération Nationale (MLN), created in December 1943, together with the Forces Françaises Libres (FFL), supervised by de Gaulle from England and North Africa.[8] In May 1943 the Comité Français de la Libération Nationale (CFLN) was created to consolidate the fusion of resistance policies in London and North Africa. Desnos's work fell into the category of the MUR, described by Azéma as part of the "civilian organization" (as opposed to essentially military organizations), which helped with the clandestine press (there were as many as 1,034 clandestine periodicals during the Occupation), liaison work with London, the fabrication of false papers, housing, and social services (156).

After the war, in 1954, Vincent Hollard, who had been active in the Resistance cell Agir together with Desnos, wrote a testimonial to Desnos's Resistance activities. He specified that the cell had been run by his own father, Col. Michel Hollard, and that the "direct and exclusive" reason for Desnos's arrest was his activity in this cell. He gives the precise date when Desnos joined Agir—25 July 1942, roughly a week after the roundup of Jews at the Vel d'Hiv on 16 and 17 July of that year. He elaborates that Desnos's duties included "direction of the clandestine press" and information pertaining to all aspects of clandestine publication as well as the creation and fabrication of materials helpful to members of the cell and to Jews. He further attests that these activities were "highly appreciated" and refers to an accompanying certificate, written in English and signed by Field Marshal B. L. Montgomery. Montgomery writes: "I record my appreciation of the aid rendered by Desnos Robert Pierre who, as a volunteer of the United Nations laid down his life that Europe might be free" (DSN 462).

André Verdet, who met Desnos through Jacques Prévert and who worked with the Combat Resistance movement, told me in an interview that roughly four days before Desnos's arrest, when they were having dinner together with Prévert, Paul Eluard came in and commented: "We're being watched; there are lots of arrests these days" (interview, 15 Nov. 1999). He referred to help Desnos had given him in his own Resistance work by transmitting "some diplomatic information," mostly about the Vichy government, gathered at the press conferences Desnos was able to attend as a journalist. Jean Galtier-Boissière claimed that everyone knew he was in danger of arrest. He told Henri Margraff, who was deported with Desnos: "We told him to hurry up and leave. But he was so stubborn [con comme la lune]!" (interview, 7 June 1996).

In the long run, however, it was perhaps an old rivalry that was the most dangerous to Desnos. He had never gotten along with right-wing journalist Alain Laubreaux, who was well connected with prominent Nazi officers in Paris and wrote throughout the Occupation for the collaborationist paper Je Suis Partout (I Am Everywhere) (which Jeanson nicknamed "Je chie partout"—"I bother everybody everywhere" [Galtier-Boissièrre 34]). He and Desnos had both worked in the 1930s for the same newspapers and magazines—Paris-Matinal, Le Soir, Vu, Voilà—and had never liked each other (Dumas 606). When Desnos was in Normandy at the end of the phony war in June 1940, he had written to Youki: "Yesterday I was delighted to learn of the arrest of Alain Laubreaux. That repugnant SOB was one of the people following us one night as we were leaving the Brasserie Lipp" (D 508). (Clearly, Laubreaux was released the following month, after Pétain's armistice with Hitler.)

Youki claims that Desnos was widely known to have said about Laubreaux: "I'll kick him until he spills his guts" (323). Desnos was not alone in hating Laubreaux. In June 1941 the actor Jean Marais, who had resented Laubreaux's criticism of Jean Cocteau's play La Machine à écrire, approached him in a restaurant and slapped him. A friend of Galtier-Boissière's commented afterward, " 'Now that I know it's possible to punch Laubreaux, I won't hesitate to do so, the first chance I get!' " (37). Maurice Bourdet, who had worked on the radio, also slapped him the following year, in March 1942, upon which Galtière-Boissière commented in his diary, "he joins the crowd" (*il joue la série*) (95). A month later, when Desnos took his turn and slapped Laubreaux in public in April 1942, he was following an established tradition (Dumas 266). It was, however, a slight Laubreaux would not forget.

From Fresnes to Compiègne

Desnos's first destination was the Rue des Saussaies for a preliminary interrogation. "No. 11 Rue des Saussaies, just round the corner from the Palais de l'Elysée," explains Ian Ousby in *Occupation*, "was the Gestapo headquarters. . . . Everyone knew that. Indeed, rather than saying that someone had been picked up by the Gestapo, people would often just say they had been taken to the Avenue Foch or Rue des Saussaies." On the morning of his arrest, when Galtier-Boissière called Youki back, she told him the German police had been there when he had called earlier: " 'They took Robert away. I'm going to try to take him something to eat at the Rue des Saussaies. Luckily he took a heavy coat' " (173–74).

The coat in question, Brieux's cape, was not the herringbone tweed overcoat worn by Desnos in several photographs from the 1940s (see fig. 16). That coat was left behind in the apartment. Two years later, in 1946, Youki gave it to the collaborator Jean Luchaire, who published a pro-German journal, *Les Nouveaux Temps*, during the Occupation (which Desnos's had had the idea to spoof with the title *Les Nouveaux Taons* [The New Gadflies]), when Luchaire was condemned to death by a firing squad. Luchaire had even published some poems by Youki in an earlier pro-German review, *Notre Temps*, poems that may, in fact, have been written by Desnos (DSN 913). Out of friendship for Luchaire and loyalty to his sister, Fraenkel's wife Ghita, Youki had testified for Luchaire at his trial (*Libération* reported on the status of his trial the day of Desnos's funeral). She had had pity on him when she learned that he was cold in his prison cell and terrified of dying; she gave him the coat to comfort him, and he died in it. Luchaire, condemned for acts of collaboration, died in the overcoat, pierced with post-Vichy government bullets, which had belonged to his old friend Desnos, who had also died but for acts of resistance.[9]

In February 1944, when Desnos was arrested, *Bonsoir Mesdames, Bonsoir Messieurs*—named for the first words ever heard on Radiola (later Radio-Paris), in 1922—had just opened in Paris, and there were posters for it around town. Desnos had attended the opening at the Paramount on 16 February (DSN 465). The film was by Roland Tual, who had participated in the hypnotic sleeps of 1922 and 1923 and had been a regular at the Rue Blomet. The delightful story, cowritten by Desnos and Jeanson, takes place in a radio station, where a happy-go-lucky employee, who resembles a younger Desnos, falls in love, organizes a radio singing contest, and has for his best friend a photographer resembling Man Ray. After the arrest Tual offered to help Youki pay for an Alsatian lawyer—Alsatians had the advantage of speaking fluent German. But the lawyer received her in a German military uniform, and she decided he was untrustworthy. She would have been a good judge. It was generally known that Youki, who believed in free love, had not been impervious to the ready cash of the German officers who had arrived in Paris in droves after 1940.

Despite the openness Youki had insisted upon throughout their relationship, however, Julia Tardy Marcus, who stayed at Rue Mazarine with Youki while Desnos was away during the phony war, insists that Youki loved Desnos "authentically" and did everything possible to get him released. Those who knew her have no doubt.[10] With the help of a friend she was able to talk her way into seeing someone at the Rue des Saussaies offices, where she learned that Desnos had already been taken to Fresnes prison just outside of Paris, and she was told that "German justice does not hold innocent men" (300).[11] Not in the least reassured, Youki hastened to take a large suitcase to Fresnes with Marcus in tow. Marcus was helpful because she was a native German speaker, having left Germany for France when Hitler came into power. Despite Youki's efforts, the suitcase was only delivered to Desnos on 6 March exactly two weeks after his arrest. He was interrogated twice while at Fresnes, on 3 and 4 March (DSN 878.382). Youki claims she managed to send him her photograph, using the willing prison chaplain as an intermediary (307–08).

On 20 March, when Desnos was transferred to the camp of Royallieu in Compiègne, Youki found out only when one of her packages was refused. In an extended quest to discover his whereabouts, she succeeded in reaching the director of the Red Cross, the count of Grammont, who gave her Desnos's identification number and location but advised her: "You don't know me" (310). This information was precious because care packages could only be sent with the correct prisoner identification number.

Youki also managed to obtain from Gerhard Heller at the Propaganda Office the private telephone number of Doctor Illers, the head of the Gestapo offices on Avenue Foch, who supposedly had the power to liberate any prisoner in France. She persuaded Marcus to call Illers and speak to him in German and learned that, although he would not receive her, he would accept a letter from Georges Suarez, the collaborationist editor of *Aujourd'hui*. Suarez allowed Youki to dictate the letter in question, to which he added effusive pages attesting to Desnos's "European qualities" and the caveat that, in his opinion, Desnos was a "perfect collaborationist" (of *parfaite moralité col-*

laborationiste) (315).[12] Youki's greatest hope was to keep Desnos at Royallieu, for she had learned that it was a transit station for concentration camps in Germany with terrible conditions.

"Marvelous Days"

Life at Royallieu was luxurious by comparison with what life would become for Desnos and his companions after their departure. Public talks and theatrical presentations were organized; priests said mass on a regular basis (Bessière interview, 12 July 2000). One former prisoner, Pierre Dumas, remembers that it was even possible to play soccer there (65). André Bessière, who lived through the same deportation trajectory as Desnos and who survived, explains in *Le Convoi des tatoués* that the camp had been built initially as a boot camp for new recruits in 1910 (28). It was then transformed into a military hospital between the wars before being taken over by the Nazis for prisoners of war in June 1940. Rebaptized "Frontstalag 122" in 1942, it became a deportation transit camp. The first deportation, of Jews, took place on 27 March 1942. The last transport was sent out on 26 August 1944, the day after Paris was liberated. (The train was stopped while still in France, and the final 300 prisoners were liberated.) A total of 53,787 men and women were deported out of Royallieu.

Having learned she was only allowed to provide Desnos with fruit at Compiègne, Youki assembled a package of apples, pears, grapes, and a lemon, a rare treat at the time. Despite the regulations, she made a roast, which she packed up with canned foods, a half-chicken in aspic, jars of jam and mustard, sardines, tuna, and crawfish, and even a small jar of honey. She also packed clothing—including a leather jacket, khaki trousers and boots, a hat, pajamas, cutlery, tobacco, and a pipe (DSN 462). This care package was of legendary proportions: the soldier who brought it to Desnos commented: "Your wife doesn't want you to come home, she's sending you all your things!" She soon learned that she could attach as much bread as she liked to the allowed five-kilo fruit package. By April she was delivering three kilos of bread at one time, obtained with ersatz bread tickets she made herself.

Youki went back to Compiègne to deliver another care package on 7 April, accompanied by her cousin Mitsou (a nickname, like Youki's, received from Foujita). Making conversation in the train with a "giant" of a man from Brittany, they learned that he was bringing wine for his son, something that Youki had not considered, since it was forbidden. As soon as she got to Compiègne, she added port and champagne to her package, which already included eau de cologne, nine packs of cigarettes, sausages, and chocolate (DSN 462). They met a man on the four-kilometer walk to the camp who found them later and told them he worked at Royallieu as a cook.[13] "Louis," a soldier from Bavaria, took down a brief message for Desnos as well as Youki's address and telephone number (318).

When she returned to Paris, Youki heard the reassuring news that Illers had telephoned Suarez to reassure him that "his protégé" Robert Desnos could remain at Royallieu, as a special favor. But then, just as she thought their ordeal was coming to an end, Suarez himself called and asked to see her, after receiving a very different message from the Avenue Foch. He curtly informed her: "May Madame Desnos consider herself lucky not to be arrested, since we assume she knows nothing. As for her husband, we have taken the necessary actions" (322).

Youki learned that the change in attitude had transpired at a dinner at Maxim's. Illers had announced to a group of Parisian journalists, including Laubreaux, that he was reviewing the dossier of a fellow journalist interned at Royallieu, whom he intended to keep there and then to release, and that his name was Robert Desnos. Apparently, Laubreaux interjected: " 'But Robert Desnos has no respect for you. He's anti-Hitler and a communist' " (323). Heller in his memoir, *Un Allemand à Paris,* confirms that this statement by Laubreaux was sufficient to make Illers change his mind and put Desnos on the list for deportation (183).

The train ride from Paris on Youki's next trip to Compiègne took twelve hours. This time Louis gave her a letter from Desnos, dated 19 April, in which he told her that he liked the people at Royallieu: "communists, Gaullists, royalists, priests, nobles, peasants. It's an extraordinary salad, which will make you laugh when I tell you about it" (320).[14] He mentioned Bourdet (who was not deported with Desnos), thanked her for the care packages, and wrote that he hoped she had bought the hat she wanted to match her new suit. He told her that he and seven or eight others shared their food packages among themselves. "The wine was a genius idea," he noted, "but they confiscate medicines and writing paper." He hoped she could get permission to visit him. He closed with the reassurance that: "everything will work out fine, and there is no doubt that this adventure is preparing marvelous days for us" (322).[15]

The next day, as Youki and Mitsou were delivering their care package, Mitsou recognized a German captain whom they had met at their pension. Youki boldly asked to visit the camp. He told her she was crazy, like all the French, who "have always hated us" and who are attached to Poincaré. To this comment she replied, "quite sincerely, 'Down with Poincaré,' " who, of course, from her point of view, had been an undesirable president because of his right-wing policies (324). The captain then spontaneously told her he would allow her to enter the camp, because it turned out to be 20 April, Hitler's birthday. Desnos was summoned. The wish from his letter written the day before was about to be granted. He wore his habitual buzz cut (*en brosse*) and the jodhpurs and leather jacket she had sent him: "Robert was looking wonderful" (*Robert était superbe*). When the officer left them alone for a few minutes, Youki blurted out that she knew he was going to be deported, despite all her efforts. Because "she had been careful to mention no names," she was astonished when he said, " 'Alain Laubreaux had something to do with this.' " " 'But don't worry,' " he promised " 'I'll come back,' " (325).

From Dreams of Soup to "Spring"

Bessière told me in an interview that he met Desnos at Royallieu, even though he was just out of high school and not at all in the same social circle (interview, 20 June 1996). He accompanied a friend, who took him to meet Desnos in his barracks. When they arrived, he was impressed by "Robert" in his elegant outfit—the khakis Youki had sent, which, to Bessière, resembled a military uniform. Desnos was laughing and explaining a dream he had had, which he had only just deciphered as a play on words. He said, " 'I was dreaming that I was drinking soup, all kinds of soup, and I was being forced to drink it, I don't know how much, and so it was spilling out all over the place . . . I was drowning in soup and I felt sick from it, sick from soup. So I said to myself, I've got to figure out what my dream means. Soup, soup. *Potage, potage.* How many syllables in *potage?* Three: *po-ta-ges* (he pronounced the *s*). Do you get it? *Po-ta-ges?* Ges-ta-po!' And everybody started laughing" (interview, 20 June 1996; 12 July 2000).

Bessière and Jean Bezaut, a friendly acquaintance of Desnos's from Compiègne, remember Desnos enveloped in Brieux's cape. Bezaut also recalls Desnos creating "Rrose Sélavy" one-line poems at Compiègne: *Tulipe en pot et pipe en terre* (Potted tulip and earthen pipes) and *A Coeur payant, un rien vaut cible* (Paid by the heart, a nothing merits a target).[16] Bessière went to hear Desnos give a talk on surrealism, although at the time he did not respond to the ideas. Nevertheless, he managed to make an impression on Desnos on another occasion, when Desnos and some friends from his radio days at the Poste Parisien—Bourdet, Rémi Roure, and René Hilsum—organized a couple of contests. The first, called the "The Unbeatables," *Club des Incollables,* involved fielding questions on any topic and knowing all the answers. Straight off, young Bessière won their respect by stumping them with a question about one of Napoléon's generals. He also performed well at the "Floral Games" of Compiègne, which were named for an annual poetry contest established by troubadours in Toulouse in the fourteenth century, the Jeux Floraux, and had "floral" prizes—"The Rose Prize" for the best poem on the night, for example, or "The Daisy Prize" for the best song about Compiègne (DSN 878; interview, 12 July 2000).[17] Bessière remembers well that the final contest, in which he was due to participate, was set for 26 April. It never took place because that afternoon seventeen hundred men were called up for deportation the following day, including Bessière, Desnos, and two others finalists of the Floral Games who would wind up at Flöha: Michel Garder and Henri Rödel (interview, 12 July 2000).

Also at Compiègne was the painter Jean Py Eirisch, for whom Desnos wrote an article extolling "the exaltation of the sense of sight" (*Ecrits* 184). Novelist and scholar Pierre Lartigue met Eirisch by chance in Compiègne years after the war, in 1969, when they were both waiting for their daughters to come out of school (Lartigue interview, 20 June 1996). Lartigue told me in an interview that he learned from Eirisch that at Compiègne Eirisch got cigarettes from the Nazi guards, in exchange for portraits. He was willing to barter some of his cigarettes with Desnos for poems. In this way Eirisch obtained and kept three poems written by Desnos at Compiègne. He in turn gave them to Lartigue in a notebook of his own sketches. They included two works written for musical settings that had already been published shortly after the war, "Song of the Road," which was dedicated to Eirisch, and the cantata "Soil of Compiègne." The third, the sonnet "Spring," is Desnos's last poem. Lartigue published it for the first time in 1969, in an article in *Les Lettres Françaises,* with a reproduction of the manuscript in Desnos's hand. He explained in the article how this poem was truly Desnos's last, not the one that myth has enshrined as the "Dernier poème" and which is inscribed in the stone walls of the Memorial to the Martyrs of the Deportation in Paris.

"Spring" is a sonnet, apostrophically addressed to Desnos's familiar alter ego, Rrose Sélavy. The poem evokes a sense of time in suspension, of baroque time, beginning with the moment of a flower's greatest beauty before its petals fall and decay:

> You, Rrose Selavy, wander out of reach
> In the spring caught up in love's sweat,
> In the scent of the rose budding on tower walls,
> in the ferment of waters and earth.
>
> Bleeding, a rose in his side, the dancer's stone body
> Appears in the theater in the midst of ploughing
> A mute, blind, and deaf people
> will applaud his dance and his spring death.
>
> It is said. But the word written in soot
> Is erased by the whims of the winds under fingers of rain
> though we hear and obey it.
>
> At the wash house, where the water runs, a cloud pretends to be
> the soap and the storm as it pushes back the moment
> when the sun will break the bushes into flower. (*O* 1259; *S* 158)

Desnos signed it with the date 6 April 1944, twenty-one days before he was sent to Auschwitz-Birkenau, and with his home address, 19 Rue Mazarine, in Paris and his telephone number. He was literally in suspension at the time of writing, awaiting spring, awaiting possible release or perhaps a "spring death."

The awareness of life's mutability comes through "Spring" in the "word written in soot" that readily disappears "by the whims of the winds under fingers of rain." It may also be sensed in the cloud simulating soap as well as the oncoming storm, while visually and temporally delaying "the moment when the sun will break the bushes into flower" in a kind of suspension of time—in an example of baroque time.[18] There is a comparable awareness of weakness and death evident in the sonnet as well. The "you" to whom the poem is addressed wanders freely "out of reach" and, even more literally "outside of these boundaries" (hors de ces bornes), within which the speaking subject remains confined. The rebirth of spring as a tangible event in nature, "caught up in love's sweat," coexists with a contradictory sense of containment, not only in the expression caught up but also within the walls, which refer both to the "constraints" of the sonnet's poetic structure and to the poet's prison, which is further evoked by the "scent of the rose budding on the tower walls." Spring coexists with the warning of incipient decay in the line "in the ferment of waters and earth," a warning that strikes the senses as much as it evokes a visual image of a moment of stopped time between one season and the next. This warning is further underscored by the contradictions, in the following quatrain, of the "dancer's body of stone," whose death is nevertheless still a "spring death."

Pétain's collaborationist and idealistically agricultural France is apparent in the sonnet's second stanza, with the "mute, blind, and deaf people" who observe the "drama" of the "bleeding" artist, represented in the poem as a dancer, and "applaud" his death. Indeed, those who collaborated turned a "blind" eye and a "deaf" ear to the struggle of their compatriots in the Resistance, like the dancer, whose "body of stone" would only be commemorated in statues after the war. Members of the Resistance had to make themselves seem to be impervious, like stone, in order to survive their ordeals. Some of them also willingly sacrificed themselves for the collective good of the community and, literally, for the possible rebirth of the land.[19]

The final image of the sun causing the bushes to flower brings the poem back to the more hopeful "scent of the rose budding" of the second line. It also highlights the tension between the image itself, of pure springlike beauty, and its temporal context, which situates it in the future tense, at a remove, as an instant delayed, possibly by a "storm." This image also draws the reader back to the emblematic name from the beginning, Rrose Sélavy, which unites woman and man—a woman's name as a playful disguise for a clever man—"prey to the sweats of love."[20] In Rrose Sélavy there is a rose, a cliché for spring and for hopeful love, for life and the promise of life. In the name there is also the intentional play on words: *éros c'est la vie,* "Eros is life." The erotic undercurrent of the scents evoked in the first quatrain—of sweat, lovemaking, flowers, and fermenting water and earth—are clear. A sense of life's limitations also becomes clear in the short phrase that opens the first tercet: "It is said." This phrase rings with a finality that is corroborated by the erasure of the poet's words inscribed in soot and by the state of suspense in which he is left in the final image, waiting for the inevitable outcome of the storm announced by the cloud. This is, indeed, all that Desnos will have left to say in writing.

"Spring" evokes life in the spring in such a manner that in this beginning lie hints of the end, concluding, typically for Desnos, on a positive note despite the melancholic images. Love is more abstract here than in Desnos's youthful love poems, and its evocation spans his own lifetime as a poet. The body of his work comes full circle with "Spring." Apostrophically addressed to Rrose Sélavy, "Spring" recalls Desnos's earliest surrealist poems and confirms that he remained true to his own surrealist principles until the end of his life.

A few days after returning home from her visit to the camp, Youki received a telephone call from an M. Darras, who owned a café in Compiègne and knew the man who went by "Louis."[21] He told her to come to Compiègne on 27 April: " 'We're waiting for you' " (326). No one was supposed to know about the dates for deportation. As a result, on that morning Youki was one of only about fifteen people, mostly women, waiting along the road to the train station. Even though the exact path was supposed to be kept secret, everyone in town knew because the prison authorities sent word the night before to the people on the streets in question, telling them to keep their shutters closed the following morning. Youki finally caught sight of Desnos at the tail end of the group, carrying the cans and blankets she had sent him. Just as he caught sight of her and waved, the prisoners were forced to run. Youki and Mitsou, unable to reach Desnos to give him the cigarettes they had brought, heard him shout, " 'I'll come back soon. Say hello to all our friends!' " (*Je reviendrai vite. Amitiés et bonjour aux copains!*) (328).

Two weeks later, when Desnos was already at Auschwitz-Birkenau, Youki received this note scribbled on cigarette paper: "Dearest—my kisses before the departure. I leave with confidence in you, reassured about your life and the behavior of our friends, just as I am confident of myself and my stars. Kisses to Lucienne [his sister] and all my kisses to you. Robert" (DSN.C.672). It was sent to her thanks to Louis, who had given it to an M. Pierre, who mailed it to Youki with his respects.

The seventeen hundred men who were put on trains to Auschwitz-Birkenau that day were apparently deported in reprisal for the execution of Pierre Pucheu by de Gaulle's troops in Algeria.[22] Pucheu, executed on 20 March, the day that Desnos arrived at Compiègne, was the first Vichy statesman to be condemned by French military men. At least through June 1944 the official Vichy policy was one of complete collaboration, as reflected in the *Aujourd'hui* headlines. A notice on the front page of the 12 June 1944 issue, six days after D-Day, warns all French citizens that they will not be protected if they join the Resistance and that they will be shot in reprisal if they do so. De Gaulle's competing French government took the opposite view—that all collaborators were traitors to "Free France"—and made an example of Pucheu. (Both his arrest and death were lamented on the front page of *Aujourd'hui* by Suarez, who called Pucheu's judges "felons; fearful, stupid bureaucrats" [22 Mar. 1944].)

Pucheu was charged with exchanging "intelligence with the enemy and putting the police at the disposal of the enemy" by the French Committee of National Liberation (CFLN) (Cointet 589). As minister of the interior in 1941, he had facilitated the arrest and execution of Communist members of the Resistance.[23] Through his active part in choosing those selected for death, he took the policy of collaboration to a new level that identified him more fully with the enemy than with his compatriots (Azéma 126). In *Destination Auschwitz avec Robert Desnos* Bessière explains that he and his fellow prisoners became convinced they had been sent to Auschwitz-Birkenau because of Pucheu's execution (156).

Bessière describes the train wagons into which the prisoners were herded as the size of an average dining room and asks the revealing question: "Can you imagine one hundred to one hundred and twenty people in your dining room?" (interview, 12 July 2000). The wagons had been built for eight horses or forty men. With their cargo of over one hundred men apiece, they became like "rolling coffins." The voyage began with a two-hour wait, as the sun beat down on the metal roofs. They had been given some bread and spicy sausage to eat but no water. Some died during the journey, which lasted four days and three nights. Thirst was the greatest hardship; some were driven to drink their own urine. Others went mad for lack of air, food, and space and from being forced to share the train cars with corpses.

When Desnos's convoy arrived at Auschwitz-Birkenau on Sunday evening, 30 April, a couple of eyewitnesses recall that those who acted out—like the man who ran off the train and tried to commandeer a Nazi motorcycle—were summarily shot. The group was then taken to "Camp Canada." Their barracks had dirt floors dotted with puddles from a recent rainstorm. Bessière said that "the after-taste of death" there was unforgettable. The next day they were stripped, shaved, showered, and dressed in striped uniforms.[24] They were tattooed on their forearms, with consecutive numbers from 184,936 to 186,590. Desnos's number was 185,443. It was his second tattoo; his upper arm still bore the Great Bear tattooed on him by Foujita in 1929, which was later seen by both Robert Laurence and Pierre Volmer at Flöha. Their tattoos bound this particular group; after the war they formed a survivor's association from the "convoy of the tattooed men," which continues to meet regularly to this day.

Alfred Smoular, who wrote about his deportation with Desnos in 1951, explains that once they were sent back to the barracks, Desnos had the inspiration to cheer up his comrades by telling fortunes. Smoular remembers Desnos saying to him: " 'Listen, we're going to make the time pass by giving them sweeter ideas. You interpret their dreams and I'll read their palms' " (6). He recalls that Desnos's predictions were often correct: on the men's characters, on a possible future accident in the south of France, of things to watch out for much later on. Bessière remembers Desnos cheering up a young man by telling him he would live to have three wives, who would wear him out when he was older (interview, 12 July 2000). Bessière also remembers that they were supervised by Polish "kapos" who hated the French because of their failure to protect Poland in 1939 and who taunted them, saying they would be gassed the following day. For thirteen days they had no idea what their fate would be.

On 12 May, after more men had died, 1,563 of the original group of 1,700 were sent to Buchenwald. Ninety-two, those too sick for the journey, were left behind. André Verdet wrote in 1974 that he believed they were spared at Auschwitz-Birkenau because de Gaulle had threatened to execute four thousand German prisoners of war if the convoy of the tattooed men was not released (O 1281; interview, 15 Nov. 1999). Some of the men believe it was because none of them was Jewish: Margraff, for example, claims that the commander of Auschwitz-Birkenau was very surprised to learn they were not Jewish (interview, 12 July 1996). Youki wrote in her notes on Desnos's deportation that, because they were a group of "Aryans," there had been "protests" about their fate (DSN 462.10).[25] Whatever the reason, for the two-day journey to Buchenwald their travel conditions were more humane: with only fifty men to a train wagon, they were fed bread and tea—what Verdet called "double rations" (interview, 15 Nov. 1999).

They arrived at Buchenwald on 14 May and were put into quarantine at the "little camp." They were assigned new numbers as well as red triangles with the letter *F* in black in the middle, to signify that they were French political prisoners, as opposed to regular prisoners, *de droit commun*, who were commingled with them. Desnos's acquaintance Robert Antelme, who arrived at Buchenwald three months later and stayed longer, explains in *The Human*

Race that he was told by his kapo on one of his first days at the camp: " 'Here, there aren't any sick. There are only the living and the dead' " (15–16).[26] Antelme explains how his will to survive arose from the fact that for him, "the calling into question of our quality as men provokes an almost biological claim of belonging to the human race" (5–6). Bessière insists, nevertheless, that Buchenwald was the best camp at the time: "death was not an everyday concern" (*la mort n'était pas au rendez-vous de tous les jours*).

One thousand of the tattooed were sent off again, ten days later, to Flossen-bürg, where they arrived on 25 May. Some of the convoy of the tattooed men remained at Buchenwald, including Verdet.[27] Verdet claims that, when they parted, Desnos said he wanted to leave because he wanted to "see more" of Germany; he told him, "I prefer not to contradict my stars, even if they lead me towards death, little brother" (qtd. in *O* 1281). Smoular confirms that a friend who had influence at Buchenwald tried to keep as many of the tattooed men with him there as possible, including Desnos, but that Desnos let himself be put onto the list of those slated to go onward (something Smoular thinks Desnos was in a position to resist) and said " 'I'm going to allow myself to be led by my destiny. I want to see as many camps as possible' " (5).

Near the Czech border in eastern Bavaria, Flossenbürg was dominated by a huge quarry, where many lost their lives. Bessière calls it an "extermination camp" (interview, 12 July 2000). It was also the main camp for a whole series of kommandos up and down the German-Czech border. At Flossenbürg yet another division of the group took place. Margraff, who was originally from Alsace and capable of speaking German, acted as interpreter. He remembers feeling frustrated with Desnos's stubbornness. For example, when the "thou-sand tattooed men" were told they could write a short letter to their families, Desnos asked Margraff to translate his letter into German. As soon as Margraff read it, he lost his temper and said: "I can translate it for you, but I can tell you right now that when the Germans see that, they'll throw it away along with everyone else's. Because when the s.s. say, 'You write: I'm here, I'm in good health, you can send me a package,' that's *all* you can write.' I called him names. . . . But then some mutual friends came along and straightened things out and we got over it. But it was a trick, anyway. They never sent our letters." Margraff saw Desnos as courageous but imprudent (interview, 12 July 1996).

When it came time to select the prisoners who were to go to Flöha, Mar-graff was summoned to accompany the s.s. officer in charge down the lineup and translate each prisoner's occupation. Desnos objected to being described as a "writer" and insisted that Margraff tell the officer he was a "man of letters." Only some quick editing on Margraff's part—the explanation that Desnos meant he was a journalist, "a correspondent"—saved him from a kick in the gut. The upshot was that on 2 June Desnos was selected to go with almost two hundred other men to a small kommando at Flöha, a town north of Flossenbürg near Chemnitz, close to the German-Czech border. Margraff stayed behind and almost died of typhus as a result of hard labor in the Flossenbürg quarry.

Desnos, with the others selected for Flöha, arrived at their new destination the next day, on 3 June 1944. In the previous month in Paris two of Desnos's books had been published: *Contrée* and *Trente chantefables pour les enfants sages à chanter sur n'importe quel air,* together with the pseudonymous poem "The Watchman of the Pont-au-Change" in the underground volume *L'Honneur des poètes.* The new prisoners worked and were housed in a "Tüllfabrik," an old red brick building that had formerly served as a textile factory, where they remained for eleven months, until mid-April 1945. They worked on the fuselages of Messerschmitt planes. Alongside them worked "voluntary" factory employees from the town of Flöha and from Belgium and Holland. These men would sometimes leave newspapers lying about, so that the prisoners knew about the advance of the Allied troops across France (Volmer interview, 10 June 1996). With the help of Pierre Volmer and Michel Garder, Desnos got the relatively easy job of sweeper, after showing himself to be almost incapable of making rivets, in perhaps yet another act of resistance (since his friends from the radio consistently praised his practical skills). Almost nine months later Desnos earned the admiration of the camp thanks to an act of foolishness or bravery that cost him twenty-five lashes and the destruction of his glasses.

The "Victim's Fate"

Life at Flöha fell quickly into a routine. The approximately two hundred Frenchmen lived under the eaves, on the top floor of the factory building. The factory was on the first three floors. They shared their lives with a majority of Russians, who numbered close to four hundred.[28] Desnos worked with Bessière and Volmer on the third floor (Bessière interview, 12 July 2000). They slept in three-decker beds that were comfortable compared with their lodgings at Auschwitz or Buchenwald, but they were tormented by fleas. Bessière remembers that Desnos made jokes about wishing he had some of the Marie Rose flea powder for which he used to write advertising jingles on the radio (*Destination* 223). There were roughly fifty faucets for the use of approximately six hundred men. Each man was provided with a sack filled with wood shavings for a mattress, a kind of pillow, and a blanket.

Habits were formed and friendships. Desnos and Bessière slept side by side on the top bunks, barely two inches apart (interview, 12 July 2000). Bessière and Volmer remember Desnos being most friendly with men closer to his age and social milieu—among them Henri Rödel, who became close to Desnos, told fortunes with him, wrote poetry, and died in deportation.[29] Also friendly with Desnos were Robert Laurence and Jean Baumel, both of whom survived and recorded their memories of Flöha. Laurence remembers playing bridge with makeshift cards with Desnos, Rödel, and a Parisian named Boynton (who, like Volmer, had not been part of the convoy of the tattooed men). Bessière remembers listening to them and noticing that Desnos was losing because the agreement was that the loser would treat the others to dinner and Desnos kept changing his mind about which of his favorite Montparnasse haunts would be the best place to celebrate his defeat (Laurence 143; interview, 20 June 1996). Like Bessière and Volmer, Clément Degueille remembers Desnos spending time with fellow Parisians of his own generation, although he was kind to everyone: "He always found the right words of comfort" (interview, 10 Nov. 1999).

The day after their arrival they were allowed to send a letter in which they were supposed to say they were in good health, adequately fed, and treated well. Thus, Youki received Desnos's first letter from Flöha, in which he requested food, socks, toothbrushes, soap, handkerchiefs, tobacco, and a pipe. No clothing. He closed: "I'm happy to have a wife like you and friends I can count on. I kiss you with all my heart, Robert" (O 1276). Only the signature, "Robert," is in Desnos's handwriting (DSN.C.673). On 6 June the prisoners learned from Michel Garder, who acted as a leader partly because of his ability to speak German and Russian, that the Allies had landed in Normandy (Volmer interview, 10 June 1996).

For the first six months Saturday afternoons and Sundays were free. With chits earned for good behavior, it was possible to buy extra food in the form of beets or pickled cabbage in the cantina. They were allowed to sleep from nine in the evening to five in the morning. Their exhaustion came mostly from hunger (Volmer interview, 10 June 1996). That Volmer saves as keepsakes the menus from the tattooed men convoy reunions is not coincidental. His major memory of his experience of everyday life at Flöha was hunger: "I was hungry. I was *hungry*. I was *hungry*. I dreamed about it at night." Baumel, citing a testimonial written by Jean Buisson, affirms: " 'If you asked those who survived Flöha what they suffered from the most, I think they would all answer: from hunger and cold' " (154). Desnos, together with Rödel, Baumel, and Laurence, was one of those who soothed his hunger pangs with food fantasies and inventive recipes. He liked to cook and had already written a "Précis de cuisine pour les jours heureux" (Handbook for Cooking on Happy Days), which was published posthumously (in *Rue de la Gaîté*). Bessière claims that he planned to publish his fantasy recipes after the war under the title "Imprécis de cuisine pour les jours peureux" (Non-handbook for Cooking on Fearful Days) (220).[30] Bessière said he himself could not bear to listen to these exchanges; he had no interest in "nourishment in the abstract" (interview, 12 July 2000).

Desnos persisted in his efforts to cheer up his fellow prisoners. He would tell bedtime stories for the high school boys, helping them to "escape" their hard living conditions. Bessière says he will never forget the sound of Desnos's voice as he fell asleep at night: "We explored the streets of Montparnasse from the 1920s; we had adventures with Picasso; we heard about the gossip from the Poste Parisien radio days; we learned details about the lives of the stars—Jean-Louis Barrault and Madeleine Renaud," although he never discussed his own personal life. Desnos also interpreted dreams, as he had on the radio, claiming the dreams he heard about were almost all erotic: " 'You dreamt about the Eiffel Tower? Oh boy, that's an erotic dream. You dreamt about a snake, last night? That's even worse.' " When Bessière questioned him on his interpretations one night, Desnos admitted that he made an effort to accentuate positive thoughts: " 'You can't tell someone who dreams he's hungry here that all he needs to do is eat more' " (interview, 12 July 2000).

Desnos also continued to tell fortunes, together with Rödel. Volmer remembers Desnos warning him that he would die at sea, which is why, he claims, he refuses to travel to the Isle of Jersey to this day. Bessière recounts that Desnos predicted he would marry twice and have three children—which turned out to be true. He also said that he would be rich when he reached the final third of his life; Bessière laughs at this prediction, saying "I don't think I've reached the last third of my life yet!" (interview, 20 June 1996). By casting himself as a seer, Desnos was making of himself an agent of the marvelous—of supernatural hope and blind faith in the future—in the lives of those around him and for himself.

The prisoners were fed one ladle of brownish hot water "called coffee" for breakfast, with fifty grams of bread and possibly some margarine. At noon they had soup made from dehydrated vegetables, a hunk of black bread with a round of sausage, a small spoonful of synthetic fruit jam, or perhaps a small chunk of margarine. For dinner they got two to three hundred grams of bread, depending on the day (*Convoi* 24).[31] Up until the end of December Desnos was one of the "privileged few," together with Rödel, who received care packages from home (the last one was sent by Youki on 14 Dec.) (Bessière interview, 12 July 2000; DSN 462). The combination of a relatively easy job as a sweeper—which he used as a means to pass news from one side of the factory to the other—together with the extra rations meant that Desnos maintained his equanimity until early 1945. Henri Pfihl, for instance, remembers his erudite charm as they waited in line for their "pittance" of food: "The poet had traveled, read, and observed a lot; his conversation was particularly interesting, and he would explain with a smile and good humor, which never deserted him, the origin of a word, the definition of another, or gave details about recipes—about which he was very knowledgeable" (*O* 1282). Bessière believes that it was because of his relatively easy circumstances that Desnos had the energy to tell stories and fortunes at the end of the workday and to devote time to others (interview, 12 July 2000).

When the extra rations stopped, however, Desnos's temperament changed, and he became cantankerous. Bessière explains that those, like him, who had been limited all along to the meals served at Flöha had grown somewhat accustomed to hunger. But for Desnos and Rödel hunger came as an unpleasant shock. Desnos stopped inventing recipes and began paying close attention to the thickness of their bread slices and the quantity of soup received. This fixation only got worse as the months passed because, as the Allied troops marched eastward and commandeered the land and the crops that fed the camps on the eastern border, the rations at Flöha were diminished even further. Moreover, the prisoners were all short of sleep because of regular air alerts, starting in January 1945, which forced them to spend hours in close air raid shelters and to work nights to make up for lost time in the factory.

The thickness of the soup dispensed at noon depended entirely on the whim of the server, who was normally a Czech named Anton. One day, Bessière thinks it was in mid-March 1945, they had only fifteen minutes in which to eat. When Desnos's turn came, Anton had himself spelled by "Willy the Kid," the head of the camp's personal favorite.[32] With a smile Desnos gestured to Willy, a young German Gypsy of sixteen, to dip the ladle deep into the tureen in order to get some of the vegetable bits from the bottom with the broth. Willy shouted, instead, and slapped him hard. Desnos, who had already part of his ration of hot barley soup in his bowl, reacted instantly by flinging it in Willy's face and burning him. Willy ran screaming to the head of the camp, while the head kapo grabbed Desnos, threw him to the ground—sending his glasses flying—and beat him brutally with kicks and with his fists. Desnos was left bloody on the ground, unable to see without his glasses. He dragged himself to the washbasin and refused to go the infirmary. Pfihl wrote that he had a very deep cut in his forehead that left a scar.

Desnos remained upstairs while the others went to the afternoon shift, because the camp commanders did not want the factory workers from the town to see evidence of their brutality. Pfihl and the others learned later that he had received twenty-five lashes without a single cry. They saw him unable to sit or lie down for days afterward, capable of walking only with small steps. He was given the worst assignments from them on, which he endured with "magnificent courage." He was told by the head of the camp that he would suffer the "victim's fate": had Willy died from his burns, Desnos would have been put to death.[33] He thus won the respect of everyone at the kommando, including that of the Russians, who, for the most part, took little interest in the French.[34]

Youki received two letters from Desnos at Flöha and was able to send at least two. In her first letter of response she explains that she had succeeded in finding Flöha on a map (DSN.C.818). She told Desnos that food was scarce because by July 1944 Paris had been cut off from Normandy. Even their cats had grown accustomed to eating soup. She told him that *Contrée* had just appeared and that it was a beautiful volume; Picasso's etching was "admirable."

Desnos's last letters, from July 1944 and January 1945, are well known and have been reprinted in the *Oeuvres*. They arrived in German on s.s. letterhead and had to be translated for Youki. The first one, from 15 July, opens: "Mein Liebling!" but has his signature at the end. It begins optimistically, as ever: "Our suffering would be unbearable if we couldn't think of it as a passing and sentimental illness. Our rediscoveries will adorn our life for at least thirty years. As for me, I'm taking a deep drink of youth, and I'll come back to you full of love and strength!" (*O* 1277; *S* 171). It is his most moving letter. He mentions working on his own birthday and sends greetings for hers, on 31 July: "I would have liked to give you 100,000 American cigarettes, a dozen dresses from the great couturiers, an apartment on the rue Seine, a car, the cottage in the Compiègne forest, the one on Belle-Isle, and a little four-sous bouquet." He also states that he has "a lot of ideas for poems and novels. I regret not having the time or the freedom to write them. But you can tell Gallimard that within three months after I get back he'll have the manuscript of a love story in an entirely new genre" (*S* 171–72).

In the very last letter, from 7 January 1945, when he and his fellow prisoners knew the Allied armies were getting closer, he included a power of attorney for Youki, since she was legally not his wife.[35] He mentioned his friends Galtier-Boissière, Jeanson, Barrault, and Hemingway as well as his sister, Lucienne. (His father had died just four months before his arrest, his mother in the 1930s.) He asked for tobacco and soap. And he sent comforting words: "I find shelter in poetry. It is truly the horse that runs free over the mountains that Rrose Sélavy talks about in one of her poems which, for me, still rings completely true." He is referring to the twenty-second poem from "Rrose Sélavy": "*Rrose Sélavy peut revêtir la bure du bagne, elle a une monture qui franchit les montagnes*" (Rrose Sélavy may don the homespun cloth of the prisoner sentenced to hard labor, yet she still has a mount capable of flying over the mountains) (*O* 503). The noun *monture* here clearly refers to a horse; at the same time, with Desnos's love of puns, it is possible to see the noun as also meaning "setting" or "frame," as in a setting for jewelry—that which holds the jewel in place, "constrains" it. He closes: "And to you, my darling, all of my love which will reach you somewhat cooled by the trip and translation. See you soon! All my love! R.D."

Nine months after completing "Spring," Desnos was still thinking of Rrose Sélavy as a person representing at once poetry itself and pure freedom. This sentence in Desnos's final letter to Youki confirms the idea expressed in his afterword to *Etat de veille:* it is not poetry that must be free, it is the poet. Every stretch of the imagination is conceivable within the kind of formal games typified by Desnos's "Rrose Sélavy" poems, which allow for at least two readings or meanings to overlap, to share one linguistic space, to "make love." He himself, at his least free, found emotional shelter in poetry, which within his imagination remained perpetually unconstrained.

Death March

On 14 April 1945, almost eleven months after their arrival, the Nazi soldiers in charge of Flöha evacuated the camp. American troops were just seven kilometers away, on the highway to Dresden.[36] Only seventeen men from the convoy of the tattooed men had died during that time, although they had been forced to watch the death by hanging of two Russians and a Pole who had tried to escape, in August 1944. Fifty-seven men were forced onto a wagon, while others were divided into two groups and sent eastward on foot, still minded by guards. Degueille remembers trying to climb onto the wagon and being pushed off (interview, 10 Nov. 1999). This turned out to be lucky for him, because the men in the wagon, all of whom were deemed weak or sick, were taken to a woods and shot. Rödel was one of the victims, together with twenty-three other Frenchmen (DSN 463).

Volmer and Bessière walked with Desnos on the "death march" that led from the town of Flöha, through the German-occupied Sudentenland of eastern Czechoslovakia—land that had been ceded to Hitler as part of the Munich Accord in 1938—toward Terezin, known to the Nazis as Theresienstadt, the large concentration camp northeast of Prague, which remained under Nazi authority until the war ended on 8 May. They walked for three weeks, with few days of rest. Some of them were shot; others died of exhaustion. Volmer remembers that they walked in columns of five; Bessière claims they progressed at the rhythm of approximately twenty kilometers a day. They received little to eat—two cups of ersatz coffee and four partially cooked potatoes a day—and had to watch their guards eat and drink as much as they wanted. They spent their nights in barns that André Lechevallier refers to as their "prisons" in a typed manuscript about "the march." Bessière credits the survival of himself and Desnos to wooden clogs that Christian Leininger found for them, taken from the feet of men who had died (242, 248).

Bessière remembers Desnos screaming one night because some Russians were trying to take his clothing from him, deeming him too weak to defend himself. All the prisoners at Flöha were dressed in the clothes they had been given upon arrival; since many of the Russians had arrived up to two years before the Frenchmen, they were literally dressed in rags by this time. Desnos had been severely weakened by his beating and the sustained lack of food; moreover, he was at least twenty years older than Bessière and Volmer, who had been seventeen and twenty-one, respectively, when they had been arrested. But Garder, together with Bessière and Leininger, intervened and rescued him. He was not wearing glasses and had trouble seeing. Bessière says that it was the first time Desnos had been heard to say: " 'I feel old now' " (interview, 20 June 1996).

One Hopeful Morning

Almost three weeks later, on a road not far from Terezin, Volmer, Desnos, and the others were loaded onto trucks and driven the rest of the way. They arrived at Terezin on the night of 7 May (see fig. 17). The next day the Allies won the war, and the former prisoners' guards disappeared. The night of their arrival they all slept in a group. Lechevallier writes in his manuscript, and in a letter to Youki from 1965, that they spent their first night in "a building of what had been the ghetto" of the town of Terezin (DSN 463). Many of them were suffering from dysentery, including Desnos. The first night in Terezin the stench was terrible, according to Bessière. The next day, 8 May, they were given showers, stripped of their flea-infested striped uniforms, offered civilian clothing, and sent to the then former concentration camp, a short distance out of town. Members of the Czech Resistance were present in the camp, and Russian troops showed up shortly thereafter to administer it.

Volmer remembers vividly the food care packages distributed to them by the Red Cross, because there were none for the Russians, since the Soviet Union was not recognized by the Red Cross. These care packages included sardines, paté, and chocolate (interview, 10 June 1996). Those who shared their rations with the Russians were fine. But the food was too rich for men fed for months on nothing but watery soup and diminishing quantities of bread. It was possible to die from too rich a diet ingested suddenly, and some of them fell ill, as a result. Once they were settled, the Soviet army fed them well, according to Volmer—that is to say, they were fed poorly, with only slightly more nourishment than what they had been given at Flöha or on the road: soup, a little vodka, and noodles. Such a meager regimen was what they needed to recover at a pace that would not shock their depleted systems.

Terezin was chaotic, filled with thousands of people speaking a variety of languages including Czech, French, Yiddish, Polish, Hungarian, Dutch, Romanian, Greek, and Russian. Rations were scarce, and Bessière remembers being given a Soviet uniform and a machine gun and being drafted to go to local farms in search of food (interview, 20 June 1996). Medical volunteers arrived from Prague. The entire camp was transformed into a free-form hospital, as former deportees arrived from all along the German border to mix with the newly freed prisoners from Terezin.

Originally an eighteenth-century fortress, Terezin had been transformed into a prison by the Nazis in 1940. It was used by the Prague Gestapo and as an offshoot of Flossenbürg throughout the war; by the spring of 1945 the prison was overcrowded with almost 5,500 prisoners, many of whom became patients once the camp was freed (Benesova 18). The entrance to the main camp, the "small fortress," is marked by a distinctive pattern of black-and-white stripes within massive brick walls. Inside those walls were directed the healthy prisoners, including Bessière. Others, including Desnos, were housed in barracks located outside the broad fortifications. Lechevallier remembers that Desnos was cared for in what was called the "Russian hospital" section of the camp. Alena Kalouskova Tesarova, a Czech medical student, claimed that there were over 100 patients in each barrack (O 1284).

Bessière remembers seeing Desnos one last time at Terezin, probably around 25 May. He was leaning on the arm of a man Bessière did not know and said to him, " 'I think I'm going to make it' " (interview, 20 June 1996). Bessière says he spoke extremely slowly and that he looked terrible (*il avait une tête de mort*), but he still was making jokes. He told Bessière: "I think I'm going to fart flames because of eating so much charcoal," referring to charcoal's legendary capacity to moderate diarrhea (interview, 12 July 2000).[37] Bessière never saw Desnos again; he caught typhus and had to remain in quarantine. He was repatriated in early June, along with several others. Volmer remembers lying in a Parisian hospital after his return and receiving a visit from Jean-Louis Barrault, wearing white pancake makeup for his role in *Les Enfants du paradis* (written by Prévert). Volmer was unable to tell him news of Desnos's fate at the time; he was so weak his own mother did not recognize him (interview, 10 June 1996).

There is a mystery about Desnos's last weeks, transformed into a myth by Youki and repeated in *Le Monde* in June 1995. In letters to Gaston Gallimard and Lechevallier, from 1958 and 1965 she claimed that Desnos could have left Terezin on a truck bound for Paris in late May or early June but that he had stayed behind to look for a metal box that had once contained chocolates. He had supposedly started a novel while he was at Flöha that he kept in a metal box together with letters from Youki and poems by his friend Rödel.[38] She believed that he refused the opportunity to return to Paris because he wanted to find the box before leaving Czechoslovakia and that he subsequently caught typhus from a flea in his sock (DSN 493).[39] That he refused the possibility of returning to Paris while he was at Terezin, or that he was even capable of making the trip, seems highly unlikely and is most certainly a myth. Whether or not the box existed, however, is more of a mystery. He had received chocolates from Youki at Royallieu, but it is very unlikely that the box could have survived the trip through Auschwitz to Flöha. Bessière told me in 1996 that Desnos had a small metal box containing his writings, which had possibly been made in the factory at Flöha (such boxes were not uncommon, given the materials available in the factory where they worked). He said at the time that he thought that Desnos had given the box to Rödel, who was shot in the forest outside of Flöha the day after the kommando was evacuated, and that it had been buried with him.

In his more recent written work on Desnos's deportation, however, Bessière suggests that Desnos had the chocolate box on their death march and that he lost it to the Russians, when he was attacked in a barn in western Czechoslovakia because they mistakenly thought it still contained chocolates (254). I have found no other confirmation of this story. There is no record of Youki having sent a box of chocolates in one of her packages to Flöha; it seems unlikely that the conditions of the march would have allowed a man of Desnos's age and weakened condition to carry anything at all. If the box ever existed, it has never been recovered.

On the morning of 4 June Josef Stuna, a Czech medical student who liked surrealist poetry, thought he recognized the name Robert Desnos on his roster of French patients. He approached the man in question and asked him: " 'Do you know the poet Robert Desnos?' " The man replied: "I am Robert Desnos, the French poet.' " Stuna confirmed: "The resemblance with the photograph of him in Breton's *Nadja* left no doubt" (DSN 986) (see fig. 15). Desnos told him that he had remained friendly with Breton and Eluard, that Breton had gone to America during the war but that Eluard had stayed in Paris. He promised to send him his new book on Picasso. He told Stuna the Germans had never learned his "principal crime," the result of his journalism, and that he had been arrested for a "triviality."

By that time he was suffering from diarrhea and a high fever that he had had for some time. He could not seem to keep down food and was tormented by thirst. The sanitary conditions at Terezin left a lot to be desired. When he was found by Stuna and Tesarova, he was in a room with roughly one hundred others, all of whom were suffering from thirst. Tesarova, a petite woman with green eyes and a soft voice who spoke French well and who helped care for him, remembers that Desnos smiled incessantly (Roy 2; O 1285).[40] He found the morning when he was discovered by these two French-speaking Czechs to be his "most hopeful morning" (*mon matin le plus matinal*). He marveled at the chance to communicate in French with people who knew something of his world. He asked many questions about Czech literature and was delighted with the pronunciation of the names of Czech authors. He invited them to visit him in Paris. Tesarova explains that he asked her to distract him by telling stories. She tried "to evoke a world of beauty where living in the everyday was normal" (*O* 1285). He would listen and smile. "He showed himself to be dignified, proud, tall." She found a rose and brought it to him. He would not allow her to take it away when it faded. It was incinerated with his body. He died at 5:30 A.M. on 8 June, less than a month before his forty-fifth birthday.

There is nothing surprising in Desnos's enthusiastic response to Tesarova's rose. It must have reminded him of poetry itself in the guise of his alter ego, Rrose Sélavy, and of "the scent of the rose budding on tower walls" of the fortress boundaries evoked in "Spring," written just a year earlier at Compiègne. This particular flower may have seemed like an ultimate confirmation of his belief that the marvelous lives in the everyday.

A Tender, Crazy Pirate

In early June 1945 at least seven newspapers reported that Desnos had survived deportation, that he was liberated and was on his way home.[41] Consequently, a little over a month after his death, in July 1945, Youki thought he was still alive. She wrote him her last letter in blue ink and in tiny handwriting to conserve paper. At the top she added afterward, in black: "Alas, Robert was already dead" (DSN.C.819). She told him she had seen Garder and Volmer and that Leininger was planning to leave for Czechoslovakia in search of him. She told him of the loyalty of their friends and that their cats Minouche and Jules were fine but that Zouzou, sick from cancer, had been put to sleep and died peacefully in her arms. She gave him the news that Suarez had already been shot and that she had testified at his trial because he had been helpful to her.[42] She also told him that Laubreaux had fled Paris.[43] She claimed that she had learned that Laubreaux had managed to get an order issued to have Desnos shot before he was deported from Royallieu but that Captain Muller, the officer who allowed her into the camp to see Desnos, had destroyed the order. Finally, she made him a moving declaration of her love: "I know what you've been through and the courage you've shown. I will devote my life to making you forget these nightmares—to loving you and to surrounding you with happiness. I'll see you soon, my darling. I send you a kiss as big as the Eiffel Tower. Your Youki."

Stuna managed to have Desnos's body cremated individually and his ashes sent to the French embassy in Prague. On 6 August Leininger wrote Youki a letter from Prague officially announcing Desnos's decease from dysentery and paratyphoid fever, based on a death certificate signed by two witnesses, no doubt Stuna and Tesarova (DSN 463.21).[44] About the same time, Youki recalls that a friend, Pierre Bost, telephoned to tell her the news of Desnos's death. He brought her a copy of the anonymous obituary article that had appeared in the Czech newspaper *Svobodne Noviny* on 31 July, together with a translation of the obituary into French he had received in a letter from someone named L. Vittet (332–33; DSN 463.16).[45] An adapted version of Vittet's translation, which had already somewhat altered the Czech original, appeared anonymously in *Les Lettres Françaises* five days later, on 11 August 1945. This anonymous mistranslation of the original article led to the creation of the myth that Desnos had managed to write a "last poem" on his deathbed at Terezin. Desnos's ashes were only repatriated two months later, on 15 October, the day of Pierre Laval's execution at Fresnes prison. Claude Roy describes the arrival of the plane at Le Bourget that Monday morning: a heavily laden man awkwardly emerged from the airplane with a cigarette in his mouth, carrying his hat, his luggage, his gloves, and an urn under his arm. Stuna and Tesarova were with him. A photograph on the front page of the Wednesday, 17 October, edition of *Libération* identities this man as an M. Lacombe. Shown in profile, he does indeed have a cigarette in his mouth and a black metal hexagonal object under his arm inscribed with Desnos's name and dates. The main feature in *Libération* that day was Laval's execution.

A personal letter from Lacombe's son Fabien to Pierre Volmer in 1987 attests that the unnamed man in Roy's article was indeed his father, who had been working at the French embassy in Prague at the time. He tells a somewhat conflicting story about the ashes by identifying the object under his father's arm as a cocktail shaker, not an urn, that his father had bought at his own expense because the French embassy refused to pay for an urn. He had it engraved with Desnos's name and dates and used it to transport the ashes. He explains that after Stuna and Tesarova brought him the shoebox with Desnos's ashes he had contacted Aragon, who asked Lacombe to bring back the ashes in person. Fabien Lacombe further explains that, in the excitement of his father's arrival at Le Bourget, he ended up with the ashes still in his possession at the end of the day. He decided to deliver them to Youki the next morning, who, half-asleep, "placed the cocktail shaker on the marble mantel, in between silk stockings and beauty creams." In the opinion of Fabien Lacombe, "this was a sign of Desnos's poetic posterity" (letter, 24 July 1987).

However the ashes actually arrived, by the following afternoon what looked like an urn containing Desnos's ashes was formally presented by a delegation of Czech writers to the French National Committee of Writers, of which Desnos had been a member. Speeches were made at the ceremony by Paul Eluard, Col. Michel Hollard, the head of the Agir Resistance network, and a representative of the Ministry of Education. Eluard described Desnos as a man with a double character: "Two men co-existed within Robert Desnos, each one worthy of admiration: one man was honest, conscientious, with a strong sense of his rights and obligations, and the other man was a tender, crazy pirate, utterly faithful to his loves, his friends, and all flesh and blood beings whose happiness and sadness, small miseries and small pleasures, he could feel passionately" (*O* 1289).

A funeral service for Desnos was held one week later, on Wednesday, 24 October, at the Church of Saint-Germain-des-Prés, across from the Deux Magots café. Galtier-Boissière describes it as a "first class funeral, church entirely draped in black, monumental hearse draped in the flag, hundreds of flickering candles, rain of silver tears, great music." Guests included Stuna, Tesarova, Eluard, and François Mauriac, who prayed for the surrealist poet's soul. Youki promised those who protested that Desnos had been an atheist that she would give him a Communist ceremony at their apartment, to which Galtier-Boissière retorted: "Robert Desnos was no more a communist than he was a believer. He was a man who was free [*C'était un homme libre*]" (543).

The Myth of the "Dernier Poème"

The myth that Desnos wrote a "last poem" on his deathbed has been much more persistent than Youki's story of the metal chocolate box. Although it seems obvious from the descriptions of the conditions at Terezin during the month of June 1945 that there was no spare paper with which to write, this myth continues to persist within French culture. Initially, the story was demythified by Adolf Kroupa in 1960. It was then explained again by Lartigue with the publication of Desnos's true last poem, "Spring," in 1969, and then the story of the myth was reiterated once by Kroupa in 1970. This has not prevented scholars from referring to the "Dernier poème" as authentic as recently as 1995. More specifically, on 31 July 1945, three weeks after Desnos's death, the Czech newspaper *Svobodné Noviny* (Free Gazette) published a short article about him in the manner of an obituary, whose title, in Czech, is a quotation from "I Have Dreamed So Much of You": "A hundred times more of a shadow than the shadow" (my translation from Adolf Kroupa's 1970 article in French, which includes his translations into French from the Czech). This short article concludes with the sentence: "His poetic lines therefore acquire a meaning at once more singular and more tragic," followed by a colon and the final paragraph of "I Have Dreamed So Much of You" translated into Czech. These lines from "I Have Dreamed So Much of You," in Czech, have been reordered so that, instead of reading like a poetic paragraph in prose form, as in the original French, they read like a verse poem.

Today it is clear that the supposed "Dernier poème" is a rewritten version of the last paragraph of Desnos's 1926 poem "I Have Dreamed So Much of You." Here is the "Dernier poème":

> I have dreamed so very much of you,
> I have walked so much, talked so much,
> Loved your shadow so much,
> That nothing more is left to me of you.
> All that remains to me is to be the shadow among shadows
> To be a hundred times more of a shadow than the shadow
> To be the shadow that will come and come again into
> your sunny life.[46] (*Domaine* 408)

And here is the final stanza of "I Have Dreamed So Much of You":

> I have dreamed so much of you, walked so much, talked, slept
> with your phantom, that all that is yet left to me perhaps,
> is to be a phantom among phantoms and a hundred
> times more of a shadow than the shadow that walks and
> will continue to walk gaily on the sundial of your life.
> (*O* 539)

Why has the myth of the "Dernier poème" been so successful? It developed through a slow process of mistranslation—a process driven, I believe, by a psychological response to the trauma of the war that provoked at least two individuals to "act out" rather than "work through" their emotions during the immediate postwar period.[47] Instead of working through the fact that Desnos died without leaving a final poem and accepting the sad fact, two individuals acted out in response to what they knew about the story of Desnos's death and, through a process of mistranslation, unconsciously created a fitting "final" poem for him. Such a process is not surprising, considering the fact that France as a nation is arguably still experiencing difficulty in reconciling the official policy of collaboration with its consequences—namely, the arrest and deportation of thousands of French citizens, most particularly French Jews.

The letter from L. Vittet to Youki's friend Pierre Bost, mentioned earlier, was dated 4 August 1945 and discussed with Youki shortly thereafter. It included two copies of the *Svobodné Noviny* article and a preliminary translation of it. A first mistranslation occurs in Vittet's version of the article's last line (which is, significantly, not followed by lines from "I Have Dreamed So Much of You"). Once again, the last line in the Czech article reads: "His poetic lines therefore acquire a meaning at once more singular and more tragic." Vittet's translation added keywords: "A singular and tragic *destiny* has given a concrete meaning to the contents of *his last verses, written for his companion* (*Svobodne Noviny* Newspaper, July 1st, 1945)" (my emph.; DSN 463).

Seven days after Vittet sent his translation to Bost, on 11 August 1945, *Les Lettres Françaises* published an unsigned French version of the article that was almost identical to the one by Vittet, except, once again, for a significant change in the last line. This time the last line was adapted partly because it was followed by an excerpt from "I Have Dreamed So Much of You," as in the Czech version. The excerpt is not identified as from *Corps et biens*, however, nor is it identical to the original from "A la mystérieuse": as in the Czech version, the lines have been rearranged to look like a verse poem. The last line of the *Lettres Françaises* translation reads: "[A] singular and tragic destiny has given a concrete meaning to the content of this poem *found on him* and probably dedicated to his romantic partner" (my emph.). Vittet's changes to the Czech obituary had already added the concept of "destiny" and implied that Desnos's "last verses" had been composed on his deathbed. The *Lettres Françaises* version changes Vittet's translation by adding the words *found on him*. It created the myth that when Desnos died he had a piece of paper in his pocket with the "last poem" written on it and that this poem was dedicated to Youki. The poem became known as the "Dernier poème" in large part because of the new title ascribed to the article in *Les Lettres Françaises:* "Le Dernier poème de Robert Desnos" (The Last Poem of Robert Desnos).

This article made the myth. As Adolf Kroupa clearly explained in 1960 and then explained again more explicitly in his 1970 *Lettres Françaises* article (in which he reproduced the documents in question), the 1945 *Lettres Françaises* translation claimed to relate "the final moments of Robert Desnos's life." It effected three significant changes from the Czech, to which it is otherwise identical. First, the title of the article was changed from "A hundred times more of a shadow than the shadow" to "Last poem of Robert Desnos." Second, the last line of the French article changed the meaning of the last line in Czech, which had already been changed once by Vittet. Third, the last paragraph of "I Have Dreamed So Much of You" is not cited from the original but retranslated from the Czech with certain liberties taken, so that it reads like a new poem. The addition of a variation on Vittet's last line for the article—"a singular and tragic destiny has given a concrete meaning to the content of this poem found on him and probably dedicated to his romantic partner"—becomes a self-fulfilling prophecy. It anticipates how French culture will preserve the legacy of Robert Desnos as a hero of World War II and as a poet: by blocking from memory Lartigue's discovery of Desnos's true last poem, "Spring."

It is possible to speculate that Vittet began the process of mistranslation unconsciously out of concern for Youki. His letter to Bost refers to a "telephone conversation" that may conceivably have involved Bost's expressions of concern about Youki, which could have precipitated an unintentional flourish by Vittet at the end of his translation. Knowing Youki was about to read his translation could have unconsciously influenced him. Yet this embellishment of the Czech obituary by Vittet seems to belong to a larger phenomenon because of the way in which the exact same sentence was once again adapted by another anonymous writer-editor at *Les Lettres Françaises*. This series of changes—from the original Czech article to the translation in Vittet's letter to the anonymous translation subsequently published in *Les Lettres Françaises*—goes beyond sympathy. It demonstrates how two French people—Vittet and the writer-editor for *Les Lettres Françaises*—responded emblematically not simply to Desnos's death but to the greater tragedy of the war experience. The result of these changes has been a myth that endures today, partly because, I believe, it relates to the nature of the French cultural memory of World War II.

Desnos has earned enough of a place in French cultural memory that two citations of his poems are inscribed on the walls of the Monument to the Martyrs of the Deportation in Paris. He is the only poet to be so honored. The monument, completed in 1962 by architect Georges Henri Pingusson, is memorable. It is constructed underground, behind Notre Dame cathedral, in such a way as to give the visitor the impression of entering a holding cell.[48] The remains of an unknown deportee are buried there. The romanticism with which the monument was planned is demonstrated in a 1962 brochure sponsored by the group Réseau du Souvenir, which was founded by survivors of German concentration camps and was instrumental in the monument's planning. This brochure describes it as a crypt, "hollowed out of the sacred isle [the Ile de la Cité], the cradle of our nation, which incarnates the soul of France—a place where its spirit dwells." The way the monument continued to be made sacred, specifically by de Gaulle in 1964, is illustrated by Henry Rousso in *The Vichy Syndrome*, in which he describes how it was used to romanticize further the myth of the Resistance. The cortège organized to take Resistance hero Jean Moulin's ashes to the Pantheon from Père-Lachaise cemetery first took the casket to the monument's crypt before bearing it to its final destination (84–90). Janet Flanner (signed Genêt), in her 1 May 1962 *New Yorker* "Letter from Paris," also lends it a sacred quality, likening its modernist style to Romanesque "holy architecture" (149). An article in the British *Architectural Review* adds that the monument was "financed by the State and partly from other sources, notably donations from school children sent from all over France" ("War Memorial, Paris" 186).

Based on the references I have been able to find to the monument, including a brief reference in the 14 April 1962 issue of *Le Monde* to its inauguration by de Gaulle, Flanner's may possibly be the only article to refer specifically to the inscriptions on the walls, which she describes as "difficult to read but rewarding" (150).[49] I have found no references to the manner in which the texts were selected, including the two ascribed to Desnos: "This Heart That Hated War" from 1943 and the "Dernier poème."

The ambivalence of the French regarding their role during the German Occupation in World War II has provided fertile ground for mythmaking.

Foremost among these myths is that of the French Resistance, created by de Gaulle after the war and finely elucidated by Rousso and by Paxton in *Vichy France*. This myth promulgated the belief that everyone in France belonged to the Resistance during the war. The "Dernier poème," like the other inscriptions in the Monument to the Martyrs of the Deportation, permits French visitors not to see what France has periodically sought to erase from memory about its participation in that war—namely, the fact that many French citizens collaborated with the Nazis in persecuting their own people, particularly the Jews (see Marrus and Paxton). I believe that the cultural force of the myth of the Resistance, together with the poem's appeal, have perpetuated the myth of the "Dernier poème," despite the fact that it was discredited convincingly in *Les Lettres Françaises* in 1960, 1969, and 1970, by both Kroupa and Lartigue.

There are many examples of the persistence of the myth, most significantly from the inclusion of the poem in René Bertelé's 1953 Desnos anthology, *Domaine public*, to the description by Carolyn Forché, of seeing the poem in the Paris Memorial and writing it down in its entirety because she was so impressed by it. Forché, who, together with William Kulik, translated Desnos's poems for the 1991 Ecco Press *Selected Poems of Robert Desnos*, notes that she has since learned, with regret, that the poem is thought to be "spurious" (Desnos 1991, xii).[50] Roy, in his article about the arrival of Desnos's ashes, Dumas, and Michel Murat all discredit the myth by omission. Lartigue reiterates his demythifying article in 1996, in a published version of a talk given at a conference in Reims sponsored by the Fédération Nationale des Déportés et Internés Résistants et Patriotes: "Desnos meurt à Terezin, le 8 juin 1945." The published debate after the talk communicates some of the emotion expressed at the conference regarding the poem: at least one listener, Henri Pouzol, publisher of a 1975 book on concentration camp poetry that includes the "Dernier poème," was upset to learn that it was not really Desnos's last poem, as he had believed since the 1960s. Lartigue told me of his own surprise at the vehemence of Pouzol's reaction. Lartigue responded with the argument that only the truth honors the memory of those who died (interview, 20 June 1996).

Differing Memories

The questions that come to mind include the following: why did the myth catch hold, and why has it had such a successful career? I believe there are several possible ways of considering the mythical poem that work together to form an answer and which rely both on its effectiveness as a moving poem and also on its sentimental value. Roland Barthes describes myth as functioning unconsciously, in a systematic way, on a collective group of people. He specifies that the experience of myth tends to be innocent, "not because its intentions are hidden" but because they are "naturalized" (*Reader* 118). I propose six readings of the "Dernier poème" that illustrate the ways in which it has been absorbed and naturalized by French culture. Since the creation of the myth, I believe the poem has been understood as: (1) a concentration camp poem; (2) a rewritten surrealist poem; (3) a patriotic love poem to France; (4) a reassuring Resistance poem; (5) a true Resistance poem; and (6) a touchstone poem for remembering Desnos's life.

First, it is not difficult to understand how a reader accepting the story of the last poem would find it haunting to consider that Desnos wrote this particular poem at the end of his life, in a concentration camp. Forché gives strong testimony to this reading: "I prefer to imagine that Desnos might have retrieved these lines from his wounded memory and spoken them again during the delirium of typhus; that they were perhaps taken down by the young Czech medical student who attended the dying poet, or by the young nurse, then made into Czech to be shared with others in the open-air hospital village that Terezin had become. The only support I have for this theory is that it seems plausible to my heart" (xii). Forché's response shows, in microcosm, how the myth caught hold and its sentimental power. Reading the love poem through an awareness of Desnos's experience in the camps makes the focus on the beloved even more poignant than reading the poem as a testament to love lost, the way "I Have Dreamed So Much of You" may be read. In the context of the last year of Desnos's life, the longing for an absent lover takes on a different meaning: she is no longer rejecting but loyal, while he suffers their separation as a result of imprisonment instead of the heartbreak of a failed love affair. The speaker's plight is more pathetic, even tragic, while the lover's response is no longer indifferent.

Similarly, when read through the belief that this poem was Desnos's last, the line "That nothing more is left to me of you," while still evoking an image of restless nights, calls to mind a nothingness coming from hunger and exhaustion more than from unhappiness in love. This sense is confirmed when the poet declares, "All that remains to me is to be the shadow among shadows." No longer the whimsical shadow of a surrealist poet who often played at crossing the boundaries between life and death in his automatically inspired writings, this "shadow" may be seen more tangibly as an accurate description of a man who, from starvation and overwork, became a "ghost" of his former self. The poem may be understood to anticipate the loss of life, not the potential loss of love. For within the poem the poet and his beloved change places—he becomes the shadow she had been in his dreams, while she takes the place of the dreamer who, in her dreams, perpetuates his memory.

A second reading of the poem involves seeing it as a rewriting, roughly twenty years later, of a previous, surrealist poem. To give credence to the notion that Desnos rewrote his most famous surrealist poem at the end of his life is to give credence to the thought that he remained surrealist throughout his life and retained his faith in the surrealist marvelous. It confirms the claim he made in the "third" manifesto from 1930, that the most surrealist surrealists were those who left the group. Accepting the thought that it would have been "natural" for him to rewrite one of his surrealist poems fifteen years after his split with Breton lends consistency to his work because it suggests that Desnos remained fundamentally capable of living as vividly in his dreams as in his conscious life. It gives hope that on an essential level Desnos was unbroken by the concentration camp experience, that his optimistic appreciation of the marvelous remained undaunted—as his references to poetry and Rrose Sélavy in his final letter to Youki suggest. This belief also carries sentimental weight because it would mean that Desnos rewrote a poem originally dedicated to Yvonne George for Youki.

A myth takes time to develop. By including the "Dernier poème" in *Domaine public,* the 1953 anthology of Desnos's poems, René Bertelé made sure that the mythmaking August 1945 *Lettres Françaises* article would be read as true. The inclusion of the poem on the walls of the 1962 Monument to the Martyrs of the Deportation had the same effect. Together with the other inscriptions, it was clearly intended to have a pedagogical impact, too, as the funding by donations from France's schoolchildren suggests. I believe that French readers sustained the myth, particularly in the 1960s, when the myth of the Resistance was strongest, because of the power it had in French cultural memory.

A third reading of the poem indicates why the myth could have taken hold in France. It is a love poem addressed to a French woman by a Resistance hero—who was heroic partly because he died, martyrdom having a canonizing effect. It is easy to see how someone who believes in the reality of the poem could project onto the last line, in which the poet is a shadow ("that will come and come again into your sunny life"), a patriotic vision of the woman to whom the poem is addressed, a woman who may substitute for France itself. She could be seen as loyally awaiting the poet in Paris and as the living being who will survive the war to lead a "sunny life" and to preserve his memory. The beloved in the poem, in fact, may be seen as both a long-suffering wife and as France, often represented by the symbolic female figure Marianne. To the credulous reader the poem's hopefulness about love could be interpreted as a Resistance poet's optimism about France, just as Desnos's bravery in the face of separation in love could be seen as an extension of his bravery during the Occupation and his acts of continued defiance in the camps.

It is no accident that the most famous Resistance poem, Paul Eluard's 1942 "Liberty," dropped by airplane over Occupied France, started out as a love poem to his wife, Nusch, only to become afterward a poem dedicated to "Liberty."[51] *Liberté* in the French tradition has often been represented as a patriotic woman, as in Delacroix's famous painting of Liberty marching on the barricades. Eluard's poem ends with the name anticipated in each preceding stanza:

> And with the power of one word
> I begin my life anew
> I was born to know you
> To name you
>
> Liberty. (oc 1, 1107)

This equation of romantic love with patriotic feeling in World War II captured the French imagination. In a talk from 1952 Eluard described his thinking in 1941: "Thus the woman I loved incarnated a desire that was greater than she. I equated her with my most sublime aspiration" (oc 2, 941). Behind the patriotism of Eluard's poem a passionate love story lingers, as, I would argue, behind Desnos's intimate love poem patriotism hovers. In both cases free France, long-suffering and patient, is conflated with a beloved woman. (This was not unusual, as indicated by a farewell letter written by a man who died for the Resistance, in which he refers specifically to France as "a great lady" [*la France est une grande dame*].)[52] Eluard and Desnos's poems reflect the revolutionary ideals of both poets and of the slogan "Liberty, Equality, Fraternity" in a way that consolidates a vision of France remaining true to its earliest republican roots. At the same time, in their evocation of love for a French woman, both poems are also quite nationalistic—as pronatalist policies before, during, and after the war indicate—because it was patriotic to make love to a French woman if the result was a French child and consequently an additional French citizen.[53] In leaving behind a love poem to his companion in Paris, Desnos could be seen as leaving a sign of hope for the next French generation.

Eluard's well-known poem paved the way for the mythologizing of Desnos's false "Dernier poème," leading to a fourth reading of the poem as a reassuring Resistance poem. As a patriotic poem by a Resistance hero—though it is also significant that Desnos was not a member of the armed Resistance, about which many French citizens had mixed feelings (Paxton 295)—it is emblematic of the heroism of those who worked in the Resistance, but it is also a safe touchstone for remembering the involvement of French citizens in World War II. The prominent display of this poem in the Paris Deportation memorial puts a soft focus on what is missing from that monument: a clear statement about those who suffered most from the war, the French Jews. Remembering someone like Desnos, who was heroic in his way but not Jewish, was easier for the French conscience, not only in the 1960s, when the myth of the Resistance was strongest, but also still today, as the belated and only very recent memorialization of the roundups of the Vel d'Hiv would suggest.[54] Thus, this false poem feeds into the myth of the Resistance because it is false. As a poem that was misread, mistranslated, and misrepresented, it encapsulates the process of revisionism, of acting out, that went into creating the myth of the French Resistance after the war.

Yet, at the same time, a fifth reading of the poem focuses on it as a true Resistance poem and points to a genuine admiration for Desnos's bravery as a member of the Resistance. It is perhaps easier to remember Desnos more as a loyal lover than as a man whose impassioned call to resistance sometimes fell on deaf ears and to admire him as a Resistance poet in the "Dernier poème," because it only indirectly evokes his actions in the Resistance. I believe the "Dernier poème" acts as a screen, or surrogate, for more combatively patriotic poems such as the one that is noticeably absent from the Monument to the Martyrs of the Deportation, "The Watchman of the Pont-au-Change." As a screen, it becomes a kind of site of memory in itself, onto which other memories about wartime French behavior get projected.

Finally, a sixth reading of the poem situates it in reference to Desnos's life and emerges from an attachment to the poet himself. Desnos, who was born on 4 July 1900 and died in a concentration camp not quite forty-five years later, may be viewed as a symbol for the vigor of intellectual experimentation in Paris between the wars and during the Occupation: because of his work as a surrealist and on the radio, because of his verses for children, which became instantly popular upon their publication in 1944, and because of his work as a journalist.[55] Just as a patriotic reading of his mythic poem evokes France as the lover looming behind the specific Frenchwoman from Desnos's dreams, so does a patriotic reading of Desnos's life transform him also into a symbol for France—dead young, brave, and passionate about love and freedom.

The myth of the "Dernier poème" probably will not fade completely, even though the poem does not appear in current textbooks.[56] It is fitting that it should be reevaluated at this time, when French culture is continuing to rethink its memory of World War II, because it reveals a multitude of French responses to the war—from a desire to perpetuate the myth of the Resistance by some to a tendency to represent patriotic emotion as an intimate love affair and a willingness to disguise weakness in patriotic feeling behind the soft focus of romantic sensibility. Most important, this myth has served the purpose well of keeping alive the memory of one of the twentieth-century's most prolific poets. A recent article about Desnos in *Europe* expresses the hope that the myth will never die because it helps to perpetuate a love for the marvelous: "They thought the various proofs would kill the legend. But in vain: the

'Dernier poème' by Robert Desnos is still cited here and there. How can we block the ears of those hungry for the marvelous, how can we refuse to hear the poignant song that rises beyond the leaning milestone?" (Cartier 129).

As we reconsider what I have called the "surrealist conversation" now, a half-century after World War II, Desnos's role in that conversation has been modified by his place in history and by the myth of his so-called last poem, which confirms his surrealist legacy. Certainly for his old friend Michel Leiris, writing in 1985, Desnos was consistently "surrealist all the time" (*Langage* 90). For one of the effects of the myth is the widespread recognition that Desnos returned to surrealism with his last words. In this the myth is correct for, as we have seen, he indeed returned to Rrose Sélavy at Compiègne and in his last letter to Youki from Flöha. As we have also seen, in his own terms, according to the principles of Desnosian surrealism, he never ceased to be surrealist, even when he was outside the Bretonian surrealist "conversation." He reentered the greater surrealist conversation at a juncture that, from the vantage point of the early twenty-first century, confirms his own, and surrealism's, commitment to one of the slogans that helped to launch the movement in its earliest years, Rimbaud's cry: "Change life!"

The Poetry of Courage and a Legacy of Liberty

When Desnos identified Victor Hugo's legacy as "liberty" in his clandestine poem "The Legacy" from 1943, he could have been predicting his own. Liberty was indeed the legacy attributed to him by Eluard in the week of Desnos's funeral: "To the very end, Desnos fought for liberty. The idea of liberty runs like a terrible fire through his poems, the word 'liberty' snaps out like a flag from his most surprising images; his most violent ones, as well. Desnos's poetry is the poetry of courage" (*O* 1289). Eluard was echoing Desnos's own words from the flyer for *Corps et biens: Toutes licences!* "Every liberty!"

"With the greatest liberty" was also the injunction Desnos gave musicians who might wish to set his words to music, in the afterword to *Etat de veille*. To his everyday poems he added songs, couplets, "composed with the ambition to propose to musicians texts resembling Spanish 'couplets' [*coplas*], Cuban 'sounds' [*sons*], or American 'blues.' They could use these with the greatest freedom—in cutting, the repetition of sentences, even in adding what they would like to add, with the hope that they would extend to the orchestras the same freedom for the execution of their music" (*O* 999; *S* 133).

This modesty may be seen as well in the self-effacing "Epitaph" he wrote for himself, as the final poem of *Contrée*. Describing a man who lived a hounded life yet remained "free amongst masked slaves," Desnos asks those who live after him whether they think about the past and whether they have built a better future:

You who are living, what have you done with these treasures?
Do you regret the time of my struggle?
Have you raised your crops for a common harvest?
Have you made my town a richer place? (*O* 1175; *S* 176)

This ability to imagine a future beyond his own death in which he himself has become anonymous is complemented by his grave in Montparnasse Cemetery. Made of simple stone in the shape of a casket, with nothing other than the family name inscribed on top, he shares his tomb with others in a communal family plot. No plaque signals the fact that the poet's ashes are buried here or that he died for his work in the Resistance during World War II. He has, in effect, become an "everyman" within French culture because of the way he lives on in the imagination of every French person today through his children's verses, internalized as the first poems learned, just as he had predicted in the two weeks before his arrest.

My term *Desnosian surrealism* has served as a way to think about the theories and practices of the surrealist movement overall—from the point of view of the one "closest to surrealist truth." Seeing surrealism through the figure of Desnos makes clear the extent to which his vision of surrealism was consistent from the beginning of the movement to the end of his life. Both Desnosian and Bretonian surrealism departed from the same starting point: Desnos's automatic performances during the period of sleeps. Desnosian surrealism, with its consistent adherence to the principles with which the movement began, represents a significant alternative to Bretonian surrealism. It shows how surrealism remained successfully pluralistic, playful, political, and dedicated to the marvelous in everyday life, as embodied in the person and the goals of Robert Desnos.

Most important, I hope that the concept of Desnosian surrealism has shed light upon the way that Desnos's own works and acts operate. From the 1920s through the Occupation Desnos showed how pliable and alive language can be, using poetic energy to illuminate baroque time, to focus intently on the oscillating present moment of experiencing poetry. His poetic legacy appropriately highlights the in-between frontier that fascinated him, the one that distinguishes high from low culture—the elite domain of high art from the public domain of publicity and popular culture. His ability to think while poised in the in-between of dream and waking consciousness during his earliest experiments with automatism helped to keep him alive through his final months by maintaining intact the sustaining power of his imagination.

Capable of maintaining his inner light in the face of crushing conditions while in deportation, Desnos the medium between his own unconscious and conscious minds, Desnos the poet who used the popular medium of the radio to interpret the dreams of a mass audience, became Desnos the medium capable of reading his fellow prisoners' fortunes at Auschwitz-Birkenau, Buchenwald, and Flöha in order to lift their spirits with hope. Desnos the love poet who longed for reciprocal love with one person became Desnos the political poet who finally achieved his goal in a reciprocal love that bound him to an entire country. Finally, his faith in poetry allowed him to persist in believing in the marvelous in everyday life. Poetry remained perpetually marvelous to him, despite all the indignities visited upon him.

The final word on Desnos indeed is *liberty* but only insofar as it remains linked to *love* in an echo of his own title, *Liberty or Love!* Just as he returned to his earliest surrealist pseudonym, Rrose Sélavy, in his last letter to his human beloved, he returned to Rrose's most salient characteristic for him—her absolute freedom, even in the most trying circumstances. Love within freedom, apparent oppositions reconciled through their equal vitality, constituted poetry for Desnos—liberty and/in constraint. This conflation of love and liberty was also life for him. As Desnos proclaims through and about Rrose Sélavy at the beginning and at the end of his poetic life: for him love is not only free; love is life.

Notes

Introduction

1. This vignette, like the ones that open the following chapters, is a fictionalized impression of a moment in Desnos's life, based on facts and interviews.
2. I date surrealism from 1922, when Breton first defines the word, to 1969, when the movement was declared officially finished in *Le Monde*.
3. Where possible, all references are to the *Oeuvres* from 1999. Those texts not included in the *Oeuvres* will be referenced to other volumes. All translations are my own, unless otherwise indicated. They are intentionally as close to the original French as possible. I have included all available translations in the selected bibliography; the English titles in the text refer to these editions. Parenthetical references are to the French editions listed in the bibliography; where a translation is used, both references are given with the French first. Where only a translation is used, only the English version is listed in the bibliography.
4. The important early studies by Anna Balakian, *Surrealism: Road to the Absolute* and *André Breton: Magus of Surrealism*, have also contributed to equating Breton with surrealism.
5. See Suzanne Guerlac's *Literary Polemics* for an excellent description of the Breton/Bataille polemic and Michele Richman's *Reading Bataille* for a study of the philosophical differences between the two.
6. See Chénieux-Gendron's *Surrealism*, Hubert's *Magnifying Mirrors*, Durozoi's *History of the Surrealist Movement*, and in particular Antle's *Cultures du surréalisme*.
7. See my article "La Nature double des yeux (regardés/regardants) de la femme dans le surréalisme."
8. Kiyoko Ishikawa's more recent *Paris dans quatre textes narratifs du surréalisme*, from 1998, devotes a chapter to Desnos. One of the first biographies of Desnos was written by William Kulik in his introduction to his translations of Desnos poems collected in the volume from 1972, *The Voice*.

9. See Guerlac's adept challenge to Sartre's view of the surrealist artist as occupying a "passive subject position," a stance she sees as defensive (46, 156).

10. He literally believed he had been visited by a ghost: in his "Journal d'Apparition" from 1927 Desnos recorded his visions of a ghostly female presence at night in his room (*O* 395–400).

11. The colors white, red, green, and black are connected to the alchemical transformations that allow the alchemist to transmute one substance into another, as is the smell of sulfur (Aromatico 69, 80, 82).

12. Gordon Wright gives the following statistic on literacy in France: "In 1870 probably a third of the peasants were still illiterate; by 1914, thanks to the Ferry school laws, almost all could read and write" (280).

13. Desnos would certainly have had to read the textbook *Le Tour de France par deux enfants,* for example. Its sermonizing preface concludes: "By thus grouping together all moral and civic knowledge around the idea of France, we wanted to present to French children, under the most noble guise, this idea of France as great, in honor, work, and profound respect for duty and justice" (Bruno 4). See Spector for more on the educational system during the Third Republic and its effects on the generation of the surrealists.

14. Marie-Claire Dumas specified to me the fact that the phrase *pour enfants sages* in the title was added by Desnos's editor, Gründ, whereas the subtitle, *à chanter sur n'importe quel air,* was requested by Desnos.

15. See Jean-Charles Chabanne's and Daniel Lançon's articles for evidence that Desnos is still one of the most widely read poets in French schools today.

16. De Certeau's approach to the everyday includes an evaluation of the "popular" in terms that Desnos might have appreciated because of his own resistance to categorization. Jeremy Ahearne explains that for de Certeau the popular "works as an unstable term for the analysis of hierarchical social organizations which divide a culturally 'productive' minority from a vast majority of apparently consumers" (161).

17. In *Non-Places* Augé focuses on the traveler whose anonymity in a crowd results in "entirely new experiences and ordeals of solitude" (93).

Chapter 1

1. The description of the group in Breton's apartment responding to Desnos's voice in the manner of "surprised utensils" comes from Louis Aragon's *Treatise on Style* (104).

2. Since 1974 the site has been transformed into a Métro station; the park above ground is traversed by paths named for poets, including André Breton and Louis Aragon.

3. Between the ages of sixteen and twenty Desnos had a variety of small jobs, including writing and translating pharmaceutical prospectuses for a neighborhood general store and working as the secretary to the writer-journalist Jean de Bonnefon, who gave him access to his own library, out of which Desnos read voraciously, and a card to the Bibliothèque Nationale; he was also mentored by the established poet Louis de Gonzague Frick (*O* 1356–57).

4. Jean-Jacques Becker and Serge Berstein give the statistic as 1.3 million in *Victoire et frustrations, 1914–1929* (156). Tony Judt, in his 27 June 1999 review of John Keegan's *First World War* in the *New York Times Books Review,* gives the statistic as 1.7 million.

5. Apollinaire first used the word *sur-réalisme* in the program notes for the ballet *Parade*—a joint venture by Jean Cocteau, Pablo Picasso, Léonide Massine, and Erik Satie—in May 1917. A month later, in June 1917, he identified his own play, *Les Mamelles de Tirésias* as "surrealist." The meaning and use of the word *surrealism* was contested by Ivan Goll and Paul Dermée, before Breton's adoption of the word became accepted (Durozoi 65–66). Adrianna Paliyenko further analyzes the Breton's ambivalence with regard to Apollinaire, specifically in light of the word *surrealism,* in her "Rereading Breton's Debt to Apollinaire."

6. In "Trois Notes sur *Corps et Biens*" Etienne-Alain Hubert qualifies Breton's choice of words to describe Desnos's aphorisms as suggesting "the homogeneity of a word establishing itself between light and shadow. . . . This process credits word games with a power of revelation as if they were so many infallible flashes from a projector" (119).

7. *Littérature* 6, 4. Murat points to the eerie coincidence that, in "predicting" Péret's death on that first evening, he in fact predicted an aspect of his own: "He will die in a train car full of people." In effect, Desnos died as a result of being deported, a voyage that began in an infernally crowded train car (*Robert Desnos* 13).

8. While in Barcelona, on 17 November, Breton gave a talk in which he praised Desnos as "the knight who has so far ridden furthest of all [*le cavalier le plus avancé*]. . . . Robert Desnos, who will be able to carry the torch far enough" (*OC* 1, 307; *LS* 125).

9. The apartment where I visited Breton's widow, Elisa Breton, in 1992 is situated directly upstairs from the one where Breton lived with Simone in the 1920s and is arranged in the same way, judging from photographs. Many of the objects from Breton's study may be seen in a temporary display at the Centre Pompidou in Paris.

10. In her essay about Breton's apartment Isabelle Monod-Fontaine quotes one of Simone's letters: "A room with noise and light, silence and shadow" (qtd. in *André Breton* 64).

11. I thank Janis Ekdahl, chief librarian, for facilitating my viewing of these drawings at the Museum of Modern Art. Mary Ann Caws has reproduced them in *The Surrealist Voice of Robert Desnos;* they have been reproduced in color by the Editions des Cendres's edition of Desnos's unfinished play from about the same time, 1925, *Le Bois d'amour.* They show to what extent the same man produced these lines and the automatic lyricism of his earliest surrealist writings (138–43).

12. The purpose of Breton's footnote is to reinforce the clarity and legitimacy of the first phrase he heard automatically ("There is a man cut in two by the window") by claiming that, as it came into his mind, it was accompanied "by the faint visual image" (oc 1, 325; *M* 21).

13. Desnos's drawings and paintings may be seen in the appendix to *Ecrits sur les peintres* and in the exhibition catalog *Robert Desnos, des mots, des images.* See the two catalog essays by Anne Egger in *Robert Desnos: Des Images et des mots* as well as her essay in *D* for more analyses of his drawings.

14. Dumas further notes that even Duchamp, who could have been offended by having his invented alter ego, Rrose Sélavy, appropriated by Desnos while in an automatic trance, responded to Desnos's antics with humor (47).

15. Limbour confirmed that " 'Robert Desnos could put himself into a second state when he wanted to.' " Desanti says that Desnos told her: " 'it's possible to be outside of oneself: here, it can happen to me even now as we speak: I can drop off like that, the way you are in the morning when you've first woken up' " (Desanti interview, 3 Mar. 1999).

16. In his talk "Robert Desnos parle surréaliste à volonté" Rothwell made the insightful point that the question of Desnos's sincerity still troubles critics today ("Surrealism in 2000: Celebrating Robert Desnos" conference in London, Nov. 2000 [volume coedited by Marie-Claire Barnet, Eric Robertson, and Nigel Saint, forthcoming with Philomel]).

17. Man Ray, who attended at least one session, comments on this as well (223).

18. Gérard Durozoi recounts that France was widely compared to the canonical literary giants Goethe and Montaigne (74).

19. The scandalous effect of the pamphlet was extreme enough to cause the wealthy couturier Jacques Doucet to suspend temporarily the financial support he gave to Breton and Aragon.

20. This classic example was published as part of a drawing in Picabia's journal *391,* in July 1924 (123). The artwork was then published again on the spring 1925 cover of the *Little Review.*

21. I explore this argument at greater length in the introduction to *Automatic Woman*. For an extended reading of the flacon Belle Haleine, see Richard Stamelman's "La Culture du parfum."

22. My reading of the visibility of Duchamp's masculine sexuality in Man Ray's photograph differs from that of Dickran Tashjian, who argues that Duchamp was not well enough known at the time to be recognizable through his disguise (43).

23. For more on Desnos as "not a nervous woman," see my article " 'Not a Nervous Woman': Robert Desnos and Surrealist Literary History," forthcoming in *South Central Review* (2003).

24. They were published in numbered form (1–150) in Desnos's 1930 collected volume of poetry, *Corps et biens*, and dated 1922–23. This publication differs from the original in *Littérature*, which included 138 unnumbered poems covering over eight pages. In the 1930 edition Desnos cut 24 of the original poems (reproduced in Dumas's book) and added 36. Manuscripts kept at the Doucet Library show that he actually wrote 199 of these poems, 25 of which were never published (Murat reproduces these in an appendix to *Robert Desnos*). I will focus here on the text published in *Littérature* in 1922.

25. For he does not, as Dumas explains, exactly repeat Rimbaud's formulation but, rather, something like "I seem like another" (*j'ai l'air d'être un autre*), which is different, because "under the appearance of another, the 'I' lives on unchanged" (*Etude* 132).

26. Twice in 1928 he implicitly postulated the notion of the fundamental bisexuality of human beings: first, in a newspaper article entitled "Madame! Qu'aimez-vous chez l'homme? . . . et vice versa" on the mysteries of the attraction of sexes, he used a pseudnoym, Pierre Guillais, composed of his own middle name and his mother's maiden name. With the use of his mother's surname he in a sense situated himself "under" the name of a woman, thus joining male and female identities (L'Herne 243). He questions the notion of gender as a clear-cut category again with the androgynous names Maxime and Fabrice ascribed to the hero and heroine of his play, from 1928, *La Place de l'étoile*.

27. In an essay on "new" novelist Jean Ricardou, Lynn Higgins describes anagrammatic writing in terms that also describe Desnos's project in 1923: "Rather than deriving from ideas which they purport to reflect, words themselves evolve and produce ideas, characters, stories" (473). Ishikawa makes an explicit connection between Desnos and the new novelists by comparing his writing to that of the authors of the *nouveaux romans* (184).

28. Adelaïde Russo makes a similar argument in her article on "Marcel Duchamp and Robert Desnos": "Puns change one's perception of language. The letters or units that create them become dual signs. Each exchanged

element has a 'memory' of its former position and previous context that it does not lose in its new ones. When we look at the words that comprise the pun, composition and repetition, elements of visual perception, become foremost, as when we are looking at a painting. . . . Symmetry, for instance, is irrelevant to the reader of normal prose narrative, whereas in puns, the plastic dimension is capital" (119).

29. Apart from Dumas's *L'Exploration des limites* there are several studies that look closely at the individual poems from "Rrose Sélavy," including Marie Paule Berranger's *Dépaysement de l'aphorisme,* Susan Frazer's *"Rrose Sélavy* et compagnie," Claude Debon's "La Question du sens dans *Rrose Sélavy,"* Etienne-Alain Hubert's "Trois Notes sur *Corps et Biens,"* René Plantier's "L'Ecriture et la voix," and Manuela Girod's "Mécanique et métaphysique." None of them addresses directly the question of Desnos's verbal cross-dressing.

30. My thanks to Philippe Met for talking to me about these observations of Leiris.

31. In "Sur quelques procédés verbo-visuels dans *Corps et biens*" Colette Guedj argues that the legibility of Desnos's word game poems is perturbed by their visual impact (86).

32. They are more elaborate versions of the word games played in the *Vampires* movies much admired by Desnos. For example, Irma Vep receives a message from the "Grand Vampire" on the ship that is destined to take her to a penal colony in Algeria. In disguise he hands her a card with the message "La vérité sera à nu" (Truth will be laid bare), which she immediately decodes and correctly reads as "Le navire sautera" (This ship will explode); she jumps ship and escapes back to Paris.

33. His good friend Georges Malkine addressed him as "Mon vieux Bob" in a letter from June 1924, indicating that Desnos toyed with an English identity (collection of Fern Malkine).

34. I have translated this line myself, since the word *prospectus* is lost in the existing English translation. (See n.3.)

35. Desnos had envisioned a published collection of poems that would have included the "Rrose Sélavy" poems with other word game poems from 1923, "L'Aumonyme" and "Langage cuit," in a book entitled *Désordre formel* (Formal Disorder).

36. In the 1930s and 1940s in the Marais telephones were shared, and children served as messengers to alert neighbors of a call (Costa 11).

37. Two of the episodes, numbers 6 and 10, were included under the general title "surrealist texts" in the first issue of *La Révolution Surréaliste,* in December 1924.

38. Desnos imagines death as the state that will unite him, finally, with his beloved in the *Mysterious One* poems from 1926, specifically in "If you only knew" and "No, Love is not dead" (*O* 541–43; *S* 16–19). The first chapter of *Liberty or Love!* consists entirely of an epitaph for himself: "Born in Paris, 4 July, 1900./Died in Paris, 13 December, 1924, the day on which he wrote these lines" (37).

39. *Liberty or Love!* also ends in shipwreck, which the debonair Corsair Sanglot survives, as Desnos suggests with his ending by means of suspension points (*O* 394, *LL* 30).

40. This line is from a dedication to M. Dausse, written in Desnos's hand on his manuscript for *The Night of Loveless Nights,* dated 2 April 1929 (Museum of Modern Art 2 S84 D51).

Chapter 2

1. Desnos's wax mermaid is owned by the community of Blainville Crevon; it was displayed in the Tate Modern version of the "Surrealism: Desire Unbound" show in 2001. The description of the symbiosis between Desnos and Malkine comes from an interview with Fern Malkine (20 Apr. 1996). The date of the writing of the first thirty-six stanzas of "The Night of Loveless Nights," first published as a book in 1930, is confirmed in the dedication to the 1930 edition: "A Charles Baron R.D. 1927." I thank Fern Malkine for giving me a copy of her father's inscribed copy of the 1930 edition.

2. Today Desnos's papers are stored at the Bibliothèque Littéraire Jacques Doucet.

3. This final line of Desnos's essay on Miró and the Rue Blomet studio is left out of the *Oeuvres* yet included in the earlier edition of Desnos's writings on art, *Ecrits sur les peintres* (146).

4. This portrait graces the cover of the *Oeuvres.*

5. "Exquisite corpse" is a folded-paper game in which several players compose a sentence or drawing in such a way that no one can see or know what the previous player has contributed until the work is completed. The classic example comes from the first sentence obtained in such a manner: *Le cadavre–exquis–boira–le vin–nouveau.* It was also at the Rue du Château that the surrealists began their "research into sexuality" discussions, starting in January 1928 and extending to August 1932 (see *Investigating Sex*).

6. Georges Neveux described the studio on Samy Simon's 1965 commemorative radio show dedicated to Desnos, broadcast in honor of the twentieth anniversary of Desnos's death.

7. There is a note in the Doucet Library from an M. E. Mailfert offering to buy from Desnos a drawing by Picabia, watercolors by Masson and Picabia, and paintings by Picabia and de Chirico (DSN 480).

8. This painting, in a private collection, has been reproduced in black-and-white in the *Oeuvres* (309) and in color in Dumas's article "Notes sur Robert Desnos" and in the catalog *Robert Desnos: Des Images et des mots*.

9. I also heard that this preference for women by Yvonne stemmed perhaps less from lesbianism than from a traumatic rape suffered when she was a young girl; I have not found written confirmation of these impressions.

10. This photograph may be found in *Robert Desnos,* a special issue of *Signes* from 1995 (113).

11. Fern Malkine confirms that Desnos and Malkine experimented with opium, too, but that her father told her that Desnos had the uncanny ability to resist the dependency that plagued her father throughout the 1930s.

12. See Dumas for the link between the swimmer in *La Liberty or Love!* and Youki (443–43) as well as my "Woman in the Bottle of Robert Desnos's Surrealist Dreams."

13. I am using my own translation here because it is closer to the French original.

14. I have examined the love relation and its connection to depictions of the writing process in *Liberty or Love!* in detail in my articles "Silence in the Heart," "The Woman in the Bottle of Robert Desnos's Surrealist Dreams," and "Going for Baroque in the 20th Century."

15. Unfortunately, I cannot give more precise references because I was only allowed to see the letters briefly, in the summer of 1993, and did not have permission to quote directly from them.

16. There is a postcard dated simply 29 July, with no indication of the year, but probably from 1929, that begins simply with the question: "So, it's over?" He asks, in essence, Will you really have nothing more to do with me? Have I not always expressed my affection for you? It is signed, "your friend, André Breton" (Doucet Library).

17. Breton had written a laudatory review of Trotsky's book on Lenin in the October 1925 issue of *La Révolution Surréaliste;* he and his second wife, Jacqueline Lamba, would visit Trotsky in Mexico ten years later, in March 1938.

18. Manuscripts of the *Second Manifesto* dating from September and October 1929 show that Breton began writing it just six months after the meeting at the bar of the Rue du Château (see Dumas 589 n.7 and n.8).

19. The only concession Breton makes to Desnos is to praise the curious coincidence that both of them wrote at the same time about the alchemist Nicholas Flamel (Desnos in *Documents* and Breton in the *Second Mani-*

festo). He adds a footnote pointing out that "this is not the first time that something of this kind has happened to Desnos and me" (oc 1, 819; *M* 174). Breton criticizes Desnos's choice of illustrations for the *Documents* article, but he adds that "Desnos played an essential, an unforgettable role in the evolution of Surrealism, and the present moment is probably more ill chosen than any other to deny it" (1, 811–12; *M* 165).

20. The editor of Bataille's *Oeuvres complètes*, Denis Hollier, claims that it would be "extremely risky to hazard a guess" as to the exact date of the collection of manuscripts concerning Breton published in the second volume (oc 2, 421).

21. This criticism of Breton by Bataille paradoxically seems to describe the movement of his own thinking in the 1940s, in *L'Expérience intérieur* and *Le Coupable,* according to Georges Didi-Huberman. Didi-Huberman characterizes this movement as "an *ascension towards a fall.* . . . This movement, let us note, proposes the reverse of the one favored by religious ascetic Christianity, in particular the movement according to which *humiliation,* the fall, is the best possible route to *elevation*" (355). The difference, of course, is that Bataille was drawn to the falling aspect of this movement, and, when he accused Breton of a similar trajectory, he probably assumed that Breton was not interested in the fall and was unaware that that was the direction he was headed, in Bataille's opinion. Amy Hollywood, in *Sensible Ecstasy,* also argues that in the 1940s Bataille focused increasingly on realities that stood outside everyday experience. This shift indicates the extent to which Bataille had come closer to Breton by the war and farther away from Desnos himself, who continued to be drawn to the intensification of the everyday experience. In fact, Michael Richardson's book on Bataille, *The Absence of Myth,* confirms that Bataille wrote the most on surrealism after the war, between 1945 and 1951.

22. In February 1930, when *The Night of Loveless Nights* was published in Anvers in book form, with illustrations by Malkine, Desnos dedicated a copy to his old friend without acrimony (collection of Fern Malkine).

23. Concerning Breton's personal life, Polizzotti explains that "Simone, although now living with Morise, still considered Rue Fontaine and its extensive art collection her domain, and over Breton's repeated objections she used the apartment as she saw fit. Matters were further complicated when Suzanne, whose marriage to Berl had settled nothing, returned to live with Breton that January. In an attempt to forestall Simone and establish her own domaine, Suzanne rearranged the entire studio, moving furniture, hiding paintings and books, and sending manuscript out for safekeeping" (311).

24. This photograph is reproduced in *Signes* (1995): 151.

25. The wedding was announced in the first (Feb.) 1929 issue of *Paris-Montparnasse:* "Foujita, the great, unequaled Foujita has just entered into appropriate matrimony with Youki" (Dumas 572 n.8).

26. The lease was in Desnos's own name, probably to spare Foujita any further difficulties with the French government.

27. Fragments of "Night of Loveless Nights" were published in 1928 (*Cahiers du Sud*) and 1929 (*Variétés,* in the same special issue as "A Suivre"). It was published in book form with illustrations by Georges Malkine in 1930 and later included in *Fortunes* (1942). "Sirène-Anémone" was published in *Corps et biens* in 1930 and dated 1929. "Siramour" was published in *Commerce* in 1931 and later included in *Fortunes*.

28. Paradoxically, these "liberties" taken by Desnos, as Michel Murat points out, coincide with a statement encouraging comparable liberties in Breton and Eluard's parody of Paul Valéry "Notes sur la poésie," published in the final 1929 issue of *La Révolution Surréaliste,* the same issue that includes the first version of the *Second Manifesto* (146). Murat has thoroughly analyzed Desnos's verse forms, both in *Robert Desnos* and in his earlier essay, "Desnos poète régulier."

29. The manuscript at the Museum of Modern Art in New York is handwritten on the back of "La Hune" letterhead—a bimonthly magazine "of the arts and of the sea" bearing a nautical mast heading.

30. Claude Cahun, who photographed Desnos (see fig. 9), wrote to him in her dedication of her own book, *Aveux non avenus,* that this poem was her favorite, she read it every day, and that for her Don Juan in the poem has "the same pearl-colored eyes as Desnos himself" (in the Guggenheim Museum show, Spring 1999, *Two Private Eyes*).

31. In her keynote speech on "Desnos and England" at the November 2000 "Surrealism in 2000: Celebrating Robert Desnos" conference, Dumas called this Desnosian hero Byronic. See Barnet, Robertson, and Saint. Perhaps Desnos was influenced by his friend Salacrou's translations of Byron at the time (Miró 101). Furthermore, Jean-Baptiste Para links both Dionysus and Bacchus to the even more primitive god Pan because of his instability and his link at once to madness and to the rescue from madness (154).

32. In *The Birth of Tragedy* Friedrich Nietzsche explains the Dionysian as "brought home to us most intimately by the analogy of intoxication" (36). "Under the charm of the Dionysian," writes Nietzsche, "not only is the union between man and man reaffirmed, but nature which has become alienated, hostile, or subjugated, celebrates once more her reconciliation with her lost son, man" (37).

33. Later Desnos would write a long poem uniting the two mythological figures: "Bacchus et Apollon" (1942).

34. Desnos's copy of the June 1929 issue of *Variétés*, which included "A Suivre" and a fragment of "Night of Loveless Nights," shows corrections by Desnos made to the text, which suggests that he continued to work on the poem until its 1930 publication in book form (Dumas 588 n.4).

35. Georges Neveux remembers, on Samy Simon's commemorative radio show (see n.6), that during the time Desnos was writing these poems he kept paper and pencil by his bed, wrote during the night, and often "discovered" what he had written in the morning, as though seeing it for the first time.

36. Armelle Chitrit sees a masculine protagonist, "Sir Amour," in the title (81). Dumas see it as a sign that Desnos has "surmounted the bipolar quality of 'Sirène-anémone,' erasing at once the dead anemone and the unlucky part of the word *sirène* (the rhyme between *ène* and *haine*, the word for hate) which figures in love" (*O* 595).

37. The line breaks differ between the original publication in *Fortunes* and the *Oeuvres;* the citations here accord with the 1945 edition of *Fortunes.*

38. This painting is reproduced in black-and-white in the *Oeuvres* (637) and in color in the exhibition catalog *Robert Desnos: Des Images et des mots.*

Chapter 3

1. Alejo Carpentier in "Robert Desnos et ses trois maisons magiques," Jean-Louis Barrault in his autobiography, Carlos Baker in his biography of Ernest Hemingway (301), and Dr. Michel Fraenkel in my interview with him all describe Desnos's Saturday parties. Baker mentions that Hemingway met the Dartmouth professor Ramon Guthrie at Desnos's apartment as well. My thanks to George O'Brien for first bringing this to my attention.

2. In the dedication of her book, *Aveux non avenus,* to Desnos in 1930, Claude Cahun calls his eyes pearl-colored, like spoiled oysters (included in the Guggenheim Museum show, Spring 1999, *Two Private Eyes*). Alejo Carpentier insists that Desnos was proud of having grown up in the neighborhood of Saint-Merri and that he fell easily into its local slang, "which contrasted curiously with the habitual care and style with which he dressed" (L'Herne 364).

3. Georges-Henri Rivière had an article in the first issue of *Documents.*

4. Desnos wrote an introduction to the first edition of Damas's poetry collection *Pigments,* in 1937.

5. This preference is linked to "fetal experience with the mother's voice." The study showed that "infants may be showing a preference for an intonation pattern characteristic of their mother's native language" (Fifer and Moon 352–54).

6. I cite here from Stephen Heath's translation in *Image-Music-Text*.

7. Mary Ann Doane calls this pleasure narcissistic because it is "derived from the image of a certain unity, cohesion and, hence, an identity grounded by the spectator's fantasmatic relation to his/her own body" (45).

8. I thank Mieke Bal for encouraging me to reread Silverman in the context of Desnos's radio work.

9. I thank Amy Smiley for discussing this aspect of the Duchamp/Desnos connection with me.

10. Marc Martin argues that, after the separation in 1933 between public and private radio stations, the combination of good programming and inventive ads (by such writers as Desnos, Jean Cocteau, Jacques Prévert, and Jean Anouilh) made advertising socially acceptable. Another indicator of this acceptance took place on the level of taxation. After 1934 products that were advertised were no longer taxed more than those that were not (237–39). Kirk Varnedoe and Adam Gopnik report that René Magritte also worked in advertising, as a designer and packager of advertisements (302).

11. He also switched from publishing in the journal of the first movement, *La Flèche*, to publishing in the journal of the second, *Commune* (Dumas 248). His timing may have had something to do with the fact that in 1936 Bergery published anti-Semitic remarks in *La Flèche* (Borne and Dubief 180). (Bergery later supported Pétain and worked for the Vichy government [*D* 520].)

12. He met the Chilean poet Neruda in the context of his connection to the Association des Ecrivains et Artistes Révolutionnaires (AEAR) (Desanti 283). He met Lorca through Carpentier. Desanti describes a friendship between poets who could read each other's work but not speak to each other: Neruda and Carpentier played the role of interpreters in discussions ranging from poetry to songs to folklore. Desanti writes: "each repeated 'Brother, brother' in the language of the other" (286).

13. That such enthusiasm for the Popular Front turned fairly quickly into disenchantment and an increasing number of strikes is not reflected in his poem.

14. Borne and Dubief explain that Hitler's generals warned him not to violate the treaty by entering the Rhineland and that Germany was prepared to retreat if the French army had crossed the border. But the army at the Maginot line was prepared only to cover the borders, not to penetrate into German territory: "The premier army in the world, theoretically capable

of including three million soldiers, seemed completely bereft of opera-
tional capacities. The army was organized for the defense of the country"
(55–56).

15. The Stavisky affair began when it was discovered that Alexandre Stavisky, a
con man, was being protected by the Parliament. He had appropriated
two hundred million francs worth of funds from fake bonds put out by
the Crédit Municipal de Bayonne in December 1933. In January 1934 the
police claimed to have found him dying in a mountain chalet. It was
widely believed at the time, however, that Stavisky had in fact been killed
by the police in order to cover up the government's involvement in his
scheme. There were antigovernment demonstrations in January. On 29
January 1934 President Albert Lebrun asked Daladier, a Radical, to head a
new government. One of Daladier's first decisions was to send the police
chief, Jean Chiappe, who had had personal connections to Stavisky, to
Morocco. The leagues of the far Right decide to demonstrate on 6 February to protest the dismissal of Chiappe. Gunfire was exchanged between
members of the Left and Right in the streets that night. Over the combined demonstrations, which stretched from 6 February through 9 and
12 February, there were thirty-seven deaths. By midnight on 6 February
two thousand people had been wounded (Borne and Dubief 109–11, 125).

16. Rosalind Krauss understands "listening" as an effect that not only produces surrealist writing but is produced by it, in her reading of The
Magnetic Fields, which she describes according to the "voice the reader
hears." That voice creates "an auditory space in which the tone of the
teller, 'speaking in the present,' emerges at each moment of the reading."
She cites Desnos as the originator of the explicit insistence on the "present
tense" within surrealist automatism ("Magnetic" 12–13).

17. Jennifer Gibson notes that Breton's idea for the "modest recording instruments" probably came from French psychiatrist Emmanuel Régis's Précis
de psychiatrie, which Breton borrowed from Dr. Raoul Leroy during his
service as an orderly at Saint-Dizier in Nantes in 1916 during World War I:
"Explaining the attitude necessary to conduct successful free association,
Régis compared the subject to a 'simple recording instrument'" (57).
Again in 1944 Breton claims pride of place for auditory experience: "The
great poets were 'listeners,' not 'visionaries'" (qtd. in Dumas "Le Chant"
234). In "Silence Is Golden" he asserted that "verbo-auditory automatism
creates for the reader visual images far more exciting than any of the visual
images that may be produced by verbo-visual automatism" (Free Rein 74).

18. In the early days, of course, the phonograph both recorded and played
back recordings from metal cylinders. Irma Vep, played by Musidora in
Les Vampires and so admired by Desnos, uses a phonograph in an episode

of the 1913 serial both to record and to play back the recording in a plot to swindle an American millionaire. (For Desnos's admiration for Musidora, see *O* 411.)

19. The serial was revived in *Le Petit Journal*. The name Fantômas had also been in the news in 1933 in connection with an espionage scandal in the navy known as "le complot 'Fantômas' " (Borne and Dubief 87). See Robin Walz's "Lament of Fantômas" in *Pulp Surrealism* for an extended study of Fantômas in French popular culture.

20. Simultaneously, Desnos wrote the scenario of an opera based on Fantômas, which was only published in the 1999 *Oeuvres* (759–65).

21. In a retrospective newspaper article for *Aujourd'hui*, 15 September 1942.

22. In 1932 Desnos wrote "La Ménagerie de Tristan" and "Le Parterre d'Hyacinthe" for the Deharme children (*O* 717–29). He wrote "La Géométrie de Daniel" for the son of Darius Milhaud (*Destinée* 146–50). These poems have been translated by Todd Sanders in *The Circle and the Star* (2000).

23. I thank Linda Simon at the Maison de la Radio for her time and generosity on 19 June 1996, when I visited the Desnos archives.

24. Simon made this comment in a commemorative radio program played in June 1965 to honor the twentieth anniversary of Desnos's death, into which Simon incorporated this brief recording of Desnos's voice.

25. Desnos was a fan of American jazz, blues, and big band music and had in his personal record collection albums by Ellington, Armstrong, Bechet, Goodman, Tommy Dorsey, Count Basie, Bessie Smith, Fats Waller, Jelly Roll Morton, and the Mills Brothers (listed at the Doucet Library).

26. Dumas credits this show with a political message, since it was aired "at the moment when fascism and mounting censorship were on the rise in Europe" ("Robert Desnos sur les ondes," *Signes* 121).

27. Another short show that ran concurrently with "La Clef des songes" was also interactive: "Le Quart d'heure de recreation," which Desnos broadcast on the Poste Parisien from May 1938 until February 1939. For this show Desnos would propose themes such as haunted houses or sundial inscriptions. The listeners would write in their responses, and Desnos would quote them on the air and respond to their opinions (Dumas 211 and 597 n.19).

28. One has to wonder if this invitation does not cast retrospective light on Desnos's hypnotic performances from 1922, suggesting that, while he may have occasionally simulated autohypnosis in order to push himself into a "real" second state, he found simulated and real automatic "dreams" equally productive of poetic material.

29. Selections of Desnos's radio scripts appear in the *Oeuvres* (850–51).

30. I thank Marie-Claire Dumas and France Culture Radio in France for making it possible for me to hear this recording.

31. This last phrase, of course, also echoes the opening to Breton's *Nadja:* "Who am I? If, exceptionally, I were to refer to an old adage: in effect does not everything come down to whom I 'haunt' or frequent?" (OC 1, 647).

32. Desanti claims (probably from conversations with Carpentier) that the tune used in the "Vin de Frileuse" advertisements were based on "l'air de la cucaracha," which Desnos had brought back from Cuba (interview, 3 Mar. 1999).

33. Examples of Masson's etchings may be found in the *Oeuvres* (778–79); as well as examples of Desnos's own drawings added to a copy given to his friend Jeander (Jean Derobe) (780–81).

34. Bataille's fascination with the symbol of the headless man led to the creation of a short-lived journal, in the 1930s, with the title *Acéphale*, although, as Dumas reminds us, the image of a man "cut in two by a window" was also at the origin of Bretonian surrealist automatism ("Guillotine" 76 n.1). In his diary from October 1979 Leiris refers to Desnos's poems and the journal *Acéphale* in a list with the notation: "Something that was 'in the air' from the start of the 1930s, the theme of the headless man" (*Journal* 721). The contemporary political scene may have reminded intellectuals of the bloody revolutions of the previous century.

35. Olivier Barbarant calls this collection a "condensed" Desnos in the sense that all of Desnos's idealisms and poetic experimentations are present within it; he compares it with Desnos's final statement about poetry, "L'Art Poétique" from 1943 ("Pétale" 160).

36. I have translated this line in the following manner: " 'You have the hello, / The hello of Robert Desnos, of Robert the Devil, of Robert Macaire, of Robert Houdini, of Robert Robert, of Bob's your uncle.' "

37. I thank the participants in the Humanities Institute on "Cultural Memory and the Present," conducted at Dartmouth during the spring of 1996, for stimulating discussions on the nature of memory and how it functions in the present.

38. This same issue of *Les Lettres Françaises* from 1945 launched the "myth" of the so-called "Dernier poème," which is discussed at length in chapter 5.

Chapter 4

1. In his review of Ernest May's *Strange Victory* in the *New York Review of Books* from 22 February 2001, Tony Judt points out that this standard view of France's defeat dates to Marc Bloch's *Strange Defeat* from 1940 but that some recent historians have contested the assumption that France was doomed to lose to the Germans in 1940.

2. Pierre Laborie describes the paradoxical nature of the French disengagement from loyalty to the Vichy régime while preserving a strong sense of loyalty to the person of Pétain: "Hoping for Germany's defeat and listening faithfully to English radio were reconcilable activities in the fall of 1942, with an intact loyalty to a 'purely French policy' for which the representation of Marshal Pétain remained the dominant symbol" (232, 236). A letter from 1954 by Vincent Hollard, whose father commanded the Agir network, attests that Desnos was arrested for his participation in Agir (DSN 462).

3. *Contrée* was partly financed by Youki's seamstress, Mme Lefèvre, according to her son Alain Brieux, who hid in the Desnos apartment for over a year (29). The new translation by Timothy Ades with the title *Against the Grain* (2003) was not yet available when I was writing this chapter.

4. In *La Guerre des écrivains* Gisèle Sapiro uses the expression *sémi-légale* to refer to Jean Lescure's literary journal *Messages,* in which Desnos published a series of six slang poems under the title "A la Caille" in November 1944.

5. The exact print run is listed in Imbert (80). As of 28 September 1940, the Nazi Propaganda-Staffel in Paris issued an official "convention" on the censorship of books stipulating that all publishers had to hand in two copies of their books to the Propaganda-Staffel (Loiseaux 74–75). It issued a total of four official lists of censored books: the "liste Bernhardt" in the summer of 1940 and three "listes Otto" in October 1940, July 1942, and May 1943 (Sapiro 34).

6. Babette Godet gave as an example of risk the name of Grou Abenz, who had printed works by Desnos and Michaux; he was eventually arrested almost at the same time as Desnos, and he never returned.

7. Michèle Cone writes that Picasso helped his surrealist friends earn money so that they would not be obliged to "get too wet with the Germans" by working together with him—since his work sold consistently—and that his contribution to *Contrée* was partly made in this spirit (L'Herne 208).

8. London radio transmissions, presented as "personal messages," were simple encoded sentences: "Andromache perfumes herself with lavender." "The postman has fallen asleep." "Grandmother is one hundred." "Jeanne is hungry." "We repeat: we will arrive ahead of you" (*Andromache se parfume à la lavande. Le facteur s'est endormi. Grand-mère a cent ans. Jeanne a faim. Nous répétons: nous arrivons avant toi*) (CHED).

9. Quoted by Hélène Eck in "La Radio" (190).

10. This essay is not included in the translation of the main text, *Strange Defeat.*

11. There is a lovely new translation of this poem by Stephen Romer in his edition of *20th-Century French Poems* (72).

12. See Desnos's November 1942 article in *Aujourd'hui* on mushrooms (*O* 877–79); he also wrote a "Précis de cuisine pour les jours heureux," which was published posthumously in *Rue de la Gaîté* (81–89).

13. My thanks to Dominique Carlat and Olivier Bara for discussing this poem with me.

14. The correspondence between Desnos and Youki from 1939 and 1940, while Desnos was mobilized, is at the Jacques Doucet Literary Library in Paris. Desnos's letters have been published in *Desnos pour l'an 2000*. References to the published letters will be identified by the abbreviation *D*.

15. Not before 1952 were the "chantefleurs" written by Desnos published together with the *Chantefables* in a joint, illustrated volume.

16. This and the other *Chantefables* appear thanks to the amiable authorization of Editions Gründ in Paris.

17. See Olivier Barbarant's "La Rime en 1943" for an analysis of how Aragon's and Desnos's approach to fixed-form poems differed in style (*D* 244–47).

18. In the 1964 preface to a new edition of *Le Libertinage* (not included in the English translation by Jo Levy [New York: Riverrun P, 1987]), Aragon explained his reasons for keeping the original dedication to Drieu: "I do not accept that the fascist he later became should erase for me today the face of our shared youth" (17).

19. It should be noted that, as the years passed, Parisians took measures to get food supplies through rural connections. Galtier-Boissière mentions that the first winter (1940–41) was the hardest: "From year to year we got better organized with food supplies. This winter [1943–1944], all of us, on every single floor of our building, from the Concierge's door up to the lodgers under the mansard roof, receive packages from the provinces. We are fed from the Mayenne, Brittany, Normandy, and Puy-de-Dôme, at more or less regular prices" (172).

20. Galtier-Boissière claims that, in an effort to prevent Suarez from taking over, the chief administrator of *Aujourd'hui* took an anti-Hitler article published by Suarez to the German propaganda office but that this document (entitled "Hitler, Pederast and Assassin") pleased, rather than discouraged, the Germans: "they are enchanted to 'hold' their strawmen" (20).

21. Philippe Burrin insists that, while several million French followed the policy of collaboration, many of them did so only "with resignation or scepticism" (463).

22. Sapiro explains that a third of France's novelists (and half the playwrights) "opted for collaboration" (90). Yet almost two-thirds of France's poets were involved in the literary Resistance. She argues that this may have been

because the poets were "accustomed to limited print-runs, to small publications which were mostly only read among small groups of initiates," and thus "almost predisposed to clandestine work and secrecy" (90).

23. Thierry Maulnier, who quit the collaborationist newspaper *Je Suis Partout* after France's defeat by Germany, published an article entitled "L'Assaut des médiocres" in April 1941, which understands the term *médiocres* in the same way as Desnos, as those intellectuals who embraced the collaboration and saw it as an opportunity to publish and win fame easily (Sapiro 177).

24. When Aragon founded *Les Lettres Françaises,* Desnos came to one of the meetings as a sign of solidarity, even though he was not a member of the Communist Party (interview with Dominique Desanti, 3 Marc. 1999).

25. Desnos also praised those French who persisted in helping their compatriots undaunted. One example, "A l'assistance publique," published in October 1940 (which, in manuscript form, is signed by the pseudonym Pierre Louvoit), was written in praise of public hospital workers (DSN 270).

26. For a selection of Desnos's jazz reviews, included by Yannick Séité in the appendix to his article "Robert Desnos 'critique de disques,'" see "Chroniques retrouvées."

27. There is added irony to Céline's comment because, in fact, the *beaux draps* of his title refer not only to "clean sheets" but to the idiomatic expression *dans de beaux draps,* meaning "to land somebody in a fine mess," which, in a sense, Desnos's review does to Céline, who then is able to turn the table on his reviewer, thanks to the political climate of the time (Collins-Robert).

28. Vincent Hollard, who worked in Agir with Desnos, stipulates that Desnos signed up on 25 July 1942 (DSN 462). A formal document from 1949 states that Desnos was an official "chargé de mission de 3e classe" in the Agir network from 1 April 1943 to 8 June 1945. This "official" status may be related to the new provisional French government established by De Gaulle in Algiers.

29. Babette Godet told me that she also transmitted carbon copies of texts she was given to type at *Aujourd'hui* to her own Resistance network (interview, 17 Nov. 1999).

30. Jeander was the pseudonym of Jean Derobe, a journalist friend of Desnos's (*D* 525).

31. My thanks to Jacques Fraenkel for showing me a copy of this card.

32. *Corps et âmes* was the title of a best-selling novel of 1943, by Maxence Van der Meersch (my thanks to Gerald Prince for bringing this novel to my attention). The plot presents a country doctor who tries to heal the

"bodies and souls" of his patients with a proper diet. The novel lingers over descriptions of copious meals—a pleasure in itself in times of deprivation such as the Occupation. A scathing review of it was anonymously published in *Aujourd'hui* in the weekend edition of 15–16 January 1944, in language that strongly resembles Desnos's 3 December 1940 review of Montaigne's essays.

33. I have not found statistics on the extent to which this call to action may have been followed.

34. When Desnos's old friend Benjamin Péret saw the two volumes of *L'Honneur des Poètes*, from the safety of Mexico City, he had a violently negative reaction to them, seeing in these fervent poems a hypocritically right-wing return to religiosity and patriotism. In his pamphlet *Le Déshonneur des poètes*, from 1945, he nevertheless expressed a similar concern to that of his former friends: "from every *authentic* poem a breath of total, active liberty escapes" (19).

35. Bessière dates this public reading of "The Watchman of the Pont-au-Change" to 27 October, three months after the liberation of Paris. He identifies Jean Martinelli as the actor who declaimed the poem (*Destination* 195).

36. The call to kill Germans, "A chacun son Boche," was printed in *France d'Abord* in October 1942 (Azéma 252 n.173). There is no evidence that Desnos killed a German in Paris.

37. The details of the publication of these poems come from Alain Chevrier's unpublished manuscript on Desnos's slang poems, *Poèmes en argot*. My thanks to Alain Chevrier for allowing me to cite his manuscript.

38. My translation is based on Chevrier's translation in the *Oeuvres*.

39. While the poem may also reflect homophobia on Desnos's part, his friendship with Jean Cocteau, forged during the Occupation, would suggest that it was not nearly as vitriolic as the poem on its own indicates (Youki Desnos 204; Cocteau in *L'Herne*).

40. Richard Zakarian wrote of Desnos's faith in poetry's regenerative powers in "Le Fard des Argonauts," from 1919, in terms appropriate to "Calixto": "Would it not be possible to interpret the poem as self-reflective and the poem and poet, incarnate in the ship Argo, illuminating the lie/*fard* through the beacon/*phare* of the written word and correcting obvious abuses exemplified in the glorified but nevertheless dishonest myth created by society for personal and interested reasons? Can the ship-poet rewrite the scenario and redirect society's energies by eradicating the legend/lie and redirecting life through the regenerative power of language and the poem?" (81).

Chapter 5

1. "Vaincre le jour, vaincre la nuit" was first published two years after his death, in July 1947, in *Les Regrets de Paris*. I am using my own translation here because, in the *Selected Poems,* Carolyn Forché's rendering of the verb *vaincre* as "to conquer" diminishes the resemblance I seek to underscore between the repeated word *vaincre* in Desnos's poem and the repetition of *vienne* in Apollinaire's "Pont Mirabeau" (*S* 162).

2. These insights into Villon's poetry, by Jean Frappier, are included in Emmanuèle Baumgartner's study of Villon's works (62–71).

3. An old friend of Brieux's, Lucien Scheler, specifies that the package was a packet of blank identities cards—with which he had made false ID's, like the one he had made for Michel Fraenkel (373). While living in the Desnos apartment, Brieux had created a design for "Sens" with the ambition of publishing it himself someday, under the imprint "La Margelle" (29–30). Brieux's name is still visible on the bookstore he later owned on the Rue Jacob, near the Desnos apartment.

4. A document in the Desnos archives indicates that Desnos was arrested at the order of "Herr Doktor Lang" from the Propaganda Office (DSN 462.13).

5. Valéry Hugotte argues that this reminiscence, which Desnos describes as persistent and recurrent, beginning with he was twenty, coincides with his commitment to poetry and that its record here confirms that he fulfilled, and remained true to, his own childhood dreams (*D* 219).

6. He wrote about this phenomenon in a 1929 *Documents* article.

7. In *Artists under Vichy* Michèle Cone tells the story that "Desnos was arrested when a young boy carrying tracts was stopped and searched by the Nazi, and revealed, among other names, that of Desnos and his address" (232 n.53). I have found no corroboration of this story.

8. The Forces Françaises de l'Intérieur (FFI) was created only in the late spring of 1944 and reorganized all the various Resistance groups under the leadership of General Koenig in London (Azéma 193).

9. This story was reported to me by Marie-Claire Dumas, who knew Youki and interviewed her extensively (Nov. 1999).

10. In the Desnos archives is a letter Youki wrote to a former model of Foujita's, Minima Becker, wife of Arno Becker, whose paintings were celebrated during the Occupation. Her draft for the letter, with sentences crossed out, communicates the anguish she felt and the hope she had that this former friend would come to her rescue: "Robert Desnos is an exquisite human being, a great poet—a man of letters, in short—who has nothing to do with politics. . . . If only you and your husband could intervene on his behalf." There is no reply in her files (DSN 462.57).

11. The story of Desnos's arrest and deportation from Youki's point of view comes from her memoir, *Les Confidances de Youki*.

12. In the Desnos archives is a draft of the letter by Youki from Suarez to Illers in which she attests that Otto Abetz himself had asked for clemency for and begs for an audience for Desnos's wife, who is "assured of her husband's innocence" (DSN 462.52).

13. Renée Coppin-Belleville gives the distance to the camp as four kilometers in her memoir, *Si Compiègne fut cela . . .*

14. This letter, reproduced in *Les Confidances de Youki*, is in the Desnos archives at the Doucet Library and is written in the handwriting of "Louis," as indicated in red at the top of the letter. It must have been dictated by Desnos at Royallieu (DSN.C.671).

15. The expression *marvelous days for us* is not included in the letter in the archives, which is unfinished. Perhaps "Louis" added the final words orally, from memory.

16. Bezaut's memories of Desnos were printed in the autumn 1986 edition of the newsletter of the Association des Amis de Robert Desnos.

17. A notebook listing the "Floral Games" of Compiègne survives in the Doucet archives, in which Desnos noted his cell number at Fresnes, the dates of his interrogations, and the date of his departure from Compiègne. It was possibly included in a trunk he managed to have sent to a café in Compiègne for Youki to collect and to which he makes reference in his penultimate letter from Flöha, from July 1944 (O 1277; see n.23).

18. Soap and its *mousse,* its bubbles, had, for a long time, represented aspects of the marvelous in the everyday for Desnos. In *Liberty or Love!* Bébé Cadum, the baby used in the soap commercials, plays a role as a marvelous superhuman creature who is a "visible god within different kinds of soap bubbles" (*O* 334). Here soap is seen by Desnos in its most poignant incarnation, as a substance capable of transforming experience. Mary Ann Caws underscores the baroque quality of soap in *The Surrealist Look:* "Baroque poetry relies on such images as soap bubbles for their formal change and their fragility" (5).

19. The last letter of Jacques Bingen, who killed himself with cyanide in captivity, knowing he was going to be tortured, is displayed at the Liberation Museum at the Invalides in Paris. Written in anticipation of his death, the letter urges his friends to support de Gaulle and to help him "conserve his nobility and purity."

20. Laurent Flieder sees in the first line a phonetic anagram of Desnos's own name, "hORs DES BOrNES Erres," because of the "strange" liaison that transforms the final *s* from *bornes* into a *z* sound (53).

21. In the Desnos archive is a note from a Mme Darral (or Darras) letting Youki know that Desnos never collected a suitcase in his name, dated 16 November 1944.

22. The facts in this narration were taken from the *Convoi des tatoués,* edited by André Bessière, from documents at the Doucet Library, and from the interviews I conducted with Bessière (20 June and 12 July 1996), Henri Margraff (7 June 1996), Pierre Volmer (10 June 1996), Clément Degueille (10 Nov. 1999), and André Verdet (15 Nov. 1999). Bessière, Verdet, and Youki all propose the hypothesis that the convoy was sent to Auschwitz-Birkenau in reprisal for the execution of Pucheu. I identify my sources wherever possible; I was given access to certain materials from which I could not quote directly.

23. The German authorities had determined that one hundred "hostages" should be shot from the camp of Châteaubriant near Nantes in reprisal for the murder of a German officer (as of 23 August 1941, all French citizens arrested by the German authorities in France were considered "hostages"). Pucheu bargained down the quantity of "hostages" from one hundred to fifty and took the initiative to substitute the names of Communists for the "good Frenchmen" originally on the list (Dank 110–15).

24. In *Destination Auschwitz avec Robert Desnos* Bessière speculates that Desnos's "Watchman of the Pont-au-Change" was published in Paris at the time he was waiting to have his head shaved at Auschwitz-Birkenau; the timing is accurate (144). Bessière has already published two books about his own deportation experience, *L'Engrenage* and *D'un enfer à l'autre.*

25. Bessière adds the possible hypothesis that it was the family members of the count of Chandon-Moët who had used their influence to allow them to leave Auschwitz-Birkenau. Others believed their own Resistance network had managed to exercise influence. He notes, however: "Many years later, those who survived still ask themselves why" (156).

26. There are at least three references to Antelme's wife, Marguerite Duras, in Desnos's agenda from 1943. Dumas told me that she had heard from men who had been at Flöha that to get even a cut could be fatal to the prisoners working there, since absolutely no care, no disinfectant, was administered to them (July 2000).

27. Margraff and Bessière explained that those who stayed behind were protected by Marcel Paul, who seemed to have special privileges. He was a Communist and would do his best to protect members of the Party who showed up at Buchenwald. Another source also said that "you could stay at Buchenwald if you were communist."

28. These numbers were provided by Bessière and confirmed in a letter from André Lechevallier to Youki (DSN 463).

29. An exchange of notes between Youki and Rödel's widow after the war confirms this closeness—Rödel's wife wrote to ask if Youki had any samples of his handwriting to pass on to their children (DSN 463).

30. Smoular remembers the recipe book envisioned by Desnos, as having the simpler title of *Manuel de cuisine* (4).

31. This food distribution was more or less confirmed by another source, who described the food at Flöha as follows: half a liter of barley soup for breakfast, a thicker soup at lunch, and, for supper, four hundred grams of bread with either a little margarine or sausage and some ersatz coffee.

32. This same story is told in my two interviews with Bessière and in *Destination Auschwitz avec Robert Desnos;* by Volmer in my interview with him and in "Avec Desnos à Flöha," published in L'Herne; by Pffihl in the *Oeuvres;* and by Baumel in his memoir.

33. These quotations, cited by Volmer, are from Christian Leininger's memoirs (Volmer 377).

34. Desnos's act of defiance was not the only act of bravery by the French prisoners: on Christmas eve, when asked to sing a carol by one of their guards, Volmer sang a patriotic song:

> You won't have Alsace and Lorraine
> And despite everything we will remain French
> You will never win our hearts.

Perhaps because of the day, he went unpunished (Bessière, *Destination* 207).

35. The Desnos archives show records of two attempts by Youki to obtain a divorce, once in 1932 and once again in 1939. The first time failed because of Foujita's departure for Japan. The second time she apparently had difficulty obtaining all the papers required (DSN 463; 480). Desnos himself wrote to his father in October 1939, asking for advice about marriage while in the army (DSN 431). In 1938 Desnos took out life insurance with Youki as the beneficiary (DSN 480). Youki did not obtain her divorce until well after the war.

36. This and other facts come from a typed manuscript by André Lechevallier, who gives a day-by-day account of the march from Flöha to Terezin.

37. My thanks to Kate Goldsborough for showing me "The Falling Leaf and Other Descents," her manuscript about her father's experiences as a prisoner of war in a German POW camp, in which she explains about charcoal in World War II lore.

38. According to Robert Laurence, the title of Desnos's novel from Flöha was *Le Cuirassier nègre* (The Negro Sailor) (142).

39. Another document in the Doucet archives claims that she learned this story from Christian Leininger, who also told her that Desnos was careful not to eat too much of the Red Cross care packages they received upon arrival at Terezin and that he promised half of his rations to anyone who could find the box for him (DSN 463).

40. Roy, who interviewed her carefully, clearly identifies Tesarova as a medical student, like Stuna. Elsewhere she is referred to as a nurse, possibly because of her sex.

41. These include notices in *Le Canard Enchaîné* from 30 May 1945, the *Dépêche de Paris* from 31 May, *Libération-Soir* from 1 June, *France-Soir* and *Lettres Françaises* from 2 June, *Le Tigre* from 30 June, and *Paysage Dimanche* from 22 July (DSN 478).

42. The last issue of *Aujourd'hui* came out on 16 August 1944, just ten days before Paris was liberated. The headline announced that the American troops were on the defensive, and the main story on the front page was about stamp collecting coming back into fashion.

43. Laubreaux fled to Spain in 1945, where he died in 1968. He was condemned to death in France in 1947 (Cointet 430).

44. Leininger said he would return to Paris with "the urn" containing Desnos's ashes, although this seems not to have taken place. He also said he had Desnos's glasses, in his letter to Youki. Neither Bessière nor Volmer remembers seeing Desnos with glasses on their three-week march or at Terezin, and it seems impossible that he could have obtained a new pair. The only explanation is that either Leininger was mistaken or that Desnos had saved his smashed glasses somehow and that they had managed to survive in his possession until his death. Stuna and Tesarova make no mention of them in their testimonials.

45. The date 31 July is given by Adolf Kroupa in his *Lettres Françaises* article from 1960. Vittet's letter in the Desnos archives refers to the date of the article as 1 July.

46. I use my own translation here for the sake of literalness in discussing the mistranslation involved in the creation of this poem (xii). As in chapter 2, I also use my own translation of the last paragraph of "I Have Dreamed So Much of You."

47. These expressions are borrowed from Dominick LaCapra, who explains his use of these psychoanalytic terms, after Freud, in *Representing the Holocaust:* "Working-through. . . . involves the attempt to counteract the projective reprocessing of the past through which we deny certain of its features and act out our own desires for self-confirming or identity-forming meaning" (64). My thanks to Marianne Hirsch for bringing LaCapra's work to my attention.

48. "The site was made available on condition that there should be no *structure* visible above ground," perhaps due to the proximity to Notre Dame (see "War Memorial, Paris" 186).

49. The "Réseau du souvenir" brochure, *Memorial to the Martyrs of Deportation,* offers a kind of subliminal reading by reproducing some of the inscriptions, without commenting upon them.

50. The poem is mentioned in, among other places, an article in the Swiss monthly *Labyrinthe* in November 1945 by L.P. and in Pierre Berger's volume on Desnos from 1949 as well as in Ilya Ehrenburg's 1955 *Memoirs,* in Rosa Buchole's 1956 book on Desnos, in the Hartley edition of *The Penguin Book of French Verse* from 1959, in the 1974 memoirs of Jean Baumel, Desnos's fellow prisoner at Flöha, in Henri Pouzol's 1975 anthology of concentration camp poetry, in a 1985 article by Roger Arnould published in *Poésie,* in Martica Sawin's 1995 *Surrealism in Exile,* and finally in a 1995 article by Mary Ann Caws, "Poetry, Passion and the Holocaust," although she makes no mention of it in her 1977 volume, *The Surrealist Voice of Robert Desnos.*

51. In "Poésie de circonstance," Eluard explains, "for the conclusion of the poem I thought to reveal the name of the woman I loved, to whom the poem was dedicated. But I quickly realized that the only word I had in my mind was *liberty*" (oc 2, 941).

52. The letter, by Jacques Bingen, is cited in n.19.

53. See Fishman for an analysis of France's pronatalist policies during World War II specifically, esp. 185–86. My thanks to Margaret Darrow for her help with this question.

54. See the article by Robert M. Webster, "Remembering *La Rafle du Vel d'Hiv,*" which begins with a 1992 commemoration. A memorial plaque was not dedicated before Sunday, 7 August 1994, by President François Mittérand, and it was not until 16 July 1995 that President Jacques Chirac gave a speech publicly recognizing France's responsibility in the roundups of the "Vel d'Hiv" and the deportation of thousands of Jews to their death.

55. In two contemporary textbooks on twentieth-century French literature, Desnos is mentioned and anthologized as both a surrealist poet (the edition edited by Henri Mittérand includes "I Have Dreamed So Much of You") and as a Resistant poet (Mittérand 226–27, 442–43; Lagarde and Michard 348–50, 537).

56. Daniel Lançon shows that many of Desnos's poems for children are included in contemporary textbooks; some of Desnos's love poetry from the 1920s is also taught, along with a small selection of his Resistance poetry.

Selected Bibliography

Adamowicz, Elza. *Surrealist Collage in Text and Image*. Cambridge: Cambridge UP, 1998.

Adelen, Claude. "L'Oeil bleu du tamanoir." *Europe* 78.851 (2000): 138–42.

Adereth, Max. *Aragon: The Resistance Poems*. London: Grant & Culler, 1985.

Ahearne, Jeremy. *Michel de Certeau: Interpretation and Its Other*. Stanford: Stanford UP, 1995.

Alexandrian, Sarane. *Le Surréalisme et le rêve*. Paris: Gallimard, 1974.

André Breton: La Beauté convulsive. Paris: Editions du Centre Pompidou, 1991.

Antelme, Robert. *The Human Race*. Trans. Jeffrey Haight and Annie Mahler. Marlboro, VT: Marlboro, 1992.

Antle, Martine. *Cultures du surréalisme*. Paris: Editions Acoria, 2001.

Anzieu, Didier. "L'Envelope sonore du soi." *Nouvelle Revue de la Psychanalyse* 13 (1976): 161–79.

Apollinaire, Guillaume. *Alcools*. Paris: Gallimard, Coll. Poésie, 1920.

——. *Calligrammes*. Trans. Anne Hyde Greet. Berkeley: U of California P, 1980.

——. *Selected Writings*. Trans. Roger Shattuck. New York: New Directions, 1971.

Aragon, Louis. "Corps, âmes et biens." *Le Surréalisme au Service de la Révolution* 1 (1930): 13–15.

——. *Le Crève-Coeur*. Paris: 1946.

——. "Du Sonnet." *Les Lettres Françaises* 504 (1954): 1, 5.

——. *Le Libertinage*. Paris: Gallimard, Coll. Imaginaire, 1977.

——. *Paris Peasant*. Trans. Simon Watson Taylor. Boston: Exact Change, 1994.

——. *Treatise on Style*. Trans. Alyson Waters. Lincoln: U of Nebraska P, 1991.

——. *Une Vague de rêves*. 1924. Paris: Seghers, 1990.

Aragon, Louis, et al. *Hommage à Malkine*. Paris: Galerie Mona Lisa, 1966.

Arnould, Roger. "Robert Desnos." *Poésie* 85.10 (1985): 35–44.

Aromatico, Andrea. *Alchemy: The Great Secret*. Trans. Jack Hawkes. New York: Harry Abrams–Discoveries, 2000.

Augé, Marc. *Non-Places: Introduction to an Anthropology of Supermodernity*. Trans. John Howe. London. New York: Verso, 1995.

Azéma, Jean-Pierre. *From Munich to the Liberation*. Trans. Janet Lloyd. Cambridge: Cambridge UP, 1984.

Baker, Carlos. *Ernest Hemingway.* New York: Scribner's, 1969.

Balakian, Anna. *André Breton: Magus of Surrealism.* 1971.

——. *Surrealism: The Road to the Absolute.* New York: Noonday P, 1959.

Barbarant, Olivier. "Un Pétale de rose tombe sur un lit vide." *Europe* 78.851 (2000): 159–64.

——. "La Rime en 1943." *Robert Desnos pour l'an 2000.* Ed. Katharine Conley and Marie-Claire Dumas. Paris: Gallimard, 2000. 237–49.

Barrault, Jean-Louis. *Memories for Tomorrow.* Trans. Jonathan Griffin. New York: Dutton, 1974.

Barthes, Roland. *A Barthes Reader.* Ed. Susan Sontag. New York: Hill & Wang, 1982.

——. *The Grain of the Voice.* Trans. Linda Coverdale. New York: Hill & Wang, 1985.

——. *Image-Music-Text.* Trans. Stephen Heath. New York: Hill & Wang, 1977.

——. *The Pleasure of the Text.* Trans. Richard Miller. New York: Hill & Wang, 1975.

——. *The Responsibility of Forms.* Trans. Richard Howard. New York: Hill & Wang, 1985.

Bataille, Georges. *Oeuvres complètes.* Vol. 2. Paris: Gallimard, 1970.

——. *Visions of Excess: Selected Writings.* Trans. Allan Stoekl. Minneapolis: U of Minnesota P, 1985.

Baumel, Jean. *De la guerre aux camps de concentration.* Montpellier: CGC, 1974.

Baumgartner, Emmanuèle. *Poésies de François Villon.* Paris: Gallimard, Coll. Folio., 1998.

Becker, Jean-Jacques, and Serge Berstein. *Victoire et frustrations, 1914–1929.* Paris: Editions du Seuil, 1990.

Béhar, Henri. *André Breton: Le grand indésirable.* Paris: Calmann-Lévy, 1990.

Benesova, Miroslava, Vjtech Blodig, Market Poloncarz, and Petr Liebl. *Terezin, The Small Forteress, 1940–1945.* Terezin: Terezin Memorial, 1996.

Berger, Pierre. "Mon Copain Robert Desnos." *Poésie* 45.26–27 (1945): 31–38.

——. *Robert Desnos.* Paris: Seghers, 1949.

Berranger, Marie Paule. *Dépaysement de l'aphorisme.* Paris: Corti, 1988.

Bessière, André, ed. *Le Convoi des tatoués.* Amicale des Déportés Tatoués du 27–4-44. Viry-Chatillon: privately published, 1999.

——. *Destination Auschwitz avec Robert Desnos.* Paris: L'Harmattan, 2001.

——. *L'Engrenage.* Paris: Buchet-Chastel, 1991.

——. *D'un enfer à l'autre.* Paris: Buchet-Chastel, 1997.

Blanchot, Maurice. "Everyday Speech." *Yale French Studies: Everyday Life.* Ed. Alice Kaplan and Kristin Ross. New Haven: Yale UP, 1987. 12–20.

Blessing, Jennifer. "Rrose is a Rrose is a Rrose: Gender Performance in Photography." *Rrose is a Rrose is a Rrose.* Ed. Jennifer Blessing. New York: Guggenheim Museum, 1997. 18–49.

Bloch, Marc. *L'Etrange défaite*. Paris: Gallimard, Coll. Folio., 1990.

——. *Strange Defeat*. Trans. Gerard Hopkins. Oxford: Oxford UP, 1949.

Bonnet, Marguerite. *André Breton: Naissance de l'aventure surréaliste*. Paris: Corti, 1975, 1988.

Borne, Dominique, and Henri Dubief. *La Crise des années 30: 1928–1938*. Paris: Editions du Seuil, 1976, 1989.

Breton, André. *Conversations: The Autobiography of Surrealism*. Trans. Mark Polizzotti. New York: Marlowe, 1993.

——. *Oeuvres complètes*. Vols. 1 and 3. Paris: Gallimard-Pléiade, 1988, 1999.

——. *Free Rein*. Trans. Michel Parmentier and Jacqueline d'Amboise. Lincoln: U of Nebraska P, 1995.

——. *The Lost Steps*. Trans. Mark Polizzotti. Lincoln: U of Nebraska P, 1996.

——. *Manifestoes of Surrealism*. Trans. Richard Seaver and Helen Lane. Ann Arbor: U of Michigan P, 1972.

——. *Nadja*. Trans. Richard Howard. New York: Grove, 1960.

——. *Surrealism and Painting*. Trans. Simon Watson Taylor. New York: Harper & Row, 1992.

Breton, André, and Philippe Soupault. *Magnetic Fields*. Trans. David Gascoyne. London: Atlas Press, 1985.

Brieux, Alain. "Robert Desnos et son petit copain." *Robert Desnos*. Ed. Marie-Claire Dumas. Paris: Editions de l'Herne, 1987. 23–32.

Brochand, Christian. "L'Année Radiophonique 1924." *Cahiers d'Histoire de la Radiodiffusion* 41 (1994): 4–48.

Brun, Guy. "Robert Desnos restera vivant grâce au prix radiophonique de *L'Etoile*." *L'Etoile de Paris* 52 (Nov. 1945): 1–2.

Bruno, G. *Le Tour de la France par deux enfants*. Paris: Librairie Classique Eugène Belin.

Buchole, Rosa. *L'Evolution poétique de Robert Desnos*. Brussels: Palais des Académies, 1956.

Burrin, Philippe. *Living with Defeat*. Trans. Janet Lloyd. London: Arnold, 1996.

Butler, Judith. *Gender Trouble*. New York: Routledge, 1990.

Cantaloube-Ferrieu, Lucienne. "La Présence d'Yvonne George dans *Corps et Biens*." *Textuel* 34–44.5 (1985): 56–68.

Carpentier, Alejo. "La Havane, Cuba, la musique . . . et Robert Desnos." *Simoun* 22–23 (1956): 32–46.

——. "Un Homme de contraste." *Robert Desnos*. Ed. Marie-Claire Dumas. Paris: Editions de l'Herne, 1987. 363–66.

——. "L'Homme qui traversait les ponts." *Chroniques*. Paris: Gallimard, 1983.

——. "Robert Desnos et ses trois maisons magiques." *Robert Desnos*. Ed. Marie-Claire Dumas. Paris: Editions de l'Herne, 1987. 329–34.

Cartier, Gérard. "La Boîte de fer blanc." *Europe* 78.851 (2000): 127–30.

Caws, Mary Ann. *The Poetry of Dada and Surrealism.* Princeton: Princeton UP, 1970.

——. "Poetry, Passion and the Holocaust." *Romance Notes* 35.3 (1995): 249–53.

——. *The Surrealist Look.* Cambridge, MA: MIT P, 1997.

——. *The Surrealist Voice of Robert Desnos.* Amherst: U of Massachusetts P, 1977.

Certeau, Michel de. *The Practice of Everyday Life.* Trans. Steven Rendall. Berkeley: U of California P, 1984.

Chabanne, Jean-Charles. "Présence de Robert Desnos dans les manuels de l'école élémentaire." *Poétiques de Robert Desnos.* Ed. Laurent Flieder. Paris: ENS Editions, 1996. 83–100.

Chénieux-Gendron, Jacqueline. *Surrealism.* Trans. Vivian Folkenflik. New York: Columbia UP, 1990.

Chevrier, Alain. "Les Sonnets de Desnos." *Poétiques de Robert Desnos.* Ed. Laurent Flieder. Fontenay–St. Cloud: ENS Editions, 1995. 119–39.

Chion, Michel. *The Voice in Cinema.* Trans. Claudia Gorbman. New York: Columbia UP, 1999.

Chitrit, Armelle. *Robert Desnos: Le Poème entre temps.* Montreal & Lyon: XYZ & PUL, 1996.

Clifford, James. *The Predicament of Culture.* Cambridge, MA: Harvard UP, 1988.

Cointet, Michèle, and Jean-Paul. *Dictionnaire historique de la France sous l'Occupation.* Paris: Editions Tallandier, 2000.

Cone, Michèle. *Artists under Vichy.* Princeton: Princeton UP, 1992.

——. "Desnos, Picasso, Girodias, trois comparses de fortune." *Robert Desnos.* Ed. Marie-Claire Dumas. Paris: Editions de l'Herne, 1987. 205–11.

Conley, Katharine. *Automatic Woman: The Representation of Woman in Surrealism.* Lincoln: U of Nebraska P, 1996.

——. "Going for Baroque in the 20th Century: From Desnos to Brossard." *Québec Studies* 31 (2001): 12–23.

——. "La Nature double des yeux (regardés/regardants) de la femme dans le surréalisme." *La Femme s'entête: La Part du féminin dans le surréalisme.* Paris: Collection Pleine Marge, 1998.

——. "Silence in the Heart: The Feminine in Desnos's *La Liberté ou l'amour!*" *French Review* 63.3 (1990): 475–83.

——. "The Woman in the Bottle of Robert Desnos's Surrealist Dreams." *French Forum* 16.2 (1991): 199–208.

Conley, Katharine, and Marie-Claire Dumas, eds. *Desnos pour l'an 2000.* Paris: Gallimard, 2000.

Coppin-Belleville, Renée. *Si Compiègne ce fut cela . . .* Paris: La Pensée Universelle, 1983.

Costa, Bernadette. *Je me souviens du Marais.* Paris: Parigramme, 1995.

Daix, Pierre. *La Vie quotidienne des surréalistes.* Paris: Hachette, 1993.

Dank, Milton. *The French against the French.* Philadelphia: Lippincott, 1974.

Darle, Juliette. "La 'Cantate pour l'inauguration du Musée de l'Homme." *Europe* 50.517–18 (1972): 41–50.

Debon, Claude. "La Question du sens dans *Rrose Sélavy, L'Aumonyme,* et *Langage Cuit* de R. Desnos." *Textuel* 34–44.16 (1985): 92–99.

Deharme, Paul. "Proposition d'un art radiophonique." *Nouvelle Revue Française* 174 (1928): 413–22.

Deleuze, Gilles. *Le Pli: Leibniz et le baroque.* Paris: Minuit, 1988.

Delporte, Christian. *Les Journalistes en France, 1880–1950.* Paris: Seuil, 1999.

Desanti, Dominique. *Robert Desnos, Le roman d'une vie.* Paris: Mercure de France, 1999.

Deshays, Daniel. *De l'écriture sonore.* Marseille: Editions Entre/Vues, 1999.

Desnos, Robert. *Le Bois d'amour.* Paris: Edition des Cendres, 1995.

——. "Chroniques retrouvées." *Europe* 75.820–21 (1997): 68–79.

——. *The Circle and the Star.* Trans. Todd Sanders. Pittsburgh: Air and Nothing P, 2000.

——. *Corps et biens.* Paris: Gallimard, 1930.

——. *Destinée arbitraire.* Ed. Marie-Claire Dumas. Paris: Gallimard, 1975.

——. *Domaine public.* Ed. René Bertelé. Paris: Gallimard, 1953.

——. *Ecrits sur les peintres.* Ed. Marie-Claire Dumas. Paris: Flammarion, 1984.

——. *Fortunes.* Paris: Gallimard, Coll. Poésie, 1945.

——. "Introduction." *Pigments.* By Léon-Gontran Damas. Paris: GLM, 1937.

——. *Le Livre secret de Youki.* Paris: Editions des Cendres, 1999.

——. *The Secret Book for Youki and Other Poems.* Trans. Todd Sanders. Pittsburgh: Air and Nothing P, 2001.

——. *Mines de Rien.* Ed. Marie-Claire Dumas. Paris: Le Temps Qu'il Fait, 1985.

——. *Nouvelles Hébrides.* Ed. Marie-Claire Dumas. Paris: Gallimard, 1978.

——. *Oeuvres.* Ed. Marie-Claire Dumas. Paris: Gallimard, Quarto, 1999.

——. *Against the Grain.* Trans. Timothy Ades. London: Hearing Eye, 2003.

——. *Mourning for Mourning.* Trans. Terry Hale. *The Automatic Muse.* London: Atlas, 1994. 7–59.

——. *Liberty or Love!* Trans. Terry Hale. London: Atlas, 1993.

——. *The Selected Poems of Robert Desnos.* Trans. Carolyn Forché and Williams Kulik. New York: Ecco, 1991.

——. *Les Rayons et les ombres.* Ed. Marie-Claire Dumas. Paris: Gallimard, 1992.

——. *Rue de la gaité.* Paris: Les 13 Epis, 1947.

——. *Les Voix intérieures.* Ed. Lucienne Cantaloube-Ferrieu. Nantes: Les Editions du Petit Véhicule, 1987.

Desnos, Youki. *Les Confidences de Youki.* Paris: Fayard-Opéra Mundi, 1957.

Didi-Huberman. *La Ressemblance informe*. Paris: Editions Macula, 1995.

Doane, Mary Ann. *Femmes Fatales*. New York: Routledge, 1991.

Drieu la Rochelle, Pierre. *La Suite des idées*. Paris: Au Sens Pareil, 1927.

Ducasse, Isidore. Comte de Lautréamont. *Maldoror and the Complete Works of the Comte de Lautréamont*. Trans. Alexis Lykiard. Boston: Exact Change, 1994.

Duchamp, Marcel. Poems by Rrose Sélavy. *Littérature* 5 (1922).

Duhamel, Marcel. *Raconte pas ta vie*. Paris: Mercure de France, 1972.

Dumas, Marie-Claire. "Avant-Propos." *Europe* 517–18 (1972): 3–14.

——. "Le Chant de l'image." *André Breton*. Ed. Michel Murat with Marie-Claire Dumas. Paris: Editions de l'Herne, 1998. 229–43.

——. *Etude de* Corps et biens *de Robert Desnos*. Geneva: Slatkine, 1984.

——. "La Guillotine sans couperet." *Poétiques de Robert Desnos*. Ed. Laurent Flieder. Paris: ENS Editions, 1996. 65–81.

——. "Introduction." *Mines de riens*. Paris: Le Temps Qu'il Fait, 1985. 7–12.

——. "Notes sur Robert Desnos." *Folie et psychanalyse dans l'expérience surréaliste*. Ed. Fabienne Hulak. Paris: Le Singleton, 1992. 102–12.

——. "Robert Desnos, journaliste." *Robert Desnos*. Ed. Marie-Claire Dumas. Paris: Editions de l'Herne, 1987. 274–79.

——. "Un Scénario exemplaire de Robert Desnos." *Etudes Cinématographiques* 38–39 (1965): 135–39.

——. *Robert Desnos ou l'exploration des limites*. Paris: Klincksieck, 1980.

——. "Robert Desnos sur les ondes." *Signes* 18 (1995): 117–21.

——, ed. *André Breton en perspective cavalière*. Paris: Gallimard, 1996.

——, ed. *"Moi qui suis Robert Desnos."* Paris: Corti, 1987.

——, ed. *Robert Desnos*. Paris: Editions de l'Herne, 1987.

Dumas, Marie-Claire, and Thomas Simonnet. *"Aujourd'hui* 10 septembre 1940–17 août 1944." *Etoile de Mer* 5 (2001): 4–10.

Dumas, Pierre. *La Forêt de Hêtres*. Villemandeur: Editions JPB, 1989.

Dumoulin, Olivier. "L'Histoire et les historiens." *La Vie culturelle sous Vichy*. Ed. Jean-Pierre Rioux. Paris: Editions Complexe, 1990. 241–68.

Durozoi, Gérard. *History of the Surrealist Movement*. Trans. Alison Anderson. Chicago: U of Chicago P, 2002.

Eck, Hélène. *La Guerre des ondes*. Paris: Armand, Colin, 1985.

——. "La Radio." *La Propagande sous Vichy*. Ed. Laurent Gervereau and Denis Peschanski. Paris: Musée d'Histoire Contemporaine de la Bibliothèque de Documentation Internationale Contemporaine, 1990. 188–94.

Egger, Anne. "L'Activité plastique de Robert Desnos." *Robert Desnos: Des Images et des mots*. Ed. Yves Peyré. Paris: Editions des Cendres, 1999. 98–108.

——. "De la poésie à l'enluminure." *Robert Desnos: Des Images et des mots*. Ed. Yves Peyré. Paris: Editions des Cendres, 1999. 83–87.

———. "Desnos à contre-jour." *Robert Desnos pour l'an 2000.* Ed. Katharine Conley and Marie-Claire Dumas. Paris: Gallimard, 2000. 123–43.

Ehrenburg, Ilya. *Memoirs: 1921–1941.* New York: World Publishing, 1955.

Eluard, Paul. *Oeuvres complètes.* Vols. 1. & 2. Paris: Gallimard, 1968.

———. "Robert Desnos." *Les Lettres Françaises* 5.68 (1945): 1, 3.

Faure, Christian. *Le Projet culturel de Vichy.* Lyon: PUF, 1989.

Fer, Briony. "Surrealism, Myth, and Psychoanalysis." *Realism, Rationalism, Surrealism.* By Briony Fer, David Batchelor, and Paul Wood. New Haven: Yale UP, 1993. 170–249.

Ferdière, Gaston. *Les Mauvaises fréquentations.* Paris: Jean-Claude Simoën, 1978.

Fifer, William, and Chris Moon. "The Effects of Fetal Experience with Sound." *Fetal Development: A Psychobiological Perspective.* Ed. Jean-Pierre Lecanuet, William Fifer, Norman Krasnegor, and William Smotherman. Hillsdale, NJ: Lawrence Erlbaum Associates, 1995. 351–66.

Fishman, Sarah. "Waiting for the Captive Sons of France: Prisoner of War Wives, 1940–1945." *Behind the Lines.* Ed. Margaret Higgonet, Jane Jenson, Sonya Michel, and Margaret Weitz. New Haven: Yale UP, 1987. 182–93.

Flanner, Janet (Genêt). "Letter from Paris." *New Yorker* May 12, 1962, 146–50.

Flieder, Laurent. "Dan 63–41 ou l'hypothèse d'un testament poétique." *Poétiques de Robert Desnos.* Ed. Laurent Flieder. Paris: ENS Editions, 1996. 39–56.

Flonneau, Jean-Marie. "Evolution de l'opinion publique: 1940–1944." *Le Régime de Vichy et les français.* Ed. Jean-Pierre Azéma and François Bédarida. Paris: Fayard, 1992. 506–22.

Fontaine, David. " 'L'Art Poétique' de Desnos: Genèse ou dislocation de l'alexandrin." *Poétiques de Robert Desnos.* Ed. Laurent Flieder. Fontenay–St. Cloud: ENS Editions, 1995. 101–17.

Forché, Carolyn. "Translator's Note." *The Selected Poems of Robert Desnos.* Trans. Carolyn Forché and William Kulik. New York: Ecco P, 1991. ix–xiv.

Fraenkel, Théodore, and Samy Simon. "Biographie de Robert Desnos." *Robert Desnos.* Ed. Marie-Claire Dumas. Paris: Editions de l'Herne, 1987. 317–27. Reprinted from *Critique* 3–4 (1946): 215–28.

Frazer, Susan. " 'Rrose Sélavy' et compagnie." *Robert Desnos.* Ed. Marie-Claire Dumas. Paris: Editions de l'Herne, 1987. 109–19.

Freud, Sigmund. *Introductory Lectures.* Trans. James Strachy. New York: Norton, 1966.

Galtier-Boissière, Jean. *Journal, 1940–1950.* Paris: Quai Voltaire, 1992.

Garber, Marjorie. *Vested Interests.* New York: Routledge, 1997.

Gateau, Jean-Charles. *Paul Eluard ou le frère voyant*. Paris: Editions Robert Laffont, 1988.

Gaucheron, Jacques. *La Poésie, la résistance*. Paris: Messidor, 1991.

Gervereau, Laurent, and Denis Peschanski, eds. *La Propagande sous Vichy*. Paris: Musée d'Histoire Contemporaine de la Bibliothèque de Documentation Internationale Contemporaine, 1990.

——. "Y-a-t-il un 'style Vichy'?" *La Propagande sous Vichy*. Ed. Laurent Gervereau and Denis Peschanski. Paris: Musée d'Histoire Contemporaine de la Bibliothèque de Documentation Internationale Contemporaine, 1990. 110–47.

Gibson, Jennifer. "Surrealism before Freud: Dynamic Psychiatry's 'Simple Recording Instrument.'" *Art Journal* 46 (Spring 1987): 56–60.

Girod, Manuela. "Mécanique et métaphysique." *Europe* 50.517–18 (1972): 97–104.

Golan, Romy. *Modernity and Nostalgia*. New Haven: Yale University Press, 1995.

Goldsborough, Kate. *The Falling Leaf and Other Descents*. Master's thesis. Dartmouth College, 1999.

Guedj, Colette. "Sur Quelques procédés verbo-visuels dans *Corps et biens*." *Signes* 18 (1995): 86–93.

Guerlac, Suzanne. *Literary Polemics: Bataille, Sartre, Valéry, Breton*. Stanford: Stanford UP, 1997.

Hartly, Anthony. *The Penguin Book of French Verse: 4. The Twentieth Century*. Harmondsworth: Penguin, 1959.

Hedges, Inez. "Robert Desnos's and Man Ray's Manuscript Scenario for *L'Etoile de mer*." *Dada/Surrealism* 15 (1986): 207–19.

Heller, Gerhard. *Un Allemand à Paris*. Paris: Editions du Seuil, 1981.

Higgins, Lynn. "Literature 'à la lettre': Ricardou and the Poetics of Anagram." *Romanic Review* 73.4 (1982): 473–88.

Hollier, Denis. "La Valeur d'usage de l'impossible." *Documents*. Paris: Jean-Michel Place, 1991. vii–xxxiv.

Hollywood, Amy. *Sensible Ecstasy: Mysticism, Sexual Difference and the Demands of History*. Chicago: Chicago UP, 2002.

Hubert, Etienne-Alain. "Trois Notes sur *Corps et Biens*." *Textuel* 34–44.16 (1985): 112–31.

Hubert, Renée, Riese. *Magnifying Mirrors*. Lincoln: U of Nebraska P, 1994.

Hugnet, Georges. "Souvenirs de l'occupation nazie." *Robert Desnos*. Ed. Marie-Claire Dumas. Paris: Editions de l'Herne, 1987. 348–54.

Hugotte, Valéry. "Comme dans une image enfantine." *Robert Desnos pour l'an 2000*. Ed. Katharine Conley and Marie-Claire Dumas. Paris: Gallimard, 2000. 208–19.

Hulak, Fabienne. "Une Modalité du transfert: Desnos et Breton." *Signes* 18 (1995): 96–101.

Imbert, Maurice. "Robert J. Godet, éditeur de Bataille, Michaux et Desnos," *Histoires Littéraires* 3 (Aug. 2000): 71–82.

Investigating Sex. Trans. Malcolm Imrie. London: Verso, 1992.

Ishikawa, Kiyoko. *Paris dans quatre textes narratifs du surréalisme.* Paris: L'Harmattan, 1998.

Jeander. "Ce pas qui ne pourra jamais s'éloigner." *Simoun* 22–23 (1956): 33–35.

Jeanneney, Jean-Noël. *Une Histoire des médias.* Paris: Editions du Seuil, Coll. Points, 1996.

Jeronimidis, Anna. "L'Outrage du sonnet: *A la caille* de Robert Desnos." *Micromégas* 50–52 (1991): 185–200.

Jones, Amelia. *Postmodernism and the En-Gendering of Marcel Duchamp.* Cambridge: Cambridge UP, 1994.

Josephson, Matthew. *Life among the Surrealists.* New York: Holt, Rinehart and Winston, 1962.

Judt, Tony. "The End of the War." *New York Times Book Review* 104, 27 June 1999, 10–12.

——. "Could the French Have Won?" *New York Review of Books,* 48.3, 22 Feb. 2001, 37–40.

Kahn, Douglas. "Introduction." Ed. Douglas Kahn and Gregory Whitehead. *Wireless Imagination: Sound, Radio, and the Avant-Garde.* Cambridge: MIT P, 1992. 1–138.

Krauss, Rosalind. "Corpus Delicti." *L'Amour Fou: Photography and Surrealism.* Ed. Rosalind Krauss and Jane Livingston. Washington, DC, & New York: Corcoran Gallery–Abbeville, 1985. 54–112.

——. "Magnetic Fields: The Structure." *Joan Miró: Magnetic Fields.* New York: Solomon R. Guggenheim Foundation, 1972. 11–38.

Kroupa, Adolf. "Desnos est mort sans poème." *Les Lettres Françaises* 19–25 Aug. 1970, 3–5.

——. "La Légende du dernier poème de Robert Desnos." *Les Lettres Françaises* 9–15 June 1960, 1, 5.

Kulik, William. "Introduction." *The Voice: Selected Poems of Robert Desnos.* Trans. William Kulik with Carole Frankel. New York: Grossman-Mushinsha, 1971. v–xii.

L.P. "Robert Desnos." *Labyrinthe* 2.14 (1945): 1–2.

Laborie, Pierre, "L'Evolution de l'opinion publique." *La Propagande sous Vichy.* Ed. Laurent Gervereau and Denis Peschanski. Paris: Musée d'Histoire Contemporaine de la Bibliothèque de Documentation Internationale Contemporaine, 1990. 224–39.

LaCapra, Dominick. *Representing the Holocaust.* Ithaca, NY: Cornell UP, 1994.

Lagarde, André, and Laurent Michard, Eds. *XXe Siècle*. Paris: Bordas, 1985.

Lamireau, Gilbert. "Lettre ouverte à Robert Desnos." *Signes du Temps* 5 (1951): 41–42.

Lançon, Daniel. "Robert Desnos dans les manuels scolaires: (Mé)connaissance et enjeux." *Robert Desnos pour l'an 2000*. Ed. Katharine Conley and Marie-Claire Dumas. Paris: Gallimard, 2000. 329–43.

Lartigue, Pierre. "Le Dernier carnet de Desnos." *Les Lettres Françaises* 2–8 Apr. 1969, 3–5.

——. "Desnos meurt à Terezin, le 8 juin 1945." *Créer pour survivre*. Paris: Fédération Nationale des Déportés et Internés Résistants et Patriotes, 1996. 105–11.

Laurence, Robert. "Souvenirs de déportation avec Robert Desnos." *Europe* 517–18 (1972): 138–45.

Lefebvre. Henri. *Critique de la vie quotidienne*, vol. 2. Paris: L'Arche, 1958.

Leiris, Michel. *Journal, 1922–1989*. Paris: Gallimard, 1992.

——. *Langage Tangage*. Paris: Gallimard, 1985.

——. "45, rue Blomet," *Zébrages*. Paris: Gallimard-Folio, 1992. 219–29.

——. "Robert Desnos: Une Parole d'or." *Robert Desnos*. Ed. Marie-Claire Dumas. Paris: Editions de l'Herne, 1987. 367–69.

Lescure, Jean. "La Radio et la littérature." *Histoire des littératures*. Vol. 3. Ed. Raymond Queneau. Paris: Gallimard, Coll. La Pléiade, 1958.

Levaillant, Françoise. *André Masson: Le Rebelle du surréalisme*. Paris: Hermann, 1994.

L'Honneur des poètes. Paris: Editions de Minuit, 1944.

Loiseaux, Gérard. *La Littérature de la défaite et de la collaboration*. Paris: Fayard, 1995.

Maffesoli, Michel. *Au Creux des apparences: Pour une éthique de l'esthétique*. Paris: Plon, 1990.

Marchand, Bertrand. *Paris, histoire d'une ville (XIX–XX siècle*. Paris: Seuil, 1993.

Marcus, Julia Tardy. "Sacrée Youki." *L'Etoile de mer: Youki et Robert Desnos*. 4 (1999): 3–11.

Marrus, Michael R., and Robert O. Paxton. *Vichy France and the Jews*. Stanford: Stanford UP, 1995.

Martin, Marc. *Trois siècles de publicité en France*. Paris: Editions Odile Jacob, 1992.

Masson, André. "45, Rue Blomet." *André Masson: Le Rebelle du surréalisme*. Ed. Françoise Levaillant. Paris: Hermann, 1994.

Memorial to the Martyrs of Deportation. Pamphlet. Paris: Réseau du Souvenir, avec le ministre des Anciens Combattants et le Commissariat Général du Tourisme.

Miró, Joan. *Selected Writings and Interviews*. Trans. Paul Auster and Patricia Matthews. Ed. Margit Rowell. New York: Da Capo, 1992.

Mittérand, Henri. *Littérature: XXe Siècle*. Paris: Nathan, 1989.

Mollgaard, Lou. *Kiki: Reine de Montparnasse*. Paris: Robert Laffont, 1988.

Monod-Fontaine, Isabelle. "Le Tour des objets." *André Breton*. Paris: Editions du Centre Pompidou, 1991. 64–83.

Mouloudji. *Le Petit invité*. Paris: Balland, 1989.

Muel-Dreyfus, Francine. *Vichy and the Eternal Feminine*. Trans. Kathleen A. Johnson. Durham: Duke UP, 2001.

Murat, Michel. "Desnos poète régulier." *Textuel* 34–44.5 (1985): 37–55.

——. *Robert Desnos: Les Grands jours du poète*. Paris: Corti, 1988.

Nadeau, Maurice. *The History of Surrealism*. Trans. Roger Shattuck. Cambridge, MA: Harvard UP, 1989.

Nietzsche, Friedrich. *The Birth of Tragedy*. Trans. Walter Kaufmann. New York: Vintage, 1967.

Nunley, Charles. "Choses lues: Pratiques desnosiennes de la lecture, 1940–1944." *Robert Desnos pour l'an 2000*. Ed. Katharine Conley and Marie-Claire Dumas. Paris: Gallimard, 2000. 275–85.

Ory, Pascal. *Les Collaborateurs, 1940–1945*. Paris: Editions du Seuil, 1980.

——. *La France allemande*. Paris: Gallimard, 1995.

——. "La Politique culturelle de Vichy: ruptures et continuités." *La Vie culturelle sous Vichy*. Ed. Jean-Pierre Rioux. Paris: Editions Complexe, 1990. 225–38.

Ottavi, André. "De la poésie aux poèmes." *Europe* 50.517–18 (1972): 75–83.

Ousby, Ian. *Occupation*. New York: St. Martin's, 1997.

Paliyenko, Adrianna. "Rereading Breton's Debt to Apollinaire." *Romance Quarterly* 42.1 (1995): 18–27.

Para, Jean-Baptiste. "Le Dieu innommé." *Europe* 78.851 (2000): 150–58. Reprinted in *Robert Desnos: Des Images et des mots*. Ed. Yves Peyré. Paris: Editions des Cendres, 1999. 37–44.

Parrot, Louis. *L'Intelligence en guerre: Panorama de la pensé française dans la clandestinité*. Paris: La Jeune Parque, 1946.

Paxton, Robert O. *Vichy France: Old Guard and New Order, 1940–1944*. New York: Knopf, 1972.

Péret, Benjamin. *Le Déshonneur des poètes*. Mexico: Poésie et Révolution 1945; Paris: Editions Mille et une Nuits, 1996.

Peschanski, Denis. "Une Politique de la censure." *La Vie culturelle sous Vichy*. Ed. Jean-Pierre Rioux. Paris: Editions Complexe, 1990. 63–115.

——. *Vichy, 1940–1944: Contrôle et exclusion*. Paris: Editions Complexe, 1997.

Plantier, René. "L'Ecriture et la voix." *Europe* 50.517–18 (1972): 51–74.

Poirion, Daniel. *Le Merveilleux dans la littérature française du Moyen Age*. Paris: PUF, 1982.

Polizzotti, Mark. *Revolution of the Mind: The Life of André Breton.* New York: Farrar, Straus & Giroux, 1995.

Pouzol, Henri. *La Poésie concentrationnaire.* Paris: Seghers, 1975.

Prévert, Jacques. *Oeuvres complètes.* Paris: Gallimard, Coll. La Pléiade, 1996.

Prin, Alice. *Kiki's Memoirs.* Trans. Samuel Putnam. New York: Ecco Press, 1996.

Ray, Man. *Self-Portrait.* Boston: Little, Brown, 1963.

Rearick, Charles. *The French in Love and War.* New Haven: Yale UP, 1997.

Récanati, François. *Meaning and Force: The Pragmatics of Performative Utterances.* Cambridge: Cambridge UP, 1987.

Reynolds, Siân. *France between the Wars.* London: Routledge, 1996.

Richardson, Michael. "Introduction." *The Absence of Myth: Writings on Surrealism.* By Georges Bataille. London: Verso, 1994. 1–27.

Richman, Michèle H. *Reading Bataille.* Baltimore: Johns Hopkins UP, 1982.

Riffaterre, Michael. *Text Production.* Trans. Terese Lyons. New York: Columbia UP, 1983.

Rimbaud, Arthur. *Oeuvres.* Paris: Garnier, 1960.

Rioux, Jean-Pierre. Ed. *La Vie culturelle sous Vichy.* Paris: Editions Complexe, 1990.

Rivière, Joan. "Womanliness as a Masquerade." *Formations of Fantasy.* Ed. V. Burgin, J. Donald, and C. Kaplan. London: Methuen, 1986. 35–44.

Robert Desnos. Special Issue of *Signes* 18 (1995).

Robert Desnos: Corps et biens. Textuel 34–44.5. Paris: Paris 7, 1985.

Robert Desnos: Des Images et des mots. Bibliothèque Historique de la Ville de Paris. Paris: Edition des Cendres, 1999.

Roberts, Mary Louise. *Civilization without Sexes: Reconstructing Gender in Postwar France, 1917–1927.* Chicago: Chicago UP, 1994.

Romer, Stephen, ed. *20th-Century French Poems.* London: Faber & Faber, 2002.

Rosolato, Guy. "La Voix: entre corps et langage." *Revue Française de Psychanalyse* 1 (1974): 75–94.

Rousso, Henry. *Les Années noires.* Paris: Gallimard, 1992.

——. *The Vichy Syndrome.* Trans. Arthur Goldhammer. Cambridge: Harvard UP, 1991.

Roy, Claude. "Robert Desnos et deux enfants de Prague." *Les Lettres Françaises* 5.78 (1945): 1–2.

Russo, Adelaide. "Marcel Duchamp and Robert Desnos: A Necessary and an Arbitrary Analogy." *Dada/Surrealism* 9 (1979): 115–23.

Salacrou, Armand Robert Desnos et la publicité radiophonique." *Simoun* 22–23 (1956): 39–41.

Sapiro, Gisèle. *La Guerre des écrivains.* Paris: Fayard, 1999.

Sawin, Martica. *Surrealism in Exile*. Cambridge: MIT P, 1995.

Scannell, Paddy. *Radio, Television and Modern Life*. London: Blackwell, 1996.

Scheler, Lucien. "Ultime rencontre." *Robert Desnos*. Ed. Marie-Claire Dumas. Paris: Editions de l'Herne, 1987. 372–73.

Sebbagh, Antoine. *La Radio: Rendez-vous sur les ondes*. Paris: Gallimard, 1995.

Séité, Yannick. "Robert Desnos 'critique de disques." *Europe* 75.820–21 (1997): 62–66.

Sheringham, Michael. "La Mort et les lois du désir dans l'écriture automatique de Desnos." *"Moi qui suis Robert Desnos": Permanence d'une voix*. Ed. Marie-Claire Dumas. Paris: Corti, 1987. 69–84.

———. "Du Surréel à l'infraordinaire: Avatars du quotidien dans le surréalisme, l'ethnographie et le postmodernisme de Georges Perec." *L'Autre et le sacré*. Ed. C. W. Thompson. Paris: L'Harmattan, 1995. 219–36.

Silverman, Kaja. *The Acoustic Mirror*. Bloomington: Indiana UP, 1988.

Simonnet, Thomas. "Desnos/Théatre." *Robert Desnos pour l'an 2000*. Ed. Katharine Conley and Marie-Claire Dumas. Paris: Gallimard, 2000. 102–12.

Smiley, Amy. "La Voix qui cire dans l'infini: Philippe Soupault et la radio (1938–1943)." *Cahiers d'Histoire de la Radiodiffusion* 41 (1994): 107–25.

Smoular, Alfred. "Robert Desnos: Deux cantates, Cantate pour l'inauguration du Musée de l'Homme, les Quatres éléments." *Signes du temps* 5 (1951): 2–6.

Soupault, Philippe. "Vers une poésie du cinéma et de la radio." *Fontaine* 16 (1941): 172–75.

Spector, Jack. *Surrealist Art and Writing, 1919–1939: The Gold of Time*. Cambridge: Cambridge UP, 1997.

Stamelman, Richard Howard. *The Drama of Self in Guillaume Apollinaire's "Alcools."* Chapel Hill: North Carolina Studies in Romance Languages and Literatures, 1976.

———. "La Culture du parfum." *Pleine Marge* 36 (2002): 27–54.

Stapleton, Michael. *The Illustrated Dictionary of Greek and Roman Mythology*. New York: Peter Bedrick, 1978.

Tashjian, Dickran. "'Vous pour moi?' Marcel Duchamp and Transgender Coupling." *Mirror Images*. Ed. Whitney Chadwic. Cambridge, MA: MIT P, 1998. 36–65.

Tomkins, Calvin. *Duchamp*. New York: Holt, 1996.

Varnedoe, Kirk, and Adam Gopnik. *High and Low: Popular Culture and Modern Art*. New York: Museum of Modern Art–Harry Abrams, 1991.

Vasquez, Carmen. "A travers la forêt obscure et touffue: De Gongora à Desnos." *"Moi qui suis Robert Desnos."* Ed. Marie-Claire Dumas. Paris: Corti, 1987. 173–89.

Villon, François. *The Poems of François Villon.* Trans. Galway Kinnell. Boston: Houghton Mifflin, 1977.

Volmer, Pierre. "Avec Desnos à Flöha." *Robert Desnos.* Ed. Marie-Claire Dumas. Paris: Editions de l'Herne, 1987. 374–81.

Waldberg, Patrick. "Retour de Malkine." *Hommage à Malkine.* Paris: Galerie Mona Lisa, 1966.

Walz, Robin. *Pulp Surrealism: Insolent Popular Culture in Early Twentieth-Century Paris.* Berkeley: U of California P, 2000.

"War Memorial, Paris." *Architectural Review* 133.793 (1963): 186–89.

Weber, Eugen. *France, Fin de Siècle.* Cambridge: Harvard UP–Belknap P, 1986.

——. *The Hollow Years.* New York: Norton, 1994.

Webster, Robert M. "Remembering *La Rafle du Vel d'Hiv.*" *Contemporary French Civilization* 28.1 (1994): 72–97.

Weiss, Allen S. *Phantasmic Radio.* Durham: Duke UP, 1995.

Wölfflin, Heinrich. *Principles of Art History.* London: G. Bell & Sons, 1932.

Wright, Gordon. *France in Modern Times.* New York: Norton, 1987.

Zakarian, Richard H. "Desnos and a Mythic *Fard.*" *Dada/Surrealism* 8 (1978): 78–83.

SELECTED BIBLIOGRAPHY

Index

Abetz, Otto, 123, 141
The Acoustic Mirror, 93 94. *See also* Sil
    verman, Kaja
Adamowicz, Elza, 22
Adereth, Max, 131, 141
Ades, Timothy, 230 n.3
advertising jingles, 112–14
Agir, 13, 153, 154, 179, 180, 202
"A la Caille," 114, 160, 166, 179. *See also*
    Desnos, Robert, Slang poems
"A la mystérieuse," 4, 47, 49, 51, 205. *See*
    also Desnos, Robert, Poetry
alchemy, 9
Alexandrian, Sarane, 18
alexandrine (verses), 49, 74, 75, 83, 140
Un Allemand à Paris, 184. *See also* Heller,
    Gerhard
Alsace, 135, 136, 191
Alsatian, 135, 182
Andier, Pierre, 121, 156. *See also* Desnos,
    Robert, pseudonymous name
André Breton: Magus of Surrealism, 215
    n.4
les années folles, 54, 84
Les Années noires, 121. *See also* Rousso,
    Henry
Antelme, Robert, 89, 190; and *The
    Human Race*, 191
anti-Semitism, 152, 154
Antle, Martine, 5; and *Cultures du sur-
    réalisme*, 215 n.6
Anzieu, Didier, 94
Apollinaire, Guillaume, 16, 36, 140, 172–
    74
—Works: *Calligrammes*, 36; "Monday in
    Christine Street," 36–37; "Le Pont
    Mirabeau," 172–74

"Aquarelle," 142. *See also* Desnos, Robert,
    Poetry
Aragon, Louis: on automatic simulation,
    21; and circular letter (1929), 55–60;
    and Desnos's word-mirrors, 19, 43; on
    hypnotic sleeps, 16; journalism of, 53;
    and *Littérature*, 26; and Resistance
    work, 6; and review of *Corps et biens*,
    74–75; as soldier in World War I, 15; in
    World War II, 140
—Works: *A Corpse* (1924), 24–25, 31, 66,
    145; *Le Crève-coeur*, 141, 149; "Du son-
    net," 151; "Les Lilas et les roses," 140; *Le
    Mouvement perpétuel*, 83; "A Suivre"
    (with André Breton), 58–59; *Paris
    Peasant*, 148; "La Rime en 1940," 140–
    41; *Une Vague de rêves*, 19, 40, 94
Arbatz, Michel, 96
Arcanum 17, 2. *See also* Breton, André,
    Works
Argo, 163–64
Arma, Paul, 96
Armstrong, Louis, 107, 151. *See also* jazz
Arnaud, Jérôme, 108
"Ars Poetica," 167, 169–72. *See also* Des-
    nos, Robert, Poetry
Artaud, Antonin, 45, 55, 60, 66, 69, 89,
    103, 133
Asturias, Miguel Angel, 88
"A Suivre," 58–59. *See also* Aragon, Louis;
    Breton, André
Atget, Eugène, 10, 67, 126 fig. 2, 126 fig. 13
"Au Crayon," 149–50, 157. *See also* Des-
    nos, Robert, Journalism
auditory imagination, 90–94
Augé, Marc, 11
Augustine, 22

Aujourd'hui, 13, 124, 137, 140, 142–53, 171, 174, 179, 182, 189
"Auprès de ma blonde," 114
Auschwitz-Birkenau, 138, 166, 169, 178, 188, 189–90, 192, 200, 214
"Author's Note" to *Fortunes*, 122. *See also* Desnos, Robert, Essays
automatic: experience, 3, 12, 20, 90; performance, 17, 22–23, 31, 213; simulation, 21–23; writing, 31–36, 40–43
automatism, 1, 3, 12, 18, 20, 22, 36, 139, 213
Avachanne, Etienne, 179
Avenue Foch, 181–82, 184
Azéma, Jean-Pierre, 121, 136, 179

Bacchus, 75, 84, 127
Bacchus-Dionysus, 129. *See also* Dionysus
Badoud, Lucie. *See* Desnos, Youki Foujita
Balakian, Anna, 215 n.4
"Ballade des pendus," 172–73. *See also* Villon, François
bar at the Rue du Château (meeting, 1929), 57–60, 68
Barbarant, Olivier, 229 n.35, 231 n.17
Baron, Jacques, 60, 66
baroque, 12, 33, 36, 164; double, 76; etymology of, 36; fulcrum of, 33; materiality, 36; poetry, 164; time, 12, 20, 34, 53, 213
Barrault, Jean-Louis, 9, 87, 99, 118, 134, 135, 196, 199
Barthes, Roland, 90–93, 104, 119, 207
bassesse, 63, 65
Bataille, Georges, 3, 4, 6, 45, 88, 116, 171; and *bassesse*, 63, 64; and the Bataille-Breton polemic, 3–4, 55–70; and *informe*, 62; and *materialism*, 62, 80
—Works: "The Big Toe," 63; *Le Coupable*, 70; "critical dictionary," 62; *L'Expérience intérieure*, 70; "The Language of Flowers," 62–66; "The 'Old Mole' and the Prefix *Sur* in the Words *Surhomme* and *Surrealist*," 65
Bataillean surrealism, 3, 80
Baumel, Jean, 193
bear: symbol for Desnos, 98–99, 162; tattoo, 72, 98, 190. *See also* Desnos, Robert, symbols for
Beauvoir, Simone de, 89

Les Beaux draps, 152
Bébé Cadum, 64
Bechet, Sidney, 107. *See also* jazz
Becker, Jean-Jacques, 26
"Before, After," 66. *See also* Breton, André, Works
Belle Haleine, 27–29. *See also* Duchamp, Marcel; Ray, Man
Belle-Ile, 133, 161, 196
Beloeil, Hormidas, 115. *See also* Desnos, Robert, pseudonymous name
Berger, Pierre, 147
Bergery, Gason, 96
Bernhardt, Sarah, 27
Berranger, Marie-Paule, 33, 112
Berstein, Serge, 26
Bertelé, René, 207, 209
Bessière, André: on Auschwitz-Birkenau, 189–90; on the death march to Terezin, 197–98; on Flöha, 192–95; on Royal-lieu, 178, 183, 185; on Terezin, 198–99, 200
—Works, *Le Convoi des tatoués*, 183, 236 n.22; *Destination Auschwitz avec Robert Desnos*, 236 n.24, 237 n.32; *D'un enfer à l'autre*, 236 n.24; *L'Engrenage*, 236 n.24
Bezaut, Jean, 185
"The Big Toe," 63
The Birth of the World, 70. *See also* Miró, Joan
The Birth of Tragedy, 84
Blanchot, Maurice, 11
Blessing, Jennifer, 28
blitzkrieg, 121, 137
Bloch, Marc, 127
Bloc national, 24, 54
Blondin, Germaine, 107
Blum, Léon, 98, 127
Boiffard, Jacques-André, 66
"Le Bon bouillon," 162. *See also* Desnos, Robert, Slang poems
Bonnard, Abel, 156, 162
Bonnet, Marguerite, 7, 18
Bonsoir Mesdames, Bonsoir Messieurs: in film, 17, 153, 181–82; as first phrase pronounced on the radio, 95. *See also* Desnos, Robert, Film scenarios
Borne, Dominique, 54, 97, 99
Bost, Pierre, 201, 204–5

Bourdet, Maurice, 181, 185
Breton, André: apartment of, 15, 18; as
    author of the definition of surrealism,
    3; and the Breton-Bataille polemic, 4,
    61–67; and circular letter with Aragon
    (1929), 55–66; and *A Corpse* (1930),
    24–26, 31; and friendship with Desnos,
    54, 56–57, 60, 67–69, 89, 104; and hyp-
    notic sleeps, 15–23; and journalism, 53,
    60; as leader of the surrealist move-
    ment, 2, 5, 10; and *Littérature*, 26; and
    "modest *recording instruments*," 100–
    102; as "Pope," 67; and surrealist
    image, 7; and telepathy, 95; and "words
    are making love," 31–36, 77
—Works: *Arcanum 17*, 2; "Before, After,"
    66; *Clair de terre*, 83; *Communicating
    Vessels*, 2; *A Corpse* (1924), 66–67;
    Immaculate Conception (with Paul
    Eluard), 22; *Mad Love*, 2; *The Magnetic
    Fields* (with Philippe Soupault), 2, 3,
    30; *Manifesto of surrealism*, 2, 7, 40, 43,
    169; "The Mediums Enter," 16–18, 146,
    100–101; *Nadja*, 2, 17, 55, 63, 200; *Sec-
    ond Manifesto of Surrealism*, 2; *Soluble
    Fish*, 3; "A Suivre" (with Louis Ara-
    gon), 58–59; "Words without
    Wrinkles," 31, 95
Breton, Simone, 17, 18, 23, 29, 53, 55, 66
Bretonian surrealism, 2, 4, 6, 7, 55, 61, 67,
    80, 89, 213
Briand, Aristide, 24, 54
Brieux, Alain, 88, 126 fig. 10, 154, 174–75,
    181, 185
Brinon, Fernand de, 156
Brittany, 133, 134, 161. *See also* Belle-Ile
Brochand, Christian, 96
Brun, Guy, 98, 119
Buchenwald, 138, 166, 190–91, 192, 214
Buisson, Jean, 193
Buñuel, Luis, 55
Burrin, Philippe, 231 n.21
Butler, Judith, 30
Byron, Lord, 45
Byronic, Desnos as, 224 n.31

Le Cabinet du Docteur Caligari, 67
Cahier du sud, 165
Les Cahiers du Rhône, 161

Cahun, Claude, 126 fig. 9, 224 n.30
Caillois, Roger, 63, 116
"Calixto," 72, 100, 155, 160, 162–67. *See
    also* Desnos, Robert, Poetry; "Notes
    Calixto"
"Call for Resistance," by Charles de
    Gaulle, 122, 125
Calligrammes, 36. *See also* Apollinaire,
    Guillaume
Callisto, 98, 162
"Cancale," 160–61. *See also* Desnos,
    Robert, pseudonymous name
"Canrobert," 166. *See also* Desnos,
    Robert, pseudonymous name
Cantaloube-Ferrieu, Lucienne, 47, 81
"Cantate pour l'inauguration du Musée
    de l'Homme," 117
Capitale de la douleur, 83. *See also* Eluard,
    Paul
Carpentier, Alejo, 66, 73, 87, 88, 97, 103,
    106, 107, 161
"Cascade," 131–33. *See also* Desnos,
    Robert, Poetry
Caws, Mary Ann, 6, 36
Céline, Louis Ferdinand, 152
Cendrars, Blaise, 16, 21
Certeau, Michel de, 11
*C'est les bottes de 7 lieues cette phrase "Je
    me vois*," 28. *See also* Desnos, Robert,
    Poetry
"Chansons de l'Empire française," 107.
    See also Desnos, Robert, Radio shows
Char, René, 6, 55, 66, 145, 161
Charcot, Dr., 22
Chemnitz, 192
Chénieux-Gendron, Jacqueline, 5
Chevalier, Maurice, 105, 107
Chevrier, Alain, 162
Chiappe, Jean, 58, 227 n.15
Un Chien andalou, 67
children's verse, 104, 137–40, 211
Chion, Michel, 92
Chirico, Giorgio, 17, 18, 47
Chitrit, Armelle, 6, 225 n.36
chocolate box. *See* myths
"Chroniques des temps présent," 150. *See
    also* Desnos, Robert, Journalism
circular letter of February 1929 (Breton
    and Aragon), 55–58, 64

The Circus, 71

Clair de terre, 83. *See also* Breton, André

clandestine writing, 146, 153–67

Clarté, 55

"La Clef des Songes," 89, 104, 107–12. *See also* Desnos, Robert, Radio shows

"La Clef des songes," 108. *See also* Desnos, Robert, Songs

Clérou, Paul, 106

Clifford, James, 11

Cliquet-Pleyel, 96

Cocteau, Jean, 19, 180, 233 n.39

Coleman, Bill, 151. *See also* jazz

Les Collaborateurs, 145

collaboration, 146, 148, 173; policies, 143, 153, 187; and STO, 143

collage, 22, 37

College of Sociology, 63, 116

Combat, 179, 180. *See also* Resistance, groups

Comité Français de la Libération Nationale (CFLN), 179. *See also* Resistance, groups

Common Front, 96–97

Communicating Vessels, 2. *See also* Breton, André, Works

Communist Party, 55, 56, 58, 59

Compiègne, 13, 176, 178, 182, 183, 184, 185–88, 196, 212

concentration camp poetry, 207

concentration camps. *See* Nazi, camps

Cone, Michèle, 230 n.7, 234 n.7

"Confessions d'un enfant du siècle," 36. *See also* Desnos, Robert, Essays

Confluences, 161

Conseil National de la Résistance (CNR), 179. *See also* Resistance, groups

Contre-Attaque, 70

Contrée, 122, 123–33, 153, 155, 156, 165, 167, 192, 196, 212. *See also* Desnos, Robert, Poetry

Le Convoi des tatoués, 183. *See also* Bessière, André

Convoy of the tattooed men, 190, 193, 197

A Corpse: 1924 version of, 24, 41, 60, 145; 1930 version of, 66, 72

corps et âmes, 72, 156

Corps et biens, 49, 72, 74, 78, 140, 142, 205. *See also* Desnos, Robert, Poetry

"Le Coteau," 128. *See also* Desnos, Robert, Poetry

Count Basie, 151. *See also* jazz

Le Coupable, 70. *See also* Bataille, Georges, Works

Le Courrier Littéraire, 67

Le Crève-coeur, 141, 149. *See also* Aragon, Louis, Works

Crevel, René, 17–18, 26

Critique de la vie quotidienne, 11, 55. *See* Lefèbvre, Henri

crossdressing, 27–31

Cuba, 71, 88

"La Cucaracha," 114

Le Cuirassier nègre, 237 n.38. *See also* Desnos, Robert, Novels

Cultures du surréalisme, 215 n.6. *See also* Antle, Martine

Cupid, 133, 165, 167

Dada, 16, 26, 64, 102, 106, 172

Daix, Pierre, 142

Daladier, Edouard, 134, 227 n.15

Dalí, Salvador, 55, 66, 84

Damas, Léon-Gontran, 88, 225 n.4

Damia, 87, 105, 107

Darle, Juliette, 69

Darras, M., 188

Darrieux, Danielle, 96

D-Day, 193

death, as a theme, 17–18

death march, 197–98

de Gaulle, Charles, 122, 125, 158, 179, 189, 190, 206, 107

Degueille, Clément, 193, 197

Deharme, Lise, 103, 104, 138

Deharme, Paul, 11, 89, 102, 104–7, 119

"De l'érotisme," 35. *See also* Desnos, Robert, Essays

Deleuze, Gilles, 20

Delteil, Joseph, 24, 31, 60, 66

Demeter, 129

"La Demi-Heure de la vie pratique," 106. *See also* Desnos, Robert, Radio shows

Demosthenes, 39

denunciation, 148–49, 152–53

"Dernier poème," 14, 186, 203–12. *See also* myths

"Le Dernier poème de Robert Desnos,"
205

Desanti, Dominique, 21, 61, 68, 89, 178–
79

Desbordes-Valmore, Marceline, 106

Dehays, Daniel, 90

Le Déshonneur des poètes, 233 n.34

Desnos, Claire Guillais (mother), 15, 177,
219 n.26; death of, 196

Desnos, Lucien (father), 15, 86, 237 n.35;
death of, 196

Desnos, Lucienne (sister), 15, 188, 196

Desnos, Robert: birth of, 15; death of,
202; as antifascist, 96–97; arrest and
deportation of, 174–75, 181–86, 188–
201; journal of, 175–78; as a journalist,
53, 58, 60, 191; legacy of: 212–14; letter
to Eluard by, 122; letters to Youki by,
61, 134–36, 180, 192, 196, 209, 212; military service of, 16; neighborhoods of,
in Marais, 7–10, 15–16, 34, 47, 64, 87,
89, 119, 150, 161, 172, 177; —, in
Montparnasse, 12, 45–49, 74, 82, 84; —,
in Saint-Germain-des-Prés, 87, 134,
144, 151, 154, 172, 182, 187, 203; nicknames of, 9, 116; as prophet of surrealism, 3, 6, 15, 17, 169–70; pseudonymous
name, of Andier, Pierre, 121, 156; —, of
Beloeil, Hormidas, 115; —, of Cancale,
160–61; —, of Canrobert, 166; —, of
Gallois, Lucien, 121, 156; —, of Guillais,
Pierre, 219 n.26; —, of Guillois, Valentin, 159; symbol for, as bear, 72, 98–99,
162; —, as horse, 79, 118; —, as seahorse, 81, 83, 139; on tattoos, 72, 98, 190

—Advertising jingles, 112–14

—Automatic texts: *Mourning for Mourning*, 36, 40–43, 157; "Three Books of
Prophecies," 169

—Book reviews, 147–49, 152–53, 171

—Cantata: "Cantate pour l'inauguration
du Musée de l'Homme," 117

—Essays: "Author's Note" to *Fortunes*,
122; "Confessions d'un enfant du siècle," 36; "De l'érotisme," 35; "Le Génie
sans miroir," 19; "L'Imagerie moderne," 64; "Journal d'une Apparition,"
216 n.10; "Précis de cuisine pour les
jours heureux," 193; "Pygmalion et le
sphinx," 64; "Quand le peintre ouvre
l'oeil," 176; "Les Sources de la création:
Le Buffet du Catalan," 176; "third"
manifesto of surrealism, 4, 66–67, 119

—Film reviews, 67

—Film scenarios: *Bonsoir Mesdames,
Bonsoir Messieurs*: 17, 153, 181–82;
L'Etoile de mer, 71; "Minuit à quatorze
heures," 7

—Flyer: *prière d'insérer* for *Corps et biens*,
74, 123, 212

—Jazz reviews, 151–52

—Journalism: "Au Crayon," 149–50, 157;
"Chroniques des temps présent," 150;
"Du temps où l'Abbé Bethléem lacérait les affiches," 149; "L'Homme de
jour," 151; "Interlignes," 152; "J'irai le
dire à la Kommandantur," 148; *Mines
de rien*, 146; "La Revanche des médiocres," 147–50; "Sous le pied d'un
cheval," 150

—Novels: *Le Cuirassier nègre*, 237 n.38;
Liberty or Love!, 1, 7, 11, 26, 40, 43, 48–
49, 51, 99, 122, 157, 214; *Le Vin est
tiré . . .* , 2, 47, 155

—Poetry: "A la mystérieuse," 4, 47, 49, 51,
205; "Aquarelle," 142; "Ars Poetica," 167,
169–72; "Calixto," 72, 100, 155, 160,
162–67; "Cascade," 131–33; *C'est les
bottes de 7 lieues cette phrase "Je me
vois"*, 28; *Contrée*, 122, 123–33, 153, 155,
156, 165, 167, 192, 196, 212; *Corps et
biens*, 49, 72, 74, 78, 140, 142, 205; "Le
Coteau," 128; "Dernier poème," 14, 186,
203–12; *Destinée arbitraire*, 72, 160;
"Door to the Second Infinity," 38–40;
"Epitaph," 124, 212–13; *Etat de veille*,
10, 98, 100, 123, 153, 155, 212; "Le Fard
des Argonauts," 75, 164; *Fortunes*, 10,
115, 142, 153; "La Fourmi," 140; "L'Hippocampe," 139; "I Have Dreamed So
Much of You," 4, 49–52, 203–5, 208;
"Infinitif," 52; "The Landscape," 129;
"The Legacy," 156, 212; "Le Livre Secret
de Youki," 74; "La Maison," 129; "Mon
tombeau," 100–103; "My mermaid," 72;
"Never Anyone but You," 51; "The
Night of Loveless Nights," 45, 46, 58,
74–78, 79; "Ode à Coco," 75; "Le Péli-

—Poetry: (*continued*)
can," 138; "La Peste," 128; "La Plage," 127–28, 131; "Prospectus," 35, 36–37, 106; "Quand le peintre ouvre l'oeil," 176; "Les Quatre sans cou," 115–16; "Le Réveil," 124, 128; "Rrose Sélavy," 29, 31–37, 39, 94, 185; *Les Sans cou*, 115–16; "Sens," 167, 169, 172; "La Sieste," 124; "Siramour," 74, 75, 80–83; "Sirène-Anémone," 74, 75, 78–80, 118; "Soil of Compiègne," 186; "Song of the Road," 186; "Spring," 13, 186–88, 197; "Tale of a Bear," 72, 98–100, 110, 123, 162; "Les Ténèbres," 52–53; "Tomorrow," 123; "To the Headless," 115–16; *Trente chantefables pour des enfants sages à chanter sur n'importe quel air*, 11, 137–40, 155, 192; "Vaincre le jour, vaincre la nuit," 172–74, 178; "La Vendange," 127; "The Voice," 124–25; "The Watchman of the Pont-au-Change," 158–60, 192, 211; "Words from the Rocks," 53
—Play: *La Place de l'Etoile*, 71, 155, 219 n.26
—Radio shows: "Chansons de l'Empire française," 107; "La Clef des Songes," 89, 104, 107–12; "La Demi-Heure de la vie pratique," 106; "Ephémérides radiophoniques," 106; "Essai d'anesthésie," 104; "La Grande Complainte de Fantômas," 103, 106; "Persil-Trois siècles de chanson," 107; "Salut au monde," 107
—Slang poems: "A la Caille," 114, 160, 166, 179; "Le Bon bouillon," 162; "Calixto," 72, 100, 155, 160, 162–67; "Le Frère au pétard," 162; "Les Frères mirotons," 162; "Maréchal Ducono," 161, 179; "Minute," 162; "Pétrus d'Aubervilliers," 161
—Songs: "La Clef des songes," 108; "Front Commun," 96; "No Pasaran," 97; "Sangre y sombra," 97
Desnos, Youki Foujita: on Desnos's arrest, 174–75, 179, 182–85, 188; as Desnos's "mermaid," 49, 70, 72, 78, 81–83; and funeral for Desnos, 203; last letter to Desnos of, 201; and life with Desnos, 13, 87–89, 137, 143–44, 137, 154, 173; and life with Tsuguhara Foujita, 57,

70–74, 81; and Marcel Noll, 57, 80; as the model for the "swimmer" from "The Night-Watch," 49, 83; and myth of the chocolate box, 199–200; and myth of the "Dernier poème," 204–5; and Picasso's etching, 132; and romance with Desnos, 70–74, 99, 133; on the Rue Blomet studio, 47–48; during transition in Desnos's affections from Yvonne George, 49, 70, 78, 80–81, 160
Desnosian marvelous, 7, 13. *See also* marvelous
Desnosian surrealism, 1, 5, 6, 10, 13, 80, 212
"Desnos meurt à Terezin, le 8 juin 1945," 207. *See also* Lartigue, Pierre
Destination Auschwitz avec Robert Desnos, 189. *See also* Bessière, André
Destinée arbitraire, 72, 160. *See also* Desnos, Robert, Poetry
Didi-Huberman, Georges, 223 n.21
Dionysus, 76, 84
Doane, Mary Ann, 93
Documents, 4, 59, 61–66, 72, 81, 88
Don Juan, 75–76, 81
"Door to the Second Infinity," 38–40. *See also* Desnos, Robert, Poetry
Dorgelès, Roland, 135
Dormans, Mady, 73
Dos Passos, John, 88, 135
double-take, 30
Doucet, Jacques, 45, 68; Literary Library of, 5
Drieu la Rochelle, Pierre: collaboration, 146; *A Corpse* (1924), 24–25, 31, 66; *Les Feuilles Libres*, 19; and *La Nouvelle Revue Française*, 141–42; 153; suicide, 142
drôle de guerre. See phony war
drugs, 2, 48
Dubas, Marie, 105
Du Bellay, Joachim, 131. *See also* Renaissance poetry
Dubief, Henri, 54, 97, 99
Ducasse, Isidore, 5, 60, 64
Duchamp, Marcel, 15, 18, 26–33, 94
Dudziak, Francis, 96
Duhamel, Marcel, 55, 88, 147

Dumas, Marie-Claire, 5, 21–22, 31, 116, 123, 132, 146, 151, 155, 160, 207, 224 n.31
Dumas, Pierre, 183
Duras, Marguerite, 89, 236 n.26
Durkheim, Emile, 117
Durozoi, Gérard, 5, 66
"Du sonnet," 151. *See also* Aragon, Louis
"Du temps où l'Abbé Bethléem lacérait les affiches," 149. *See also* Desnos, Robert, Journalism

Editions de Minuit, 154, 156
Egger, Anne, 218 n.13
Eirisch, Jean Py, 176, 186
Ellington, Duke, 107, 151. *See also* jazz
Eluard, Gala, 17, 55
Eluard, Nusch, 89, 144
Eluard, Paul: and eulogy for Desnos, 202–3; and *Les Feuilles Libres* hoax, 19; friendship with Desnos of, 89, 122, 144, 200; and hypnotic sleeps, 16–18, 21, 34, 66; marriage of, 55; and memorial article to Desnos, 119, 212; mobilization of (1939), 134; and Occupation, 180; and Resistance, 6
—Works: *Capitale de la douleur*, 83; *A Corpse* (1924), 24–25, 31; *Immaculate Conception* (with André Breton), 22; "Liberté," 209–10
Les Enfants du Paradis, 199. *See also* Barrault, Jean-Louis
"Ephémérides radiophoniques," 106. *See also* Desnos, Robert, Radio shows
"Epitaph," 124, 212–13. *See also* Desnos, Robert, Poetry
"Epitaphe," 172–73
Ernst, Max, 17, 22, 84
l'esprit français, 142
l'esprit parisien, 145
"Essai d'anesthésie," 104. *See also* Desnos, Robert, Radio shows
Etat de veille, 10, 98, 100, 123, 153, 155, 212. *See also* Desnos, Robert, Poetry
Eternal France, 125
L'Eternelle Revue, 158
ethnographic surrealism, 11
ethnography, 127
L'Etoile de mer, 71. *See also* Desnos, Robert, Film scenarios

Europe, 211
Everling, Germaine, 17, 34
everyday, 6, 7, 10–12, 23, 143, 174, 176, 201
L'Expérience intérieur, 70. *See also* Bataille, Georges, Works
"Exquisite corpse," 221 n.5

Fandor, 53, 103
Fantômas, 10, 64
Fantômas, 10, 53, 103–4
la Fantômas, 81
"Le Fard des Argonauts," 75, 164. *See also* Desnos, Robert, Poetry
Faure, Christian, 126
femininity, 28
Ferdière, Gaston, 89, 133, 155
Fernandel, 105
Feuillade, Louis, 10, 53
Les Feuilles Libres, 19
Le Figaro, 140, 148
fixed-form verse, 83, 140–42, 160
Flamel, Nicholas, 8, 64
Flanner, Janet, 206
Flieder, Laurent, 235 n.20
Flöha, 166, 186, 191, 192–97, 200, 212, 214
Flonneau, Jean-Marie, 126, 153
"Floral Games," 185–86
Flossenbürg, 166, 191, 192
Foniric radio studios, 97, 103
Fontaine, 161
Fontaine, David, 171
Forché, Carolyn, 207–8
Foujita, Youki. *See* Desnos, Youki Foujita
Foujita, Tsuguhara, 13, 57, 71–73, 80–81, 183, 190
Fortunes, 10, 115, 142, 153. *See also* Desnos, Robert, Poetry
fortune-telling: at Auschwitz, Birkenau, 190; at Flöha, 194
"La Fourmi," 140. *See also* Desnos, Robert, Poetry
Fraenkel, Ghita, 181
Fraenkel, Michel, 87, 121, 155
Fraenkel, Théodore, 47, 48, 87, 97, 121, 134, 146
France, Anatole, 24–26, 31, 60, 66
La France Libre. *See* Free France

Franc-Tireur, 179. *See also* Resistance, groups

Free France, 179, 189

Fréhel, 96

French Committee of National Liberation (CFLN), 189. *See also* Resistance, groups

French cultural memory, 206, 209, 211

French National Committee of Writers, 202

French Republic, 129

"Le Frère au pétard," 162. *See also* Desnos, Robert, Slang poems

"Les Frères mirotons," 162. *See also* Desnos, Robert, Slang poems

Fresnes, 182, 202

Freud, Sigmund, 22, 36

From Munich to the Liberation, 179. *See also* Azéma, Jean-Pierre

"Front Commun," 96. *See also* Desnos, Robert, Songs

Frontstalag, 122, 183. *See also* Royallieu

Galiana, Chantal, 96

Gallimard (publishing house), 142, 146, 155

Gallimard, Gaston, 141, 199

Gallois, Lucien, 121, 156. *See also* Desnos, Robert, pseudonymous name

Garber, Marjorie, 27, 33

Galtier-Boissière, Charlotte, 89

Galtier-Boissière, Jean, 89, 122, 144, 145, 175, 180–81, 196, 203

Garcia Lorca, Federico, 97

Garder, Michel, 186, 192–93, 198, 201

Gaucheron, Jacques, 161

Gaullism, 153

Gaullists, 184

Gauthier, Renée, 17

Gautré, Georges, 22, 103

"Le Génie sans miroir," 19. *See also* Desnos, Robert, Essays

George, Yvonne: and Desnos's love for, 4, 13, 48–49, 68, 78, 80; and Desnos's transition to Youki, 74–83; drug addiction of, 48, 155; as inspiration for "A la mystérieuse" and "Les Ténèbres," 49–53; and the starfish, 71; symbolized as the star, 70, 81–82; and wax mermaid, 45, 49, 82

Gestapo, 122, 175, 178, 181, 182, 185

Giacometti, Alberto, 55

Gilbert-Lecomte, Roger, 58

Giraudoux, Jean, 175

Godet, Babette, 124, 129, 145

Godet, Robert J., 123–24, 153

Golan, Romy, 26

Goldsborough, Kate, 237 n.37

Goodman, Benny, 107, 151. *See also* jazz

"The *grain* of the voice," 90, 104. *See also* Barthes, Roland

"La Grande Complainte de Fantômas," 103, 106. *See also* Desnos, Robert, Radio shows

Le Grand Jeu, 55, 57

Le Grand Meaulnes, 147. *See also* Desnos, Robert, Book reviews

Great Bear. *See* bear

Greco, Juliette, 96

Gringoire, 135

Grumier, Mme, 174

Gründ, Michel, 155

Guedj, Colette, 220 n.31

Guerande, Philippe, 53

Guerlac, Suzanne, 36, 215 n.5; *Literary Polemics*, 215 n.5

Guillais, Claire. *See* Desnos, Claire Guillais

Guillais, Pierre, 219 n.26. *See also* Desnos, Robert, pseudonymous name

Guillois, Valentin, 159. *See also* Desnos, Robert, pseudonymous name

Guthrie, Ramon, xi, 225 n.1

Halles, 7, 15, 64, 161, 172. *See also* Marais

Hawkins, Coleman, 151. *See also* jazz

Heller, Gerhard, 179, 182, 184

Hemingway, Ernest, 87, 135, 196

Higgins, Lynn, 219 n.27

Hilsum, René, 185

"L'Hippocampe," 139. *See also* Desnos, Robert, Poetry

"Histoire de baleines," 119. *See also* Prévert, Jacques

Une Histoire des médias, 95. *See also* Jeanneney, Jean-Nöel

History of the Surrealist Movement, 215 n.6. *See also* Nadeau, Maurice

Hitler, Adolf, 97, 98, 121, 125, 136, 137, 144, 153, 156
Hollard, Michel, Col., 154, 180, 202
Hollard, Vincent, 179
Hollier, Denis, 3, 59
Hollywood, Amy, 223 n.21
"L'Homme de jour," 151. *See also* Desnos, Robert, Journalism
Honneger, Arthur, 96
L'Honneur des poètes, 156, 192
horse: symbol for Desnos, 79, 118. *See also* Desnos, Robert, symbol for
Hubert, Etienne-Alain, 217 n.6
Hubert, Renée Riese, 5
Hughes, Langston, 88
Hugnet, Georges, 144, 176
Hugo, Victor, 9, 16, 60, 212, 156
Hugotte, Valéry, 234 n.5
Hulak, Fabienne, 3
The Human Race, 191. *See also* Antelme, Robert
hypnotic sleeps, 18, 16–23, 36, 181–82

Icarian movement, 65, 223 n.21
"I Have Dreamed So Much of You," 4, 49–52, 203–5, 208. *See also* Desnos, Robert, Poetry
Illers, Dr., 182, 184
"L'Imagerie moderne," 64. *See also* Desnos, Robert, Essays
The Immaculate Conception, 22. *See also* Breton, André; Eluard, Paul
the in-between, 60, 213
"Infinitif," 52. *See also* Desnos, Robert, Poetry
informe, 62
"interior theater," 91, 105, 109
"Interlignes," 152. *See also* Desnos, Robert, Journalism
Introductory Lectures, 22. *See also* Freud, Sigmund

"J'ai tant rêvé de toi." *See* "I Have Dreamed So Much of You"
jazz, 151–52; Armstrong, Louis, 107, 151; Bechet, Sidney, 107; Coleman, Bill, 151; Count Basie, 151; Ellington, Duke, 107, 151; Goodman, Benny, 107, 151; Hawkins, Coleman, 151; Reinhardt,

Django, 151; Shaw, Artie, 151; Smith, Bessie, 107; Waller, Fats, 151
Jeander, 30 n.30
Jeanneney, Jean-Nöel, 95
Jeanson, Henri, 9, 142–43, 145, 149, 153, 180, 196
Je Suis Partout, 154, 180
"J'irai le dire à la Kommandantur," 148. *See also* Desnos, Robert, Journalism
Jones, Amelia, 27
Josephson, Matthew, 21
"Journal d'une Apparition," 216 n.10. *See also* Desnos, Robert, Essays
journalism, 53, 58, 60, 191
Judt, Tony, 217 n.4, 229 n.1
Juve, 103

Kahn, Douglas, 89
Kaiser, Dr., 141
Kiki of Montparnasse, 17, 71, 87, 88
Klee, Paul, 88
Krauss, Rosalind, 3, 63
Kroupa, Adolf, 203–5, 207
Kulik, William, 207, 215 n.8

Labisse, Félix, 155
Laborie, Pierre, 122, 124, 153
Lacan, Jacques, 94
Lacombe, Fabien, 202
Lacombe, M. 202
Lame, Louise, 7, 11, 511. *See also Liberty or Love!*
Lamireau, Gilbert, 137
Lançon, Daniel, 239 n.56
"The Landscape," 129. *See also* Desnos, Robert, Poetry
"The Language of Flowers," 62–66. *See also* Bataille, Georges, Works
Lartigue, Pierre, 186, 203–5, 207
Laubreaux, Alain, 137, 146, 154, 180, 181, 184, 185
Laurence, Robert, 190, 193
Lautréamont, Count of. *See* Ducasse, Isidore
Laval, Pierre: and collaboration policies, 143, 153, 156; Desnos's "Pétrus d'Auberviliers," 161; execution of, 202; and meeting with Hitler, 137; in the 1930s, 54, 98; and STO policy: 143, 154

Lechevallier, André, 157, 198, 199
Lecuona Cuban Boys, 88
Lefèbvre, Henri, 11, 12
Lefèvre, Mme, 154, 175, 230 n.3
"The Legacy," 156, 212. *See also* Desnos, Robert, Poetry
Leininger, Christian, 197–98, 201
Leiris, Michel: and College of Sociology, 63; and the Communist Party, 55; and *A Corpse* (1930), 66; and *Documents*, 59; everyday practices of, 11; and friendship with Desnos, 70, 88, 212; and *Messages*, 161; and the Musée de l'Homme, 69, 116–17; response to the circular letter (1929) of, 56, 58; and the Rue Blomet group, 45–46, 63
Lescure, Jean, 118, 160
Les Lettre Françaises, 186, 202, 204–7, 209
Libération, 179. *See also* Resistance, groups
Liberté, Egalité, Fraternité. See "Liberty, Equality, Fraternity"
la liberté ou l'amour, 99–100
"Liberty, Equality, Fraternity," 35, 37, 101, 126, 150, 209–20, 210
Liberty or Love!, 1, 7, 11, 26, 40, 43, 48–49, 51, 99, 122, 157, 214
"Les Lilas et les roses," 131, 140, 148, 149. *See also* Aragon, Louis, Works
Limbour, Georges, 16, 60, 66
"listes Otto," 123–24. *See also* Abetz, Otto
Literary Polemics, 215 n.5. *See also* Guerlac, Suzanne
Littérature, 26, 29, 31, 38
Little Red Riding Hood, 139
"Le Livre Secret de Youki," 74. *See also* Desnos, Robert, Poetry
Locarno Pact, 98
loi scélérate, 25
Luchaire, Jean, 146, 181
Lycée Turgot, 151

La Machine à écrire, 180. *See also* Cocteau, Jean
Mad Love, 2. *See also* Breton, André
Maffesoli, Michel, 20
Maginot line, 54, 134
The Magnetic Fields, 2, 3, 30. *See also* Breton, André; Soupault, Philippe

Magnifying Mirrors, 215 n.6. *See also* Hubert, Renée Riese
Magritte, René, 84, 226 n.10
"La Maison," 129. *See also* Desnos, Robert, Poetry
Maldoror, 60, 64
Malkine, Fern, 46
Malkine, Georges, 45, 46, 47, 48, 55, 67, 75, 88
Mallarmé, Stéphane, 38, 102
Mandel, Georges, 95
Manifesto of Surrealism, 2, 3, 7, 17, 18, 19, 20, 24, 40, 43, 59, 169. *See also* Breton, André
maquis, 131, 132
Marais, 7–10, 15–16, 34, 47, 64, 87, 89, 119, 150, 161, 172, 177. *See also* Rue de Rivoli
Marais, Jean, 180
Marcus, Julia Tardy, 89, 143–44, 182
"Maréchal Ducono," 161, 179. *See also* Desnos, Robert, Slang poems
"Maréchal, nous voilà," 151
Margraff, Henri, 158, 190, 191
Marianne, 209
Marie Rose flea powder, 112, 192
marvelous, 7, 13, 201, 209, 213, 214
masculinity, 28
Masson, André: and costumes and scenery for *Numance de Cervantes*, 118; and *Documents*, 59, 62; illustrations for *C'est les bottes de 7 lieues cette phrase "Je me vois,"* 38; for *Les Sans cous*, 115; and response to the circular letter (1929), 56, 58, 60; and Rue Blomet group, 45–46, 60, 67
materialism, 62, 80. *See also* Bataille, Georges
mathematics, 122–23, 146
Mauriac, François, 203
Mauss, Marcel, 117
May-June war (1940), 131, 140. *See also* blitzkrieg
Mayr, Weiland, 19
les médiocres, 148, 232 n.23
"The Mediums Enter," 16–18, 146, 100–101. *See also* Breton, André
memory site, 211. *See also* French cultural memory
Merle, Eugène, 67

mermaid: symbol for Youki, 49, 70, 72, 81–83. *See also* Desnos, Youki Foujita; wax mermaid
Messages, 160–61
Milhaud, Darius, 116, 138
Milhaud, Madeleine, 117, 138
Mines de rien, 146. *See also* Desnos, Robert, Journalism
"Minuit à quatorze heures," 7. *See also* Desnos, Robert, Film scenarios
"Minute," 162. *See also* Desnos, Robert, Slang poems
Mireille, 96, 135
Miró, Joan, 46, 70, 88
Mistinguett, 105
Mitsou, 183–84, 188
mobilization (World War II), 134–37
"modest *recording instruments*," 101–2. *See also* Breton, André
"Monday in Christine Street," 36–37. *See also* Apollinaire, Guillaume
Montaigne, Michel de 149, 233 n.32
Montand, Yves, 96
Montgomery, Field Marshal B. L., 180
"Mon tombeau," 100–103. *See also* Desnos, Robert, Poetry
Montparnasse, 71, 88, 119
Monument to the Martyrs of the Deportation, 206–7, 209, 211
Morise, Max, 17, 55, 66
Morocco, 2, 16, 55
Mossé, Sonia, 144
Mother Goose, 138
Moulin, Jean, 179, 206
Mouloudji, 144
Mourning for Mourning, 36, 40–43, 157. *See also* Desnos, Robert, Automatic texts
Mouvement de Libération Nationale (MLN), 179. *See also* Resistance, groups
Le Mouvement perpétuel, 83. *See also* Aragon, Louis
Mouvements Unis de la Résistance (MUR), 156, 179. *See also* Resistance, groups
Muller, Capitain, 184, 201
Munich Accord, 134
Murat, Michel, 5, 83, 157, 207
Musée de l'Homme, 69, 116–19

music-hall *chanteuse*, 48, 51, 81. *See also* *Liberty or Love!*
Muzard, Suzanne, 55, 57, 63, 68
"My mermaid," 72. *See also* Desnos, Robert, Poetry
Les Mystères de New York, 67. *See also* Desnos, Robert, Film reviews
myth, 207–8
myths: metal chocolate box, 199–200; "Dernier poème," 203–12; the French Resistance, 206–7, 211

Nadcau, Maurice, 2. *See also* *History of the Surrealist Movement*
Nadja, 2, 17, 55, 63, 200. *See also* Breton, André
National Block, 24, 54
National Museum of Popular Arts and Traditions, 126
National Revolution, 125, 137
Naville, Pierre, 66
Nazi camps, 2, 13; Auschwitz-Birkenau, 138, 166, 169, 178, 188, 189–90, 192, 200, 214; Buchenwald, 138, 166, 190–91, 192, 214; Flöha, 166, 186, 191, 192–97, 200, 212, 214; Flossenbürg, 166, 191, 192; Terezin, 118, 169, 179, 197, 198–201, 202
Nazis: ideology of, 129, 183; as Occupiers, 148; Propaganda-Stafel of, 124, 146; régime of, 140
Neruda, Pablo, 97
"Never Anyone but You," 51. *See also* Desnos, Robert, Poetry
New York Dada, 27
Nietzsche, Friedrich, 84
"The Night of Loveless Nights," 45, 46, 58, 74–78, 79. *See also* Desnos, Robert, Poetry
"The Night-Watch," 49, 60, 68, 74, 83. *See also* *Liberty or Love!*
Noailles, Anna de, 19, 106
Noll, Marcel, 55, 57, 71, 80
non-Occupied zone, 122, 141, 151, 153
"No Pasaran," 97. *See also* Desnos, Robert, Songs
Normandy, 136
Nosferatu Le Vampire, 67. *See also* Desnos, Robert, Film reviews
"Notes Calixto," 160, 173

Les Nouveaux Temps, 181. *See also* Luchaire, Jean

Nouvelles Hébrides, 68

La Nouvelle Revue Française (*La* NRF), 135, 141

Numance de Cervantes, 118. *See also* Barrault, Jean-Louis

Nunley, Charles, 147

Occupation, 6, 13, 115, 124–25, 139, 141, 143–47, 160, 162, 167, 179, 206, 211, 213

Occupation, 181. *See also* Ousby, Ian

Occupied France, 122, 130, 141, 149, 165, 209

Occupied Paris, 9, 142–44

Occupied zone, 122

"Ode à Coco," 75. *See also* Desnos, Robert, Poetry

Oeuvres (by Robert Desnos), 5, 196, 215 n.3

"Les Oiseaux de Paris," 114

"The 'Old Mole' and the Prefix *Sur* in the Words *Surhomme* and *Surrealist*," 65. *See also* Bataille, Georges, Works

"Operation Spring Wind." *See* Vel d'Hiv roundup

oracular, 17. *See also* prophet

Orpheus, 172

Ory, Pascal, 145

Oswald, Marianne, 96

Ousby, Ian, 148, 181

Paliyenko, Adrianna, 217 n.5

Para, Jean-Baptiste, 224 n.31

parapraxis, 22

Paris Peasant, 148

Parrot, Louis, 158

Pascal, Pierre, 152

Paulhan, Jean, 141, 152–53

Paule, Colette, 108

Paxton, Robert O., 178, 207

"Le Pélican," 138. *See also* Desnos, Robert, Poetry

Péret, Benjamin, 16–17, 55, 58, 233 n.34

performative utterance, 22

Perrault, Charles, 138

"Persil-Trois siècles de chanson," 107. *See also* Desnos, Robert, Radio shows

"La Peste," 128. *See also* Desnos, Robert, Poetry

Pétain, Marshal Philippe: collaboration policy of, 143, 148, 153, 156, 187; as Desnos's "Maréchal Ducono," 161, 179; as head of Vichy state, 54, 122–23; and National Revolution, 136–37; and return-to-the-land policy, 126–27, 129, 187

"Pétrus d'Aubervilliers," 161. *See also* Desnos, Robert, Slang poems; Laval, Pierre

Pfihl, Henri, 194–95

Phantasmatic Radio, 103. *See also* Weiss, Allen

phony war, 2, 98, 124, 133–37, 143, 161

Picabia, Francis, 17, 19, 23, 31, 45

Picasso, Pablo, 46, 62, 71, 89, 132, 176, 196, 200

Pierre, José, 59, 61

Pingusson, Georges Henri, 206

La Place de l'Etoile, 71, 155, 219 n.26

"La Plage," 127–28, 131. *See also* Desnos, Robert, Poetry

Plantier, René, 35, 159

Pléiade poets, 131–33, 141. *See also* Renaissance poetry

poem-conversation, 36. *See also* Apollinaire, Guillaume

Poésie, 161

La Poésie, la résistance, 161

poetic constraint, 74, 139, 214

Poincaré, Raymond, 24, 53–54, 59, 66, 69, 184

Poirion, Daniel, 7

Polizzotti, Mark, 21, 68, 71

Ponge, Francis, 66

"Le Pont Mirabeau," 172–74. *See also* Apollinaire, Guillaume

popular culture, 1, 10, 127, 213

Popular Front, 97–99, 126–27

populist surrealism, 67

Pour mes amis, 124. *See also* Godet, Robert J.

"Pourquoi je suis républicain," 127

Pouzol, Henri, 207

"Précis de cuisine pour les jours heureux," 193. *See also* Desnos, Robert, Essays

Prévert, Jacques, 55, 112, 119, 180, 199
prière d'insérer for *Corps et biens*, 74, 123, 212
Prin, Alice. *See* Kiki of Montparnasse
Privat, Maurice, 96
pronatalism, 25–26, 210
Propaganda-Stafel, 124, 142
prophet, 3, 6, 15, 169–70
"Proposition d'un art radiophonique," 105. *See also* Deharme, Paul
"Prospectus," 35, 36–37, 106. *See also* Desnos, Robert, Poetry
Proust, Marcel, 92
public domain, 4, 67, 119
publishing in Occupied France, 123–24
Pucheu, Pierre, 127, 189, 236 n.23
Pupier Chocolate, 114, 119
"Pygmalion et le sphinx," 64. *See also* Desnos, Robert, Essays

"Quand le peintre ouvre l'oeil," 176. *See also* Desnos, Robert, Essays
"Les Quatre sans cou," 115–16. *See also* Desnos, Robert, Poetry
Queneau, Raymond, 11, 55, 66, 146, 161
quotidian, 74. *See also* everyday

Radiguet, Raymond, 16
radio, 4, 23, 89, 92, 94, 95–96, 98, 153, 211, 213
Radio Magazine, 89, 107
Ray, Man, 15, 10, 18, 21, 27–29, 56, 71, 126 fig 4, 169, 182
Reading Bataille, 215 n.5
readymade, 22, 34
Rearick, Charles, 24
Récanati, François, 22
recording instruments. See "modest recording instruments"
Red Cross, 198
"refusal," 146
Reinhardt, Django, 151. *See also* jazz
Renaissance poetry, 131–33, 165, 167. *See* Pléiade poets
Renaud, Madeleine, 9, 87, 197
Rénier, Max, 109
Réseau du souvenir, 206
Resistance: armed, 131–32; Desnos and the, 144, 153–55, 161, 172, 175, 179, 211,

213; groups, 156, 179, 189; members, 187, 189, 210; poems, 12; poets, 6, 129, 132–33; and the STO, 154. *See also* Agir; *maquis*
"La Revanche des médiocres," 147–50. *See also* Desnos, Robert, Journalism
"Le Réveil," 124, 128. *See also* Desnos, Robert, Poetry
Reverdy, Pierre, 7
La Révolution surréaliste, 4, 18, 36, 40, 49, 56, 59, 64
Reynolds, Sian, 25
Ribemont-Dessaignes, Georges, 6, 16, 21, 56, 60, 66
Richardson, Michael, 3
Richman, Michèle, 215 n.5
Rif, War of the, 55
Riffaterre, Michael, 27, 40
Rimbaud, Arthur, 9, 16, 29, 37, 60, 212
"La Rime en 1940," 140–41. *See also* Aragon, Louis, Works
Rivet, Paul, 117, 126
Rivière, André de la, 71
Rivière, Georges-Henri, 69, 88, 116, 117, 126
Rivière, Joan, 28
Robert, Pierre, 95
Roberts, Mary Louise, 25
Robespierre, Maximillien, 17, 60
Rödel, Henri, 186, 192, 193, 194, 197, 199, 200
Romer, Stephen, 231 n.11
Ronsard, Pierre de, 131. *See also* Renaissance poetry
Rosolato, Guy, 93
Rossi, Tino, 104, 107
Rothwell, Andrew, 22
roundups, 122, 153–54, 180, 211
Roure, Rémi, 185
Rousso, Henry, 137, 151, 206
Roy, Claude, 202, 207
Royallieu, 13, 176, 178, 182, 183, 184, 185–88
"Rrose Sélavy": Aragon's criticism of, 75, 141; and automatic poems, 29, 31–37, 39, 94, 185; as crossdressing, 112; as emblematic of poetry, 196–97; as equations, 34, 122–23; formal properties of, 61, 68, 74, 171, 196. *See also* Sélavy, Rrose

Rue Blomet group, 46, 58, 60
Rue Blomet studio, 12, 45–49, 74, 82, 84.
    See also Montparnasse
Rue de Rivoli, 9, 15, 16, 177
Rue Lacretelle, 73–74
Rue Mazarine, 87, 144, 151, 154, 182, 187.
    See also Saint-Germain-des-Prés
Rue Saint-Bon, 9, 15, 150, 178. *See also*
    Marais
Rue Saint Merri, 8, 119, 177. *See also*
    Marais
Rue Saint-Martin, 150, 177. *See also*
    Marais
Rue des Saussaies, 175, 181. *See also*
    Gestapo
Russian hospital at Terezin, 199
Russo, Adelaïde, 219 n.28

sacred union, 24, 54, 59. *See also* Poin-
    caré, Raymond
Sadoul, Georges, 55
Saint-Germain-des-Prés, 87, 134, 172, 203.
    See also Rue Mazarine
Salacrou, Armand, 45, 106, 112
"Salut au monde," 107. *See also* Desnos,
    Robert, Radio shows
Sand, George, 106
Sanglot, Corsair, 1, 7, 11, 20, 51, 52. See
    also *Liberty or Love!*
"Sangre y sombra," 97. *See also* Desnos,
    Robert, Songs
Les Sans cou, 115–16. *See also* Desnos,
    Robert, Poetry
Sapiro, Gisèle, 142, 146
Sartre, 89
Savitry, Emile, 56, 58
Scannell, Paddy, 22, 90, 105
seahorse, 81, 83, 139. *See also* Desnos,
    symbol for
Second Manifesto of Surrealism, 2, 4, 59–
    60, 61–66, 69, 72, 74. *See also* Breton,
    André, Works
Séité, Yannick, 151
Sélavy, Rrose: alterego for Desnos, 29–31,
    98, 112–13, 170, 186–8, 196–97, 201, 209,
    212, 214; for Duchamp, 18, 26–33; for
    poetry, 197, 209
Selected Poems of Robert Desnos, 207. *See
    also* Kulik, William

semilegal: poetry, 123; journal (*Messages*),
    160
"Sens," 167, 169, 172. *See also* Desnos,
    Robert, Poetry
Serman, Elisabeth, 96
Service de Travail Obligatoire (STO), 143,
    154
Shaw, Artie, 151. *See also* jazz
Sheringham, Michael, 11, 157
Shipman, Evan, 135
"La Sieste," 124. *See also* Desnos, Robert,
    Poetry
Silverman, Kaja, 93–94; *The Acoustic
    Mirror*, 93–94
Simon, Samy, 97, 105, 112, 142
Simonnet, Thomas, 17
simulation, 21
"Siramour," 74, 75, 80–83. *See also* Des-
    nos, Robert, Poetry
"Sirène-Anémone," 74, 75, 78–80, 118. *See
    also* Desnos, Robert, Poetry
slang, 37, 160–67, 170–72, 173
slogan for French Republic. *See* "Liberty,
    Equality, Fraternity"
slogan for Vichy State. *See* "Work, Fam-
    ily, Homeland"
Smiley, Amy, 93
Smith, Bessie, 107. *See also* jazz
Smoular, Alfred, 190, 191
"Soil of Compiègne," 186. *See also* Des-
    nos, Robert, Poetry
Soluble Fish, 3. *See also* Breton, André,
    Works
"Song of the Road," 186. *See also* Desnos,
    Robert, Poetry
Soupault, Philippe: as co-author (with
    André Breton) of *The Magnetic Fields*,
    2, 30; and *A Corpse* (1924), 24–26, 31,
    66; excluded by Breton, 55; on the
    radio, 89
"La Source de la création: Le Buffet du
    Catalan," 176. *See also* Desnos, Robert,
    Essays
"Sous le pied d'un cheval," 150. *See also*
    Desnos, Robert, Journalism
Spanish Civil War, 97, 118
Spector, Jack, 2
"Spring," 13, 186–88, 197. *See also* Desnos,
    Robert, Poetry

"Le Stade du miroir," 94
Staël, Mme de, 106
Stamelman, Richard, 29, 219 n.21
star: as symbol for Yvonne, 48, 70, 78, 82, 83. *See also* George, Yvonne
starfish: as symbol for Yvonne, 49
Stavisky affair, 99, 227 n.15
STO. *See* Service du Travail Obligatoire
Stuna, Josef, 169, 200, 201, 202, 203
Suarez, George, 145, 149, 182, 184, 189
surrealism, 3, 16, 18–19
Surrealism, 215 n.6. *See also* Chénieux-Gendron, Jacqueline
"Surrealism and Painting, 66–67
"Surrealism in 2000: Celebrating Robert Desnos," 218 n.16
Le Surréalisme au service de la révolution, 74
Surrealism: Road to the Absolute, 215 n.4
surrealist "conversation," 5, 14, 212
surrealist image, 7, 70
Svobodné Noviny, 202–6
swimmer, 49, 78, 83, 99. *See also* Desnos, Youki Foujita; *Liberty or Love!*; "The-Night Watch"

"Tale of a Bear," 72, 98–100, 110, 123, 162. *See also* Desnos, Robert, Poetry
Tardieu, André, 54, 66
tattoos, 72, 98, 190
telepathy, 94–95
"Les Ténèbres," 52–53. *See also* Desnos, Robert, Poetry
Terezin, 118, 169, 179, 197, 198–201, 202
Tesarova, Alena Kalouskova, 169, 199, 202, 203
théâtre intérieur, 91, 105, 109
Theresienstadt, 197. *See* Terezin
"third" manifesto of surrealism, 4, 66–67, 119. *See also* Desnos, Robert, Essays
Third Reich, 129, 143
Third Republic, 10, 136
"This Heart that Hated War," 156–57, 206. *See also* Desnos, Robert, Poetry
"Three Books of Prophecies," 169. *See also* Desnos, Robert, Automatic texts
tirailleur algérien, 16
Tomkins, Calvin, 26

"Tomorrow," 123. *See also* Desnos, Robert, Poetry
"To the Headless," 115–16. *See also* Desnos, Robert, Poetry
Trenet, Charles, 96, 114, 134
Trente chantefables pour des enfants sages à chanter sur n'importe quel air, 11, 137–40, 155, 192. *See also* children's verse; Desnos, Robert, Poetry
"Troisième manifeste du surréalisme." *See* "third" manifesto of surrealism
Trotsky, Leon, 57
Truffaut, François, 96
Tual, Roland, 17, 45, 181
Tzara, Tristan, 16, 19, 66

Une Vague de rêves, 19, 40, 94. *See also* Aragon, Louis, Works
Unik, Pierre, 55
Union nationale, 24

Vailland, Roger, 57, 58
"Vaincre le jour, vaincre la nuit," 172–74, 178. *See also* Desnos, Robert, Poetry
Les Vampires, 10, 53
Variétés, 58–59
Vasquez, Carmen, 155, 156
Vel d'Hiv roundup, 153–54, 180, 211. *See also* roundups
"La Vendange," 127. *See also* Desnos, Robert, Poetry
Vep, Irma, 10
Verdet, André, 89, 180, 190, 191
Versailles Treaty, 98
Vested Interests, 27. *See also* Garber, Marjorie
Vichy: jazz, 151; Jews, 145, 147, 207, 210–11; slogan, 126; youth camps, 151; state, 54, 114, 122, 123, 125–27, 129, 136, 161, 167, 178, 180
Vichy France, 207. *See also* Paxton, Robert O.
The Vichy Syndrome, 206. *See also* Rousso, Henry
Vigilance Committee of Antifascist Intellectuals, 97
Villon, François, 172–73
Le Vin est tiré . . . , 2, 47, 155. *See also* Desnos, Robert, Novels

Vitrac, Roger, 16, 17, 55, 60, 66
Vittet, L. 202, 204–6
voice, 20, 35, 39, 90–94, 118–19, 124, 150, 159
"The Voice," 124–25. *See also* Desnos, Robert, Poetry
Volmer, Pierre, 190, 192, 194, 197, 198, 199, 201, 237 n.34

Waldberg, Patrick, 46
Waller, Fats, 151. *See also* jazz
Wall Street crash, 54, 69
Walz, Robin, 228 n.19
"The Watchman of the Pont-au-Change," 158–60, 192, 211. *See also* Desnos, Robert, Poetry
wax mermaid, 45, 49, 82. *See also* George, Yvonne
Weber, Eugen, 40
Webster, Robert M., 239 n.54
Weill, Kurt, 193
Weiner, Jean, 138
Weiss, Allen, 102
Whitman, Walt, 107

Why Not Sneeze Rrose Sélavy?, 34. *See also* Duchamp, Marcel
Winnicott, D. W., 94
Wölfflin, Heinrich, 33
woman swimmer. *See* swimmer
"Womanliness as a masquerade," 28
word-mirror, 19, 43. *See also* Aragon, Louis
"words are making love," 31, 77. *See also* Breton, André
"Words from the Rocks, 53. *See also* Desnos, Robert, Poetry
"Words without Wrinkles," 31. *See also* Breton, André, Works
"Work, Family, Homeland," 126
World War I, 10, 13, 15, 16, 23, 24, 25, 64, 121, 136, 142, 145
World War II, 14, 54, 118, 206, 210–13

Youki, déesse de la neige, 71. *See also* Desnos, Youki Foujita

Zakarian, Richard, 233 n.40
zazous, 151–52. *See also* jazz